WHO'S WHO OF ASTON VILLA

WHO'S WHO OF
ASTON VILLA

Tony Matthews

MAINSTREAM
PUBLISHING
EDINBURGH AND LONDON

First published in Great Britain in 2004 by
MAINSTREAM PUBLISHING COMPANY (EDINBURGH) LTD
7 Albany Street
Edinburgh EH1 3UG

ISBN 1 84018 821 9

A catalogue record for this book is available from the British Library

Typeset in Caslon and Gill Condensed
Printed and bound in Great Britain by
Antony Rowe Ltd, Chippenham, Wiltshire

CONTENTS

Acknowledgements 7

Introduction 9

Who's Who of Aston Villa, 1874–2004 11

Appendix: Aston Villa's Managers and Chairmen 311

Bibliography 313

ACKNOWLEDGEMENTS

First and foremost I must say a special big thank you to two people – Bill Campbell of Mainstream Publishing (Edinburgh) for agreeing to produce and publish this book, and John Farrelly, an ardent Villa supporter who has worked wonders in amending and adding to the players' biogs.

Also a huge thank you to David Barber (Football Association), Zoe Ward (FA Premier League), Adrian Faber (the *Express and Star* picture library editor), the late Norman Edwards (cartoonist extraordinaire), all the past employees, reporters and photographers (freelance and librarians) of the *Birmingham Evening Mail, Birmingham Post, Birmingham Gazette, Sunday Mercury* and *Sport Argus*.

I acknowledge, too, those who have contributed with regards to loaning photographs, cuttings, scrapbooks and other memorabilia, namely Paul Sturgess (Sports-Line Photographic for the David Platt picture), Dave and Pam Bridgewater, Paul Yeomans, Paul Delaney, Terry Chorley, Dave Hodges, Jim Creasy, David Goodyear, Reg Thacker, Charlie Poultney, Geoff Allman, Andy Porter, Roger Wash and John Cross. Likewise I thank Jim Brown, Graham Hughes, statisticians representing Coventry City and Wolverhampton Wanderers respectively, plus ex-players Jim Cumbes, Jimmy Dugdale, the late Stan Lynn and Jock Mulraney, Nigel Sims, Leslie Smith, Dave Walsh and members of the Dorsett family.

Thank you, also – and 'sorry, darling' for the inconvenience caused – to my loving wife Margaret, who once again has had to put up without me for hours upon end while I've sat thrashing away on the computer keyboard, thumbing through old reference books, matchday programmes and soccer magazines, checking and re-checking the thousands of statistics and stories as well as travelling up and down the country from picturesque and sunny Devon.

IMPORTANT NOTICE

INTRODUCTION

I am certain that all supporters of Aston Villa, young and old, male and female, have, at some time or another, been involved in an argument concerning a past or present player.

I know for sure that in numerous pubs and clubs, inside street cafés, bars and restaurants, at schools, colleges and universities, at home, in office blocks, on the shop floor, at various grounds, in cars, on trains and buses, even when travelling in an aircraft or walking down the road, perhaps sitting on the beach, discussions have certainly taken place about one or more players and also a few managers who have been associated with Villa down the years.

Some of these discussions, for sure, have turned into heated arguments, with questions being asked but no definite answer given. As a result, wagers have been laid as to who is right and who is wrong!

Some questions revolve around the obvious, such as the following. (1) When did the player join the club? (2) Where did he come from? (3) How many goals did he score? (4) Where did he go after leaving Villa? (5) Did he play for England or Wales, or Scotland etc.? (6) Was he a defender or midfielder, a left- or right-winger? and (7) Did he play in a cup final?

Hopefully this elaborated players' *Who's Who* can answer most, if not all of these questions, as well as offering you a lot more information besides. It will also satisfy that laudable curiosity without a shadow of a doubt.

On the following pages you will find multitudinous authentic personal details of every single player who has appeared for Villa in a competitive League or Cup match from December 1879 (when the club first entered the FA Cup) up to and including the 2003–04 Premiership season. There are lists, too, of Villa's managers and chairmen.

Included in the pen-picture portraits are details of all junior and non-League clubs the player assisted, any transfer fees involved (if known), honours won at club and international level, plus the respective senior appearance and goalscoring records (for Villa) which appear at the head of each individual player's write-up. The total number of appearances after a player's name is for all major domestic and European competitions only; wartime games, friendlies, youth and other matches are not included. All statistics appertaining to individual players are correct up to May 2004.

It has not been possible to obtain details of every player's birthplace or birthday, date or place of death, and these have been stated where known.

Virtually throughout this book, the name of the club – Aston Villa – is referred to as 'Villa'. Few abbreviations have been used, but among the more common ones are: FC (Football Club), PFA (Professional Footballers Association), FAC (FA Cup), FLC (Football League Cup), AWS (Auto-Windscreen Shield), FRT (Freight Rover Trophy), SVT (Sherpa Van Trophy), NPL (National Players League), NASL (North American Soccer League), YTS (Youth Training Scheme), ZDS (Zenith Data Systems), apps (appearances), sub (substitute), (N) for (North) and (S) for (South). Figures after the + sign in the players' records indicate the number of substitute appearances they made for the club.

Where a single year appears in the text (when referring to an individual player's career), this indicates, in most cases, the second half of a season: i.e., 1975 is 1974–75. However, when the figures (dates) such as 1975–80 appear, this means seasons 1975–76 to 1979–80 inclusive and not 1974–80.

If you spot any discrepancies, errors, even omissions, I would appreciate it very much if you could contact me (via the publishers) so that all can be amended in any future publications about Aston Villa Football Club. If you have anything to add, this would also be most welcome, as people tend to reveal unknown facts from all sources when football is the topic of conversation.

WHO'S WHO OF
ASTON VILLA,
1874—2004

ADAM, JAMES
Winger: 25 apps, 3 goals
Born: Glasgow, 13 May 1931
Career: Blantyre Celtic (amateur), Aldershot (amateur, 1948; professional, August 1951), Spennymoor United (August 1952), Luton Town (July 1953), VILLA (August 1959), Stoke City (July 1961), Falkirk (July 1963), South Melbourne/Australia (June 1964; later Australian staff coach and physical education teacher; became Victoria staff coach and assistant coach to the Australian national team), Stourbridge (August 1967), Oxford United (assistant trainer, November 1968, then manager for four weeks)

A fast winger able to occupy both flanks, Adam spent two seasons at Villa Park, gaining a Second Division championship medal in 1960. He made over 150 appearances for Luton.

AITKEN, CHARLES ALEXANDER
Left-back: 657+3 apps, 16 goals
Born: Edinburgh, 1 May 1942
Career: Gorsebridge Juniors, Edinburgh Thistle, VILLA (August 1959), New York Cosmos (May 1976), Worcester City (1977–78), VILLA Old Stars (from 1979), Talbot Tankards FC; later ran an antiques shop in Acocks Green (Birmingham)

Aitken spent 17 years with Villa and holds the club's appearance record of 660 games (of which 561 were in the Football League). He missed only 18 out of 252 First Division matches between April 1961 and May 1967. His first and last League games were against Sheffield Wednesday; he won a League Cup-winner's tankard in 1975, having earlier collected two runner's-up medals, 1963 and 1971. A member of Villa's Third Division championship-winning side in 1972, he was voted 'Midland Footballer of the Year' three years later. Capped once by Scotland at Under-23 level, Aitken had a testimonial match against

Coventry in 1970. An all-time Villa great, he skippered the side on several occasions and was a terrific club man.

ALDIS, BASIL PETER
Left-back: 295 apps, 1 goal
Born: Kings Heath, Birmingham, 11 April 1927
Career: Pineapple School/Stirchley, Cadbury Works, Hay Green (1947), VILLA (amateur, November 1948; professional, January 1949), Hinckley Athletic (July 1960); Slavia FC/Australia (player/coach, February 1964), FC Wilhelmina/Australia (coach, 1965–66), Melbourne Lions /Australia (coach, 1966–69); Alvechurch (player/manager, July 1969–May 1970); Mitchell and Butler's works side (player/coach, 1971–72); later worked for a firm in Earlswood, was an education and welfare officer in Redditch and also a groundsman at a Solihull school

Aldis, like Aitken, also occupied the left-back position and he, too, gave Villa tremendous service. An ex-Cadbury chocolate-maker, Aldis had a sunshine smile and during his time with Villa scored just one goal – a spectacular 35-yard header in the League game against Sunderland in 1952. He helped Villa win the FA Cup in 1957 and in 1966 was voted Australia's 'Footballer of the Year'. When he was with Hinckley, Aldis became one of only two players ever to appear in 13 different rounds of the FA Cup!

ALDRIDGE, ALBERT ARTHUR JAMES
Full-back: 14 apps
Born: Walsall, 13 April 1864 – *Died*: Birmingham, May 1891
Career: Walsall Council and Pleck Schools, Walsall Swifts (August 1881), West Bromwich Albion (March 1886; professional, July 1886), Walsall Town Swifts (July 1888), VILLA (August 1889; retired, April 1891)

An England international full-back (two caps gained), Aldridge presented a formidable barrier, being hardy, resolute and unyielding: the harder the tussle, the better he played. An FA Cup winner with WBA in 1888, after being a runner-up the previous year (against Villa), he was forced to retire through poor health and sadly died aged 27.

ALLBACK, MARCUS
Striker: 20+24 apps, 7 goals
Born: Stockholm, Sweden, 5 July 1973
Career: Orgryte IS/Sweden (August 1990), Lyngby BK/Denmark (loan, March 1998), Bari/Italy (loan, August–November 1998), SC Heerenveen/Holland (September 2000), VILLA (£2m, May 2002), FC Hansa Rostock/Germany (August 2004)

Allback, a Swedish international, World Cup and Euro 2004 striker (6 ft tall, 12 st. 4 lb in weight), struggled to get into Villa's first team. Indeed, he had to wait until the last two months of the 2002–03 season before getting a decent run in the side. A strong, forceful player, he ended his first campaign in English soccer with five goals in 20 Premiership games, 11 as a substitute. Capped over 30 times by his country (20 goals) he made more substitute appearances than he started games for Villa, having scored 114 times in 271 League games for his four previous clubs (88 in 203 for Orgryte).

ALLEN, ALBERT ARTHUR

Forward: 56 apps, 33 goals
Born: Aston, Birmingham, 7 April 1867 – *Died*: Birmingham, 13 October 1899
Career: St Phillips FC/Aston, VILLA (August 1884; retired, through ill-health, May 1891)

Allen was a prolific goalscorer as well as a hard-working utility forward, able to play on the wing or inside, having a wonderful understanding with Denny Hodgetts. One pen-portrait of Allen revealed: 'Lack of height and size did not affect his pluck; he dribbled like an artist and shot with force and good aim.' A modest, unassuming player, he hit a hat-trick in his only international game for England against Ireland in 1888 and also claimed Villa's first League hat-trick against Notts County six months later. Allen was forced to retire at the age of 24.

ALLEN, BARNEY WILLIAM

Outside-right: 3 apps, 1 goal
Born: Hockley, Birmingham 1885 – *Died*: *circa* 1946
Career: Hockley Hill School, Icknield Street Old Boys, Leominster, VILLA (April 1905), Chesterfield (November 1905), Kidderminster Harriers (1906–08)

Allen was an efficient winger, 5 ft 6 in. tall who deputised for Billy Brawn. He made 20 League appearances for Chesterfield.

ALLEN, JAMES PHILLIPS

Centre-half: 160 apps, 3 goals
Born: Poole, Dorset, 16 October 1909 – *Died*: Southsea, February 1995
Career: Longfleet St Mary's school, Poole Central, Poole Town (August 1927), Portsmouth (£1,200, July 1932), VILLA (£10,775, June 1934; retired, injured, May 1944); guest for Birmingham, Chelsea, Crystal Palace, Fulham, Luton Town, Portsmouth and Southampton during WW2; became Sports and Welfare Officer with Gaskell and Chambers; VILLA (colts coach, September 1946), Colchester United (manager, July 1948; retired April 1953); later a Southend licensee

Allen was a solid defender who had the ideal frame for the 'stopper' centre-half. He played 145 games for Portsmouth, appearing in the 1934 FA Cup final. A record signing by Villa, he was a Second Division championship-winner in 1938 and was capped twice by England and also represented the Football League. He guided Colchester into the Football League in 1950.

ALLEN, MALCOLM
Forward: 4 apps
Born: Caernarfon, 27 March 1967
Career: Watford (apprentice, July 1983; professional, March 1985), VILLA (loan, September–October 1987), Norwich City (£175,000, August 1988), Millwall (£400,000, March 1990), Newcastle United (£300,000, August 1993; retired, injured, December 1995); Gwynedd Council (coach and youth development officer, July 1996)
In his career, Allen, signed as a replacement forward, scored 42 goals in over 160 League games, won 14 caps for Wales and also represented his country at both youth- and 'B'-team levels.

ALPAY, OZALAN FEHMI
Defender: 69+2 apps, 1 goal
Born: Karsiyaka, near Ismir, Turkey, 29 May 1973
Career: Altay FC/Turkey (August 1992), Besiktas/Turkey (June 1993), Jet-Pa FC/Turkey (briefly, 1994), Fenerbahce/Turkey (loan, July 1999), VILLA (£5.6m, July 2000–May 2004)
When Turkish international defender Alpay signed a four-year contract with Villa there was uproar in Turkey – because everyone thought he was going to sign permanently for Fenerbahce! Vastly experienced and on a wage of £22,000 per week, he played in 14 of Turkey's Euro 2000 matches, including ten qualifying games, and was sent off for elbowing Gomes of Portugal in the quarter-finals. A well-built, hard-tackling centre-back, 6 ft 2 in. tall and 13 st. 4 lb in weight, with over 80 caps under his belt, he played in the Champions League with Besiktas and helped Fenerbahce to fourth place in the Turkish First Division in 2000. Made only 12 Premiership appearances in his last two seasons with Villa having scored 12 goals in 200 games in eight years of Turkish football.

ANDERSON, DAVID WALTER
Wing-half: 5 apps
Born: Hockley, Birmingham, 1861 – *Deceased*
Career: Hockley Belmont, VILLA (August 1881), Abbey FC (June 1883)
Anderson, a well-built wing-half, made his senior appearances for Villa in the FA Cup of 1882–83. A spate of niggling injuries led to him leaving the club.

ANDERSON, WILLIAM JOHN
Winger: 264+3 apps, 45 goals
Born: Liverpool, 24 January 1947
Career: Liverpool and Merseyside Boys, Manchester United (junior, April 1962; professional, February 1964), VILLA (£20,000, January 1967), Cardiff City (£60,000, February 1973), Portland Timbers (July 1977; retired May 1979); later an executive with a commercial radio station in Oregon (USA)
Anderson, a fast raiding left-winger and reserve to George Best at Old Trafford,

had film-star looks and was a huge favourite with the female supporters everywhere he went. An FA Youth Cup winner with the Reds, he also gained England youth international honours and played for Villa in the 1971 League Cup final against Spurs, also helping them win the Third Division championship the following season. Top marksman with six League goals in 1968–69, he scored in all five matches against Wrexham in 1971–72.

ANGEL, JUAN PABLO ARANZO
Striker: 86+17 apps, 43 goals
Born: Medelin, Colombia, 24 October 1975
Career: Colombian junior football, Atletico Nacional/Colombia (1993), River Plate/Argentina (July 1995), VILLA (£9.5m, January 2001)
Colombian international striker Pablo Angel was Villa's record signing when he joined in 2001 after tedious on–off negotiations. Already an established marksman, he scored 17 goals in 17 games during the 2000–01 season before Villa secured his signature after boss John Gregory had flown 6,000 miles to Buenos Aires to watch him play. 'He has all the qualities to become a real star in the Premiership,' said Gregory. Capped over 20 times by his country, having earlier played at youth-team level, Angel has pace, power, accuracy, ability and commitment. After his debut at Manchester United, he struck his first goal in a 3–2 win over Coventry in May 2003 (his eighth game in the Premiership). He notched 16 goals in 2001–02, netted just once the following year and then top-scored with 23 in 2003–04.

ANSELL, BARRY
Left-back: 1 app.
Born: Small Heath, Birmingham, 29 September 1947
Career: Waverley Grammar School, VILLA (junior, June 1965; professional, October 1967–May 1969); non-League football (1969–74)
Reserve left-back Ansell's only League outing for Villa was at Cardiff in December 1967 when he replaced Charlie Aitken.

ANSTEY, BRENDEL
Goalkeeper: 45 apps
Born: Bristol, 1887 – *Died*: Wednesbury, 12 December 1933
Career: Hanham Juniors, Bristol Rovers (August 1910), VILLA (February 1911); guest for Bellis and Morcom FC, Birmingham, BSA and Lincoln City during WW1; Leicester City (September 1919), Mid-Rhondda (July 1920), Wednesbury (June 1922)
Anstey was a competent goalkeeper, signed initially as a replacement for Billy George, before understudying England international Sam Hardy.

APPERLEY, CHARLES WILLIAM
Defender: 8 apps
Born: Birmingham, 1861 – *Died*: South Africa, 1926
Career: Birmingham St George's, VILLA (August 1882); emigrated to South
    Africa, summer of 1884
A well-built defender, able to play at right-half or centre-half, Apperley was a
regular in Villa's first team during his two seasons with the club, appearing in
eight successive FA Cup games. He was reserve for England in 1883–84.

ARMFIELD, WILLIAM CHARLES WASSELL
Winger: 12 apps, 2 goals
Born: Handsworth, Birmingham 7 July 1903 – *Died*: *circa* 1970
Career: Ellison's FC/Birmingham (August 1920), VILLA (March 1922), Exeter
    City (August 1929), Gillingham (August 1932), Droitwich (briefly), Brierley
    Hill Alliance (August 1933; retired November 1933); later a member of the
    Woodpecker Bowling Club; worked for H.W. Perion Ltd (nuts and bolts)
A tall, skilful winger, Armfield was mainly reserve to Dicky York for most of his
seven seasons at Villa Park. He netted 17 times in 80 outings for Exeter, figuring
in the Grecians' FA Cup giant-killing side of 1930–31. Two weeks after joining
Brierley Hill he broke his right leg in a friendly and two months later had the
limb amputated. A junior international, capped in 1925, he played for the
Colours against the Whites in an international trial that same year.

ASHE, NORMAN JAMES
Outside-right: 5 apps
Born: Bloxwich, 16 November 1943
Career: Brierley Hill schoolboys, VILLA (amateur, July 1958; professional,
    November 1960), Rotherham United (£2,000, March 1963), Nuneaton
    Borough (July 1964–69)
Right-winger 'Tosh' Ashe made his League debut for Villa at the age of 16
years, 48 days in January 1960 against Swansea Town (Division Two). He joined
the club with Alan Baker and won England schoolboy and youth international
honours.

ASHFIELD, GEORGE OWEN
Defender: 10 apps
Born: Manchester, 7 April 1934
Career: Stockport County, VILLA (March 1954), Chester (February 1959),
    Rhyl (September 1960; retired, injured, May 1967)
A reserve full-back or centre-half, Ashfield remained loyal to Villa for five years
before slipping down two divisions.

ASHMORE, WALTER WILLIAM

Goalkeeper: 1 app.
Born: Smethwick, 1867 – *Died*: 1940
Career: West Bromwich Standard (1886), VILLA (August 1888), Aston Unity
   FC (April 1889–May 1891)
Reserve keeper Ashmore's only League game for Villa was against Everton in
September 1888 when he deputised for Jimmy Warner. Besides soccer, he also
played cricket for Aston Unity CC.

ASHTON, DEREK O.

Defender: 10 apps
Born: Worksop, Notts, 4 July 1922
Career: Worksop Schools, Wolverhampton Wanderers (amateur, April 1940;
   professional, September 1941); guest for Leicester City (March 1946);
   VILLA (May 1946), Wellington Town (August 1951–May 1953; later coach,
   June 1959)
'Paleface' Ashton, a former coalminer in South Yorkshire, spent six years at
Molineux, during which time he failed to establish himself in the first XI. A
versatile defender, he made his debut for Villa against Blackpool in September
1946, having his next outing two years later.

ASKEW, LESLIE WALTER

Half-back: 2 apps
Born: Marylebone, London, 1886 – *Died*: 1955
Career: Xylonite FC, Tottenham Gothic Works FC, Chadwell Heath, Finchley
   FC, Southend United, Norwich City (briefly 1909), VILLA (August 1910),
   West Ham United (May 1912–May 1917)
Askew spent most of his two years at Villa Park playing in the second team. He
later made over 100 appearances for West Ham but did not figure after WW1.
He was banned from football for quite some time when registered with
Chadwell Heath.

ASPINALL, WARREN

Forward: 45+5 apps, 16 goals
Born: Wigan, 13 September 1967
Career: Wigan Athletic (junior, 1983; professional, August 1985), Everton
   (£150,000, February 1986), Wigan Athletic (loan, February 1986), VILLA
   (£300,000, February 1987), Portsmouth (£315,000, August 1988),
   Bournemouth (loan, August 1993), Swansea City (loan, October 1993),
   Bournemouth (£20,000, December 1993), Carlisle United (free, March
   1995), Brentford (£50,000, November 1997), Colchester United (free,
   February 1999), Brighton and Hove Albion (free, September 1999; retired,
   injured, November 2000; appointed scout, January 2001)
The only player recruited by Villa manager Billy McNeill, Aspinall was a useful

marksman who developed into an efficient midfielder. An England youth international, he helped Wigan win the FRT in 1985, Carlisle the AWS in 1997 and gained promotion from Division Three with Colchester in 1999. After making his senior debut in 1985, he went on to amass over 575 appearances and scored 110 goals.

ASTLEY, DAVID JOHN
Forward: 173 apps, 100 goals
Born: Dowlais, near Merthyr, Glamorgan, 11 October 1909 – *Died*: Birchington, Kent, 7 November 1989
Career: New Road Amateurs, Dowlais Welfare (1923), Merthyr Town (amateur, July 1927; professional, August 1927), Charlton Athletic (£100, January 1928), VILLA (£1,500, June 1931), Derby County (£5,250, November 1936), Blackpool (January 1939); guest for Charlton Athletic and Clapton Orient during WW2; later coach of Inter Milan/Italy (June 1948), Genoa/Italy (June 1949), Djurgardens IF/Sweden (June 1951), Sandvikens/Sweden (until May 1956); later landlord of the White Horse pub (Ramsgate)
One of the best marksmen to come out of Wales, ex-miner Dai Astley had a fine career, spanning 15 years. In that time he scored 200 goals including 172 in 376 League games, won 13 caps for Wales (12 goals) and played in WW2 internationals against England. His best season with Villa came in 1933–34 when he netted 33 times in 44 outings. He was Villa's top scorer in three successive seasons (1933–36).

ASTON, CHARLES LANE
Right-back: 24 apps
Born: Bilston, 1875 – *Died*: Leytonstone, 9 January 1931
Career: Willenhall White Star, Bilston United, Walsall (December 1895), VILLA (£300, April 1898), Queens Park Rangers (June 1901), Burton United (August 1902), Gresley Rovers (August 1903), Burton United (August 1904), Watford (May 1905), Leyton (August 1908; retired May 1910); VILLA (trainer, after WW1)
An efficient full-back who enjoyed floating long passes down the wing or across the field, Aston never established himself at Villa Park, yet later took his career appearance-tally past the 300 mark (106 with Watford).

ATHERSMITH, WILLIAM CHARLES
Outside-right: 311 apps, 86 goals
Born: Bloxwich, Staffordshire, 10 May 1872 – *Died*: Shifnal, 18 September 1910
Career: Walsall Road Council School, Bloxwich Wanderers, Bloxwich Strollers, Unity Gas Depot, VILLA (February 1891), Birmingham (June 1901), Grimsby Town (trainer, May 1908–May 1909)
One of the fastest right-wingers of his era, Athersmith reigned supreme on his

day with only Billy Bassett (WBA) comparable to him for speed and ability. A great touchline player, he centred with unerring precision but at times was a trifle wayward, frequently straying offside, so eager was he to get forward. In his ten years with Villa he won five League championship medals (1894, 1895, 1897, 1899, 1900), two FA Cup-winner's medals (1895, 1897) and was instrumental when the double was achieved in 1897. Capped 12 times by England, he played in 100 games for Birmingham and was suspended by the FA in 1906 for taking part in the Tagg and Campbell tour to Germany. It is also on record that during a League game against Sheffield United in November 1894, the rain was so severe that Athersmith and his colleague Tom Wilkes both borrowed umbrellas from spectators to protect themselves from the elements.

ATKINSON, DALIAN ROBERT
Striker: 106+10 apps, 34 goals
Born: Shrewsbury, 21 March 1968
Career: Ipswich Town (apprentice, June 1984; professional, June 1987), Sheffield Wednesday (£450,000, June 1989), Real Sociedad/Spain (£1.7m, August 1990), VILLA (£1.6m, July 1991), Fenerbahce/Turkey (June 1996)

A stocky, well-built striker, Atkinson had mixed fortunes at Villa. On his day he was terrific but could also be mediocre! Capped by England 'B', he battled against injury for long periods but nevertheless was a fine player who gained a League Cup-winner's medal in 1994 and scored a goal every three games for Villa before leaving for Turkey.

BACHE, JOSEPH WILLIAM
Forward: 474 apps, 184 goals
Born: Stourbridge, 8 February 1880 – *Died*: 10 November 1960
Career: Bewdley Victoria, Stourbridge (July 1897), VILLA (professional, December 1900); guest for Notts County (1915–16); Mid-Rhondda (player/manager, July 1919), Grimsby Town (player/coach, July 1920), Rot-Weiss FC Frankfurt/Germany (coach/trainer, May 1921), Mannheim FC/Germany (player, November 1924), VILLA (reserve-team coach, July 1927); Mannheim FC/Germany (coach, July 1928), Rot-Weiss FC Frankfurt/Germany (coach, 1929); later hospital clerical worker and landlord of Traveller's Rest, Aston Cross, and the Coaching House, Evesham; then worked for gents' outfitters, Bristol Road South, Northfield (Birmingham)

A cultured inside-forward and occasional left-winger, Bache had few equals in the art of dribbling, although at times he could be somewhat selfish. A good-tempered, brainy footballer he displayed a masterly technique on the pitch and gave Villa great service for some 15 years. An international trialist and also reserve for his country, he won seven full England caps (1903–11) and succeeded Howard Spencer as Villa's captain. Forming a wonderful left-wing partnership with Albert Hall, he gained two FA Cup-winner's medals (1905,

1913) and a First Division championship medal (1910) and represented the Birmingham County FA and Birmingham against London in 1909 and 1913 respectively. His two brothers were also at Stourbridge.

BAIRD, JOHN

Defender: 69 apps

Born: Dumbartonshire, Scotland, 1871 – *Died:* 31 July 1905

Career: Vale Athletic, Vale of Leven (1886), Vale Wanderers (1887), Kidderminster, VILLA (briefly, 1889), Kidderminster Olympic (1888), Kidderminster Harriers (1889), VILLA (October 1891), Leicester Fosse (August 1895; retired April 1896); later returned to Scotland

Strength, skill and stamina were Baird's attributes. A real teak-tough defender, he could play at full-back or left-half and appeared in Villa's 1892 FA Cup final defeat by WBA. He died from a heart attack.

BAKER, ALAN REEVES

Inside-forward: 109 apps, 17 goals

Born: Tipton, 22 June 1944

Career: Brierley Hill Schoolboys, VILLA (junior, June 1958; professional, July 1961), Walsall (£10,000, July 1966; retired May 1971); later a leather-cutter in Walsall

Inside-forward Baker was highly rated as a youngster and played alongside Norman Ashe as a schoolboy and also with Villa. He had a good career, gaining a League Cup runner's-up prize in 1963, and scored 36 goals in 164 appearances for the Saddlers.

BALABAN, BOSKO

Striker: 2+9 apps

Born: Croatia, 15 October 1978

Career: NK Rijeka/Croatia (professional, October 1995), Dinamo Zagreb/Croatia (season 2000–01), VILLA (£6m, August 2001), Dinamo Zagreb/Croatia (loan, August 2002), Empoli/Italy (December 2003)

When he joined Villa on a £15,000-a-week contract, striker Balaban was already an established Croatian international with 13 caps to his credit. He was also a proven goalscorer with a huge reputation, having fired Croatia towards the World Cup finals. But he simply couldn't get into Villa's side and struggled throughout his stay with the club, failing to find the net at senior level.

BALL, JOHN HENRY

Goalkeeper: 2 apps

Born: Birmingham, 1857 – *Died:* Birmingham, 1940

Career: Arcadians (1877), VILLA (August 1879), Walsall Town Swifts (July 1880–May 1884)

Ball, 5 ft 6 in. tall, made the first of his two senior appearances for Villa in the club's initial FA Cup tie against Stafford Road in December 1879. He did not play competitive football after 1884.

BALL, THOMAS EDGAR

Centre-half: 77 apps

Born: Usworth, County Durham, 11 February 1899 – *Died*: Perry Barr, Birmingham, 19 November 1923

Career: Usworth Central School, Wadley Colliery (Tyneside Amateur League, 1913–17), Felling Colliery FC (1917), Newcastle United (July 1919), VILLA (January 1920–November 1923)

Ball was only 24 when he was shot dead in Brick Kiln Lane, Perry Barr, by his policeman neighbour George Stagg, who was sentenced to death for murder, later reduced to life imprisonment. A strapping centre-half, he was being groomed to replace Barson in Villa's defence and was a gentleman off the field and a real lion on it! His death came as a bitter blow to the club, for Ball was destined for international honours. His mother was Italian.

BANKS, HERBERT EDWARD

Inside-forward: 56 apps

Born: Coventry, 1874 – *Died*: Smethwick, 1947

Career: Leamington junior football, 72nd Seaforth Highlanders, Everton (October 1896), St Mirren (loan, January 1897), Third Lanark (August 1897), Millwall Athletic (March 1899), VILLA (April 1901), Bristol City (November 1901), Watford (May 1903), Coventry City (August 1904), Stafford Rangers (December 1905), Verity's Athletic (October 1906; reinstated as an amateur May 1907; retired April 1910); later worked for a Birmingham-based engineering firm

Banks joined Villa a month after playing for England against Ireland. He made only a handful of appearances for the club but later scored 18 goals in 40 League games for Bristol City and 21 in 19 starts for Watford.

BARBER, THOMAS

Wing-half: 68 apps, 10 goals

Born: West Stanley, 20 February 1888 – *Died*: Nuneaton, 18 September 1925

Career: Todd's Nook Board School, Hamotley FC, West Stanley FC (1904), Bolton Wanderers (junior, August 1907; professional, May 1908), VILLA (December 1912), served with the Footballers' battalion during WW1; Celtic (guest, August 1918), Partick Thistle (guest, December 1918), Linfield (guest, January 1919), Belfast Celtic (guest, January 1919), Stalybridge Celtic (August 1919), Crystal Palace (October 1919), Merthyr Town (September 1920), Pontypridd (briefly, January 1921), Walsall (August–December 1921), Darlaston (February 1922), Hinckley Athletic (August 1922; retired May 1923), Boscombe FC (trainer/coach, June 1923–25)

Wing-half Barber was a clever, enterprising player who won a Second Division championship medal with Bolton in 1910 and headed the winning goal for Villa in the 1913 FA Cup final against Sunderland. He suffered serious leg wounds on the Western Front (Battle of the Somme) and was laid up in an Aberdeen infirmary in August 1916. Told he would never play football again, he defied doctors' orders, and turned out in an Inter Hospital Fund game at Celtic Park in June 1918. Sent to work in a munitions department in Glasgow, he helped Celtic to two wins out of two. Barber was admitted to hospital with pleurisy in September 1918; five years later he was hospitalised again, suffering from tuberculosis, but this time he never recovered.

BARKER, JEFFREY
Left-half: 3 apps
Born: Scunthorpe, 16 October 1915 – *Died:* 1985
Career: Brigg Town/Goole Town, Sheffield United (amateur), Scunthorpe United, VILLA (£400, November 1936); guest for Blackpool, Rochdale, Walsall, Watford, Solihull Town and Huddersfield Town during WW2; Huddersfield Town (November 1945), Scunthorpe United (August 1948), Goole Town (1951; retired July 1952)

Barker stepped into Bob Iverson's boots for his three League games for Villa against Burnley, Sheffield United and Spurs in 1937. After WW2 he starred in Scunthorpe's first season in the League (1950–51) and made over 150 appearances during his career, playing for Birmingham against a Services XI in 1940 and for the FA XI against the British Army of the Rhine in Germany in 1945. His brother, Josh Barker, played for Derby and England.

BARNIE-ADSHEAD, DR WILLIAM EWART
Centre-half: 2 apps
Born: Dudley, 10 April 1901 – *Died:* Birmingham, 28 January 1951
Career: Birmingham University, Corinthians (1918–19), VILLA (August 1920), Birmingham University (1922–23), Corinthians (June 1923–May 1924), Dudley Town

An amateur throughout his career, Barnie-Adshead appeared in only two first-team games for Villa owing to his university studies. Also a very keen county cricketer with Worcestershire, he averaged 11.61 from 22 innings in 12 games. He won England amateur international honours at soccer whilst at university, where he qualified as a surgeon. His father was the mayor of Dudley.

BARRETT, EARL DELLISER
Defender: 142+1 apps, 2 goals
Born: Rochdale, 28 April 1967
Career: Manchester City (juniors, 1983; professional, April 1985), Chester City (loan, March 1986), Oldham Athletic (November 1987), VILLA (£1.7m, February 1992), Everton (£1.7m, January 1995), Sheffield United (loan,

January 1998), Sheffield Wednesday (February 1998; retired July 1999)
Stylish defender, able to play at right-back or centre-back, Barrett was capped
three times by England, represented his country at 'B' and Under-21 levels and
played for the Football League. He gained a Second Division championship in
1991 with Oldham and a League Cup-winner's medal in 1994 with Villa,
picking up a Charity Shield prize with Everton in 1995. Barrett made over 400
League appearances in all.

BARRETT, KENNETH BRIAN

Winger: 5 apps, 3 goals
Born: Bromsgrove, 5 May 1938
Career: Stoke Works/Bromsgrove, VILLA (amateur, January 1957; professional,
February 1957), Lincoln City (June 1959), Weymouth (loan,
September–November 1960), Stourbridge (June 1963; retired February
1968); later manager of a bookmaker's shop
Winger Barrett, small in stature with attacking ideas, was spotted by former
Villa player Frank Shell starring in the Bromsgrove and District League. He was
adequate cover for Les Smith and Peter McParland during his time with Villa.
He served as a soldier when with Lincoln, based mainly at Blandford Camp, and
played for his unit in several representative matches.

BARRY, GARETH

Midfield: 222+14 apps, 12 goals
Born: Hastings, 23 February 1981
Career: Brighton and Hove Albion (associate schoolboy forms), VILLA
(apprentice, June 1997; professional, February 1998)
A versatile performer, Barry made rapid strides, reaching the top of the football
ladder after just two years at Villa Park. Despite being nurtured by Brighton, he
joined Villa as a 16 year old and initially played in midfield. He made his debut
as a substitute in the penultimate Premiership game of the 1997–98 season at
Sheffield Wednesday, with his full debut following in the last match against
Arsenal. Barry got better and better and has now topped the 200 appearance
mark for Villa while also being a full England international, having gained the
first of his eight senior caps as a 'sub' against Ukraine prior to Euro 2000. He
has also represented his country in 25 Under-21 matches and a handful of
youth-team games.

BARSON, FRANK

Centre-half: 108 apps, 10 goals
Born: Grimethorpe, Sheffield, 10 April 1891 – *Died*: Winson Green,
Birmingham, 13 September 1968
Career: Grimethorpe Road County School, Albion FC/Sheffield, Cammell
Laird FC/Sheffield, Barnsley (August 1911); guest for Burnley (1916–17);
VILLA (£2,850, October 1919), Manchester United (August 1922), Watford

(May 1928), Hartlepool United (player/coach, May 1929), Wigan Borough (initially as an amateur; professional, July 1930), Rhyl Athletic (player/manager, June 1931), Stourbridge (manager, July–August 1935), VILLA (coach/head trainer, October 1935), Solihull Town ('B' team manager, 1940), Swansea Town (trainer, July 1947–February 1954), Lye Town (trainer, September 1954; manager, October 1954; retired April 1956); was a bailiff during WW2

Barson was a bastion in defence. He was a captain and centre-half, who was a great inspiration to the rest of the team. A hard, tough, rugged Yorkshireman, he gained an FA Cup-winner's medal when Villa defeated Huddersfield in the 1920 final. Barson also won one England cap that same season, against Wales at Highbury (19 March). He switched his allegiance to Manchester United in 1922 – after refusing to move from his Yorkshire home and live in Birmingham! He was adamant that he would never move to 'Brummagem' and often had heated words with the Villa directors. On Boxing Day 1920, so determined was he to play for Villa, and due to a train derailment, he trudged seven miles through heavy snow to make sure he arrived in time for the game at Old Trafford. Playing out of his skin, he helped Villa win 3–1 in front of a record crowd of 70,504.

With United, he performed even better, appearing in 152 games for the Reds (four goals). Highly controversial, Barson was often in trouble with referees and during his career was sent off at least 12 times (twice with Villa). Overall he was suspended for a year, having a ban of six months during his Watford days. He also received an eight-week suspension following an incident in the Manchester United against Manchester City FA Cup semi-final in March 1926, when it was alleged that he punched City's centre-half Sam Cowan unconscious.

Barson was promised a pub if he skippered Manchester United back to the First Division. He did just that and was given a hotel in Ardwick Green. Scores of punters turned up for the official opening. However, after 15 minutes behind the bar, Barson, utterly fed up, handed the keys over to the head waiter and walked out, never to return.

BAXTER, WILLIAM
Wing-half: 108 apps, 6 goals
Born: Leven, near Methil, Fife, 21 September 1924 – *Died*: East Wemyss, Fife, 9 November 2002
Career: Vale of Leven Schools, Wolverhampton Wanderers (junior, 1939; professional, September 1945), VILLA (November 1953; retired May 1957, became reserve-team coach, later assistant trainer, then senior trainer, July 1964–June 1968), St Mirren (coach, July 1968; manager, August 1969–October 1970), Raith Rovers (manager, October 1970–November 1971); later Raa IF Helsingborgs/Sweden (coach, November 1976–March 1977)

Baxter spent 38 years in football: as an aggressive, workmanlike wing-half, then coach, trainer and finally as manager. Despite a record 213 Central League appearances for Wolves, he was unable to gain a regular first-team place at Molineux due to the quality of the half-backs at the club. A totally committed player, he served Villa well.

BEARD, MALCOLM

Wing-half: 6+1 apps

Born: Cannock, 3 May 1942

Career: Birmingham City (junior, June 1957; professional, May 1959), VILLA (July 1971–May 1972), Atherstone United (1972–73), Saudi Arabia (coach, 1994), Birmingham City (scout, mid-1970s), VILLA (chief scout, 1982), Middlesbrough (coach, 1987), Portsmouth (coach, 1990), Atherstone (July 1994), VILLA (reserve-team coach/manager, 1997–98)

Before joining Villa, ever-reliable wing-half Beard scored 32 goals in 405 senior appearances for the Blues, gaining England youth international honours and playing in both the final of the Inter-Cities Fairs Cup (1961) and the final of the League Cup (1963) when Villa were beaten over two legs.

BEATON, WILLIAM

Goalkeeper: 1 app.

Born: Kincardine-on-Forth, Scotland, 30 September 1935

Career: Dunfermline Athletic, VILLA (£30,000, October 1958), Airdrieonians (February 1960–May 1963)

As a lad, Beaton preferred rugby but quickly took up soccer and was 15 when he made his debut for Dunfermline against Leith. He developed into a competent custodian and was signed by Villa as cover for Nigel Sims. His only first-team outing was away at Leicester soon after signing, when the Foxes won 6–3. After manager Eric Houghton had been sacked and Joe Mercer installed, Beaton became surplus to requirements and returned to Scotland.

BEDINGFIELD, FRANK

Centre-forward: 1 app.

Born: Sunderland, March 1877 – *Died*: South Africa, 3 November 1904

Career: South Shields Schools, Yarmouth Town (briefly), Rushden (1896), VILLA (June 1898), Queens Park Rangers (August 1899), Portsmouth (May 1900; collapsed after playing in an FA Cup tie for Pompey in 1902); later went to South Africa

Very useful at reserve-team level, Bedingfield didn't complete a first-team game for Villa! He was one of the 11 players who lined up in the unfinished League game at Sheffield Wednesday in November 1898 (it was abandoned with only 11 minutes to go), scoring his side's only goal. When Villa travelled back to play out the remaining few minutes, in March 1899, he was replaced by Billy Garraty. After leaving Villa, he scored 21 goals in 32 games for QPR and 58 in 69 for Pompey. He died of consumption.

BEESON, GEORGE WILLIAM
Full-back: 71 apps
Born: Clay Cross, Chesterfield, 31 August 1906 – *Died*: Wythall, near Kings Heath, Birmingham, January 1999
Career: Clay Cross FC, Bury (trialist), North Wingfield FC, New Tupton FC, Chesterfield (August 1927), Sheffield Wednesday (March 1929), VILLA (August 1934 in exchange for Joe Nibloe), New Tupton FC (1936), Walsall (June 1938; retired May 1940), Djerv/Norway (coach, July 1946), Ollerton Colliery (November 1946), Brodsworth Main Colliery (June 1948); later ran a fish and chip business in Birmingham (bought initially in May 1939); also worked at George Ellisons Ltd for whom he played cricket and coached the football team, occasionally playing himself

A fine figure of a man, Beeson who was initially a goalkeeper, was a strong-tackling, full-back who never shirked a tackle. An England reserve, he represented the Football League, the Central League against London Combination (1936), was reserve for an England international trial (1935) and made 75 appearances for Sheffield Wednesday. He often ate two pre-match dinners to give him strength. He died from Alzheimer's disease.

BEINLICH, STEFAN
Utility: 7+9 apps, 1 goal
Born: Germany, 13 January 1972
Career: PFV Bergmann Borsig (German Second Division), VILLA (October 1991); returned to Germany (April 1993)

A defender who could also man midfield (if required), Beinlich was only 19 when he signed for Villa with fellow countryman Matthias Breitkreutz in 1991. He failed to hold down a regular first-team place and returned 'home' after 18 months in England.

BENWELL, LOUIS ARTHUR
Goalkeeper: 1 app.
Born: Worcester, 1870 – *Died*: Worcester, 28 October 1936
Career: Singers FC/Coventry, Berwick Rangers/Worcester (August 1890), VILLA (June 1893), Berwick Rangers/Worcester (briefly), Walsall Town Swifts (August 1894), Worcester City, Berwick Rangers/Worcester (May 1895–April 1896); later a county cricket umpire and Midland hockey player

Deputy to goalkeeper Bill Dunning, Benwell's only League outing for Villa was at Bolton in November 1893. He had three separate spells with Berwick Rangers.

BERESFORD, JOSEPH
Forward: 251 apps, 73 goals
Born: Chesterfield, 26 February 1906 – *Died*: Birmingham, 26 February 1978
Career: Bentley Toll Bar School (1917), Bentley New Village Old Boys (1920),

Doncaster Schools, Ashern Road Working Men's Club/Doncaster (1922), Bartley Colliery, Mexborough Athletic (1923), Mansfield Town (May 1926), VILLA (May 1927), Preston North End (September 1935), Swansea Town (December 1937), Stourbridge (August 1938), Sutton Town (September 1939; retired May 1941); returned as guest for Hartlepool United (1943); opened a fish shop in Stourbridge (May 1939); later employed for 11 years at ICI, Witton

Inside- or centre-forward Beresford was Villa's 'human dynamo' for eight years (1927–35). After bedding himself in at the club, he became a fitting partner to 'Pongo' Waring and Billy Walker in Villa's attack. Capped by England against Czechoslovakia in Prague in 1934, his career with Villa ended when manager Jimmy McMullan left, being transferred to Preston, for whom he appeared in the FA Cup final, collecting a loser's medal against Sunderland. He was later reunited with his former Villa colleague Alex Talbot at Stourbridge.

BETTS, ANTHONY THOMAS

Inside-forward: 1+3 apps

Born: Sandiacre, Nottinghamshire, 31 October 1953

Career: VILLA (junior, May 1969; professional, March 1972), Southport (loan, December 1974–February 1975), Portland Timbers (July–August 1975), Port Vale (trial, September 1975), Boldmere St Michael's (November 1975), Portland Timbers (June–August 1976, June–August 1977), Minnesota Kicks/USA (season 1978–79)

Betts won both amateur and youth international caps for England but made only a handful of first-team appearances for Villa before transferring to Port Vale. An FA Youth Cup winner with Villa in 1972, he now lives in Portland, Oregon.

BEWERS, JONATHAN

Utility: 0+2 apps

Born: Kettering, 10 September 1982

Career: Schoolboy football, VILLA (YTS, June 1998; professional, 16 September 1999), Macclesfield Town (trialist, January 2004), Notts County (February–May 2004)

Bewers, a full-back, central defender or midfielder, made his Premiership debut for Villa at Tottenham in April 2000, coming on as a substitute, having already been capped by England at schoolboy, Under-16 and Under-17 levels.

BIDDLESTONE, THOMAS FREDERICK

Goalkeeper: 160 apps

Born: Pensnett, Dudley, 26 November 1906 – *Died*: Great Barr, Birmingham, 7 April 1977

Career: Bilston Boys' Club, Hickmans Park Rangers (1921), Moxley Wesleyans (1922), Wednesbury Town, Sunbeam Motors (1925–27), Bloxwich Strollers,

Walsall (professional, April 1929), VILLA (£1,750, April 1930), Mansfield Town (August 1939); guest for Walsall (1939–42; retired May 1944); Victorians FC/Blackpool (coach, 1948–49)

Biddlestone was a centre-half before becoming a goalkeeper. He did very well at non-League level, especially with Wednesbury Town and Bloxwich Strollers, and in 1929 signed for Walsall, switching to Villa in 1930 following a brilliant display in an FA Cup tie at Villa Park. Nicknamed 'The Councillor', he was sound rather than spectacular and helped Villa win the Second Division title in 1938.

BIRCH, JAMES

Centre-forward: 3 apps, 2 goals
Born: Blackwell, Derbyshire, 1888 – *Died*: London, 1940
Career: Riddings FC (Derbyshire), Buxton Lime Firms, Burton United (April 1906), VILLA (May 1906), Stourbridge (on loan), Queens Park Rangers (June 1912); guest for Nottingham Forest (1915–16); Brentford (April 1926), Queens Park Rangers (coach, June 1926; retired May 1927)

A strongly built, aggressive forward, unassuming in his manner, Birch deputised for Harry Hampton. He did exceedingly well with QPR (144 goals in 363 games) before spending a season in Brentford's second team. He was an above-average cricketer.

BIRCH, PAUL

Midfield: 201+27 apps, 25 goals
Born: West Bromwich, 20 November 1962
Career: West Bromwich Boys, VILLA (apprentice, June 1978; professional, July 1980), Wolverhampton Wanderers (£400,000, February 1991), Preston North End (loan, March 1996), Doncaster Rovers (July 1996), Exeter City (March 1997–May 1998), Halesowen Town (1998–2000), Forest Green Rovers (player/coach, 2000–03), Birmingham City (Youth Academy coach, 2003–04)

Birch, a totally committed footballer, preferred to play wide on the right side of midfield. He gained a European Super Cup-winner's medal in 1982, helped Villa win promotion from Division Two in 1988 and collected an FA Youth Cup-winner's medal in 1980. He was awarded a testimonial in August 1991 (Villa against Wolves) and when he quit top-class football in 1998, he had amassed 465 appearances and scored 53 goals.

His brother, Alan, played for Walsall, Chesterfield, Wolves, Barnsley, Rotherham United, Scunthorpe United and Stockport between 1973 and 1988.

BIRCH, TREVOR

Right-half: 22 apps
Born: West Bromwich, 20 November 1933
Career: Accles and Pollock FC, VILLA (amateur, July 1949; professional, 1952),

Stockport County (November 1960), Nuneaton Borough (July 1962; retired May 1965)

Trevor 'Clamp' Birch was spotted playing in the Birmingham Works League. He signed professional forms within three years of joining the club and acted, in the main, as reserve to Danny Blanchflower, Vic Crowe and Bill Baxter before leaving in 1960.

BLACKBURN, GEORGE FREDERICK

Left-half: 145 apps, 2 goals

Born: Willesden Green, London, 8 March 1899 – *Died*: Cheltenham, 3 July 1957

Career: Pound Lane School/Willesden, London Juniors, Willesden Juniors, St Francis's FC, Essex Yeomanry, Hampstead Town (January 1919), Army football (1917–19), Hampstead Town, VILLA (amateur, December 1920; professional, January 1921), Cardiff City (June 1926), Mansfield Town (June 1931), Cheltenham Town (player/manager, July 1932), Moor Green (coach, August 1934), Birmingham (trainer, July 1937; coach, 1946; retired May 1948)

Blackburn became a 'pro' at Villa Park four weeks after joining the club. A sound performer, preferring the left-half berth, he quickly established himself in the first XI and produced many outstanding displays, lining up in the 1924 FA Cup final defeat by Newcastle. A month after that Wembley encounter he was capped by England against France in Paris. Blackburn missed out on Cardiff's FA Cup final win over Arsenal the following year even though he was a regular in the side. He netted once in 116 games for the Welsh club.

BLACKBURN, ROBERT ERNEST

Full-back: 33 apps

Born: Crawshaw Booth, near Rawtenstall, Manchester, 23 April 1892 – *Died*: Birkenhead, 13 July 1964

Career: Loveclough FC (1907), Manchester Youth Club (1911), served in Army (1915–18), VILLA (April 1919), Bradford City (May 1922; retired October 1923), Accrington Stanley (trainer, August 1924; manager, November 1924–January 1932), Wrexham (manager, January 1932–January 1936), Hull City (manager, December 1937–January 1946), Tranmere Rovers (manager, September 1946–May 1955; club secretary, June 1955; retired from football, May 1959)

Blackburn served with the Royal Medical Corps before becoming an effective full-back with Villa. He was at the club for three seasons, but unfortunately his career was cut short by injury in 1923. As a manager he worked under considerable pressure at Accrington (no money) and was the first boss to lose his job after WW2. Blackburn earned a reputation as a hard worker, a fine judge of players and a financial economist.

BLAIR, ANDREW

Midfield: 48+14 apps, 2 goals

Born: Kirkcaldy, Fife, 18 December 1959

Career: Nicholas Chamberlain School, Bedworth Juniors, Warwickshire Schools, Coventry City (YTS, July 1975; professional, October 1977), VILLA (£300,000, August 1981), Wolverhampton Wanderers (loan, October–November 1983), Sheffield Wednesday (£60,000, August 1984), VILLA (March 1986), Barnsley (loan, March–April 1988), Northampton Town (October 1988), Kidderminster Harriers (August 1989–May 1990)

Capped five times by Scotland at Under-21 level, midfielder Blair appeared in over 100 games for Coventry before moving to Villa, for whom he made his debut as a substitute in the FA Charity Shield game against Spurs in 1981. He helped Villa win the European Super Cup and after moving to Hillsborough, scored a hat-trick of penalties in a Milk Cup tie against Luton. When he pulled out of senior football in 1989, his record stood at 224 League appearances and 10 goals. Collected European Cup-winner's medal in 1982 as a non-playing substitute.

BLAIR, DANIEL

Full-back: 138 apps

Born: Parkhead, Glasgow, 2 February 1906 – *Died*: Blackpool, 1976

Career: Whitehall Higher Grade School (Glasgow), Parkhead Juniors, Rasharkin FC and Cullybackey/Ireland; then Devonport Albion, Toronto Scottish FC, Rhode Island, Willy's Overland Motor Works' FC, Providence FC (all in Canada and USA); Parkhead Juniors/Glasgow (1924), Clyde (April 1925), VILLA (£7,000 plus player, November 1931), Blackpool (June 1936), Cardiff City (briefly, 1939–40; retired during WW2), Blackpool (coach, 1946–52); thereafter a market gardener in Blackpool

Despite being on the small side, left-back Blair was a competitive footballer, honest and efficient. After studying agriculture in Ireland, he did the same job in North America. He joined Villa for what was the second-highest fee splashed out by the club at that time. Capped eight times by Scotland (1929–33), Blair also represented the Scottish League on three occasions, having earlier played for his country at schoolboy level. When he left Villa Park, his place went to George Cummings. His son, J.A. Blair, played for Blackpool and Hereford United.

BLAKE, MARK ANTONY

Midfield: 31+5 apps, 2 goals

Born: Nottingham, 16 December 1970

Career: VILLA (apprentice, April 1987; professional, July 1989), Wolverhampton Wanderers (on loan, January 1991), Portsmouth (£400,000, August 1993), Leicester City (£360,000, March 1994), Walsall (free, August 1996), Mansfield Town (free, August 1999), Kidderminster Harriers (free, July 2001; retired December 2002)

Blake, who could also play as an emergency right-back, occupied both wide positions across midfield and although performing with credit, he was never regarded as a first-team regular at Villa Park. Capped by England at schoolboy, youth and Under-21 levels (gaining nine caps in the latter category), he retired with a snapped Achilles tendon with well over 300 senior appearances under his belt (26 goals).

BLAKE, NOEL LLOYD GEORGE

Defender: 4 apps

Born: Jamaica, 12 January 1962

Career: Sutton Coldfield (August 1977), VILLA (professional, August 1979), Shrewsbury Town (loan, March 1982), Birmingham City (£55,000, September 1982), Portsmouth (£150,000, August 1984), Leeds United (July 1988), Stoke City (February 1990), Bradford City (loan, February 1992, signing permanently, July 1992), Dundee (December 1993), Exeter City (as a player/assistant manager, August 1995; coach/caretaker boss, January 1999; manager, May 2000; retired as a player, May 2001; continued as manager to October 2001), Barnsley (coach, July 2003), Stoke City (coach)

A rugged, no-nonsense centre-half, Blake had a fine playing career that spanned 20 years. One of the elite band of players to move from Villa Park to St Andrew's (reunited with his former boss, Ron Saunders), Blake made 694 first-class appearances and scored 40 goals.

BLANCHFLOWER, ROBERT DENNIS (DANNY)

Wing-half: 155 apps, 10 goals

Born: Belfast, 10 February 1926 – *Died*: Surrey, 9 December 1993

Career: 19th Belfast Wolf Cubs, Ravenscroft Elementary School (Belfast), Boys' Brigade, Belfast College of Technology, ATC, Bloomfield United (East Belfast, 1939–44), Connsbrook (Gaelic football, 1940), RAF (based in Scotland), Glentoran (amateur, December 1945; professional, January 1946), Swindon Town (WW2 guest), Barnsley (£6,000, April 1949), VILLA (£15,000, March 1951), Tottenham Hotspur (£30,000, October 1954–June 1964, when he retired as a player), Showbiz XI, Northern Ireland (manager, June 1976–November 1978), Chelsea (manager, December 1978–September 1979); also a sports journalist for *Sunday Express* (1964–88)

Blanchflower served in the RAF during WW2. Entering League football as a wing-half with Barnsley in 1949, he developed fast, bringing the scouts flooding to Oakwell. On transfer deadline day in 1951, Villa boss George Martin swooped to bring him to the Midlands to fill the right-half berth vacated by Ivor Powell. Blanchflower, cool and composed, a thinker and tremendous passer of the ball, spent three and a half years at Villa Park, skippering the side on many occasions. A master tactician with the ability to spot weaknesses in the opposition defence and exploit them visibly, Blanchflower then became a member of one of the greatest midfield units in post-WW2 football as he linked up with two Scots, Jimmy White and Dave Mackay, in the Spurs side. Twice voted 'Footballer of the Year' (1958, 1961), the latter after Spurs had completed the double, Blanchflower also lifted the FA Cup again in 1962, the European Cup-winners' Cup in 1963 and went on to gain 50 caps for Northern Ireland. He toured Canada with the Irish FA in 1953 (playing in 8 games out of 10) and in 1955 represented Great Britain against the Rest of Europe. He also played for the Football League against the Irish League (1960) and captained London against Basel and Barcelona in the semi-final and final respectively of the Inter-Cities Fairs Cup in 1958. A knee injury forced him into retirement in 1964 after he had appeared in 720 matches. In May 1990, Spurs met a Northern Ireland XI in a benefit match for one of the club's all-time greats.

Blanchflower was the first player to skipper two successive FA Cup-winning teams, and during WW2 played rugby union, Gaelic football, soccer, hockey, cricket, golf, squash, table tennis and badminton. His brother, Jackie Blanchflower, centre-half of Manchester United, was seriously injured in the Munich air disaster of 1958.

BLOOMFIELD, RAYMOND GEORGE
Midfield: 3 apps
Born: Kensington, London, 15 October 1944
Career: Kensington Boys, Arsenal (amateur, May 1960; professional, November 1961), VILLA (August 1964–August 1966), Atlanta Chiefs/NASL (August 1966–March 1969)
Bloomfield's first-team outings were restricted to just three during his two years at Villa Park. He represented England at both schoolboy and youth levels. His nephew, Jimmy, played for Arsenal and Birmingham City.

BOATENG, GEORGE
Midfield: 126+8 apps, 5 goals
Born: Nkawkaw, Ghana, 5 September 1975
Career: Excelsior FC (professional, June 1994), Feyenoord/Holland (July 1995), Coventry City (£250,000, December 1997), VILLA (£4.5m, July 1999), Middlesbrough (£5m, June 2002)
Midfielder Boateng captained Holland's Under-18 and Under-21 teams, gaining 18 caps in the latter category when with Feyenoord, for whom he made 68 League appearances. A strong-running player with good distribution and an appetite for hard work, Boateng joined Coventry after starring against the Sky Blues in a pre-season friendly. A member of Villa's 2000 FA Cup final side against Chelsea, he was reunited with two ex-Villa players, Ugo Ehiogu and Gareth Southgate, at the Riverside Stadium. He's now added two senior caps to his tally and in 2004 helped 'Boro win their first-ever major trophy, the League Cup.

BODEN, CHRISTOPHER DESMOND

Left-back: 0+1 app.

Born: Wolverhampton, 13 October 1973

Career: VILLA (YTS, 1989; professional, December 1991), Barnsley (loan, October 1993), Derby County (£150,000, March 1995–May 1996), Shrewsbury Town (loan, January–February 1996)

Full-back or left-sided midfielder Boden's only substitute appearance for Villa was in the Premiership game at Leicester in December 1994. He moved to Derby as cover for Shane Nicholson.

BODEN, JOHN ARTHUR

Centre-half: 18 apps, 2 goals

Born: Northwich, Cheshire, 1883 – *Died*: *circa* 1942

Career: Glossop North End (June 1902), Clapton Orient (£200, August 1904), VILLA (March 1906), Northwich Victoria (briefly, August 1906), Reading (August 1907), Croydon Common (August 1909), Plymouth Argyle (June 1910), New Brompton/Gillingham (May 1912), Northwich Victoria (July 1913; retired, injured, April 1914)

Boden, a well-built centre-half, was deputy to Alec Leake at Villa Park. He later occupied the left-half and centre-forward positions with Plymouth, for whom he scored 31 goals in 65 outings.

BOSNICH, MARK JOHN

Goalkeeper: 227+1 apps

Born: Sydney, Australia, 13 January 1972

Career: Croatia Sydney SFC/Australia, Liverpool (trial), Manchester United (non-contract, June 1989), Croatia Sydney SFC/Australia (June 1991), VILLA (February 1992), Manchester United (free, July 1999), Chelsea (free, January 2001; released May 2003)

Bosnich was brought up in the Croatian community of Sydney before getting the urge to move to the UK. After a trial at Anfield, he joined Manchester United and stayed at Old Trafford for two years, during which time he was a student at Manchester Polytechnic. He made three first-team appearances for the Reds before returning to Australia. Bosnich moved back to England to replace Nigel Spink at Villa Park and after 228 outings was ironically re-signed by his former club Manchester United. Capped at youth and Under-23 levels, Bosnich has also played in 17 full internationals and starred for Australia in the semi-final of the Olympic Games in Barcelona in 1992, but did not play for his 'host' country in the 2000 Games. He had a remarkable record of saving penalties, gained two League Cup-winner's medals with Villa (1994, 1996) and after helping United win the Premiership in 2000, he suddenly found himself third-choice keeper at Old Trafford. He made only seven appearances for Chelsea (in two seasons) before he was banned from the game for alleged drug-taking. Bosnich was fined £1,000 and received a stern warning from the FA for his Hitler impression ('Sieg Heil') at White Hart Lane in 1996.

BOULDING, MICHAEL THOMAS
Forward: 2 apps, 1 goal
Born: Sheffield, 8 February 1975
Career: Hallam FC, Mansfield Town (August 1999), Grimsby Town (free, August 2001), VILLA (free, July 2002), Sheffield United (loan, September–October 2002), Grimsby Town (free, January 2003), Barnsley (February 2004)
After helping Grimsby retain their place in the First Division, speedy striker Boulding joined Villa but sadly never settled down in the Premiership.

BOURNE, HUBERT EDGAR
Inside-forward: 7 apps, 2 goals
Born: Bromsgrove, 6 March 1896 – *Died*: Birmingham, 1965
Career: Bromsgrove Maypole County and Stourbridge Road Schools, Early Morning School side, Bromsgrove All Saints, Bromsgrove Rovers (1912), Austin Motors FC, Manchester United (July 1914); guest for Wolverhampton Wanderers (1918–19); VILLA (July 1919, retired March 1925; third-team coach, later second-XI trainer, then first-team trainer, August 1934–June 1953); England trainer on four occasions between 1948 and 1951
'Schubert' Bourne was a reserve inside-forward who was forced to retire with a serious knee injury. He had been at Old Trafford before WW1, but did not receive a first-team call. Very efficient in everything he did, Bourne was succeeded as Villa's trainer by the ex-Portsmouth player Jimmy Easson.

BOWEN, SAMUEL EDWARD
Full-back: 199 apps
Born: Hednesford, 17 November 1903 – *Died*: Stafford, 4 March 1981
Career: West Hill School (Hednesford), Hednesford Town (August 1918), Hednesford Primitives, Hednesford Town (1921), VILLA (August 1923), Norwich City (October 1934–May 1938), Torquay United (trial, signed November 1938), Norwich City (Midlands scout, 1938–39); later worked for the Hednesford and District Social Services Department (1947–81)
Though heavily built, Bowen was a very consistent full-back who was described in 1933 as being 'dainty, gentle, efficient and canny'. He came from a footballing family and after his schooldays were over he joined his hometown club (the Pitmen). After a brief spell with rivals the Primitives, he returned to Cross Keys for a second term, signing as professional with Villa at the start of the 1923–24 season. Bowen stayed at Villa Park for over 11 years, during which time he made almost 200 appearances (it would have been decidedly more if Messrs Mort and Smart hadn't been around). Bowen added a further 139 outings to his tally with Norwich before retiring in 1938.

BOWMAN, THOMAS
Defender: 116 apps, 2 goals
Born: Tarbolton, Strathclyde, 26 October 1873 – *Died*: Southampton, 27 August 1958
Career: Annbank, Blackpool (June 1896), VILLA (October 1897), Southampton (May 1901), Portsmouth (May 1904–June 1909), Eastleigh Athletic (August 1909–May 1912); later worked in the Southampton dockyards

Bowman played initially as a right-back, but after his transfer to Villa Park he developed into a hard-to-beat, reliable, purposeful, clean-tackling full-back or centre-half. He gained League championship-winning medals in 1899 and 1900, and a year after leaving Villa (with Albert Brown) he collected an FA Cup runner's-up medal. Bowen made well over 170 Southern League appearances for Saints and Pompey.

BOYMAN, WALTER RICHARD
Inside-forward: 22 apps, 11 goals
Born: Richmond, Surrey, 10 August 1891 – *Died*: 1970
Career: Halford Road School/Fulham, Kent County FA; served in Royal Navy (demobbed 1919); Sheffield United (guest), Cradley Heath St Luke's (July 1919), VILLA (October 1919), Nottingham Forest (October 1921), Kidderminster Harriers (June 1923), Worcester City (May 1925), Kidderminster Harriers (1928; retired 1930)

Boyman scored a hat-trick in his second game for Villa at Middlesbrough in October 1919. Having played representative football for the adjoining county of his birth (Kent) as a teenager, and also for his Royal Navy Unit (Chatham) he surprisingly moved to the Black Country to sign for Cradley Heath just after WW1. Boyman, who missed the 1920 FA Cup final (cup-tied), broke his leg on the last day of the 1920–21 season and never regained his composure.

BOYNE, REGINALD
Inside-forward: 8 apps
Born: Leeds, 10 October 1891 – *Died*: Yorkshire, 1939
Career: Yorkshire junior football, New Zealand intermediate football, VILLA (trial, September 1913; professional, December 1913), guest for Notts County and Leicester Fosse (WW1), Brentford (August 1919–May 1921); returned to New Zealand, 1922.

Inside-forward Boyne emigrated to New Zealand (with his family) as a teenager and played soccer on Long Island before returning to England. After starring in local football for a year, he was spotted by a Villa scout, who invited him along for trials. They were successful, Boyne signing as a professional shortly before Christmas, 1913. Besides his competitive outings, he had five games during WW1 and had the pleasure of scoring Brentford's first-ever League goal.

BRADLEY, DARREN MICHAEL

Utility: 19+4 apps

Born: Kings Norton, Birmingham, 24 November 1965

Career: St Thomas Aquinas School, Kings Norton Boys, West Midlands County Schools, South Birmingham Schools, Broadmeadow All Stars, VILLA (apprentice, June 1982; professional, December 1983), West Bromwich Albion (£90,000, plus Steve Hunt, March 1986), Cape Town Spurs/South Africa, Walsall (August 1995), SV Meffen/Germany (trial, June 1997), Hibernians/Malta, Solihull Borough (July 1997), Hednesford Town (season 2000–01)

After leaving Villa, Bradley amassed almost 300 appearances for WBA, skippering the Baggies to victory in the 1993 Division Two play-off final. Adaptable at full-back, in central defence or midfield, he was a totally committed player with good skills.

BRADLEY, KEITH

Full-back: 135+9 apps, 2 goals

Born: Ellesmere Port, Cheshire, 31 January 1946

Career: Everton (junior, June 1961), VILLA (apprentice, July 1962; professional, June 1963), Peterborough United (November 1972; retired May 1976), Birmingham City (youth coach), Cyprus and Middle East (coaching, under the guidance of former Bristol City manager Alan Dicks); later a bar/restaurant owner, Mojacar (Spain)

Full-back Bradley, who failed to make the grade at Goodison Park, had Charlie Aitken, Gordon Lee and Mick Wright to contest a first-team place with at Villa Park. After making steady progress, he eventually gained a place in the side and appeared in over 140 matches in ten years. He played in the 1971 League Cup final and gained a Third Division championship medal the following year.

BRAWN, WILLIAM FREDERICK

Outside-right: 107 apps, 20 goals

Born: Wellingborough, 1 August 1878 – *Died*: London, 18 August 1932

Career: Rock Street School, Wellingborough White Star, Wellingborough Principals, Northampton Town (July 1895), Sheffield United (professional, January 1900), VILLA (December 1901), Middlesbrough (March 1906), Chelsea (November 1907), Brentford (August 1911; retired May 1919 after guesting for Spurs, November 1918); later employed as advisory manager at Griffin Park; also ran a pub (the King's Arms) in Boston Road (Brentford)

It was said that Brawn was one of 'the most dangerous outside-rights in the kingdom' during the early 1900s. Renowned for his speed and shooting ability, he was unusually tall for a winger (6 ft 2 in.) and was also weighty at 13 st. 5 lb. Able to use both feet, he gained two England caps and collected an FA Cup-winner's medal with Villa in 1905. He later starred in Chelsea's first-ever season in Division One and retired with over 350 senior appearances to his name.

BREITKREUTZ, MATTHIAS
Midfield: 13+1 apps
Born: Germany, 12 May 1971
Career: PFV Bergmann Borsig/Germany (1987), VILLA (October 1991), PFV
    Bergmann Borsig/Germany (August 1993)
Breitkreutz joined Villa along with his fellow countryman Stefan Beinlich three
months into the 1991–92 season. A competent midfielder, never able to
command a regular place in the side, he duly returned to his former club.

BREMNER, DESMOND GEORGE
Midfield: 222+5 apps, 10 goals
Born: Aberchider, Kirkcaldy, 7 September 1962
Career: Kirkcaldy schoolboy football, Banks O' Dee 'A', Deverondale FC
    (Highland League), Hibernian (July 1971; professional, November 1972),
    VILLA (£250,000, September 1979 in a deal involving Joe Ward),
    Birmingham City (October 1984–May 1989), Fulham (August 1989),
    Walsall (March–May 1990), Stafford Rangers (August 1990–May 1992),
    VILLA (academy coach, 1999); later associated with the PFA
For a period of five years, the hard-working and forceful midfield play of
Bremner was always evident. He made over 225 appearances for Villa, and
besides his goals, he created several openings for his colleagues. After leaving
Villa Park, he gave the Blues excellent service, making almost 200 appearances
for the St Andrew's club prior to joining Fulham. With Villa he won a League
championship medal in 1981 and European Cup and Super Cup prizes a year
later. Capped once by Scotland at senior level and 9 times by the Under-23s, he
became the oldest player ever to appear in a League game for the Saddlers, aged
37 years 240 days against Bristol City, in May 1990.

BRIGGS, WILSON WAITE
Full-back: 2 apps
Born: Gorebridge, near Edinburgh, Scotland, 15 May 1942
Career: Armiston Rangers, Gorebridge Youths, Musselburgh Welfare, VILLA
    (August 1959–May 1964), Falkirk (April 1965–May 1968), East Fife
    (1968–70), then non-League football in Scotland until 1975
Briggs, a former apprentice butcher, played amateur football north of the border
before joining Villa on the same day as Charlie Aitken in 1959. Aitken made
the grade, Briggs didn't. In fact, he only participated in two League games
during his five-year stay at Villa Park, making his debut at right-back against
the Blues at St Andrew's in March 1962. Briggs remained a reserve at the club
until returning to Scotland in 1964.

BRITTLETON, JOHN THOMAS

Full-back: 10 apps

Born: Winsford, Cheshire, 5 May 1900 – *Died*: Cheshire, 1970

Career: Winsford Celtic (August 1920), Chester (August 1926), VILLA (November 1927; registration cancelled, November 1930), Winsford United (January 1932; retired May 1935)

A resilient defender, Brittleton started playing football with his local side Winsford Celtic before establishing himself with Chester. After leaving Sealand Road, he spent three years as a Villa reserve before signing for Winsford, retiring three years later with a knee problem. He was the son of the former England international J.T. Brittleton, who played League football for Stockport, Sheffield Wednesday and Stoke.

BROADBENT, PETER FRANK

Midfield: 65+4 apps, 4 goals

Born: Elvington, Kent, 15 May 1933

Career: Dover (1949), Brentford (professional, May 1950), Wolverhampton Wanderers (£10,000, February 1951), Shrewsbury Town (January 1965), VILLA (October 1966), Stockport County (October 1969), Bromsgrove Rovers (October 1970; retired May 1971); later ran a baby-wear shop in Halesowen

Broadbent, a brilliant inside-forward, spent 20 years in League football, 17 in the West Midlands. He was the workhorse in Wolves' centre-field, linking up with England international wingers Johnny Hancocks and Jimmy Mullen and then Norman Deeley and the South African Des Horne. He grafted hard and long, driving forward, spraying passes wide and long. He created goalscoring opportunities galore for his colleagues and netted some fine goals himself in a haul of 145 in 497 games for the Molineux club, whom he helped win three League titles in the 1950s and the FA Cup in 1960. He gained seven England caps and also represented his country at 'B' and Under-23 levels as well as playing for the Football League XI and Young England. Broadbent had the pleasure of netting Wolves' first-ever European goal versus FC Schalke 04 in 1958. He left Wolves soon after manager Stan Cullis had departed. Unfortunately, his experience failed to prevent Villa from being relegated to the Second Division and he quit the club three months into the 1969–70 season. Broadbent's wonderful career in top-class football saw him amass 631 League appearances. A very fine golfer, in 1967–68 he won the professional footballers' golf title, having finished runner-up in 1965 and 1966.

BROCKLEBANK, ROBERT EDWARD

Inside-forward: 20 apps, 2 goals

Born: Finchley, 23 May 1908 – *Died*: Brixham, Devon, 6 September 1981

Career: Finchley Boys, Finchley AFC, VILLA (May 1929), Burnley (March 1935); guest for Manchester United (1942–43), Bury (1943–44), Blackburn

Rovers (1944–45); Chesterfield (manager, September 1945–January 1949), Birmingham City (manager, January 1949–October 1954), West Bromwich Albion (scout, November 1954–March 1955), Hull City (manager, March 1955–May 1961), Bradford City (manager, May 1961; resigned October 1964)

Brocklebank, one of eight brothers, was one of Finchley's most illustrious players before leaving the amateur scene to join Villa. Nicknamed 'The Toff' or 'Brock', he had limited opportunities during his six-year stay at Villa Park but afterwards did very well with Burnley, netting 38 goals in 128 games for the Clarets, playing alongside Tommy Lawton. As manager, he guided Hull to the runners-up spot in Division Three (N) in 1959. On retiring, he moved to the Devon fishing town of Brixham. He was a very accomplished cricketer and handy golfer.

BROOKES, FRANKLIN

Forward: 1 app.

Born: Aston, February 1859 – *Died*: Birmingham, *circa* 1920

Career: Aston Pilgrims, Wesleyan Chapel FC, VILLA (August 1880), Centaurs FC/Smethwick (May 1882)

Brookes' only senior outing for Villa was against Notts County in an away FA Cup tie in 1882. Signed after doing well in local church football, he never fulfilled his promise and left after just one season with the club.

BROOME, FRANK HENRY

Forward: 151 apps, 90 goals

Born: Berkhamstead, Herts, 11 June 1915 – *Died*: Bournemouth, 10 September 1994

Career: Berkhamstead Victoria C of E School, Boxmoor United Juniors (1928), Boxworth United (September 1929–May 1932), Berkhamstead Town (August 1932), VILLA (November 1934), WW2 guest for Aldershot, Birmingham, Charlton Athletic, Chelmsford City, Chesterfield, Northampton Town, Nottingham Forest, Notts County, Revo Electric, Watford and Wolverhampton Wanderers; Derby County (September 1946), Notts County (October 1949), Brentford (July 1953), Crewe Alexandra (October 1953), Shelbourne (February 1955), Notts County (assistant trainer, June 1955; caretaker manager, January–May 1957; assistant manager, June–December 1957), Exeter City (manager, January 1958–May 1960), Southend United (manager, May–December 1960), Bankstown, NSW/Australia (manager/coach, July 1961–October 1962), Corinthians/Sydney (manager/coach, late 1962), Exeter City (manager, May 1967–February 1969); coached in the Middle East until 1976

Broome was Villa's top scorer three seasons running (1936–39). A small, thrustful winger who could also play as either centre or inside-forward, he was adept at switching positions during a game and often caused defenders all sorts of trouble. A terrific marksman, speedy and extremely dangerous inside the penalty area, he went on to score 180 goals for Villa, half in 136 WW2 appearances. He also played for the FA XI in 1944. With Villa he gained a Second Division championship medal in 1938 and a wartime League Cup (N) winner's medal in 1944, having helped Wolves win the Football League Cup in 1942. A member of Notts County's Third Division (S) championship-winning side in 1950, he occupied four different forward-line positions for England, gaining eight caps (seven at full international level, one in WW2). He also toured Australia with the FA in 1951, played for an International XI against a District XI in 1940 and amassed 600 first-class appearances, scoring over 250 goals.

BROWN, ALBERT ARTHUR

Utility: 106 apps, 54 goals
Born: Aston, Birmingham, 7 January 1862 – *Died*: Birmingham
Career: Mitchell St George's (1881), VILLA (August 1884; retired, injured, July 1894)

The younger brother of Arthur (q.v.), Albert Brown could play as a right-half, outside-right or inside-right. He was with Villa for ten years, scoring a goal every two games. He played in the 1887 FA Cup final win over WBA and lined up for Villa in their first-ever League game at Wolves in September 1888. He then had the pleasure of scoring in Villa's first League win, 5–1 against Stoke. Injured during the away game at Preston early in 1891, he struggled on for several years, mainly in the reserves, before retiring.

BROWN, ARTHUR ALFRED

Forward: 22 apps, 15 goals
Born: Aston, 15 March 1859 – *Died*: Aston, 11 July 1909
Career: Aston Park School, Florence FC (1874), Aston Unity (1876), VILLA (August 1878), Mitchell St George's (August 1879), Birchfield Trinity, Excelsior FC, VILLA (February 1880; retired through ill-health, May 1886, but remained on the club's staff as a steward until 1908)

Brown (sometimes referred to as 'AA') was a splendid, all-action forward who gave Villa grand service during his second spell at the club. Despite his height (5 ft 8 in.) he was a strong, sturdy player, determined and goal-happy, who was replaced in the side by his brother, Albert Brown, who, in fact, had starred in the same forward-line as Arthur during the 1884–86 seasons. 'AA' linked up supremely well with Archie Hunter and in 1882 appeared in 3 internationals for England, scoring 4 times on his debut against Ireland in Belfast when his Villa colleague, Howard Vaughton, scored a 5-timer in an emphatic 13–0 victory. A real opportunist, Brown had the knack of keeping his shorts clean on the muddiest of pitches!

BROWN, ARTHUR FREDERICK

Forward: 2 apps, 2 goals

Born: Tamworth, April 1879 – *Died*: Birmingham, late 1940s

Career: Atherstone County School, Atherstone Star (1894), Tamworth Swifts (1895), Brownhills Albion, West Bromwich Albion (May 1896), VILLA (February 1898), Southampton (May 1901), Queens Park Rangers (October 1902), Preston North End (May 1904), Blackpool (March 1906; retired, injured, May 1908)

Brown was a decidedly speedy outside-right or centre-forward who was aptly nicknamed the 'Tamworth Sprinter' and said to be the fastest footballer in the kingdom! With a long, raking stride, he did well for his school team and at junior and non-League levels before entering the big time with Villa in 1898. Unfortunately, he was never able to establish himself in the first XI, playing in just two matches but having the pleasure of scoring twice on his League debut at Sheffield United in November 1900 when he replaced George Johnson. Transferred (with Tommy Bowman) he quickly made his mark at The Dell and in December 1901 entered the Saints' record books by netting 7 goals out of 11 against Northampton in the Southern League. Brown scored 29 times in 34 matches that season, playing in the FA Cup final. He received bad knee injuries in 1902 and 1904.

BROWN, GEORGE

Centre-forward: 126 apps, 89 goals

Born: Mickley, Northumberland, 22 June 1903 – *Died*: Birmingham, 10 June 1948

Career: Mickley Juniors, Mickley Colliery, Huddersfield Town (trial, March 1921; professional, April 1921), VILLA (£5,000, August 1929), Burnley (£1,400, October 1934), Leeds United (£3,100, September 1935), Darlington (£1,000, player/manager, October 1936; retired October 1938); guest for Sutton Town (1939), Shirley NFS (1940–41); later licensee of the Star Vaults, Aston, and also landlord of the Plume and Feathers, Stratford Road, Shirley (for six years)

Brown, one of the most prolific marksmen in the history of the game, netted 276 goals in 444 League matches between 1921 and 1938 (his record in all competitions was 298 goals in 473 appearances). A clever dribbler, his eye for snapping up the half-chance, allied to his power and accuracy with his shooting (especially his right-foot rockets) earned him the nickname of 'Bomber'. That was particularly relevant during his Villa days, when, besides some wonderful strikes, he bagged a five-timer against Leicester in January 1932. He was, of course, part of a terrific forward-line that also comprised Tom 'Pongo' Waring, Billy Walker and Eric Houghton.

Brown worked at the local colliery and played for the pit team as a youngster. In May 1921, when on strike, he asked Huddersfield for a trial. Manager Herbert Chapman liked what he saw and signed Brown on professional forms within a fortnight. 'Bomber' went on to score 159 goals in 229 games for the Terriers, being a key member of their attack when they completed a treble of League championship triumphs in the mid-1920s. In the last of those successes (1925–26) he equalled the club's scoring record of 35 goals in a season. After missing Huddersfield's 1922 FA Cup final victory over Preston, Brown played in the 1928 final, but on this occasion Blackburn beat Huddersfield 3–1 to ruin his big day! Capped eight times by England, he also represented the Football League and added one more full cap to his collection as a Villa player. As a manager he helped Darlington avoid re-election to the Football League. Brown's uncle, Joe Spence, played for Manchester United and England.

BROWN, JAMES KEITH
Midfield: 85+3 apps, 1 goal
Born: Wallyford, Midlothian, 3 October 1953
Career: Edinburgh and District Schools, Midlothian Boys, VILLA (associated schoolboy, May 1969; professional, October 1970), Preston North End (October 1975), Ethnikos/Greece (August 1978–December 1979), Portsmouth (February 1980), Hibernian (November 1980), Worcester City (July 1981), Heart of Midlothian (1982), Worcester City (again, season 1982–83), Sutton Coldfield Town, VILLA Old Stars, then footballing coach in the local community

Brown became the youngest player ever to appear in a first-class game for Villa when, at the age of 15 years, 349 days, he made his debut against Bolton at Burnden Park in a Second Division match on 17 September 1969. After that, Brown, strong and competitive in midfield, steadily added to his appearance-tally, scoring his only goal in the away game at Brighton in January 1973 (won 3–1). Brown was capped by his country at youth-team level, gained a League Cup runner's-up tankard in 1971, helped Villa win the Third Division championship in 1972 and also received the annual Villa supporters' 'Terrace Trophy' award in 1973.

BROWN, JAMES RICHARD
Utility: 56 apps, 4 goals
Born: Renton, Scotland, June 1868 – *Died*: Leicester, January 1924
Career: Renton Union, Renton Thistle, Renton (1878), VILLA (June 1890), Leicester Fosse (October 1893), Loughborough (September 1899; retired May 1900); Football League referee (1902–05)

A moustachio'd Scottish 'professor', Brown was a useful footballer, awkward at times owing to his round-shouldered gait, but totally reliable, who could occupy a variety of positions from right-half to centre-half to centre-forward. A junior international north of the border, he joined Villa in 1890, having previously done well with three Renton-based clubs. An excellent prompter, he hit 21 goals in 153 games for Leicester.

BROWN, RALPH

Forward: 1 app.

Born: Nottingham, 26 February 1944

Career: Ilkeston Boys, Derby County (schoolboy forms), VILLA (junior, March 1959; professional, February 1961), Notts County (May 1962), Nuneaton Borough (August 1964), Ilkeston Town (June 1965–May 1966); later a Nottinghamshire coalminer

Brown, who represented the Birmingham County FA (December 1959), played just once for Villa's senior side, lining up as a 17 year old in the first leg of the 1961 League Cup final against Rotherham – thus entitling him to a winner's tankard! An inside- or centre-forward, he was an England youth trialist and became surplus to requirements at the end of the 1961–62 season.

BROWN, ROBERT ALBERT JOHN

Forward: 31 apps, 9 goals

Born: Great Yarmouth, 7 November 1915

Career: Gorleston Town (1932–34), Charlton Athletic (August 1934), guest for Newcastle United, West Ham United, Millwall, York City, Leicester City, Manchester City, Wolverhampton Wanderers and East Fife during WW2; Nottingham Forest (£6,750, May 1946), VILLA (£10,000, October 1947), Gorleston Town (player/coach, June 1949–May 1956), VILLA (scout, 1946–48); later ran sports shop (1956–59), then with Joe Jobling, ex-Charlton teammate, managed a Gorleston betting shop; also organised sporting events at a Gorleston holiday centre and worked for a timber merchant, often driving a 10-ton truck; retired from work in 1982

Inside- or centre-forward 'Sailor' Brown scored plenty of goals during his two seasons with Gorleston. His efforts were rewarded, being immediately snapped up by Charlton. He remained at The Valley for 12 years, although the conflict and disruption of WW2 severely dented his progress, despite him guesting for several clubs up and down the country. With his balding head and ambling action, he scored 23 goals in 50 League and FA Cup games for the Addicks. He served in the Greenwich Auxiliary Police from September 1939 to January 1940 before joining the RAF, representing both the FA and FA Services in 1945. After returning to The Valley, he scored once in Charlton's 1946 FA Cup run, which ended in defeat by Derby in the final. A year later, after a brief spell with Forest, he was recruited by Villa to accompany Trevor Ford, but after a decent first season and a moderate second, he announced his retirement from first-class football after suffering a badly fractured jaw in a game against Portsmouth. During May–June 1939 Brown toured South Africa with the FA, playing in one Test match. He skippered the RAF team in Norway, Denmark and Sweden during WW2, gained two League Cup (S)-runner's-up medals, with Charlton against Chelsea in 1944 and with Millwall against Chelsea in 1945, and also played for England in seven wartime/victory internationals (1945–46).

BROWN, WALTER GEORGE
Full-back: 13 apps
Born: Hurlford, near Kilmarnock, September 1876 – *Died*: Birmingham, 1950
Career: Hurlford Thistle Juniors, Hurlford Seniors, Beith, Bolton Wanderers (1898), VILLA (April 1904), Plymouth Argyle (May 1905)
Brown made over 100 appearances for Bolton before joining Villa as cover for Albert Evans and Howard Spencer, but surprisingly made his debut for the club as an emergency outside-right against Preston on the opening day of the 1904–05 season.

BROWNE, PAUL
Defender: 2 apps
Born: Glasgow, 17 February 1975
Career: VILLA (YTS, June 1991; professional, July 1993; released May 1996)
A central back, highly rated at one stage, Brown appeared in just two League games before leaving Villa at the end of the 1995–96 season.

BRYAN, THOMAS
Left-back: 2 apps
Born: Walsall, 1859 – *Died*: May 1913
Career: Saltley College, Wednesbury Strollers (August 1879), VILLA (August 1881), Bilston (April 1883), Darlaston (August 1887–April 1889)
Strong and thrustful, Bryan's two outings for Villa came in 1882 against Walsall Swifts and Wednesbury Old Athletic, both in the FA Cup. He also represented the Birmingham Association several times.

BUCKLEY, CHRISTOPHER SEBASTIAN
Centre-half: 144 apps, 3 goals
Born: Urmston, Manchester, 9 November 1886 – *Died*: 11 January 1973
Career: Manchester Catholic Collegiate Institute, Victoria Park, Manchester Ship Canal FC, Manchester City (amateur, 1903), West Bromwich Albion (trial, 1904), Xaverian Brothers' College, West Bromwich Albion (trial, 1904), Brighton and Hove Albion (May 1905), VILLA (May 1906), Arsenal (July 1914–May 1921); guest for Birmingham (1916–17), Manchester United (1916–17), Coventry City (1917–19); and non-League football (May 1921, retired April 1922), VILLA (director, 1936–67; also club chairman)
A relatively small man (he stood 5 ft 9 in. tall and weighed barely 11 st.), Buckley only played in Manchester City's second team and made 17 Southern League appearances for Brighton before establishing himself in Villa's first XI as a wing-half in 1907. He was then sidelined for a year after breaking an ankle but returned to action in a determined fashion and helped Villa win the League in 1910. Nicknamed 'Ticker', he played in an international trial in January 1911 and represented Birmingham against London a year later. After WW1, having made 60 appearances for Arsenal, he entered non-League football, only to

fracture his leg again in 1922, the injury effectively ending his career. He then took up farming in Redditch and became co-owner of a large Manchester warehouse. In 1936 Buckley joined the board of directors at Villa, later taking over as club chairman. He resigned his seat in 1967, handing over the duties to Norman Smith after serving on the board for 31 years. A typical English sportsman, he participated in athletics, cricket, cycling, golf and of course soccer.

In September 1912, Buckley, one of five brothers including Major Frank, was suspended by Villa over the payment of a benefit cheque. The matter was quickly resolved and Buckley eventually received a cheque for £450.

BULLIVANT, TERENCE PAUL

Midfield: 11+4 apps
Born: Lambeth, London, 23 September 1956
Career: Fulham (schoolboy forms, 1969; apprentice, 1972; professional, May 1974), VILLA (£220,000, November 1979), Charlton Athletic (£90,000, June 1982), Brentford (July 1983), Reading (loan, March–April 1984; retired 1986), Barnet (manager), Reading (manager, June 1997–March 1998), Fulham (part-time youth coach, later first-team coach), Crystal Palace (coach, then assistant manager 2002, Technical Advisor/Football, December 2003)

Bullivant was unable to command a regular first-team place at Villa Park and subsequently returned to London. He began to struggle with injuries in the mid-1980s and was forced to quit the professional game at the age of 30. At that juncture he rejoined the Cottagers as a part-time youth coach and was called into action for a reserve-team game in 1988–89. All told, Bullivant netted 7 goals in 181 League games for his 5 clubs. He gained England youth caps and collected a runner's-up medal with Brentford (against Wigan) in the FRT final in 1985.

BURKE, MARK STEPHEN

Winger: 5+3 apps
Born: Solihull, 12 February 1969
Career: Solihull and District Schools, VILLA (YTS, June 1985; professional, February 1987), Middlesbrough (December 1987), Darlington (loan, October 1990), Wolverhampton Wanderers (March 1991), Luton Town (March 1994), Port Vale (August 1994), Tottenham Hotspur (trial, June–July 1995), Sporting Lisbon/Portugal (trial, late July 1995), Fortuna Sittard/Holland (August 1995), B'Karna/Finland (trial), Tiru'su/Finland (trial, one week), TopOss/Holland (trial), OM Ya Ardlja/Tokyo (June 1997), Rapid Bucharest (March 2001); retired May 2001; now taking his coaching badge

Burke played for England youths before turning professional at Villa Park. He tasted first-team football only spasmodically before joining Middlesbrough, for whom he made 60 League appearances and helped win promotion from the Second Division in 1988.

BURRIDGE, JOHN

Goalkeeper: 80 apps

Born: Workington, 3 December 1951

Career: Workington (apprentice, June 1968; professional, December 1969), Blackpool (£10,000, April 1971), VILLA (£100,000, September 1975), Southend United (loan, January 1978), Crystal Palace (£65,000, March 1978), Queens Park Rangers (£200,000, December 1980), Wolverhampton Wanderers (£75,000, August 1982), Derby County (loan, September 1984), Sheffield United (£10,000, October 1984), Southampton (£30,000, August 1987 – signed to replace Peter Shilton!), Newcastle United (£25,000, October 1989), Hibernian (July 1991), Newcastle again (free, August 1993), Scarborough (non-contract, October 1993), Lincoln City (non-contract, December 1993), Enfield (loan, February 1994), Aberdeen (non-contract, March 1994), Barrow (non-contract, September 1994), Dumbarton (October 1994), Falkirk (November 1994), Manchester City (free, December 1994), Notts County (free, August 1995), Witton Albion (October 1995), Darlington (free, November 1995), Grimsby Town (free, December 1995), Northampton Town (non-contract/reserve, January 1996), Gateshead (March 1996), Queen of the South (March–April 1996), Blyth Spartans (player, July 1996), Scarborough (loan, December 1996), Blyth Spartans (player/manager, March 1997), China (goalkeeping coach, May 1997), Blyth Spartans (November–December 1997); retired as a player in December 1997 on leaving Blyth Spartans, also goalkeeping coach at Leeds United and Newcastle United (1995)

A fitness fanatic, Burridge's wonderful career spanned four decades and when he quit the game (as a player) in 1997, having joined his first club, Workington, 29 years earlier, he had accumulated an appearance record bettered by only one other keeper – Peter Shilton. Burridge played in 915 competitive matches (League and Cup) and over 1,000 matches altogether, including friendlies, tour games and charity matches.

He made his League debut for Workington in a 3–2 win over Newport County in May 1969. Then, 28 years and 6 months later – just short of his 46th birthday – he played his last competitive game for Blyth Spartans in the first round of the FA Cup against Blackpool, November 1997, having appeared in his last Football League game in May 1995 – 26 years and 6 days after appearing in his first!

He was aged 45 when he turned out for Scarborough in the AWS game against Notts County in December 1996 – making him the oldest player ever to appear for the seaside club. He became Scarborough's oldest League player in 1993 (aged 41 years, 338 days) and likewise is Darlington's oldest player, at 44 years, 6 days, in December 1995 when he lined up against Scarborough. Besides these landmarks, the effervescent 'Budgie' Burridge is the oldest player so far to appear in the Premiership – aged 43 years, 5 months, 11 days when in goal for Manchester City against QPR in May 1995. Burridge won an Anglo-Italian

46

Cup-winner's medal with Blackpool in 1970, a League Cup-winner's medal with Villa in 1977, a Division Two championship medal with Palace in 1979 and a Scottish Premier League Cup-winner's medal with Hibs in 1991. He also helped Wolves win promotion from Division Two in 1983 and the following season was voted the Molineux club's 'Player of the Year', going on to make 81 appearances. Burridge either served with and/or was associated with 23 different League clubs (18 English, 5 Scottish), playing for 22 of them. He lined up against 89 other League clubs (out of a possible 101) and played against 22 of the 40 Scottish League clubs. He conceded 1,080 goals in his 915 senior games, keeping 298 clean sheets and was beaten 899 times in his 771 League games (255 of them shut-outs). With Burridge still involved in football, his wife said: 'We've been married for 17 years. John's had 14 clubs, we've lived in 6 different houses and 7 rented places. He's so wrapped up in football, I've heard him giving commentator Gerald Sinstadt a TV interview in his sleep.'

BURROWS, HENRY
Outside-left: 181 apps, 73 goals
Born: Haydock, 17 March 1941
Career: VILLA (amateur, April 1956; professional, March 1958), Stoke City (£30,000, March 1965), Plymouth Argyle (August 1973–May 1974), VILLA Old Stars; played non-League football to 1976; later a publican in Stoke before running a sub-post office in Abbots Bromley
'Harry' Burrows bided his time at Villa Park before making the outside-left position his own in 1961–62, having acted as reserve to international Peter McParland. Fast and direct, with a fair amount of skill and a cracking left-foot shot, Burrows was an old-fashioned winger with an eye for goal. He attended the same school as Walter Hazelden before signing for Villa. Nicknamed 'The Blast', he gained one England Under-23 cap and helped Villa win the Second Division championship and the Football League Cup in successive years (1960 and 1961). He also played in the 1963 losing League Cup final against the Blues and was twice top scorer (1961–62 and 1962–63) before transferring to Stoke. He did a shade better at The Victoria Ground than he'd done at Villa Park, netting 75 goals in almost 270 outings for the Potters.

BURTON, GEORGE FRANK
Wing-half: 53 apps, 3 goals
Born: Aston, Birmingham, June 1868 – *Died*: Birmingham, *circa* 1935
Career: Aston Park School, Birmingham St Luke's, Walsall Town, VILLA (August 1892), Bristol Eastville Rovers (October 1898; retired, injured, June 1899)
Burton, a hard-tackling wing-half, spent six years with Villa, but unfortunately seemed to be on the treatment table quite regularly during that time and in the end was forced to retire through injury.

BURTON, JOHN HENRY

Half-back: 47 apps, 1 goal

Born: Handsworth, Birmingham, 18 September 1863 – *Died*: Hockley, Birmingham, April 1914

Career: Grove Lane School/Handsworth, Hamstead Hall, Handsworth Victoria, Aston Park Unity, VILLA (April 1885; retired, injured, August 1893)

An FA Cup winner with Villa in 1887, Burton was as strong as an ox and could kick a ball as hard as any other player. He retired with a knee injury.

BUTCHER, FREDERICK WILLIAM

Left-back: 2 apps

Born: Hemmingfield, near Barnsley, August 1913 – *Died*: May 1996

Career: Hoyland junior football, Wombwell FC (August 1929), VILLA (April 1931), Blackpool (June 1936), Swindon Town (August 1938); guest for Sutton Town (1939–40) and Kynochs FC

Butcher made 2 League appearances for Villa before fracturing his leg during the 1934–35 season, effectively ending his career, although he did play in 4 games for Blackpool and 36 for Swindon before WW2. He retired after breaking his leg for a second time.

BUTLER, LEE SIMON

Goalkeeper: 10 apps

Born: Sheffield, 30 May 1966

Career: Harworth Colliery, Lincoln City (professional, June 1986), VILLA (£100,000, August 1987), Hull City (loan, March 1991), Barnsley (July 1991), Scunthorpe United (loan, February 1996), Wigan Athletic (July 1996), Dunfermline Athletic (July 1998), Halifax Town (September 1999), Doncaster Rovers (January 2002; retired, with a knee injury, May 2002)

Butler deputised for Nigel Spink for Villa. He had worked down a pit before becoming a professional at Sincil Bank. Recruited by Villa boss Graham Taylor in 1987, he couldn't resist an offer from Barnsley to play regular first-team football, and went on to appear in 120 League games for the Tykes. Voted Halifax's 'Player of the Year' for 2000, Butler amassed more than 400 senior appearances at club level, including 105 for the Shaymen.

BUTTRESS, MICHAEL DAVID

Full-back: 1+2 apps

Born: Whittlesey, near Peterborough, 23 March 1958

Career: VILLA (junior, June 1975; professional, February 1976), Gillingham (March–May 1978); served in West Midlands Police Force since 1979

Buttress (6 ft tall) was a reserve at Villa Park, making 3 first-team appearances. He surprisingly quit League football to join the West Midlands Police Force, playing for the constabulary's soccer team in the Midland Combination.

BYFIELD, DARREN

Striker: 3+7 apps

Born: Sutton Coldfield, 29 September 1976

Career: VILLA (YTS, 1992; professional, February 1994), Preston North End (loan, November 1998), Northampton Town (loan, August 1999), Cambridge United (loan, September 1999), Blackpool (loan, March 2000), Walsall (July 2000), Rotherham United (£50,000, March 2001), Sunderland (January 2004), Gillingham (June 2004)

Byfield joined Villa as a YTS player and made good progress at intermediate- and reserve-team levels. His first-team outings were limited and after loan spells with four League clubs, he was recruited for Walsall by ex-Villa player Ray Graydon to replace Michael Ricketts, sold to Bolton. He netted 17 goals in 92 games for the Saddlers, helping them win promotion to the First Division via the play-offs in 2001. Byfield gained two caps for Jamaica (April–May 2003), then helped Sunderland reach the 2004 play-offs.

CALDERWOOD, COLIN

Defender: 26+4 apps

Born: Glasgow, 20 January 1965

Career: Mansfield Town (juniors, June 1980; professional, March 1982), Swindon Town (£30,000, June 1985), Tottenham Hotspur (£1.25m, July 1995), VILLA (£225,000, March 1999), Nottingham Forest (£70,000, March 2000; retired, injured, May 2001), Northampton Town (manager, October 2003)

Despite being a Scotsman and representing his country at schoolboy level, Calderwood surprisingly started his professional career with Mansfield. Three years and 117 appearances later, he moved to Swindon. He did well at the County Ground and went on to accumulate a splendid record of over 400 games for the Robins. His performances didn't go unnoticed by Spurs manager Gerry Francis, who signed him in 1995. He gained the first of his 36 full caps for Scotland and went on to play in almost 200 games for the Londoners before transferring to Villa Park in 1999. After a bright start, when he was part of a three-man defence along with Ugo Ehiogu and Gareth Southgate, Calderwood then lost his place to Gareth Barry. He became unsettled and was eventually sold to Forest, signed by ex-Villa star David Platt. As a manager, he guided Northampton into the Third Division play-offs in 2004.

CALLAGHAN, ERNEST

Defender: 142 apps, 6 goals

Born: Newtown, Birmingham, 29 July 1907 – *Died*: Castle Vale, Birmingham, March 1972

Career: Dartmouth Council School, Barton Arms (pub side), Rose Villa, Walmer Athletic (1925), Hinckley Athletic (August 1928), Atherstone Town (July 1929), Cradley Heath, West Bromwich Albion (trial), Birmingham (trial), VILLA (September 1930; retired May 1947); guest for Solihull Town (1939–40); later worked as 'odd-job' man at Villa Park (1947–71)

'Mush' Callaghan is the oldest player ever to appear for Villa in a major game, being 39 years, 257 days old when he lined up against Grimsby in a First Division match at Villa Park in April 1947. He played non-League football for five years before signing a professional contract at Villa Park. His defensive displays were admired by players and fans alike and he went on to become a household name, amassing a fine pre-WW2 record for the club while adding another 151 outings during the hostilities when he also played for the Police and Civil Defence (1944). A magnificent partner to full-back George Cummings, later on he became a resolute centre-half and helped Villa win the Second Division championship in 1938 and the Wartime League Cup in 1944. He was awarded the BEM for 'conspicuous bravery' during the Birmingham blitz of September 1942, when serving with the Police Reserve. In 1971 Callaghan received a testimonial for his service and dedication to the club.

CALLAGHAN, NIGEL IAN

Wide midfield: 27+4 apps, 1 goal

Born: Singapore, 12 September 1962

Career: Watford and District Schools, Hertfordshire County Schools, Watford (apprentice, June 1978; professional, July 1980), Derby County (February 1987), VILLA (February 1989), Derby County (loan, September 1990), Watford (loan, March 1991), Huddersfield Town (loan, January 1992); non-League football (1993–97)

A left-sided midfielder who loved to hug the touchline, Callaghan gained 9 England Under-21 caps before joining Villa. He'd already scored 60 goals in over 375 competitive matches for the Hornets and Rams, helping the latter club win the Second Division title in 1987. He netted once for Villa, in a 2–0 win over Sheffield Wednesday in February 1989.

CAMPBELL, ARCHIBALD

Defender: 4 apps

Born: Crook, 15 August 1904 – *Died*: *circa* 1980

Career: Spennymoor United (1921), VILLA (December 1922), Lincoln City (June 1925), Craghead United (July 1927), Washington Colliery (May 1930), Dundee (briefly), Birmingham City Transport FC (January 1931–34)

'Aussie' Campbell, a rough and ready defender and nephew of John Campbell (q.v.), was a fringe player at Villa Park, although he did represent the Birmingham Juniors against the Scottish Juniors in April 1925. He was given only 4 first-team outings before switching to Lincoln, for whom he netted 4 times in 54 League games.

CAMPBELL, GEORGE

Utility: 53 apps, 1 goal

Born: Ayr, Ayrshire, February 1871 – *Died*: Kirkcaldy, 4 April 1898

Career: Renton, VILLA (October 1890), Dundee (August 1893), Renton (1895; retired, through ill-health, May 1896)

Nicknamed 'Monkey Brand' by his colleagues, Campbell was an amazing character, able to play anywhere and often did – just to get a game! He filled both full-back berths, all three half-back positions, inside-forward and even in goal. He took over between the posts against Sunderland in an away League game in March 1892 when he replaced Jimmy Warner, who had refused to play after performing so badly against WBA in the FA Cup final the previous week. Exceptionally good on the ball, Campbell was badly injured playing for Dundee and his career was cut short at the age of 27.

CAMPBELL, JOHN JAMES

Inside- or centre-forward: 63 apps, 43 goals

Born: Glasgow, September 1871 – *Died*: Scotland, December 1947

Career: St Alexandra's, Glasgow Benburb (August 1888), Celtic (professional, May 1890), VILLA (May 1895), Celtic (August 1897), Third Lanark (August 1903; retired April 1906)

Campbell scored over 50 goals in two seasons for Glasgow Benburb before joining Celtic. He became an instant hit at Parkhead, continuing to score plenty of goals, including 2 in the 1892 Scottish Cup final victory and 12 in a reserve-team game in 1891. His transfer to Villa in 1895 allowed Bob Chatt to move to wing-half and he made an immediate impact, finishing up as top scorer in the country at the end of his first season in English football with 26 goals, while also helping Villa win the League title. The following season he was again instrumental as Villa captured the double, netting once in the Cup final against Everton and having the pleasure of scoring the first goal at Villa Park in a 3–0 win over Blackburn in April 1897. An excellent dribbler, Campbell spent just two years on the English circuit, returning to Celtic. Back in Scotland he continued to find the net and went on to claim over 100 goals for the Bhoys (including 90 in 169 League appearances). He won 12 full caps for Scotland (1893–1903), represented the Scottish League on 4 occasions and also played 3 times for the Glasgow Select XI. Besides his three English medals and his initial Cup success with Celtic, Campbell won three more League titles in Scotland (1899, 1900 and 1903, the latter with Third Lanark) and 3 Scottish League runner's-up medals. He retired in the summer of 1906 and lived a further 41 years before his death, aged 76. In his League career (England and Scotland) Campbell scored 141 goals in 264 games.

CAMPBELL, LOUIS

Outside-left: 49 apps, 23 goals

Born: Edinburgh, April 1864 – *Died*: Scotland, 1938

Career: Dumbarton (1883–86), Helensburgh FC (1887), Glasgow United (1888), Hibernian (1889), VILLA (January 1890), Burslem Port Vale (August 1893), Walsall Town Swifts (May 1894), Burton Swifts (1895), Dumbarton (1896–97)

A fast and tricky winger, Campbell had done well north of the border before joining Villa, for whom he scored almost a goal every 2 games before going on to net 15 times in more than 30 outings for Port Vale.

CAMPBELL, ROBERT McFAUL (BOBBY)

Forward: 9+3 apps, 1 goal

Born: Belfast, 13 September 1956

Career: VILLA (apprentice, June 1972; professional, January 1974), Halifax Town (loan, February 1975), Huddersfield Town (£5,000, April 1975), Sheffield United (£10,000, July 1977 – after a loan spell), Vancouver Whitecaps/NASL (June 1978), Huddersfield Town (September 1978), Halifax Town (October 1978), Brisbane City/Australia (May, 1979), Bradford City (December 1979), Derby County (£70,000, August 1983), Bradford City (loan, September 1983; signed for £35,000, November 1983), Wigan Athletic (£25,000, October 1986–May 1988)

Capped by Northern Ireland at youth and senior levels (being in his country's squad for the 1982 World Cup finals), Campbell had a fine career as a striker, scoring more than 200 goals in 600 club and international matches. His League record was most impressive: 179 goals in 476 appearances, including 121 in 274 outings for Bradford. He never got a chance to show his worth during his three years with Villa.

CANNING, LAWRENCE

Utility: 41 apps, 3 goals

Born: Cowdenbeath, 1 November 1925

Career: Broughty Amateurs, Paget Rangers (March 1940), VILLA (December 1943; professional, October 1947); guest for Lincoln City (WW2); Kettering Town (August 1954), Northampton Town (June 1956), Nuneaton Borough (June 1957; retired May 1958); later a VILLA director and also a successful BBC radio sports reporter and journalist

A reserve winger, Canning, who also occupied the right- and left-half, centre-forward and outside-left berths, played in a handful of games for Villa during WW2, and just over 40 at competitive level before leaving the club. He is the cousin of the former Scottish international Alex Venters, who played for Blackburn and Glasgow Rangers.

CANTRELL, JAMES

Inside-right or centre-forward: 52 apps, 23 goals

Born: Sheepbridge, near Chesterfield, 7 May 1882 – *Died*: Basford, Notts, 31 July 1960

Career: Chesterfield Schools, Bulwell Red Rose, Bulwell White Star FC, Carey United, Hucknall Constitutionals, VILLA (July 1904), Notts County (March 1908), Tottenham Hotspur (October 1912), guest for Notts County (1915–16), Sutton Town (August 1923; retired May 1925); later became a golf professional

Cantrell, who scored on his debut for Villa, in a 4–0 home win over his future club Notts County in November 1904, gained a regular place in the forward-line halfway through the 1906–07 campaign, as partner to Charlie Millington on the right-wing with Harry Hampton to his left. Far removed from the battering-ram type of forward, Cantrell was a subtle, dainty player, smart and alert with an excellent right foot. He netted 63 goals in 131 League games for Notts County, top-scoring at Meadow Lane in 3 of his 4 seasons there. With Spurs, he continued to rattle in the goals – 95 in almost 200 competitive matches, including the winner in the 1921 FA Cup final against Wolves. He also bagged 19 in 29 outings when Spurs won the Second Division title the season before. Cantrell, who never gained a full England cap owing to the fact that there were several high-class marksmen around at the same time, is the oldest player ever to don a Spurs jersey – aged 40 years, 349 days against Birmingham in April 1923.

CAPEWELL, LEONARD KING

Inside- or centre-forward: 156 apps, 100 goals

Born: Bordesley Green, Birmingham, 8 June 1895 – *Died*: Evesham, November 1978

Career: Bordesley Green and Washwood Heath Council Schools, Saltley Baptists, Wolseley Athletic Works FC, Wellington Town, served with Royal Engineers in Belgium during WW1; VILLA (£700, January 1921; professional, August 1922), Walsall (as part of Fred Biddlestone transfer, February 1930), Wellington Town (August 1930; retired May 1939); assisted Small Heath Baptists (January–October 1947); later ran a coffee tavern and then worked at BSA (press experimental department) for 22 years before spending the rest of his life living in Droitwich

Known as the 'King' or 'Nobby' at Villa Park, Capewell was a tremendous goalscorer, a player who 'sliced his way through some of the tightest defences in the game with all the defiance of a pint-sized battleship', being an early version of Bolton's Nat Lofthouse! Villa pipped Birmingham for his signature in 1921, the club's assistant secretary, Wally Strange, signing him as he arrived at Wellington's home ground after an away game at Wrexham. Capewell spent almost two seasons in Villa's reserve team before scoring three times in five League games at the end of the 1921–22 campaign, including a goal on his debut against Blackburn. Establishing himself in the first XI in 1923–24, he hit 26 goals in 45 games, forming part of a grand forward-line of Dicky York, Billy Kirton, Billy Walker and Arthur Dorrell. Unfortunately, that campaign ended with defeat in the FA Cup final at Wembley. One of ten players to have scored a century of goals for Villa, Capewell's tally included a 5-timer in a 10–0 win over Burnley in 1925, 4 in an FA Cup triumph over Port Vale in 1926 and a hat-trick (with a dislocated shoulder) in a 5–3 League victory over Everton, which was also in 1926. He left the club following the arrival of George Brown. He was keen on golf, billiards and snooker and watched quite a bit of cricket.

CARBONE, BENITO
Forward: 28+2 apps, 8 goals
Born: Begnana, Italy, 14 August 1971
Career: Calabra Asanti/Italy, Torino/Italy (August 1989), Reggiana/Italy (1990), Casertana/Italy (July 1991), Ascoli/Italy (August 1992), Torino/Italy (June 1993), Napoli/Italy (September 1994), Inter Milan/Italy (July 1995), Sheffield Wednesday (£3m, October 1996), VILLA (undisclosed fee, believed to be £100,000, October 1999), Bradford City (Bosman free, July 2000), Derby County (loan, October 2001), Middlesbrough (loan, February–May 2002), Como/Italy (free, June 2002)

The black-haired Italian spent just seven months with Villa. His total of eight goals included a stunning hat-trick in a fifth-round FA Cup tie win over Leeds, and he was also sent off at Everton in the same competition. Very talented with tremendous on-the-ball skills, he made his senior debut at the age of 17 and appeared in over 200 games in Serie 'A' and 'B' (24 goals), gaining a UEFA Under-21 championship medal in 1994 before entering the Premiership with Wednesday. After doing very well with the Owls, scoring 26 goals in 107 appearances, a much-publicised dispute with the Yorkshire club led to his move to Villa Park. The fans took to him immediately, and his presence on the field certainly commanded respect. His three-goal salvo in the Cup against Leeds included one majestic effort that won him the 'Goal of the Season' award. He also netted a cracker against Darlington in the third round. But alas, he failed to perform in either of Villa's two games at Wembley in April–May 2000, and soon afterwards 'Benny' departed for Bradford on a Bosman free, signing a contract worth £30,000 per week.

CAREY, WILLIAM JAMES
Goalkeeper: 4 apps
Born: Prestwich, Manchester, June 1913 – *Died*: Colchester, September 1998
Career: Sedgley Park, Hereford United (briefly), VILLA (May 1936), Bury (July 1939); guest for Rochdale (1939–41), Manchester United (1940–41), Manchester City (1941–42), Coventry City (1944–45), Southport (1944–45), Hereford United; VILLA (re-signed January 1945; retired May 1945)

Reserve to Fred Biddlestone, Carey made four senior appearances for Villa during his three years with the club, although he was sidelined with injury from August 1936–January 1937. Those outings came in 1937–38 – three in the League against Newcastle, Chesterfield and Plymouth and one in the FA Cup against Charlton at Highbury. He did not concede a League goal, Villa winning all three matches on their way to taking the Second Division championship.

CARR, FRANZ ALEXANDER

Winger: 2+3 apps
Born: Preston, 24 September 1966
Career: Blackburn Rovers (apprentice, July 1982; professional, July 1984), Nottingham Forest (£100,000, August 1984), Sheffield Wednesday (loan, December 1989), West Ham United (loan, March 1991), Newcastle United (£250,000, June 1991), Sheffield United (£120,000, January 1993), Leicester City (£100,000, September 1994), VILLA (£250,000, February 1995), Reggiana/Italy (1996), Bolton Wanderers (October 1997), West Bromwich Albion (non-contract, February 1998), Grimsby Town (trial, August 1998), Runcorn (season 1999–2000)

Carr was never given a chance at Ewood Park, but after moving to Forest he developed into a fine player, winning nine England Under-21 caps to go with those he gained at youth-team level. He appeared in over 150 games for Brian Clough before losing his way, leaving the City Ground in 1991. Long periods in the wilderness disrupted Carr's progress after that and he struggled with his form at Villa Park before moving to Italy.

CARRODUS, FRANK

Midfield: 196 apps, 10 goals
Born: Manchester, 31 May 1949
Career: Manchester and District Schools, Lymm Grammar School Old Boys, Altrincham Old Boys, Heyes Albion, Altrincham (July 1964), Manchester City (£5,000, professional, November 1969), VILLA (£95,000, August 1974), Wrexham (£70,000, December 1979); on 'Rebel Tour' to South Africa (summer 1982), Birmingham City (August 1982), Bury (October 1983–May 1984), Witton Albion (season 1984–85), Runcorn (1985), Altrincham (1986), Macclesfield Town (1987); later ran his own promotions business in Altrincham

Carrodus worked as a civil servant before entering League football. A hard-working midfielder who attended regular PE classes, he helped Villa win promotion from the Second Division and gained two League Cup-winner's medals, 1975 and 1977, having collected a loser's prize in the same competition with Manchester City in 1974. After three years with Wrexham, he went on the 'Rebel Tour' to South Africa, returning unscathed and none the wiser to join the Blues. He only had a handful of outings during his short stay at St Andrew's but amassed a total of 331 in League football during his career. Carrodus is a pigeon fancier and a keen hiker.

CARRUTHERS, MARTIN GEORGE

Striker: 2+4 apps

Born: Nottingham, 7 August 1972

Career: VILLA (YTS, July 1988; professional, July 1990), Hull City (loan, October 1992), Stoke City (£100,000, July 1993), Peterborough United (November 1996), York City (loan, January 1999), Darlington (March 1999), Southend United (loan, August 1999; signed for £50,000, September 1999), Scunthorpe United (£20,000, March 2001), Macclesfield Town (July 2003), Boston United (June 2004)

Carruthers failed to make an impact under Villa managers Josef Venglos and Ron Atkinson and was subsequently transferred to Stoke. However, in later years he did very well, and ended the 2003–04 season with 130 goals to his credit in more than 450 senior games.

CARTLIDGE, ARTHUR

Goalkeeper: 55 apps

Born: Hanley, Stoke-on-Trent, 12 June 1880 – *Died*: Stoke-on-Trent, August 1940

Career: Penkhull Victoria, Market Drayton (August 1898), Stoke (September 1899), Bristol Rovers (April 1901), Stoke (briefly, May 1907, but FA subsequently refused transfer, went back to Rovers), VILLA (April 1909), Stoke (August 1911), South Shields (September 1913; retired May 1915)

Cartlidge was regarded as one of the best goalkeepers in the Southern League during his eight years with Bristol Rovers. He won a Southern League championship medal in 1905 and made almost 300 senior appearances for the Pirates before transferring to Villa Park towards the end of the 1908–09 campaign. He gained a Football League championship medal in 1910.

CASCARINO, ANTHONY GUY

Striker: 50+4 apps, 12 goals

Born: St Paul's Cray, 1 September 1962

Career: Orpington Schools, Crockenhill FC, Gillingham (professional, January 1982), Millwall (June 1987), VILLA (£1.5m, March 1990), Celtic (August 1991), Chelsea (£1.1m, February 1992), Olympique Marseille/France (July 1993), FC Nancy/France (1996), Red Star/France (1999–2000); now a football columnist

Cascarino did very well at the Priestfield Stadium, scoring 78 goals in 219 League appearances for the Gills. He continued to find the net for Millwall, claiming almost 50 goals in 128 outings. In almost two years at Villa Park he averaged roughly a goal every four matches up to 1991 when he moved to Celtic, returning to England with Chelsea seven months later. On leaving Stamford Bridge, Cascarino began a seven-year stint in France. He made 88 appearances for the Republic of Ireland at full international level (19 goals) – a record he took from ex-Villa star Paul McGrath, who won 83 caps.

CHAMBERS, JOHN FREDERICK

Forward: 1+1 apps

Born: Garretts Green, Birmingham, 7 October 1949

Career: Sheldon Heath Comprehensive, Birmingham Boys, VILLA (apprentice, June 1965; professional, October 1966), Southend United (July 1969–May 1970), Hereford United (July–August 1971), Knowle (part-time player, September 1971), Stafford Star (Sunday team), Merthyr Tydfil (February 1972), Stourbridge (June 1972), Bromsgrove Rovers, Worcester City, Kidderminster Harriers (October 1976, player/manager 1978–80), Alvechurch (player/manager), Malvern Town (player/manager), Stourbridge (player/manager, August 1988–May 1993), Dudley Town (manager, February 1995–May 1997)

Chambers was a useful youth and Central League player for Villa, for whom he made his League debut at the age of 19 against Blackburn in August 1968. He later did very well as a manager in non-League football.

CHANDLER, ROBERT WILLIAM

Goalkeeper: 1 app.

Born: Calcutta, India, September 1894 – *Died*: *circa* 1950

Career: Aston Town, Upper Thomas Street Boys, Glossop (1911), VILLA (August 1913), Walsall (September 1914), Bloxwich Strollers (August 1920; retired, injured, 1922)

A competent goalkeeper who understudied Sam Hardy during his only season at Villa Park, Chandler's only League game came in the 3–0 home win over Sheffield United on Boxing Day 1913. He was injured before he could make his first-team debut for Walsall.

CHAPMAN, HAROLD

Utility: 6 apps

Born: Liverpool, 4 March 1921

Career: Ellesmere Port (1938), Kidderminster Harriers (1945), VILLA (February 1947), Notts County (March 1949), Gorleston Town (May 1951), Cambridge United (August 1957), Bletchley Town (player/coach, October 1958–March 1959)

Chapman, a neat little player who occupied either the right-half or inside-right berths, was a reserve at Villa Park for two years and made his League debut at Charlton in March 1948. He scored once in 53 League games for Notts County. Captured at Arnhem while serving with the Airborne Division during WW2, Chapman now lives at Bow Brickhill, Herts.

CHAPMAN, ROY CLIFFORD

Forward: 19 apps, 8 goals

Born: Kingstanding, Birmingham, 18 March 1934 – *Died*: Stoke-on-Trent, 21 March 1983

Career: Dulwich Road School, Kingstanding Youth Club, 46th Perry Common Division Boys' Brigade, Kynoch's Works FC, Birmingham County Works FA, County Youth XI, Coventry City (trial, 1950), VILLA (amateur, November 1951; professional, February 1952), RAF (1955–57), Lincoln City (November 1957), Mansfield Town (£7,000, August 1961), Lincoln City (player/manager, January 1965), Port Vale (August 1967), Chester (June 1969), Nuneaton Borough (August 1969), Stafford Rangers (manager, October 1969), Stockport County (manager, September 1975–May 1976), Port Vale (coach, August 1976–May 1977), Stafford Rangers (manager, April 1977–February 1980), later Walsall SportsCo (manager, seasons 1980–82)

Chapman scored over 200 goals in a fine career. Regarded as first reserve to Johnny Dixon and Derek Pace at Villa Park, during his time with Vale he developed sciatica (October 1968) and struggled thereafter. He enjoyed his best managerial days with Stafford Rangers, guiding them to the Northern Premier League title and FA Vase double in 1972, a year after finishing runners-up in the NPL. He was also a Staffordshire Cup winner three times and played for the FA XI against South Africa. He was 49 when he died. Roy's son, Lee Chapman, played for Stoke, Arsenal, Sunderland, Sheffield Wednesday, Noort, West Ham and Leeds.

CHAPPLE, FREDERICK JAMES

Forward: 8 apps, 3 goals

Born: Treharris, South Wales, 1880 – *Died*: *circa* 1945

Career: Treharris Boys' Club, Bristol Schools, VILLA (August 1906), Birmingham (November 1908), Crewe Alexandra (June 1910), Brentford (September 1912), Bristol City (June 1913), Blyth Spartans (August 1918; retired June 1920)

A nippy footballer, elusive at times, Chapple occupied an inside-forward position, but found it tough at Villa Park. Not at his best with either Villa or the Blues, yet he still netted 16 times in 53 appearances for the latter club before moving to Crewe, later having a good spell with Brentford (12 goals in 29 League outings).

CHARLES, GARY ANDREW

Full-back: 92+13 apps, 4 goals

Born: Newham, 13 April 1970

Career: Newham and District Schools, trial with Arsenal and Leyton Orient (1985), Nottingham Forest (apprentice, June 1986; professional, November 1987), Leicester City (loan, March 1989), Derby County (£750,000, July 1993), VILLA (£1.45m, January 1995), Benfica/Portugal (£1.5m, January

1999), West Ham United (£1.2m, October 1999), Birmingham City (loan, September 2000; retired, injured, May 2002)

Right-wing-back 'Fluff' Charles was capped twice by England at senior level and four times by the Under-21s. He gained a Simod Cup-winner's medal with Nottingham Forest in 1992 and then collected a League Cup-winner's medal with Villa in 1996 – before suffering a badly fractured ankle in the end-of-season League game with West Ham. In fact, before joining Villa he'd already amassed over 160 appearances at club level. A player with great pace and balance, Charles loved to join his attack whenever possible, and he was the unfortunate victim of a reckless challenge by Spurs' midfielder Paul Gascoigne in the 1992 FA Cup final.

CHATT, ROBERT SAMUEL

Forward/right-half: 94 apps, 26 goals

Born: Barnard Castle, August 1870 – *Died*: *circa* 1935

Career: Cleator Moor, Middlesbrough Ironopolis (1889), VILLA (August 1893), Stockton (June 1898), South Shields, Willington Athletic, Doncaster Rovers (trainer, 1904), Burslem Port Vale (trainer, August 1905), Manchester City (trainer, May 1906–April 1916), South Shields (trainer, September 1919), Caerphilly (trainer, July 1921–May 1922), Newport County (trainer, July 1922–May 1931)

A very useful footballer, Chatt began his career as a centre-forward and also occupied both the inside-right and inside-left berths before switching into the half-back line, always giving a manly performance. Credited with having scored Villa's winning goal against WBA in the 1895 FA Cup final – after just 39 seconds' play – he gained 2 League championship medals with Villa (1896, 1897) and later won an FA Amateur Cup-winner's medal with Stockton. He played twice for an England XI and also represented the Football League as a Villa player.

CHATTERLEY, LAWSON COLIN (LEW)

Defender: 160+4 apps, 27 goals

Born: Birmingham, 15 February 1945

Career: Birmingham Schools, Birmingham Boys, VILLA (apprentice, June 1960; professional, February 1962), Doncaster Rovers (loan, March 1971), Northampton Town (September 1971), Grimsby Town (February 1972), Southampton (March 1974), Torquay United (player/coach, February 1975), Chicago Sting/USA (player/coach 1978), Southampton (coach, 1979), Sunderland (coach, July 1985); licensee of the Chump Inn, Southampton; Poole Town (manager, June 1987), Reading (coach, June 1988), Southampton (youth development officer, January 1990; coach, July 1991–92)

Chatterley had the distinction of being the first substitute to score for Villa – finding the Blackpool net in a 3–2 home win in January 1967. A solid defender who could also man midfield with efficiency, he won England youth honours as a teenager (1962–63) and went on to appear in over 160 senior games for Villa. He was leading marksman in 1966–67 with 13 goals, and skippered the team in Division Two the following season. Chatterley was a regular for 3 years before leaving for Northampton after 11 years at Villa Park. He went on to amass more than 350 appearances at club level (324 in the Football League) and later coached under Lawrie McMenemy at Southampton and Sunderland, having played under 'Mac' at Grimsby. He was later Ian Branfoot's right-hand man at The Dell and Reading.

CHESTER, REGINALD ARTHUR
Forward: 96 apps, 34 goals
Born: Long Eaton, 21 November 1904 – *Died*: Long Eaton, 24 April 1977
Career: College Road School, Long Eaton Juniors, Long Eaton Rangers, Notts County (trial, April 1921), Mansfield Town (trial, May–June 1921), Peterborough and Fletton United (August 1921), Stamford Town (amateur, August 1922), VILLA (amateur, December 1924; professional, April 1925), Manchester United (May 1935), Huddersfield Town (exchange for Tommy Long, December 1935), Darlington (July 1937), Arnold Town (July 1938), Woodborough United (October 1938), Grantham Town (1940); retired May 1940

A utility forward, Chester was a loyal and dedicated club man who spent eleven and a half years at Villa Park, during which time he averaged a goal every three games. Unable to command a regular place in the side, his best season was in 1929–30 (9 goals in 20 outings). He started out as a centre-forward but did not have the necessary physique or aggression to fulfil that role, choosing to play on the wing most of the time. He made his debut for Villa in September 1925 against Manchester United. Chester top-scored for Darlington in the Third Division (N) in 1937–38 with 9 goals in 28 appearances.

CLARKE, ALBERT WILLIAM
Goalkeeper: 7 apps
Born: Walsall, 7 July 1860 – *Died*: Birmingham, 1934
Career: Wednesbury Old Athletic, VILLA (August 1880), Bilston Town (May 1884); later worked as a printer
Clarke was all set to make a big name for himself in the Villa side when unfortunately he broke his right leg in a friendly game against Wednesbury Strollers in December 1882. He regained full fitness but was only second choice after that and eventually left the club in 1884.

CLARKE, GEORGE BADEN
Outside-left: 7 apps
Born: Bolsover, Derbyshire, 24 July 1900 – *Died*: London, 11 February 1977
Career: Bolsover Main County School, Welbeck Colliery (1918), Mansfield

Town (July 1921), VILLA (£500, December 1922), Crystal Palace (May 1925), Queens Park Rangers (August 1933), Folkestone (1934–35)

Reserve to Arthur Dorrell, Clarke spent three years at Villa Park, during which time he was given just seven first-team outings. He was then transferred to Crystal Palace, for whom he scored 105 goals in 299 senior appearances.

CLARKE, NORMAN FREDERICK

Wing-half: 1 app.

Born: Birmingham, 31 October 1934

Career: Aston Boys (1947–50), VILLA (juniors, April 1950; professional, July 1953), Torquay United (July 1956), Bridgwater Town (July 1958), Weston-Super-Mare (trial, August 1961; signed September 1961–May 1962)

'Nobby' Clarke set a new record by representing Birmingham Boys in each of four successive seasons (1947–51). He later won an England youth cap (against Scotland, 1952) but failed to make the grade with Villa, appearing once in the League side in place of Bill Baxter against Charlton in February 1955. He had 55 games in the Third Division (S) with Torquay.

CLARKE, WILLIAM GIBB

Winger: 43 apps, 6 goals

Born: Mauchline, Ayrshire, 1880 – *Died*: *circa* 1940

Career: Third Lanark (April 1897), Bristol Rovers (July 1900), VILLA (September 1901), Bradford City (£200, April 1905), Lincoln City (December 1909), Croydon Common (September 1911–May 1912)

When he joined Villa in 1901, Clarke was described in the local press as a 'flying winger with great ball skills'. Later reporters saw him play 'pretty and brilliant football, his retention giving much satisfaction'. Signed to replace Charlie Athersmith, unfortunately he was plagued by injuries to both knees and his right ankle, and was consequently sidelined for long periods, his best season coming in 1902–03 (20 appearances). A Second Division championship-winner with Bradford in 1908, he made 98 senior appearances during his 4 years at Valley Parade and followed up with 35 outings for the Imps.

CLARKSON, THOMAS

Wing-half: 17 apps

Born: Stourbridge, April 1865 – *Died*: West Bromwich, July 1915

Career: Stourbridge Invicta, Halesowen Town, VILLA (August 1889), Oldbury Town (June 1893–May 1895)

A strong-tackling, forceful wing-half, Clarkson spent four seasons with Villa, being a permanent reserve for the last two.

CLAYTON, JAMES GORDON THOMAS

Centre-forward: 11 apps, 1 goal

Born: Sunderland, July 1910 – *Deceased*

Career: Shotton Colliery, Wolverhampton Wanderers (October 1932), Sunderland Police Force (March–September 1935); VILLA (October 1937), Burnley (October 1938), Swansea Town (WW2 guest); retired May 1945

Clayton was a tall, strapping footballer, recruited to bolster up Villa's attack during their Second Division championship-winning season. A temperamental player, he lost his place in the Villa side to Frank Shell. Clayton scored 39 goals in 54 games for Wolves and his only strike for Villa was the winner against Sheffield United in November 1937. He notched 10 goals in 16 games for Burnley.

COBLEY, WILLIAM ARTHUR

Left-back: 47 apps

Born: Blaby, Leicester, 31 December 1913 – *Died*: Leicester, April 1989

Career: Leicester schoolboy football, Leicester Ivanhoe, VILLA (trial, January 1935), Coutisthorpe FC (February–May 1935), Nuneaton Town (July 1935), VILLA (professional, September 1935), Solus FC/Leicester (May 1939), Mellor Bromleys FC (briefly); guest for Northampton Town (1939–41), Sutton Town (1939), Solihull Town (1939–40), Fulham (1943–44), Leicester City (September–October 1944); Notts County (August 1946; retired, with leg injury, May 1947)

Left-back Cobley acted mainly as reserve to George Cummings at Villa. Ever-reliable, his best season was in 1936–37, when he starred in 34 Second Division encounters and one FA Cup tie, making his debut in the goalless home draw with Coventry in front of 63,868 fans in October. His son, Paul, played for Leicester Boys.

CODLING, ROLAND JAMES

Left-half: 82 apps

Born: Durham, October 1879 – *Died*: 1940

Career: Durham Youth Club, Stockton (1898), Swindon Town (August 1901), Stockport County (October 1903) Clapton Orient (April 1905), VILLA (March 1906), Northampton Town (July 1909), Croydon Common (October 1909), Manchester City (August 1910), Denton (July 1911; retired 1914)

Codling's career spanned 16 years, during which time he appeared in over 200 first-class matches. A sturdy defender and stern tackler with a strong shot, he was a regular in the Villa side for two full seasons (1906–08) helping the team claim runners-up spot in the First Division in the latter. He became surplus to requirements following the arrival of Frank Cornan and the improving form of Jimmy Logan.

COLLYMORE, STANLEY VICTOR

Striker: 49+12 apps, 15 goals

Born: Swynnerton, near Stafford, 22 January 1971

Career: Broomhill Primary and Sherbrook Comprehensive Schools, Cannock, Longmoor Boys, Walsall (YTS, June 1989), Wolverhampton Wanderers (non-contract, July 1989), Stafford Rangers (July 1990), Crystal Palace (£100,000, December 1990), Southend United (£100,000, November 1992), Nottingham Forest (£2.25m, July 1993), Liverpool (£8.5m, June 1995), VILLA (£7m, May 1997), Fulham (loan, July 1999), Leicester City (£250,000, rising to £500,000, February 2000), Bradford City (free, October 2000), Real Oviedo/Spain (February 2001; retired May 2001)

The son of a Barbadian tax officer, also called Stanley, Collymore did not stay long with the Saddlers, leaving to sign for Wolves (his boyhood heroes). He failed to fit in at Molineux and switched to non-League soccer before returning to the Football League with Palace. After 2 years and 20 games for the Eagles, he moved to Southend and then Forest boss Frank Clark splashed out £2.25m to bring him to the City Ground. He netted over 40 goals in 2 seasons for Forest, helping them gain promotion to the Premiership and with it a place in Europe. In 1995 he was snapped up by Liverpool and while at Anfield made his England debut and also played in the 1996 FA Cup final defeat by Manchester United. He did the business (reasonably well) at Villa Park but had his problems with manager John Gregory. Indeed, he hit the headlines for a variety of reasons with most of the clubs he served. A real character, 'Stan The Man' gained three England caps and could well have been a world-beater if he'd put his mind to playing football! Nonetheless, in his prime he was an exciting, powerful striker whose great talent was not always fully exploited. He partnered some of the finest marksmen around – Ian Wright, Ian Rush, Robbie Fowler and Tony Cottee – and scored some spectacular goals.

Injuries, suspensions and a serious incident involving the TV star Ulrika Jonsson interrupted his career, but when the curtain came down in 2001, his record at senior club level was impressive: 125 goals scored in 317 appearances.

COMYN, ANDREW JOHN

Defender: 17+4 apps

Born: Wakefield, 2 August 1968

Career: Wakefield Schools, Blackburn Rovers 'A', Manchester United (junior), Alvechurch (1987), VILLA (£34,000, August 1989), Derby County (£200,000, August 1991), Plymouth Argyle (£200,000, August 1993), Exeter City (trial), Northampton Town (trial), Preston North End (briefly), Rotherham United (reserves), West Bromwich Albion (non-contract, March 1996), Hednesford Town (August 1997), Halesowen Town (May 2000), Nuneaton Borough (season 2002–03)

Comyn was given a surprise League debut at right-back by Villa boss Graham Taylor against Liverpool just a few days after setting foot inside Villa Park as a university graduate. He wasn't overawed and helped his side to a 1–1 draw. After deputising for various defenders, he was eventually sold to Derby. In September 1992 he came on as a substitute for the Rams against Bristol City and, after just nine seconds of action and with his first touch of the ball, headed an own-goal! When with Hednesford, Comyn skippered the FA XI against Combined Services at Worcester (January 1999) and also won four semi-professional caps for England.

COOCH, HAROLD

Goalkeeper: 25 apps
Born: Birmingham, 1877 – *Died*: Birmingham, 1935
Career: Local schoolboy football, VILLA (professional, August 1901), Walsall (May 1908; retired May 1909 after losing a finger); later returned to Villa Park as coach/trainer (up to WW1)
Deputy to Billy George, Cooch made his League debut at Newcastle in April 1902 (lost 2–1) and had his last outing against Manchester United at Villa Park in September 1907 (lost 4–1). He occasionally occupied a defensive position in the second XI.

COOK, GEORGE WILLIAM

Forward: 61 apps, 40 goals
Born: Evenwood, Co. Durham, 27 February 1895 – *Died*: Colwyn Bay, 31 December 1980
Career: Evenwood Juniors (1912–14), Trindle Juniors (1914–16), Royal Field Artillery (from 1916), Bishop Auckland (August 1919), Rotherham County (May 1922), Huddersfield Town (March 1923), VILLA (February 1927), Tottenham Hotspur (June 1929–April 1931), Brentford (August 1931), Colwyn Bay (August 1932), Rhyl (May 1934–April 1935)
An accomplished footballer, Cook won many honours during his career. He made his mark with Bishop Auckland, whom he twice helped win the FA Amateur Cup (1921 and 1922). His performances around this time attracted many scouts and it was Rotherham who enticed him to turn professional. A year later he signed for Huddersfield and gained three League championship medals with the Terriers in successive seasons before joining Villa. Having scored 35 goals in 91 games for Huddersfield (as partner to George Brown, later to join Villa) he played between Joe Beresford and Billy Walker in Villa's forward-line. However, following the arrival of 'Pongo' Waring, Cook struggled to get into the side during his second season and subsequently moved to White Hart Lane. Although over 34 when he joined Spurs, he still gave the London club excellent service, notching 30 goals in 73 appearances.

COOKE, STEPHEN LEE

Midfield: 0+4 apps

Born: Walsall, 15 February 1983

Career: VILLA (YTS, April 1999; professional, February 2002), AFC Bournemouth (loan, March–April 2002)

England youth international Cooke, after gaining some experience with Bournemouth (seven appearances on loan), eventually made it into Villa's senior side and was handed three substitute appearances in the Premiership in 2002–03 to get himself going in the top flight! Despite his slight frame (5 ft 8 in. tall and 10 st. in weight), he is a talented footballer and looks set for an excellent career at top-class level.

COOPER, NEALE JAMES

Midfield: 21+1 apps, 1 goal

Born: Darjeeling, India, 24 November 1963

Career: Hazelhead Academy, Aberdeen (amateur, 1979; professional, November 1981), VILLA (£300,000, July 1986), Glasgow Rangers (October 1988), Reading (July 1991), Dunfermline Athletic (November 1991), Ross County (player, August 1996; player/coach, 1997; manager, July 1999), Hartlepool United (manager, June 2003)

Cooper, a Scottish youth and Under-21 international, played as a defender and also as a key midfield anchorman for Aberdeen. He helped the 'Dons' win three Premier Division titles, the Scottish Cup on four occasions, the League Cup once, the European Cup-winners' Cup and European Super Cup during his time at Pittodrie, netting ten goals in 245 outings for the Scottish club. Then, following his transfer to Villa, he was injured and out of the game for the first half of the 1986–87 campaign, missing most of the following season as well. His only goal for Villa came against Chelsea in a third-round FA Cup tie and, after returning to Scotland, he won another Premiership medal with Rangers. As manager, he guided Hartlepool into the Second Division play-offs in 2004.

COPLEY, GEORGE HENRY

Goalkeeper: 4 apps

Born: Birmingham, February 1861 – *Died*: Birmingham *circa* 1930

Career: Saltley College, VILLA (August 1879), Birmingham St George's (July 1881–May 1882); VILLA (season 1882–83); emigrated to Ceylon, later worked in Singapore.

Copley was a commanding figure between the posts for Villa during his two seasons with the club, making over 50 appearances in various games (4 in the FA Cup). In one home friendly he 'took out' three opposing forwards with a fierce challenge. He played for Villa's reserve side (1882–83).

CORBETT, JOSEPH

Wing-half. 7 apps

Born: Brierley Hill, 19 June 1902 – *Died*: 1973

Career: Brierley Hill Schools, Cradley Heath Victoria, VILLA (trial, July–August 1919), Brierley Hill Alliance (September 1919), VILLA (August 1921), Brierley Hill Alliance (November 1929), Stourbridge (July 1930), Worcester City (January 1931), Dudley Town (May 1932; retired, injured, October 1937); later landlord of the Boat Inn (Coseley)

'Joe' Corbett spent most of his first three years with Villa playing in the Central League side, making his senior debut at Nottingham Forest in April 1924, when he deputised for George Blackburn. He was reserve for that year's FA Cup final.

CORBETT, WALTER A SAMUEL

Full-back: 13 apps

Born: Wellington, 26 November 1880 – *Died*: Birmingham, 1955

Career: Vicarage Road Council and King Edward Grammar Schools (Birmingham), Thornhill FC, Astbury Richmond (Handsworth), Headingly FC, Soho Villa, Handsworth Victoria, Bournbrook, VILLA (June 1904), Birmingham (July 1907), Queens Park Rangers (loan, September 1907), Birmingham (October 1907), Wellington Town (loan, April 1909), Birmingham (August 1909–May 1911), Wolverhampton Old Church (August 1911; retired April 1913); later managed a Birmingham Export House (from 1922) and in 1945 became head of the wages department of Birmingham City Transport

'Watty' Corbett was a grand defender who played in 18 amateur and 3 full internationals for England before WW1. He also gained a soccer gold medal for Great Britain at the 1908 Olympic Games. One of the best amateur footballers in the game during the six-year period from 1905 to 1911, Corbett showed infinite resource, possessed a fine turn of speed, tackled well and was a consistent performer. He helped Villa's reserve side win the Birmingham and District League three seasons running, skippered Birmingham and District Juniors against Scotland (1903, 1904, 1905) and was selected to represent a mixed amateur and professional XI on tour to the continent in 1906, partnering Bob Crompton of Blackburn and England. Corbett always carried a handkerchief in his withered left hand and while a student at grammar school (where he also played rugby and cricket) he became an expert linguist. He made 46 appearances for the Blues but only one for QPR.

CORDELL, JOHN GRAHAM

Goalkeeper: 5 apps

Born: Bloxwich, 6 December 1928 – *Died*: 1984

Career: Hillary Street School (Walsall), Walsall Schoolboys, Walsall Star, VILLA (amateur, June 1949; professional, September 1949), Rochdale (May 1953), Hednesford Town (August 1955), Brush Sports (March 1958),

Hednesford Town (manager, May 1958), Stafford Rangers (manager, January 1961)

Nicknamed 'Lemon Squash' and 'Jumbo', Cordell was fifth-, sometimes sixth-choice keeper during his time with Villa. His League debut came at Spurs in October 1951 in front of 49,000 spectators and later he had 15 senior outings for Rochdale.

CORNAN, FRANK

Wing-half: 16 apps

Born: Sunderland, 5 May 1880 – *Died*: Halifax, 3 May 1971

Career: Sunderland Black Watch, Willington, Barnsley (1903), Birmingham (April 1905), VILLA (September 1908), Spennymoor United (August 1909), Barnsley (September 1909), Nelson (May 1910), Exeter City (October 1911), Barnsley (July 1912); then non-League football from August 1913; retired 1915

A steely, robust wing-half, Cornan tackled with venom. He made 89 League appearances for Barnsley (all told), 26 for the Blues and 27 for Exeter in the Southern League. His outings for Villa came during the second half of the 1908–09 season. He was almost 91 when he died.

COULTON, FRANK

Full-back: 60 apps

Born: Walsall, February 1868 – *Died*: Sparkhill, Birmingham, 11 March 1929

Career: Walsall Swifts (August 1884), VILLA (August 1886; retired, injured, April 1895)

A stylish footballer, Coulton won an FA Cup-winner's medal with Villa in 1887 and also played in the club's first-ever League game against Wolves in 1888. A damaged knee ended his career.

COWAN, JAMES

Defender: 356 apps, 26 goals

Born: Bonhill, near Renton, Dumbartonshire, 17 October 1868 – *Died*: Scotland, 12 December 1915

Career: Bonhill Council School, Jamestown, Vale of Leven (1887), VILLA (August 1889; retired June 1902; stayed at Villa Park for a short time, coaching the juniors); later licensee of The Grand Turk, High Street, Aston (May 1904–December 1906); Queens Park Rangers (manager, May 1907–November 1913); returned to Scotland

Cowan, with his untiring energy and skilful, timely tackles, was the mainstay of Villa's defence throughout the 1890s. As a centre-half, he was of immense value to the team, being undismayed and uncomplaining after the hardest of games. Known as the 'Prince of half-backs', Cowan was a shrewd tactician, surprisingly quick and certainly a fine footballer, one of Villa's all-time greats. Only 5 ft 7 in. tall and less than 11 st. in weight, he was as solid as a rock at the heart of the

Villa defence. He won three full caps for Scotland, gained two FA Cup-winner's medals (1895, 1897) and collected five League championship medals during his thirteen years with Villa. In December 1895, Cowan missed five League games when he trained away from the ground before travelling to Scotland to enter and win the famous Powderhall Sprint, which earned him £80 in prize money. He was fined four weeks' wages and suspended by a furious Villa committee, who, in fact, knew nothing about his venture north of the border. While he was away, Villa lost games at Preston and Everton. He returned to the team in early January and was at his best as Villa surged on to win the championship. Cowan, a pupil of vocation, was QPR's first-ever team manager.

COWAN, JOHN

Winger: 69 apps, 27 goals

Born: Bonhill, near Renton, Dumbartonshire, 12 December 1870 – *Died*: Scotland, May 1937

Career: Vale of Leven, Preston North End (briefly in 1893), Glasgow Rangers (September 1894), VILLA (August 1895), Dundee Harp (June 1899–May 1901)

A fast and direct winger with a strong shot, Cowan, brother of James (q.v.), spent four years with Villa, being a valuable member of two First Division championship-winning sides (1896, 1897) and playing in the FA Cup final victory over Everton, which completed the double (1897). Cowan left after losing his place to Steve Smith.

COWANS, GORDON SIDNEY

Midfield: 506+22 apps, 59 goals

Born: Cornworth, County Durham, 27 October 1958

Career: County Durham and District Schools, VILLA (apprentice, July 1974; professional, August 1976), Bari/Italy (£450,000, with Paul Rideout, valued at £400,000, June 1985), VILLA (£250,000, July 1988), Blackburn Rovers (£200,000, November 1991), VILLA (free, July 1993), Derby County (£80,000, February 1994), Wolverhampton Wanderers (£20,000, December 1994), Sheffield United (free, December 1995), Bradford City (free, July 1996), Stockport County (free, March 1997), Burnley (free, as reserve-team player/coach, August 1997–May 1998), VILLA (assistant manager/coach, August 1998)

'Sid' Cowans spent 15 years all told as a player at Villa Park and is currently lying third in the club's all-time list of appearance-makers. He helped Villa win the Football League Cup in 1977, the First Division title in 1981, the European Cup and the European Super Cup, both in 1982, and was capped ten times by England, making his international debut against Wales in February 1983 and having his last outing in a World Cup qualifier against the Republic of Ireland in Dublin in November 1990.

He also represented his country in two 'B' and five Under-21 internationals, having earlier played at youth-team level. He helped Stockport win promotion to the First Division. The much-travelled Cowans was player/coach under Chris Waddle at Turf Moor and when Waddle left, Cowans returned to Villa Park for a fourth time as assistant manager/coach to John Gregory. When he quit top-class football, he had accumulated a personal record in club and international competitions of 825 appearances (75 goals).

One of the finest left-sided midfielders in the country during the late 1970s/early 1980s, Cowans could deliver a 30–40 yard defence-splitting pass with pinpoint accuracy. He was an expert with in-swinging corner-kicks and free-kicks and he packed a fair shot himself. He was part of two exceptionally brilliant engine-room units at Villa Park – the first with John Gregory and Dennis Mortimer and then with Des Bremner and Mortimer. A ball-artist, he was voted the Barclays 'Young Player of the Year' in 1980 and was then an ever-present as Villa went on to win their first League title for 71 years (1981).

COX, GERSOM

Full-back: 102 apps

Born: Birmingham, March 1863 – *Died*: Birmingham, September 1940

Career: Excelsior FC, Walsall Town (trial), VILLA (August 1887), Willenhall Pickwick (June 1893), Walsall Brunswick (August 1895), Bloxwich Strollers (May 1898; retired May 1900 after breaking his right leg); later a successful market trader; joined the Birmingham City Police Force as a special constable; also held a brief appointment as coach of non-League side Gravesend

Cox was a well-built, versatile defender, who had the misfortune to score the first own-goal in League football, giving Wolves the lead at Dudley Road on the opening day of the competition, 8 September 1888. He was an FA Cup winner in 1892.

COX, NEIL JAMES

Defender: 37+20 apps, 4 goals

Born: Scunthorpe, 8 October 1971

Career: Scunthorpe United (YTS, June 1988; professional, March 1990), VILLA (£400,000, February 1991), Middlesbrough (£1m, July 1994), Bolton Wanderers (£1.2m, May 1997), Watford (£500,000, November 1999)

Capped six times by England at Under-21 level during the early part of his career, right-back Cox moved to Middlesbrough just a few months after gaining a League Cup-winner's medal with Villa. He then helped 'Boro climb into the Premiership in 1995. A tough-tackling, uncompromising defender, sound and committed, Cox enjoys getting forward at every opportunity and was signed by ex-Villa boss Graham Taylor for Watford in 1999.

CRABTREE, JAMES WILLIAM

Left-half: 202 apps, 7 goals

Born: Burnley, 23 December 1871 – *Died*: Birmingham, 31 May 1908

Career: Burnley Royal Swifts (1885), Burnley (August 1889) Rossendale (August 1890), Heywood Central (July 1891), Burnley (professional, August 1892), VILLA (£250, August 1895), Plymouth Argyle (January 1904; retired May 1904); coached several non-League clubs for two years; then licensee of the Royal Victoria Cross, William Street, Lozells, Birmingham (1906–08)

One of England's greatest players during the period 1894–1902, Crabtree preferred a half-back position, from where he kicked cleanly and with rare precision. A hard tackler, clever at close quarters and equally reliable in open play, he was cool, resourceful and brainy. He excelled in the finer points of the game and was one of the most versatile players in the country, being unrivalled in the left-half position for many years. Very sensitive to criticism, he often stormed off in a temper.

One of the best-paid footballers of his time, he quickly bedded himself in to Villa's first team and certainly repaid the money spent on him. Capped 14 times by England (1894–1902), Crabtree gained 4 League championship-winning medals (1896, 1897, 1899, 1900) and also helped Villa win the FA Cup in 1897, the year that they achieved the double. He skippered Burnley, Villa and his country and quit soccer with an apparent drink problem. After a number of fits (some serious) he died at the age of 36.

CRADDOCK, LEONARD MILLER

Forward: 34 apps, 10 goals

Born: Newent, Herefordshire, 21 September 1926 – *Died*: Ledbury, 21 May 1960

Career: Broomesberrow Council School (Herts); assisted Heenan and Froudin FC (WW2); Chelsea (amateur forms, August 1945), Newport County (May 1946), Hereford United (August 1947), VILLA (September 1948; retired through ill-health, May 1952); later coach to Metham United (Malvern League, 1959–60)

A sprightly forward, able to occupy several positions, Craddock's promising career came to an abrupt end when doctors ordered him to give up the game due to a heart problem. He had a nightmare League debut for Villa – a 6–0 defeat at Middlesbrough in December 1948. Craddock was awarded a benefit match in October 1955. He died at the age of 33.

CRAIG, THOMAS BROOKS

Midfield: 32 apps, 2 goals

Born: Penilee, Glasgow, 21 November 1950

Career: Avon Villa Juveniles, Drumchapel Amateurs (August 1965), Aberdeen (groundstaff, June 1966; professional, November 1968), Sheffield Wednesday (£100,000, May 1969), Newcastle United (£110,000, December 1974),

VILLA (£270,000, January 1978), Swansea City (£150,000, July 1979), Carlisle United (player/coach, March 1982), Hibernian (player/coach, October 1984), Celtic (assistant manager/coach, 1987–1990)

Craig was the first Scotsman to join an English League club for a six-figure fee when he moved to Hillsborough in 1969. He made 210 appearances for the Owls and 122 for Newcastle before joining Villa halfway through the 1977–78 season. A left-sided player, direct, skilful and an excellent shot, he was capped by Scotland against Switzerland in 1976 and also represented his country at schoolboy, youth, Under-21 and Under-23 levels. He played for Newcastle in the 1976 League Cup final defeat by Manchester City and left the Geordies after being involved in a heated argument with the club's board of directors over the 'Ninnis Affair'.

CROPLEY, ALEXANDER JAMES
Midfield: 82+2 apps, 7 goals
Born: Aldershot, 16 January 1951
Career: Edina Hearts (1966–68), Hibernian (July 1968), Arsenal (£150,000, December 1974), VILLA (£125,000, September 1976), Newcastle United (loan, February–March 1980), Toronto Blizzard (briefly, 1981), Portsmouth (September 1981), Hibernian (September 1982; retired May 1985); later a licensee and then a taxi driver in Edinburgh.

Raised in Edinburgh despite being born in deepest England, Cropley was a left-sided player who could also be used as a direct winger. He twice broke his leg in League games – first with Arsenal against Birmingham in November 1975 and with Villa against WBA in October 1977. He won two full and three Under-23 caps for Scotland before joining the Gunners. He played in two League Cup-winning sides: Hibs in 1973, Villa in 1977.

His father, John Thomas, played in over 160 League games for Aldershot (1947–63).

CROSSLAND, WILLIAM SAMUEL
Defender: 5 apps
Born: West Bromwich, February 1856 – *Died*: Birmingham, February 1923
Career: West Bromwich Baptists, Hockley Heart of Oak, Oldbury Town, VILLA (August 1879; retired May 1883 through injury); later worked in Birmingham's jewellery quarter

Crossland was a powerful player who lined up in Villa's first-ever FA Cup tie against Stafford Road in December 1879.

CROUCH, PETER JAMES
Striker: 25+18 apps, 6 goals
Born: Macclesfield, 30 January 1981
Career: Tottenham Hotspur (YTS, April 1997; professional, July 1998), Queens Park Rangers (£60,000, July 2000), Portsmouth (£1.25m, July 2001), VILLA

(£4m, March 2002), Norwich City (loan, September–December 2003), Southampton (£3m, August 2004)
A giant striker, 6 ft 6 in. tall and 12 st. in weight, Crouch failed to make Spurs' first team, scored 12 goals in 49 games for QPR and hit 19 in 39 outings for Pompey before his move to Villa Park, signed by Graham Taylor. He struggled early on in the claret and blue strip but was a better player when he returned after a loan spell at Norwich. Capped four times by England at Under-21 level, he also represented his country's youth team and gained a First Division championship medal with Norwich in 2003–04.

CROWE, VICTOR HERBERT
Wing-half. 351 apps, 12 goals
Born: Abercynon, Glamorgan, 31 January 1932
Career: Handsworth Wood School, Erdington Albion, West Bromwich Albion (amateur, May 1950), VILLA (amateur trial, March 1951), Stirling Albion (amateur player while on National Service), VILLA (professional, June 1952), Peterborough United (July 1964), Atlanta Chiefs/NASL (assistant manager, 1967–May 1969), VILLA (assistant coach, September 1969; manager, January 1970–May 1974), Portland Timbers/NASL (coach/manager, 1975–76); later scout in non-League football and advisory manager to Bilston Town (1988–89)
Crowe was brought up in Handsworth, Birmingham. He did well as an amateur and after his national service he was handed a professional contract. He went on to give Villa, and Wales, excellent service as a wing-half before joining Peterborough. Known as 'Spike', his red hair stood out like a beacon in centre-field where he performed manfully, never shirking a tackle, always totally committed and producing some sterling work for both club and country. He replaced Danny Blanchflower at right-half in the Villa side in 1954 and went on to skipper the side to the 1960 Second Division championship and victory in the 1961 League Cup final over Rotherham, but missed the 1957 FA Cup win through injury. Later Crowe played in two FA Cup semi-finals defeats (1959 and 1960), won the supporters' 'Terrace Trophy' award and was capped 16 times by Wales. A member of his national team at the 1958 World Cup finals, he eventually captained the Red Dragons for the first time in 1960. He helped Posh reach the 1966 League Cup semi-final before returning to Villa Park, where he subsequently became manager, Villa playing 192 League games under his guidance, remaining unbeaten in 140 of them while winning 86. Crowe now lives in Sutton Coldfield.

CROWTHER, STANLEY
Wing-half. 62 apps, 4 goals
Born: Bilston, Staffs, 3 September 1935
Career: Stonefield Secondary Modern School, West Bromwich Albion (amateur, May 1950), Erdington Albion (briefly), Bilston Town (August

1952), VILLA (£750, August 1955), Manchester United (£18,000, February 1958), Chelsea (£10,000, December 1958), Brighton and Hove Albion (March 1961), Solihull Town (October 1961), Rugby Town (December 1961), Hednesford Town (July 1963), Rushall Olympic (September 1965; retired May 1967); became a senior foreman for Armitage Shanks (Wolverhampton)

Crowther joined Manchester United in one of the most dramatic transfers in the game's history! One hour and 16 minutes after signing for the Reds, he stepped out in front of almost 60,000 fans at Old Trafford for an FA Cup tie against Sheffield Wednesday in the aftermath of the Munich air crash – having earlier assisted Villa against Stoke in the same competition. Crowther made over 60 appearances for Villa, helping them beat Manchester United 2–1 in the 1957 FA Cup final. He was only acquired as a stop-gap by United and after 20 outings moved to Chelsea, for whom he made over 50 League appearances before ending his career with Brighton. Orphaned at the age of 15, Crowther won three England Under-23 caps and represented the Football League as a Villa player. He was on the losing side for Manchester United in the 1958 FA Cup final.

CRUDGINGTON, GEOFFREY

Goalkeeper: 5 apps

Born: Wolverhampton, 14 February 1952

Career: Wolverhampton and District Schools, Wolverhampton Wanderers (junior, 1967–68), VILLA (professional, September 1969), Bradford City (loan, March–April 1971), Preston North End (loan, May 1971), Toronto Blizzard (summer, 1971), Crewe Alexandra (£5,000, March 1972), Swansea City (£20,000, July 1978), Plymouth Argyle (£40,000, October 1979; later coach, then football in the community officer and now School of Excellence advisory coach at Home Park)

Crudgington played for England schoolboys before standing in for John Dunn and Tommy Hughes at Villa Park. He went on to appear in over 275 games for Crewe and 374 for Argyle, playing for the latter in the 1984 FA Cup semi-final against Watford at Villa Park.

CUMBES, JAMES

Goalkeeper: 183 apps

Born: Didsbury, near Manchester, 4 May 1944

Career: Didsbury County School, Manchester Boys (trial), Whalley Range FC (Manchester Amateur League), Runcorn, Southport, Tranmere Rovers, West Bromwich Albion (£33,350, August 1969) VILLA (£36,000, November 1971), Portland Timbers (March 1976), Coventry City (non-contract, September 1976), Runcorn (semi-professional, August 1977), Southport (non-contract, January 1978), Worcester City (March 1978–May 1981), Kidderminster Harriers (September 1982–May 1984), West Bromwich Albion All Stars (1980s); also played cricket for Lancashire (1963–67, 1971),

73

Surrey (1968–69), Worcestershire (1972–81), Warwickshire (1982) and West Bromwich Dartmouth (1982–84); commercial manager of Warwickshire CCC (October 1984–August 1987) and Lancashire CCC where he is now chief executive

Tall, agile and competent with a good technique for a goalkeeper, Cumbes was also a fine fast bowler at county level. He won a Cheshire Bowl final medal with Runcorn before appearing in 137 League games for Tranmere. He then contested the number one position with John Osborne at Albion, transferring to Villa after 79 outings for the Baggies. He gained a Third Division championship medal and a League Cup-winner's prize with Villa before losing his place to John Burridge. Cumbes amassed over 400 League and Cup appearances during his career. As a cricketer, he won both county championship and knockout cup medals with Worcestershire and played in 161 first-class matches, averaging 7.56 with the bat and taking 379 wickets at 30.20 each, with a best return of 6–24. He also took 38 catches.

CUMMINGS, GEORGE WILFRED

Full-back: 232 apps

Born: Thornbridge, near Falkirk, Scotland, 5 June 1913 – *Died*: Birmingham, April 1987

Career: Laurieston School (Stirlingshire), Thornbridge Waverley (1928), Thornbridge Welfare (1930), Grange Rovers (1931), Partick Thistle (August 1932), VILLA (£9,350, November 1935); guest for Revo Electric (1939), Solihull Borough, Birmingham, Falkirk (1940), Nottingham Forest and Northampton Town (WW2); retired May 1949; VILLA (third-team coach, July 1949–July 1952), Hednesford Town (manager, May 1953–May 1954), scout for Burnley and Wolves (part-time); also employed at the Dunlop Rubber Company

Cummings, nicknamed 'Icicle' for his coolness and composure, was a masterful full-back, as hard as a block of granite with a superb physique. His kicks were strong and long, his bone-shaking tackles were thorough and positive, his attitude determined and resourceful, while his brain never stopped working. A great footballer who served Villa superbly for 14 years, making over 400 first-class appearances, including 177 during WW2, Cummings helped the team win the Second Division title in 1938 and lift the Wartime League (N) Cup in 1944. He won nine full caps for Scotland between 1935 and 1939 (six as a Villa player) and toured the USA and Canada with the Scottish FA in 1935 while also representing the Scottish League XI on two occasions. He appeared in a WW2 international and lined up for an All-British team and the Football League side in 1939 and for an International XI against the British Army in 1940. As a youngster he had played for the Scottish Junior FA (1929–30). Cummings skippered Villa for four years to 1949, taking over from Alex Massie. Cummings was suspended by Villa in 1937 after being found guilty of driving under the influence of drink. He was fined £10 and banned for a year.

CUNLIFFE, ARTHUR

Outside-right: 75 apps, 13 goals

Born: Blackrod, near Wigan, 5 February 1909 – *Died*: Bournemouth, 28 August 1986

Career: Adlington FC (aged 14, 1923), Chorley (August 1927), Blackburn Rovers (professional, January 1928), VILLA (joint deal involving Ronnie Dix, May 1933), Middlesbrough (December 1935), Burnley (April 1937), Hull City (June 1938), guest for Aldershot, Brighton and Hove Albion, Fulham, Reading, Rochdale and Stoke City (WW2); Rochdale (August 1946; trainer, July 1947), Bournemouth (trainer, July 1950; physiotherapist, 1971–May 1974)

Early in his career Cunliffe was an aggressive outside-right but in later years he developed into an international left-winger, winning two full England caps in that position. Very quick, he had good ball skills and whipped in a positive centre, given the chance. He was a regular marksman throughout his career, scoring 47 goals in 129 League games for Blackburn, 5 in 27 for Middlesbrough, 19 in 42 for Hull and 5 in 23 for Rochdale. He spent nearly 25 years with Bournemouth.

CURBISHLEY, LLEWELLYN CHARLES (ALAN)

Midfield: 41+2 apps, 1 goal

Born: Forest Gate, London, 8 November 1957

Career: West Ham United (apprentice, November 1973; professional, July 1975), Birmingham City (£225,000, July 1979), VILLA (£100,000, plus Robert Hopkins, March 1983), Charlton Athletic (£40,000, December 1984), Brighton and Hove Albion (£32,000, August 1987); Charlton Athletic (player/coach, July 1990; assistant manager, October 1990; joint manager, July 1991; manager, June 1995)

In May 1998, Curbishley celebrated when Premiership football came to The Valley for the first time. He took the Addicks up again in 2000 and later that same year was in line as an England coach.

As a player Curbishley never reached the heights he had hoped for, although he did represent England at schoolboy, youth and Under-23 levels and made well over 600 senior appearances while serving with five different clubs. He gained an FA Youth Cup runner's-up medal with West Ham (1975) and helped the Blues win promotion from Division Two (1980). After 155 appearances for the latter club he moved to Villa, for whom he scored his only League goal at Watford on Boxing Day 1983.

CURCIC, SASA

Midfield: 23+11 apps, 1 goal

Born: Belgrade, Yugoslavia, 14 February 1972

Career: OFK Belgrade/Serbia, Partizan Belgrade/Serbia, Bolton Wanderers (£1.5m, October 1995), VILLA (£4m, August 1996), Crystal Palace (£1m,

March 1998), New Jersey Metros/USA (July 1999), Rochdale (briefly), Motherwell (March–April 2000), Tranmere Rovers (trial, August–September 2000)

Capped ten times by Yugoslavia before joining Bolton for a club record fee, attacking midfielder Curcic was voted Wanderers' 'Player of the Year' in his only season with the club. He then moved to Villa (another record fee) but after an encouraging start found himself out of favour for long spells, prompting calls from the player that he should never have left Bolton! Failing to get on with manager Brian Little, Curcic submitted a transfer request in February 1997 but did not leave Villa Park until 13 months later – after his work permit had been renewed. A moody player at times, he scored his only goal for Villa against Derby in a fourth-round FA Cup tie in January 1997, while taking his tally of international caps up to 13, adding another to his total later. He played with a lot more purpose and heart under Terry Venables at Selhurst Park, but when he left the Eagles he became unsettled again and was devastated when NATO bombed his homeland.

CURTIS, GEORGE WILLIAM

Centre-half: 57 apps, 4 goals

Born: Dover, 5 May 1939

Career: Snowdown Colliery, Coventry City (amateur, May 1954; professional, May 1956), VILLA (£25,000, December 1969; retired May 1972); Coventry City (commercial staff, 1974; managing director, September 1983; joint manager with John Sillett, April 1986–May 1987; then director to 1994)

As a solid, uncompromising defender, Curtis made 538 appearances for Coventry – a club record that was eventually broken by Steve Ogrizovic in 1996. Three years after being voted 'Midland Footballer of the Year', he helped the Sky Blues gain promotion to Division One for the first time in the club's history (1967) and he played in four different divisions of the Football League with City. Bought as a stop-gap by Villa, he did well for a short while, adding a Third Division championship medal to his collection.

CUTLER, NEIL ANTHONY

Goalkeeper: 0+1 app.

Born: Birmingham, 3 September 1976

Career: West Bromwich Albion (YTS, June 1992; professional, September 1993), Chester City (loan, March 1996), Crewe Alexandra (July 1996), Chester City (loan, August 1996; signed permanently July 1998), VILLA (November, 1999), Oxford United (loan, December 2000), Stoke City (free, July 2001), Swansea City (loan, February–April 2003), Stockport County (June 2004)

Former England schoolboy and youth international, Cutler had one Premiership outing with Villa as a substitute for David James in a 4–0 win at

Middlesbrough in February 2000. In 2001–02 he helped Stoke gain promotion to the First Division.

DALEY, ANTHONY MARK

Winger: 241+49 apps, 38 goals
Born: Lozells, Birmingham, 18 October 1967
Career: Aston Manor School, Holte Comprehensive School, Birmingham Boys, VILLA (YTS, June 1983; professional, May 1985), Wolverhampton Wanderers (£1.25m, June 1994), Watford (July 1998), FC Madeira/Portugal, Hapoel Haifa/Israel, Walsall (June 1999), Nailsworth FC (briefly), Forest Green Rovers (October 1999; retired May 2003)

After playing for his country at youth-team level, dashing right- or left-winger Daley bided his time with Villa before gaining a place in the first XI. Once in, he stayed and did well, gaining one 'B' and seven full England caps as well as helping Villa win the League Cup in 1994. Direct, skilful, with an eye for goal, Daley was plagued by injuries at Molineux before linking up with his former boss Graham Taylor at Watford.

DALY, PATRICK

Defender: 4 apps
Born: Dublin, 4 December 1927
Career: Dublin City Boys, Shamrock Rovers, VILLA (November 1949), Shamrock Rovers (May 1951–54)

Chatty Irishman Daly was signed as a replacement for Dicky Dorsett but unfortunately he failed to settle at Villa Park and returned home after making just four appearances. His League debut was at Blackpool in January 1950, when he did well against Stanley Matthews. He represented the Republic of Ireland against Finland in 1951 and also starred for the League of Ireland as a Shamrock Rovers player. He's now living in Ireland.

DAVIS, ARTHUR GEORGE

Forward: 5 apps, 1 goal
Born: Edgbaston, Birmingham, 7 July 1900 – *Died*: Birmingham, 1955
Career: Handsworth Old Boys, Birmingham St George's, Evesham, guest for Coventry City (1917–18), Leicester Fosse (December 1918–January 1919), VILLA (July 1919), Queens Park Rangers (May 1922), Notts County (February 1924), Crystal Palace (May 1928), Kidderminster Harriers (August 1929–May 1931)

Davis was a reserve inside- or outside-left who was given few opportunities with Villa. He later amassed over 200 League appearances, playing for QPR, Notts County and Palace.

DAVIS, ELISHA

Winger: 21 apps, 2 goals
Born: Dudley, December 1855 – *Died*: Birmingham, 20 December 1897
Career: Hockley Hill Council School, Florence FC (Birmingham), Wednesbury
   Strollers, VILLA (August 1879; retired, injured, May 1886); later landlord of
   the Golden Lion, Aston (Birmingham)
Davis played in Villa's first-ever FA Cup tie in 1879, a 1–1 draw at Stafford
Road. A wholehearted performer, he was quite unflagging and especially good
at dribbling, although a little imprudent at times. A serious knee injury ended
his career.

DAVIS, GEORGE

Goalkeeper: 1 app.
Born: Birmingham, 1868 – *Died*: Birmingham, 1925
Career: St Phillip's, VILLA (August 1889), Witton White Star (1891–92)
Davis, a relatively unknown goalkeeper, made just one League appearance for
Villa – deputising for Jimmy Warner in a 6–2 win at Burnley in October 1889.

DAVIS, GEORGE ARCHIBALD

Centre-forward: 1 app., 1 goal
Born: Handsworth, Birmingham, 1870 – *Died*: Birmingham, *circa* 1930
Career: Victoria FC, Aston Manor, VILLA (July 1892), Smethwick Centaur
   (August 1893), Wesleyans FC
A reserve forward, Davis partnered Jack Devey and Denny Hodgetts in a 3–2
defeat at West Brom in September 1892, scoring his side's second goal.

DAVIS, NEIL

Striker: 0+3 apps
Born: Bloxwich, 15 August 1973
Career: Redditch United, VILLA (£25,000; professional, May 1991), Wycombe
   Wanderers (loan, October 1996), Walsall (August 1998), Hednesford Town
   (September 1998)
A hard-working player, two of Davis' substitute appearances for Villa came in
the Premiership.

DAVIS, RICHARD DANIEL

Centre-forward: no senior apps
Born: Birmingham, 22 January 1922 – *Died*: Bishops Stortford, August 1999
Career: Morris and James FC (Birmingham), Sunderland (February 1939),
   VILLA (WW2 guest, September 1940–October 1943); also guest for
   Aldershot, Brentford, Bristol Rovers, Notts County and Rochdale
   (1943–45), Darlington (May 1954; retired, injured, May 1957)
Davis – an England schoolboy international – was a guest player for Villa during
WW2, and what an impact he had! Only 18 when he came to the club, he gave

defenders a torrid time with his precise, all-action play and devastating marksmanship. He hit 67 goals in 53 games for Villa, including 10 hat-tricks and a 6-timer. In 1941–42 he was unstoppable, cracking in 30 goals in 18 outings. After the war, Davis returned to Roker Park and went on to score 79 goals in 154 senior games for Sunderland before netting another 32 in 93 Third Division (N) matches for Darlington. One of the game's greatest strikers, he notched more than 200 goals (all levels) during a wonderful career.

DAVIS, RICHMOND

Forward: 12 apps, 4 goals
Born: Walsall, April 1861 – *Died*: Birmingham, 1934
Career: Broadway Council School (Walsall), Walsall Swifts (1881), VILLA (August 1884; retired, injured, May 1888); enticed out of retirement to play for Walsall (1888–89)

Davis enjoyed running with the ball but was somewhat greedy at times and lost possession in dangerous situations. Able to play in all of the five forward positions, he was an FA Cup winner in 1887 against West Brom. A knee injury ended his career.

DAWSON, FREDERICK HENRY HERBERT

Wing-half: 20 apps, 2 goals
Born: Birmingham, December 1858 – *Died*: Birmingham, 19 November 1938
Career: Handsworth New Road Council School, Aston Unity, VILLA (August 1880; retired, injured, September 1889)

A key member of Villa's 1887 FA Cup-winning side, Dawson played with evident enjoyment, tenacity and constructiveness, always putting himself about! He lined up at left-half in Villa's first-ever League game against Wolves in September 1888.

DAWSON, JAMES HUBERT

Right-half: 5 apps
Born: Stoke-on-Trent, August 1859 – *Died*: Burton-on-Trent, 10 February 1927
Career: Forest Courtiers FC (Stoke), VILLA (August 1880), Burton Swifts (May 1882–May 1884)

Dawson, adept with both feet, possessed a fearsome tackle. He burst the ball when clearing his line during an FA Cup tie between Villa and Notts County in January 1882.

DAY, MERVYN RICHARD

Goalkeeper: 33 apps
Born: Chelmsford, 16 June 1955
Career: Chelmsford and Essex Schools, West Ham United (apprentice, June 1971; professional, March 1973), Leyton Orient (£100,000, July 1979), VILLA (£15,000, August 1983), Leeds United (£30,000, January 1985),

Luton Town (loan, March 1992), Sheffield United (loan, April 1992), Carlisle United (July 1993–May 1994; later coach, then Director of Coaching, January 1995; manager during season 1996–97), Charlton Athletic (first-team coach, July 1999 to date)

Possessing good technique, cool and composed with exceptional positional sense, Day made his League debut as an 18 year old. As a 'Hammer' he won England Youth and Under-23 honours, was named 'Young Footballer of the Year', gained an FA Cup-winner's medal in 1975 and played in the 1976 European Cup-winner's Cup final, while making 231 appearances. He then had 138 games for Orient and briefly displaced Nigel Spink between the posts during his time with Villa. In 1987 Day was in goal for Leeds in the play-off final against his future club Charlton.

DEACY, EAMONN STEPHEN

Full-back: 30+9 apps, 1 goal

Born: Galway, Ireland, 1 October 1958

Career: Galway Rovers, VILLA (March 1979), Derby County (loan, October 1983), Galway United (July 1984); later worked in the family fruit and vegetable business in Ireland

During the 1978–79 season, Deacy – one of nine brothers – wrote at least 20 letters in eight months to Villa asking for a trial. He finally got one and spent five years at the club. His goal came in a 3–2 home win over Norwich in March 1983. He won four caps for the Republic of Ireland in 1981–82.

DEAKIN, ALAN ROY

Wing-half: 269+1 apps, 9 goals

Born: Balsall Heath, Birmingham, 27 November 1941

Career: Mary Street Junior and Dennis Road Secondary Modern Schools (Balsall Heath), South Birmingham Boys, Cannon Hill Rovers, VILLA (juniors, 1956; professional, December 1958), Walsall (October 1969–May 1972), Tamworth (August 1972–June 1974), Metropolitan Cammell FC, VILLA Old Stars (1979–88); later a welder for the Gamwell Engineering Company (Witton)

Deakin was outstanding in the early 1960s, one of the most talented of the 'Mercer Minnows'. He successfully took over the number 6 shirt from Pat Saward, but his career took a nosedive in 1965 following a series of injuries, which included a broken leg, fractured ankle, damaged toe and twisted knee. He returned in 1966–67 and fulfilled a lifetime's ambition when asked to captain the first team, having skippered the Youths some years earlier. Deakin helped Villa win the League Cup in 1961 and collected a loser's medal two years later. He also gained six England Under-23 caps before transferring to Walsall. Deakin's brother, Mike, played for Crystal Palace, Aldershot and Northampton.

DE BILDE, GILLES ROGER GERARD

Utility: 4 apps

Born: Zellick, Belgium, 9 June 1971

Career: FC Aalst/Belgium, RSC Anderlecht/Belgium, PSV Eindhoven/ Holland, Sheffield Wednesday (£3m, July 1999), VILLA (loan, October 2000–January 2001), RSC Anderlecht/Belgium (July 2001)

Capped over 25 times by his country, de Bilde was an attacking midfielder or out-and-out striker who did well in Belgium and Holland before his big-money transfer to Hillsborough. The Owls struggled in the Premiership and were relegated, but de Bilde still top-scored with 11 goals in 45 appearances. He played for Belgium in Euro 2000 yet found it hard to fit in with Villa's style of play and returned to Wednesday after his loan spell had expired.

DE LA CRUZ, ULISES

Wing-back: 39+17 apps, 2 goals

Born: Piqulucho, Ecuador, 8 February 1974

Career: Liga Deportiva Universitaria Quito FC/Ecuador (July 1999), Hibernian (£700,000, July 2001), VILLA (£1.5m, August 2002)

De La Cruz made 20 appearances for Villa in his first Premiership campaign, having previously appeared in 32 League games (2 goals) for Hibs. A strongly built, fast and decisive player with an appetite for hard work, he enjoys a challenge. He has gained over 60 full caps for Ecuador (3 goals).

DEEHAN, JOHN MATTHEW

Striker: 135+4 apps, 50 goals

Born: Solihull, 6 August 1957

Career: St Peter's School (Solihull), Olton British Legion FC, Arsenal (trial, 1972), VILLA (apprentice, July 1973; professional, April 1975), West Bromwich Albion (£424,000, September 1979), Norwich City (£175,000, November 1981), Ipswich Town (June 1986), Manchester City (player/coach, July 1988), Barnsley (player/coach, January 1990), Norwich City (assistant manager/coach, 1991, then manager, January 1994–June 1995), Wigan Athletic (manager, November 1995–July 1998), Sheffield United (chief scout), VILLA (coach/assistant manager, July 2001), Ipswich Town (scout), Northampton Town (coach, then caretaker manager, October–November 2003); served on the PFA Management Committee during the 1980s

Deehan had an Irish father but chose to play for England and won three youth and seven Under-21 caps while also being a non-playing substitute for the senior side against Brazil in 1981. A very competent striker, he scored well for Villa before transferring to West Brom, for whom he made 50 appearances. He netted 70 goals in 199 games for Norwich, helping the Canaries win the League Cup in 1985 and the Second Division title 12 months later before playing over 50 times for Ipswich.

Positive during his coaching appointments at Maine Road and Oakwell, he replaced Mike Walker as manager at Carrow Road and guided Wigan to the Third Division title in 1996.

DELANEY, MARK ANTHONY

Full-back: 127+18 apps, 1 goal
Born: Haverfordwest, 13 May 1976
Career: Carmarthen FC (August 1994), Cardiff City (free, July 1998), VILLA (£250,000, March 1999)

Delaney established himself in Villa's first team halfway through the 1999–2000 season, having contested a place in the side with Steve Watson. Initially capped by Wales at 'B'-team level, he's now appeared in over 20 full internationals, captaining his country against Norway in May 2004. A busy player with good pace, he was sent off three times in ten matches in 2000, seeing 'red' in the FA Cup semi-final with Bolton at Wembley, in an international against Portugal soon afterwards and then in the InterToto Cup clash with Marila Pribram.

DENNINGTON, LESLIE ARTHUR

Defender: 1 app.
Born: West Bromwich, June 1902 – *Died*: *circa* 1980
Career: Dartmouth Council School, West Bromwich Sandwell, Wellington St George's (briefly), Wolseley Motors FC, VILLA (December 1924), Reading (July 1925), Exeter City (November 1928), Coventry City (October 1931)

Strongly built reserve centre-half or left-half, Dennington's only League outing for Villa was against Huddersfield in February 1925. He made 65 appearances for Exeter.

DEVEY, HARRY PERCIVAL

Wing-half: 84 apps
Born: Newtown, Birmingham, 10 March 1860 – *Died*: Birmingham, 25 April 1940
Career: Aston Hall School, Aston Clarendon (1881), Montrose (May 1884), Aston FC (December 1884), Excelsior FC/Birmingham (June 1886), VILLA (August 1887; retired, injured, May 1893)

One of identical twins (the other was Arthur, a Villa trialist), Devey came from a family of eight (seven boys, one girl). A keen, hard tackler, typical of many players of his era, he enjoyed 'carrying' the ball forward and often tried shots from long range, albeit not too successfully. He lined up in Villa's first-ever League game against Wolves in September 1888 and collected an FA Cup runner's-up medal in 1892.

DEVEY, JOHN HENRY GEORGE

Forward: 308 apps, 186 goals

Born: Newtown, Birmingham, 26 December 1866 – *Died*: Aston, Birmingham, 13 October 1940

Career: Aston Brook School, Montrose YC (Aston), Wellington Road FC, Excelsior FC/Birmingham (1883), Aston Unity, Aston Manor, West Bromwich Albion (briefly 1889), Mitchell St George's (1890), VILLA (professional, March 1891; retired April 1901; coach, 1901–03; then director, June 1904–September 1934); ran a sports outfitter's shop in Lozells and played county cricket for Warwickshire (1888–97), scoring over 6,500 first-class runs including 8 centuries

For a player so skilful, thorough and effective, Devey's merits, when in his prime, were inexplicably overlooked by the England selectors. He could play in any forward position and there is no doubt that he was one of the finest goalscorers in the country in the 1890s. A close dribbler with good pace (when required), Devey was alive to every movement on the field and possessed the rare gift of 'intelligent anticipation'. He knew the game inside out. He never lacked initiative, but was a strong believer in combination, bringing his fellow forwards and half-backs into the game as often as possible. He was exceptionally clever with his head as he was with both feet and often scored goals from distance when he caught the opposing goalkeeper off guard. Capped just twice by England, Devey helped Villa win the Football League championship five times (1894, 1896, 1897, 1899, 1900) and the FA Cup twice (1895, 1897). He also collected a Cup runner's-up medal in 1892 and was a key figure in the double-winning side of 1897, appearing in 29 of the 30 League games and in all 7 Cup matches. He was on the board of directors for 32 years. It is said that Devey made his sporting 'debut' for Villa in March 1890 – at baseball!

DEVEY, WILLIAM

Inside-right: 10 apps, 2 goals

Born: Perry Barr, Birmingham, 12 April 1865 – *Died*: Birmingham, 1935

Career: Aston Brook School, Clarendon Montrose, Aston Brook Boys, Wellington Road FC, Aston Unity (1882), Mitchell St George's (briefly), Small Heath (August 1885), Wolverhampton Wanderers (August 1891), VILLA (December 1892), Walsall Town Swifts (May 1894), Burton Wanderers (1895), Notts County (1896), Walsall (1897), Burton Wanderers (briefly), Walsall (March 1898), Small Heath (July 1898; retired May 1900)

A skilful player, occupying mainly the inside-right berth, Devey did far better with his other clubs than he did with Villa, securing 18 goals in only 13 first-class games for the Blues and 18 in 42 League outings for Wolves. He made 121 League appearances during his career (42 goals). He was the brother of John Devey (q.v.).

DICKIE, WILLIAM WALTER ARTHUR
Wing-half: 1 app.
Born: Wednesbury, September 1867 – *Died*: Birmingham, March 1931
Career: Wednesbury White Star, Walsall Swifts, VILLA (August 1889),
   Darlaston (September 1890), Bilston Town (August 1891–May 1893)
Small, industrious player, second reserve to Jack Burton and Tom Clarkson,
Dickie's only senior game for Villa was in the FA Cup at Notts County in
February 1890 (lost 4–1).

DICKSON, IAN WILLIAM
Centre-forward: 83 apps, 39 goals
Born: Maxwell, Dumfries, September 1902 – *Died*: *circa* 1976
Career: Harold Johnstone Motor Works FC (Dumfries), Maxwelltown United,
   Cheshaw Juniors, Queen of the South (October 1919), VILLA (January
   1921), Middlesbrough (£3,000, December 1923), Westborough FC (April
   1926; retired, through injury, May 1928)
A robust player who used his weight to good effect, Dickson was marvellously
adept at stealing in unnoticed behind a defence, and during a useful career he
averaged a goal every 130 minutes of football. He played for the Anglo Scots
against Home Scots in an international trial in Glasgow in 1922 and scored 12
in 38 games for Middlesbrough.

DICKSON, WILLIAM ALEXANDER
Centre-forward: 64 apps, 34 goals
Born: Crail, Fife, 27 August 1866 – *Died*: Stoke-on-Trent, 1 June 1910
Career: Dumfries Schools, Dundee Strathmore (1885), Sunderland (July 1888),
   VILLA (August 1889), Stoke (July 1892; retired, injured, May 1897; then
   coach and later director, 1907); also a licensee in Stoke-on-Trent
Dickson, a striker of the highest quality, hit four goals in his only international
outing for Scotland against Ireland in 1888. He skippered Villa on several
occasions, played in the 1892 FA Cup final defeat by West Brom and struck 48
goals in 134 senior games for Stoke.

DINSDALE, WILLIAM ARTHUR
Forward: 8 apps
Born: Darlington, 12 July 1903 – *Died*: Darlington, 21 February 1984
Career: St Phillip's School, Rise Carr Juniors, Darlington (amateur, August
   1921), Darlington Railway Athletic, Crook Town (1922), VILLA (March
   1925), Lincoln City (May 1926), Bradford Park Avenue (£1,200, February
   1929), Lincoln City (May 1930), Darlington (August 1931; retired May
   1932)
Dinsdale understudied Len Capewell and Billy Walker at Villa Park before
moving to Lincoln, where he developed into one of the Imps' all-time greats,
netting 89 goals in 125 senior games in 2 spells at Sincil Bank. A big, bustling

player with no great ball control, he took his fair share of knocks and was delighted when he scored a goal.

DIVER, EDWIN JOHN

Goalkeeper: 3 apps
Born: Cambridge, 20 March 1861 – *Died:* Portardawe, Swansea, 27 December 1924
Career: Perse School (Cambridge), Surrey AFC (1890), VILLA (August 1891; retired April 1894 to concentrate on playing cricket)

Reserve to both Albert Hinchley and Jimmy Warner, Diver made his League debut for Villa at Bolton in April 1892. Regarded as a cricketer rather than a footballer, he played in 75 matches for Surrey CCC (1883–86) and in 118 games for Warwickshire (1894–1901). An opener or middle-order right-hand batsman, he amassed 7,245 runs at an average of 23, having his best year in 1899, when he scored 1,096 runs at an average of almost 30 with a top score of 184. An occasional medium-pace bowler, he captured a handful of wickets, having a best return of 6–58. He also kept wicket on occasions. Diver assisted both Monmouthshire and Cambridgeshire cricket clubs, being joint secretary/treasurer of the latter in 1889.

DIX, RONALD WILLIAM

Inside-forward: 104 apps, 30 goals
Born: Bristol, 5 September 1912 – *Died:* 2 April 1998
Career: South Central School, Bristol Schools, Gloucestershire Schools, England Schools (aged 13), Bristol Rovers (amateur, July 1927; professional, September 1929), Blackburn Rovers (May 1932), VILLA (with Arthur Cunliffe, March 1933), Derby County (February 1937), Tottenham Hotspur (June 1939); guest for Blackpool, Bradford PA, Bristol City, Chester, Liverpool, Wrexham and York City during WW2; Reading (November 1947; retired June 1949)

The youngest player ever to score a League goal, Dix was 15 years, 180 days old when he netted for Bristol Rovers against Norwich in a Third Division (S) game in March 1928. Joining Villa after a proposed move to Everton had fallen through, he was a fine footballer, an inside-forward of high consistency who made the ball do the work. He averaged a goal every three and a half games during his four years at Villa Park and in his career bagged almost 140 in 442 senior matches. Capped by England against Norway in 1939, he had earlier represented the Football League (1926) and in 1943 won a Wartime League Cup (N) winner's medal with Blackpool, following on with a runner's-up medal 12 months later when the Seasiders lost to his old club Villa.

DIXON, ARTHUR ALBERT

Wing-half: 3 apps
Born: Matlock, July 1867 – *Died:* 1933
Career: Derby Midland (1886), VILLA (August 1888), Stoke (August 1889), Leek Alexandra (September 1891–May 1893)

Wiry and aggressive, Dixon was knocked out when making his Villa debut against his future club Stoke in September 1888 – Villa's first home game in the Football League.

DIXON, JOHN THOMAS
Inside-left: 430 apps, 144 goals
Born: Hebburn, County Durham, 10 December 1923
Career: Hebburn Boys' Club, Durham County Boys, Spennymoor United (1940), Newcastle United (amateur trialist); guest for Hull City, Middlesbrough, Newcastle United and Sunderland during WW2; VILLA (August 1944; professional, January 1946; retired May 1961; remained on coaching staff for three years; then second-team trainer, July 1964–May 1967); also played regularly for Villa Old Stars (1969–90) and was also a fully qualified FA coach
Dixon enjoyed 17 wonderful years with Villa. One of the stars of the 1950s, he skippered the team to FA Cup glory in 1957 and amassed excellent goalscoring and appearance records, being top marksman three seasons running (1950–53). Named as reserve for England against Wales in 1953, he established himself in the Villa side during the 1948–49 campaign and went on to occupy all five forward-line positions and that of left-half for the club, with inside-left undoubtedly his favourite berth. Voted the supporters' 'Terrace Trophy'-winner in 1959, Dixon broke his nose playing his last game for the club against Sheffield Wednesday in April 1961 – the day Charlie Aitken made his League debut! A teetotaller and non-smoker, he ran an ironmonger's shop in Wylde Green for many years before selling up in September 1985. He still attends the occasional match at Villa Park.

DOBSON, HENRY ARTHUR
Half-back: 7 apps
Born: Chesterton, Staffs, April 1893 – *Died*: Germany, May 1918
Career: Chesterton Foresters, Audley North Staffs (July 1911), VILLA (August 1912–May 1918); guest for Rotherham County (1917)
Tall and athletic, Dobson was sadly killed in action while serving with the North Staffordshire Regiment during WW1, after making just seven appearances for Villa – the first against Blackburn in February 1913.

DODDS, THOMAS BLACK
Forward: 1 app.
Born: South Shields, 20 December 1918
Career: Hebburn YMCA, North Shields (May 1937), VILLA (January 1939), guest for Darlington (1943–44), Swansea Town (part-exchange with Trevor Ford, January 1947), Barry Town (July 1947), Hereford United (August 1950–May 1951)
Strong and virile, Dodds' only outing for Villa was in the first League game after WW2 against Middlesbrough in August 1946. He scored twice in 11 League games for Swansea.

DONCASTER, STUART
Centre-forward: 2 apps, 1 goal
Born: Gainsborough, September 1890 – *Died*: Derbyshire, 1955
Career: Gainsborough County School, Buxton, VILLA (guest, April 1911), Stourbridge (May 1911), VILLA (May 1912), Glossop (December 1913), Army (from 1914), guest for Matlock (1915–16); did not figure after WW1

A tall, hard-working reserve centre-forward, Doncaster scored in his second outing for Villa against Liverpool in April 1913.

DONOVAN, TERENCE CHRISTOPHER
Forward: 24 apps, 11 goals
Born: Liverpool, 27 February 1958
Career: Clee Grammar School, Louth United, Grimsby Town (professional, August 1976), VILLA (£75,000, September 1979), Portland Timbers (loan, June–August 1982), Oxford United (loan, February 1983), Burnley (£25,000, February 1983), Rotherham United (£15,000, September 1983), Blackpool (loan, October 1984); moved into non-League football (1985)

Honoured by the Republic of Ireland at schoolboy level, Donovan added Under-21 and senior caps to his collection. Son of Donal Donovan (ex-Everton and Grimsby full-back), he drew up an impressive Central League record with Villa (70 goals scored in 120 matches) but failed to establish himself in the first XI. He was Grimsby's record transfer 'out' when he moved to Villa Park. His hobbies include squash and golf.

DORIGO, ANTHONY ROBERT
Left-back: 129+6 apps, 1 goal
Born: Melbourne, Australia, 31 December 1965
Career: Birmingham junior football, VILLA (apprentice, 1981; professional, January 1982), Chelsea (£475,000, July 1987), Leeds United (£300,000, May 1991), Torino/Italy (free, June 1997), Derby County (free, October 1998), Stoke City (free, July 2000; retired 2002)

Dorigo has three different passports – Australian, Italian and British. An efficient and steady defender who enjoyed his sorties upfield, he won seven England Under-21 caps while with Villa, who gave him a trial after he had pestered the club to answer his letters! He made his debut as a 'sub' on the last day of the 1983–84 League programme against Ipswich and gained a regular place in the side the following season.

After joining Chelsea, he skippered the England Under-21 side, added four more intermediate caps to his tally, played seven times for England 'B', made the first of fifteen full international appearances and helped the London club win both the Second Division title (1989) and the Full Members Cup (1990). In his spell with Leeds he gained both First Division championship and FA Charity Shield medals (1992). He retired in 2002 with well over 650 senior appearances under his belt.

DORRELL, ARTHUR REGINALD

Outside-left: 390 apps, 65 goals

Born: Small Heath, Birmingham, 30 March 1896 – *Died*: Alum Rock, Birmingham, 13 September 1942

Career: Belper Road, Loxton Street Schools (Leicester), Carey Hall Sunday School (Leicester), Army Service/RASC (from 1916), VILLA (May 1919), Port Vale (June 1931; retired August 1932); later landlord at the Pelham Arms, Alum Rock (Birmingham)

Dorrell, a fast-raiding orthodox winger, was capped four times by England in 1925–26. Nothing ruffled or disturbed him – even the most exciting game left him ice-cool – he joined Villa on his demob from the Army and spent 12 years with the club, frequently combining style and brilliance with Billy Walker. Besides his full international honours, he represented the Football League (1923) and played in two FA Cup finals (1920 and 1924), collecting a winner's medal in the first against Huddersfield. During WW1 Dorrell made quite a name for himself on the athletics track, sprinting to victory in the Army championships in France. His father, William (q.v.), also played for Villa and it was he who prompted his son to become a professional footballer. His brother played for Hinckley Athletic.

DORRELL, WILLIAM

Forward: 12 apps, 4 goals

Born: Coventry, 1872 – *Died*: *circa* 1939

Career: Hopkins and Sewell, Singers FC (1889), Leicester Fosse (1891), VILLA (April 1894), Leicester Fosse (March 1896), Burslem Port Vale (trial, August 1897), Belper Town (September 1897; retired April 1905)

Father to Arthur (q.v.), Dorrell played on the left-wing or inside-right. He had to contest a first-team place with such fine players as Steve Smith and Albert Woolley and therefore his outings were restricted. He was released in 1896.

DORSETT, RICHARD

Defender: 271 apps, 36 goals

Born: Brownhills, Staffordshire, 3 December 1919 – *Died*: Brownhills, 1998

Career: Walsall Boys, Birmingham County FA, Wolverhampton Wanderers (groundstaff, April 1935; professional December 1936); guest for Liverpool, Grimsby Town, Southampton, Brentford and Queens Park Rangers during WW2; VILLA (£3,000, September 1946; retired May 1953, then youth-team coach), Liverpool (assistant trainer, July 1957), Brownhills Boys Club (manager/coach, August 1962); was also employed by BRD and BIP (Strelly Works)

Known as the 'Iron Man', 'Brick Wall' and the 'Brownhills Bomber', Dorsett was as tough as they come, a player who never shirked a tackle, was totally committed and as rugged and as strong as an elephant! In 1946, while on tour with Wolves in Copenhagen, he was sent off after an incident with a Danish player. Recalled Dorsett: 'He kicked me in the back as I was shielding the ball. With no "Clean Air" act in operation I told him precisely what I thought. He retorted by spitting at me, so I smacked him one.'

This upset the club and Dorsett didn't play for Wolves again. He whipped in 13 goals in his first season at Villa Park, but early in 1947–48 he was moved to right-half, a position vacated by Bob Iverson. As time progressed, Dorsett was switched to left-back where he did well until Peter Aldis and Harry Parkes appeared on the scene. In January 1950 his playing days almost came to an end when he was involved in a car crash. He survived and went on to give Villa grand service. He had netted 35 times in only 52 outings for Wolves, including their goal in their 1939 FA Cup final defeat by Portsmouth. He also helped Wolves win the 1942 Wartime League Cup. Dorsett was the nephew of the former West Brom and Manchester City brothers, George and Joe Dorsett.

DOUGAN, ALEXANDER DEREK
Striker: 60 apps, 26 goals
Born: Belfast, 20 January 1938
Career: Distillery, Portsmouth (£4,000, August 1957), Blackburn Rovers (March 1959), VILLA (£15,000, August 1961), Peterborough United (£21,000, June 1963), Leicester City (£25,000, May 1965), Wolverhampton Wanderers (£50,000, March 1967; retired August 1975), Kettering Town (manager, August 1975–May 1977); also PFA chairman and a sports presenter on Yorkshire TV; Wolverhampton (chairman and chief executive, August 1982–85); later involved in fund-raising scheme for the Duncan Edwards Medical Centre (Dudley)

One of the most colourful footballers of his day, Derek Dougan shaved his head when he played for Villa. Always a big favourite with the fans, he represented his country at schoolboy, youth and amateur levels as a wing-half or central defender before joining Portsmouth in 1957. Pompey switched him to centre-forward and he went on to score 9 goals in 33 League games before moving to Ewood Park in 1959. Dougan hit 25 goals for Rovers and appeared in the 1960 FA Cup final against Wolves – despite having asked for a transfer on the eve of the match. After working as a part-time car salesman in Blackburn, Dougan was bought to replace Gerry Hitchens at Villa. Dubbed the 'Clown Prince of Soccer', 'Cheyenne' (when he was bald) and the 'Doog', he was, without doubt, a great character and fine goalscorer. After interesting spells with Peterborough and Leicester, Wolves' manager, Ronnie Allen, enticed him to Molineux – and what a signing he turned out to be, helping Wolves win promotion from the Second Division in 1967. He formed a brilliant partnership up front with John Richards and in 1974 was a League Cup winner. Leading marksman at Molineux in 1967–68, 1968–69 and 1971–72, he went on to net 123 goals for the Wanderers in 323 appearances before entering into management with Kettering Town. Capped 43 times by Northern Ireland, Dougan also gained 'B' caps for his country. Making his First Division debut for Portsmouth at Old

Trafford in October 1957, he went on to score more League goals than any other Irishman – 222 in 546 appearances. He is one of only a handful of footballers to have netted a hat-trick in both First and Second Division matches and in the FA Cup, League Cup and the UEFA Cup. The 'Doog' suffered a heart attack in 1997 but made a full recovery after treatment. Dougan's brother was married on the same day as the Queen and Prince Philip; another brother was born on the same day as Prince Charles, and the Doog himself became a father of a boy on the day the Queen gave birth to her fourth child.

DOWDS, PETER

Utility: 21 apps, 3 goals

Born: Johnstone, Renfrewshire, 12 December 1867 – *Died*: Glasgow, 2 September 1895

Career: Broxburn Shamrock, Celtic (February 1889), VILLA (May 1892), Stoke (July 1893), Celtic (May 1894–September 1895)

Dowds was a quality footballer, able to play anywhere, but preferred a wing-half position. He was an artist with the ball, always in control of the situation, always displaying a full range of tricks and graces and very creative in the process. Capped once by Scotland against Ireland in 1892, he had 2 good spells with Celtic, notching 19 goals in 49 games. A heavy drinker, he died following a chest complaint.

DRAPER, MARK ANDREW

Midfield: 141+14 apps, 11 goals

Born: Long Eaton, 11 November 1970

Career: Notts County (YTS, June 1986; professional, December 1988), Leicester City (£1.25m, July 1994), VILLA (£3.25m, July 1995), Rayo Vallecano/Spain (loan, January–May 2000), Southampton (July 2000)

Industrious midfielder Draper had already appeared in almost 320 senior games (54 goals scored) and gained 3 England Under-21 caps before joining Villa. Over the next five years he produced some fine displays, helping Villa win the League Cup in 1996. But after only one substitute outing in his last season he departed after failing to fit into manager John Gregory's plans.

DRINKWATER, CHARLES JAMES

Outside-left: 2 apps, 1 goal

Born: Willesden, north London, 25 June 1914 – *Died*: London, 1998

Career: Golder's Green, Middlesex Wanderers, Brentford (amateur, June 1933), Walthamstow Avenue (1934–35), VILLA (amateur, August 1935; professional, October 1935), Charlton Athletic (July 1936), Walsall (August 1939); guest for Watford (February 1941–46); Notts County (1943–44), Southampton (1943–44), Gillingham (1945–46), Pinner FC (trainer/coach, February 1948), Ruislip Manor (player–manager/coach, April 1952–October 1953)

Reserve left-winger, only 5 ft 4 in. tall, but reliable and nippy, Drinkwater – an England schoolboy trialist – scored once on his debut against Chelsea in November 1935 when deputising for Arthur Cunliffe. He also figured in Villa's next game at Birmingham when he set up one of Dai Astley's goals in the 2–2 draw in front of 60,250 fans.

DUBLIN, DION

Striker: 149+41 apps, 59 goals
Born: Leicester, 22 April 1969
Career: Oakham United, Norwich City (professional, March 1988), Cambridge United (free, August 1988), Manchester United (£1m, August 1992), Coventry City (£2m, September 1994), VILLA (£5.75m, November 1998), Millwall (loan, March–May 2002), Leicester City (May 2004)

Rejected by Norwich, 6 ft 2 in. striker Dublin started to score goals aplenty for Third Division Cambridge, netting a hat-trick on his League debut against Peterborough. His all-action performances quickly drew scouts and managers from several top clubs and after securing 73 goals in 201 appearances for United, finishing as top marksman 3 seasons running and gaining a Third Division championship medal in 1991, he joined Manchester United. Unfortunately, after scoring on his full debut for the Reds, he suffered a broken leg and ankle ligament damage. Out for five months, he came back late on and scored seven goals in thirteen Pontins League matches but, following the arrival of Eric Cantona, he found himself surplus to requirements and moved to Highfield Road. He weighed in with 72 goals in 171 senior appearances for the Sky Blues and then started off like a house on fire with Villa, netting 5 times in his first 2 outings, including a brace against Spurs on his debut and a hat-trick at Southampton. There were signs of a tremendous striking partnership with Stan Collymore, but that sadly never fully materialised and Dublin ended his first term with 11 goals to his name in 24 outings. He put away 12 more goals during the first part of the 1999–2000 season, but in December suffered a serious injury in the home game with Sheffield Wednesday. Fractured neck vertebrae were diagnosed and surgery was required to repair what could easily have been a life-threatening injury. Dublin was not expected to return that season – but he defied all odds and bounced back to help Villa reach the FA Cup final, scoring the deciding penalty in the semi-final shoot-out with Bolton. A powerful, sometimes awkward-looking player, exceptionally strong in the air and no mean performer on the ground, Dublin earned 4 full England caps and reached the personal milestone of 200 first-class goals in 2003. He helped Millwall reach the First Division play-offs during his loan spell with the London club.

DUCAT, ANDREW

Right-half: 87 apps, 4 goals

Born: Brixton, Surrey, 16 February 1886 – *Died*: Lord's cricket ground, Marylebone, London, 23 July 1942

Career: Brewer Road and Crompton House Schools (Southend), Westcliff Athletic, Southend Athletic, Woolwich Arsenal (amateur, January 1905; professional, February 1905), VILLA (£1,000, June 1912); guest for Birmingham, Bellis and Morcom FC, Grimsby Town and Alexander Pontorium FC (1916–18); Fulham (May 1921, retired May 1924; then manager to July 1926); Corinthians Casuals (August 1926, reinstated as an amateur); ran a sports outfitter's shop during his time with Villa and also played county cricket for Surrey (1906–31)

As a footballer, Ducat was capped six times by England (1910–12) and skippered Villa to victory in the 1920 FA Cup final, having missed the 1913 final with a broken leg. He was out of action for two years but soon made up for lost time, giving Villa tremendous service right up until 1921.

An outstanding wing-half of the unflurried, academic type and a great sportsman, he was rarely spoken to by the referee, never booked or sent off and played the game with passion and total commitment. Signed to replace George Tranter, Ducat appeared in 193 games for Arsenal (plus 47 during WW1) and starred in 69 matches for Fulham.

On the cricket field he was a top-order, right-hand batsman and occasional right-arm slow bowler. He appeared in 428 first-class matches, scored 23,373 runs, including 52 centuries, at an average of 38.63, with a best score of 306 not out against Oxford University. He took 21 wickets for 903 runs (average 43) and claimed 205 catches, the majority as a close-to-the-wicket fielder. Ducat played in one Test match, for England against Australia in 1921, batting twice. He was dismissed in unusual circumstances for a duck in his first innings when a slice of wood flew off his bat and dislodged a bail, but he recorded a fine 50 when he returned to the crease for his second knock. He was later cricketing coach at Eton College, a part-time journalist and a Surrey publican.

He played in various football and cricket matches (mainly for charity) right up until his sudden death, which occurred out on the cricket square at Lord's in 1942, when he suffered a heart attack while batting for the Surrey Home Guard against the Sussex Home Guard.

DUFFY, DARRELL GERARD

Defender: 1 app.

Born: Birmingham, 18 January 1971

Career: Archbishop Isley School, Idsall School (Shropshire), South Birmingham Boys, West Midland Schools, VILLA (schoolboy forms, March 1985; YTS, June 1987; professional, July 1989), Moor Green (August 1991), Scunthorpe United (February 1993–May 1994), Nuneaton Borough, Tamworth, West Midlands Police Force

Duffy, a former England schoolboy international, made one League appearance for Villa, stepping in at right-back for Chris Price at Derby County in May 1989, two months before he became a professional.

DUGDALE, JAMES ROBERT

Centre-half: 255 apps, 3 goals

Born: Liverpool, 15 January 1932

Career: Harrowby FC (Liverpool), West Bromwich Albion (January 1950; professional, January 1951), VILLA (£25,000, February 1956), Queens Park Rangers (October 1962; retired, injured, May 1963); became a Witton publican, later steward of Villa's Lions club, Hasbury Conservative club (Halesowen) and Moseley rugby club; had a leg amputated in 1990

Dugdale – the 'Laughing Cavalier' – was an excellent defender who shared the number 5 shirt at Albion with Joe Kennedy before moving to Villa. He had 75 games for Albion, gaining an FA Cup-winner's medal in 1954, collecting 3 England 'B' caps and also representing the Football League. Replacing Con Martin in Villa's defence, he collected his second FA Cup-winner's medal in 1957, helped Villa win the Second Division title in 1960 and was brilliant when the League Cup was won 12 months later. In 1993 Villa staged a testimonial match on his behalf (against the Blues). He is the uncle of the ex-Barnsley, Coventry and Charlton defender Alan Dugdale. He now lives in Acocks Green, Birmingham.

DUNN, JOHN ALFRED

Goalkeeper: 118 apps

Born: Barking, 21 June 1944

Career: Barking and Essex Schools, Chelsea (schoolboy forms, June 1959; apprentice, June 1960; professional, February 1962), Torquay United (October 1966), VILLA (£8,000, January 1968), Charlton Athletic (free, July 1971), Ramsgate (loan, December 1974), Tooting and Mitcham (player/coach, February 1975), Woking, Grays Athletic, Craven FC (Essex Business Houses League); then refereed in the Essex Business Houses and Sunday Corinthian Leagues (1986–90)

Due to his inconsistency, Dunn was the target of a group of fans during his last season with Villa. Prior to that, he had given the club excellent service, playing in the 1971 League Cup final at Wembley after taking over from John Phillips. He was eventually replaced by Jim Cumbes and, leaving Villa Park, replaced Charlie Wright at The Valley, going on to play in 118 games for Charlton. During his 'pro' career he amassed almost 300 appearances, 262 in the Football League, and made over 100 at non-League level. He now lives in Hornchurch, Essex.

DUNNING, WILLIAM

Goalkeeper. 69 apps

Born: Arthurlie, Scotland, 2 January 1865 – *Died*: Southampton, 4 January 1902

Career: Johnstone Juniors (1886), Celtic (May 1888), Glasgow Hibernians (1899), Bootle (1890), VILLA (£100, July 1892; retired, through ill-health, April 1895); moved to South Africa before returning to work as a docker in Southampton

Dunning, 6 ft tall and 13 st. in weight, was a daring custodian who replaced Jimmy Warner in the Villa goal. He won a League championship medal in 1894 before handing over his duties to Tom Wilkes. He died of tuberculosis.

DUTTON, THOMAS THEODORE

Inside-forward: 1 app.

Born: West Bromwich, April 1870 – *Died*: Wednesbury, February 1922

Career: Oak Lane School, Wednesbury Old Athletic (1889), VILLA (July 1891), Walsall Town (May 1892–April 1894)

A reserve with Villa, Dutton's only League appearance was against Blackburn in March 1892 when he made two goals for Louis Campbell in a 4–3 defeat.

DYKE, ARCHIBALD SAMUEL

Outside-right: 9 apps

Born: Newcastle-under-Lyme, Staffordshire, September 1886 – *Died*: *circa* 1955

Career: Chesterton FC, Newcastle Congregational, Newcastle PSA, Stoke (1908), Port Vale (August 1912), Stoke (July 1913), VILLA (February 1914), Bellis and Morcom, Port Vale (WW1 guest, 1916); later played briefly for Stafford Rangers (October 1919), Coventry City (September 1920), Blackpool (May 1921), Congleton Town (June 1922), Stafford Rangers (May 1923; retired April 1925)

A clever little winger with good speed, Dyke deputised for the more experienced Charlie Wallace in Villa's pre-WW1 attack.

ECCLES, JOSEPH

Outside-right: 10 apps

Born: Stoke-on-Trent, 5 February 1906 – *Died*: 1970

Career: Wolseley Motors (1921), Walsall (1922), Wolseley Motors, VILLA (January 1924), West Ham United (August 1926), Northampton Town (June 1928), Coventry City (June 1929), Kidderminster Harriers (July 1930)

Eccles, a speedy winger, walked into Villa Park and asked for a trial. He impressed and was signed as a professional within a fortnight. However, owing to the form of Dicky York, he found it difficult to get into the first team and left after 18 months. His father, Jack, played for Stoke and was trainer at Birmingham.

EDGLEY, HAROLD HORACE

Outside-left: 86 apps, 17 goals
Born: Crewe, January 1892 – *Died*: Nottingham, March 1966
Career: Whitchurch, Crewe Alexandra, VILLA (£50, June 1911), Stourbridge (loan, September–December 1913), VILLA (December 1913); guest for Bellis and Morcom (1915–17), West Bromwich Albion, Stourbridge (1916), Port Vale (1916–17), Chesterfield Town, Lincoln City, Birmingham, Leicester Fosse (1917–18); Queens Park Rangers (August 1921), Stockport County (August 1923), Worcester City (May 1924), then non-League football in Cheshire League (1925–27); later director of Notts County

Edgley was a positive left-winger, well built, quick with a powerful shot. He had cruel luck when he broke his leg in two places during a League game at Chelsea three weeks before Villa were due to play (and beat) Huddersfield in the 1920 FA Cup final. He was later presented with a specially designed gold medal after appearing in all the previous rounds. Edgley had 75 outings with QPR (6 goals) and 31 with Stockport (4 goals).

EDWARDS, ALFRED

Half-back: 8 apps
Born: Coventry, April 1890 – *Died*: October 1918
Career: Lord Street FC (Coventry and North Warwickshire League), Stourbridge, VILLA (July 1910), Dudley Town (August 1912), Bristol City (May 1912), Newport County (1913), Army (1914–18)

Compact, small in stature but as keen as mustard, Edwards was a natural footballer who did exceedingly well in non-League football after leaving Villa Park, where he deputised for Chris Buckley. He represented Birmingham and District Juniors against Scotland Juniors at Glasgow in April 1910. He was killed in action during WW1.

EDWARDS, GEORGE ROBERT

Forward: 152 apps, 41 goals
Born: Norwich, 1 April 1918 – *Died*: Lapworth, 21 January 1993
Career: Priory School (Great Yarmouth), Yarmouth Boys, Norfolk Boys, Yarmouth Caledonians, Norfolk County, Yarmouth Town, Norwich City (amateur, March 1935; professional, April 1936), VILLA (June 1938); WW2 guest for Birmingham (1939–40), Chelmsford (1939–40), Coventry City (1939–40), Northampton (1939–40), Norwich City (1939–40), Walsall (March 1940), Wrexham (April 1940), Nottingham Forest (1940–41), Notts County (1940–41), Leicester City (1945–46) and Worcester City; Bilston United (August 1951), Yarmouth Town (April 1955–September 1955); later ran a newsagent's/sub post-office business in Birmingham; became a VILLA shareholder

After nine appearances for Norwich, Edwards had to wait until November 1938 before making his Villa debut against Manchester United, having chipped a bone in his ankle when tackled by Bob Iverson in a practice session. The injury niggled him throughout his career and he always played with a heavy strapping around his ankle. Nevertheless, Edwards – a huge favourite and great servant to Villa – was a goalscoring master (certainly during WW2). A hard-grafting forward, he could occupy a number of positions, but was best at centre-forward. He top-scored for Villa during WW2 with 94 goals in 125 games and was a Wartime League Cup (N) winner in 1944. He also netted the fastest goal by a Villa player in the FA Cup – after just 13 seconds against Manchester United in 1948. Indeed, he was leading marksman at Villa Park in 1946–47 and 1947–48, having notched 43 goals (including two fours) in the transitional season of 1945–46.

At the age of 15, Edwards won the Norfolk County schools' 100 yards sprint title and excelled at both billiards (champion, 1939) and snooker.

EDWARDS, RICHARD THOMAS
Defender: 77 apps, 2 goals
Born: Kirkby-in-Ashfield, 20 November 1942
Career: Nottingham Forest (trial), Notts County (juniors, 1958; professional, October 1959), Mansfield Town (March 1967), VILLA (£30,000, March 1968), Torquay United (£8,000, June 1970), Mansfield Town (July 1973), Bath City (player/coach, 1974; manager, 1975–76)

An England youth international, a long-throw expert, and sturdy central half, Edwards tackled decisively and enjoyed a challenge. A former pit worker, he was manager Tommy Cummings' first signing when he took charge at Villa Park. During a fine career, Edwards made 469 League appearances, including 221 for Notts County and 102 for Mansfield. After retiring from soccer, he became a professional singer with Bruce Stuckey, a colleague at Torquay. He went on to become a star on the American country and western circuit after turning solo.

EDWARDS, ROBERT OWEN
Defender: 8+1 apps
Born: Telford, 25 December 1982
Career: VILLA (YTS, June 1999; professional, December 2000), Crystal Palace (on loan, November 2003), Derby County (on loan, January–May 2003) Wolverhampton Wanderers (£150,000, June 2004)

Reserve defender Edwards, 6 ft 1 in. tall, made eight appearances for Villa during the 2002–03 Premiership campaign, having developed strongly in the second XI over the previous three seasons. A strong, forceful right-back, he's appeared in one international for Wales (against Azerbaijan, March 2003) having earlier gained youth honours. He made his Premiership debut against Middlesbrough in December 2002.

EHIOGU, UGOCHUKA
Defender: 286+17 apps, 15 goals
Born: Hackney Marshes, London, 3 November 1972
Career: West Bromwich Albion (YTS, 1988; professional, July 1989), VILLA
  (£40,000, July 1991), Middlesbrough (£8m, October 2000)
Tall, rangy centre-back, determined, reliable, strong in the tackle and quick in
recovery, Ehiogu was 'given away' by WBA, for whom he made two substitute
League appearances. He was 'signed' with a sell-on clause and Albion later
received £2m when he was sold to Middlesbrough. Ehiogu was a star performer
with Villa, winning international honours for England at 'B', Under-21 (15
caps) and senior levels (1 cap) while gaining a Coca-Cola Cup-winner's medal
in 1996. Unfortunately, he had a disagreement with manager John Gregory
(after being left out of the team) and eventually left for the Riverside Stadium,
becoming the second costliest defender in British football (behind Manchester
United's Jaap Stam) at that time. A bad injury suffered on his debut for 'Boro at
Charlton sidelined him for almost a month, but since then he's been superb at
the heart of the Teessiders' defence, playing mainly alongside another ex-Villa
star, Gareth Southgate. Both players helped 'Boro win the Carling League Cup
in 2004.

ELLIOTT, JAMES ALEXANDER ERNEST
Defender: 25 apps
Born: Middlesbrough, 20 October 1869 – *Died*: Middlesbrough 1899
Career: Middlesbrough Ironopolis, VILLA (August 1893; retired, due to ill-
  health, April 1896)
Tall, beefy player who weighed over 14 st., Elliott, who occupied both full-back
positions, made his League debut for Villa against West Bromich Albion in
September 1893.

ELLIOTT, PAUL MARCELLUS
Defender: 68+5 apps, 7 goals
Born: Lewisham, 18 March 1964
Career: Woodhill Primary and Blackheath Bluecoat Secondary Schools, trials
  with Luton Town, Millwall and West Ham United; Charlton Athletic
  (apprentice, July 1980; professional, March 1981), Luton Town (£95,000,
  March 1983), VILLA (£400,000, December 1985), Pisa/Italy (£400,000,
  July 1987), Celtic (£600,000, June 1989), Chelsea (July 1991; retired, injured,
  1993); later a match summariser on Channel 4, covering Italy's Serie 'A'
Elliott was a well-proportioned centre-half who gained England youth honours
(1982) and England Under-21 caps (1985 and 1986). In 1990 he collected
Scottish Cup and Skol Cup runner's-up medals with Celtic. After the
disappointment of being rejected by 3 major clubs, Elliott made 70 appearances
for Charlton and 73 for Luton before joining Villa, taking over from Brendan
Ormsby. After a spell in Italy, he had 42 League outings with Chelsea before

suffering a bad injury in September 1992 when challenged by future Villa striker Dean Saunders, then of Liverpool. In May 1994, a High Court case began (*Elliott v. Saunders*) when it was suggested that Saunders had supposedly put in a dangerous tackle that effectively ended Elliott's career. The hearing lasted almost four weeks before Saunders was cleared of all charges, leaving Elliott with legal costs of £500,000.

ELSTON, ARTHUR EDWARD
Outside-left: 1 app.
Born: Liverpool, July 1882 – *Died*: 1950
Career: Crownhills FC (Liverpool), Liverpool Leek FC, VILLA (April 1905), Portsmouth (September 1906–May 1909); continued to play at non-League level until the outbreak of WW1
Elston's only League outing for Villa was against Sunderland at Roker Park in February 1906, when he deputised for Joe Bache. He went off injured late in the second half in a 2–0 defeat. Elston made 20 Southern League appearances for Pompey.

ENCKELMAN, PETER
Goalkeeper: 65+2 apps
Born: Turku, Finland, 10 March 1977
Career: Jalkapallo TPS Turku/Finland (April 1995), VILLA (£200,000, February 1999), Blackburn Rovers (June 2004)
Signed by Villa as cover for David James, Enckelman had already been honoured by Finland at Under-21 level and later added five full caps to his tally. He appeared in 79 League games for TPS before making his debut (as a substitute) for Villa in the Premiership game at Arsenal in September 1999. Retaining his place in the side for the next six games (keeping five clean sheets), he then suffered a knee injury but bounced back and gained the first of his international caps against Wales at Cardiff in March 2000. Enckelman lost his place to Thomas Sorensen (q.v.) at the start of the 2003–04 season. His father, Goran, was a Finnish international who played against England in a 1976 World Cup qualifier.

EVANS, ALBERT JAMES
Full-back: 206 apps
Born: Barnard Castle, 18 March 1874 – *Died*: Warwick, 24 March 1966
Career: Stortforth and West Auckland Schools, Egglestone Abbey Boys, Barnard Castle (1891), Small Heath (trial), VILLA (trial, signed August 1896), West Bromwich Albion (October 1907; retired May 1908; then trainer at the Hawthorns), Sarpsborg FC/Norway (coach, May–September 1919), Coventry City (manager, June 1920–November 1924); thereafter travelled the world doing many different jobs, including gold prospecting in the Yukon and sheep farming in Canada; returned to England in 1950; VILLA (scout, until 1956)

Evans was an adaptable full-back, a clean, crisp tackler who was introduced to Villa by former player Bob Chatt, who spotted his talents in the North-east. Evans gained three League championship-winning medals (1897, 1899, 1900), an FA Cup-winner's medal (1897) and represented the Football League (1900) before switching to WBA, where he partnered England left-back Jesse Pennington. Evans, who captained Villa several times, had the misfortune to suffer five broken legs in his career – three with Villa (one forcing him to miss the 1905 FA Cup final), a fourth with Albion (on Christmas Day, 1908) and his last in a charity match (1915). When he took over as Coventry manager, he was the club's third boss in three months. He inherited a poor side at Highfield Road and although he strengthened it slightly, he was always under pressure and lost his job after four years.

EVANS, ALLAN JAMES

Defender: 466+7 apps, 63 goals
Born: West Calder, Polbeath, Edinburgh, West Lothian, 12 October 1956
Career: Wood Mill High School, Dunfermline Athletic (apprentice, December 1972; professional, October 1973), VILLA (£30,000, June 1977), Leicester City (free, August 1989), Brisbane United/Australia (1990), Darlington (March 1991; retired May 1991), Leicester City (assistant manager, June 1991), VILLA (assistant manager, November 1994), Stoke City (assistant manager, February 1998), West Bromwich Albion (assistant manager, September 1999–March 2000), Greenock Morton (manager, June 2000–April 2002)

As a teenager, Evans spent four years in Malta and Cyprus before joining Dunfermline. He had the misfortune to break his right leg when making his League debut against Glasgow Rangers, but recovered within three months. In his last season in Scottish football he scored 15 goals from the centre-forward position, including hat-tricks against Clyde and Stranraer. He netted a 6-timer for Villa's reserves in a 10–0 win over Sheffield United – and this performance went a long way towards him making his League bow in March 1978, against Leicester when he donned the number 7 shirt. He had two more senior outings before establishing himself in Villa's defence. A solid performer alongside Ken McNaught and later Brendan Ormsby, Paul Elliott and Steve Sims (plus a few others), Evans was a regular in the side until 1986. He helped the team win the League title (1981) and both the European Cup and Super Cup (1982) as well as gaining four caps for Scotland. He later worked under his former playing colleague Brian Little at Darlington, Leicester, Villa, Albion and Stoke.

EVANS, ALUN WILLIAM

Forward: 62+11 apps, 117 goals
Born: Stourport, 30 September 1949
Career: Stourport Junior and Bewdley Council Schools, Mid-Worcester Boys, Birmingham and District Schools, VILLA (trial, 1964), Wolverhampton

Wanderers (apprentice, July 1965; professional, October 1966), Liverpool (£100,000, September 1968), VILLA (£72,000, June 1972), Walsall (£30,000, December 1975), South Melbourne/Australia (trial, June 1978; signed £10,000, July 1978), Hellas FC/Australia (April–July 1979), South Melbourne/Australia (August 1979; retired May 1981); now resides in Cheltenham, Victoria (Australia)

Evans, the son of a former WBA and Wales WW2 international, became Britain's costliest teenager when he left Wolves for Liverpool in 1968. After winning England caps at schoolboy, youth and Under-23 levels, he was regarded as the 'star of the future' but sadly never reached the heights expected of him. A blond with an eye for goal, Evans scored 21 times in 79 League games for Liverpool and played in the 1971 FA Cup final against Arsenal. His stay at Anfield, however, was marred by a much-publicised night-club incident, when he received a badly gashed face, leaving him scarred for life. He moved to Villa three years later and gained a League Cup-winner's medal in 1975. Nine months after that Wembley triumph he moved to Walsall, for whom he made over 100 appearances, mainly as a midfielder.

EVANS, DAVID GORDON
Defender: 3 apps
Born: West Bromwich, 20 May 1958
Career: VILLA (apprentice, June 1974; professional, February 1976), Halifax Town (loan, September 1978; signed permanently for a record £22,500, June 1979), Bradford City (June 1984), Halifax Town (August 1990)
After missing out at Villa Park and moving into midfield, Evans made over 300 appearances in three spells with Halifax and more than 230 for Bradford, helping the Bantams win the Third Division title in 1985. He made his Villa debut at right-back in the Nou Camp Stadium against Barcelona in a UEFA Cup clash in March 1978 before 50,000 fans and his League debut followed six months later against Everton.

EVANS, ORLANDO
Forward: 2 apps
Born: Hednesford, June 1878 – *Died*: *circa* 1941
Career: Hednesford Town, Hednesford Swifts (1898), VILLA (July 1900), Burton (September 1903), Leyton, Hednesford Town
A slim-looking reserve forward who deputised for Joe Bache against Bolton and Notts County in March and April 1903 respectively, Evans also played for Birmingham Juniors against Scotland Juniors in 1900–01.

EVANS, ROBERT ERNEST
Winger: 17 apps, 44 goals
Born: Chester, 21 November 1885 – *Died*: Chester, 28 November 1965
Career: Saltney Ferry, Bretton FC (August 1900), Saltney Works FC (August

1902), Chester (June 1905), Wrexham (July 1905), VILLA (£30, March 1906), Sheffield United (£1,100, plus Peter Kyle, October 1908); guest for Tranmere Rovers (1916–17), Sandycroft (1918–19); Chrichton's Athletic (£25, May 1921), Saltney Ferry (May 1923; retired May 1924), Brookhirst FC (manager, 1921–23); in the 1920s worked as a welfare supervising officer for Shell Mex (Ellesmore Port) and was trainer to the works soccer team that included a young Joe Mercer

After turning out in friendlies for Saltney Ferry at the age of 14, winger Evans joined Bretton and was 'paid' two turnips a week in lieu of travelling expenses. He won several trophies as a youngster and after a trial with Chester he scored twice on his debut for Wrexham and was offered a contract worth ten shillings (50p) per week. A splendid display against Villa's reserve side led to his transfer in 1906 and immediately his wages went up to £4 per week. Unusually tall for a wide player (5 ft 10 in.), Evans covered the ground with long, raking strides and packed a stinging left-foot shot. Before leaving for Bramall Lane, he had already won ten caps for Wales when the FA discovered, after a tip-off from the Sheffield United secretary, John Nicholson, that he'd actually been born this side of the English border in Chester, although his parents had moved to Wales when he was only three weeks old. Consequently, the FA caused great controversy in Welsh football circles when they selected Evans to represent England – and he went on to win four caps for his 'second' country. In fact, he played for England against Wales at Wrexham in 1910, having starred for Wales against England four years earlier. This led to Evans being described as 'the best winger England and Wales had ever had'.

Making the last of his 225 appearances for Sheffield United a few weeks after WW1, a broken leg the following year brought his career to an end. In 1921 Evans came out of retirement in an emergency, and sadly broke the same leg again!

EVANS, WILLIAM EMMANUEL

Inside-left: 7 apps, 3 goals

Born: Aston, Birmingham, 5 September 1921 – *Died*: August 1960

Career: Linread Works FC, VILLA (trial, August 1946; professional, September 1946), Notts County (June 1949), Gillingham (July 1953), Grimsby Town (June 1955, retired July 1958); then assistant trainer at Blundell Park until his death

Principally an inside-left, Evans was often given a roaming commission, which saw him occasionally occupy the right-wing berth. While with Notts County, he played as an out-and-out centre-forward. He helped the Magpies win the Third Division (S) title in 1950 and the Mariners lift the Third Division (N) crown in 1956. He scored a staggering 57 goals in works soccer for the Linread team in 1945–46, a record that set him on the road to a useful League career. After leaving Villa, he hit 14 goals in 96 League games for Notts County, 12 in 89 for the Gills and 28 in 102 for Grimsby. He died suddenly at work.

EVANS, WILLIAM WALTER GWYNNE
Full-back: 68 apps
Born: Builth, Radnorshire, 1867 – *Died*: Builth, 10 May 1897
Career: Builth FC, Bootle (1889–90), VILLA (July 1890), Builth FC (August 1893; retired May 1897)

Evans, the son of a Builth butcher, excelled at rugby, cricket and soccer. The Football Association of Wales' Player Assessment file, published in 1891, described him as a 'very good back, tackles unflinchingly and has a safe kick – done himself credit'. He played for Villa against West Bromich Albion in the 1892 FA Cup final and won three full caps for Wales against England – twice as a Bootle player (1890) and once as a 'Villan' (1892). In May 1897, Evans caught a chill while attending a funeral and died within days. His loss was described as 'a calamity for the Builth club'.

EWING, THOMAS
Winger: 45 apps, 7 goals
Born: Swinhill, Lanarkshire, 2 May 1937
Career: Larkhall Thistle, Partick Thistle (April 1955), VILLA (£20,000, February 1962), Partick Thistle (July 1964), Greenock Morton (August 1966), Hamilton Academical (July 1967, then Accies' manager for a year from November 1969, playing in one League match); later a licensee in Scotland

A small, clever winger, able to occupy both flanks but preferring the right, Ewing started his career as a left-back but found marking players far too strenuous. He was unlucky with injuries during his time in Scotland, although he did win two full caps in 1958 and represented the Scottish League while playing in two losing League Cup finals with Partick (1957, 1959). He took over from Jimmy MacEwan at Villa Park.

EYRE, EDMUND
Winger: 31 apps, 5 goals
Born: Worksop, December 1882 – *Died*: Worksop, 1943
Career: Worksop West End, Worksop, Rotherham Town, Birmingham (March 1907), VILLA (December 1908), Middlesbrough (April 1911), Birmingham (April 1914; retired May 1919)

'Ninty' Eyre was a direct winger who hugged the touchline. He possessed good pace, had the ability to beat a defender and could deliver a telling cross. A prolific goalscorer during the early part of his career (especially with Worksop when he played through the middle), he was converted into a winger at St Andrew's. He contested the left-wing position at Villa with Albert Hall and after leaving, took his final goal-tally for the Blues to 17 (in 82 games) and netted 15 times in 69 starts for Middlesbrough.

FARRELL, DAVID WILLIAM

Winger: 7+1 apps
Born: Birmingham, 11 November 1971
Career: Redditch United, VILLA (£45,000, January 1992), Scunthorpe United (loan, January 1993), Wycombe Wanderers (£100,000, September 1995), Peterborough United (free, July 1997)

Farrell, quick and mobile, found it difficult to adjust to League soccer following his move from Redditch. He made only eight appearances for Villa before moving to Wycombe for a record fee. He scored the first League hat-trick of his career in the 2000 Third Division semi-final play-off, which helped send Barry Fry's Peterborough through to Wembley and subsequent victory (and promotion) over Darlington. During 2002–03, Farrell reached the milestone of 350 senior appearances as a professional.

FARRELLY, GARETH

Midfield: 2+7 apps
Born: Dublin, 28 August 1975
Career: VILLA (YTS, June 1991; professional, January 1992), Rotherham United (loan, March 1995), Everton (£700,000, July 1997), Bolton Wanderers (loan, November 1998; signed permanently December 1998), Rotherham United (loan, March–May 2003), Burnley (loan, August–September 2003), Bradford City (loan), Wigan Athletic (March 2004)

Farrelly started only two first-team games for Villa before his transfer to Everton. He developed his game considerably at Goodison Park and after 30 outings for the Merseysiders, established himself at the Reebok Stadium, scoring on his debut for Bolton with his second touch of the ball at Sheffield United. He's been honoured by the Republic of Ireland at senior (6 caps), 'B' (1), Under-21 (11), youth and schoolboy levels.

FASHANU, JOHN

Striker: 14+2 apps, 3 goals
Born: Kensington, London, 18 September 1962
Career: Cambridge United (junior, 1977), Norwich City (October 1979), Crystal Palace (loan, August 1983), Lincoln City (loan, September–November 1983; signed for £15,000, December 1983), Millwall (£55,000, November 1984), Wimbledon (£125,000, March 1986), VILLA (£1.35m, June 1994; retired May 1996); later a TV personality, featuring in *The Gladiators* and *I'm A Celebrity – Get Me Out Of Here* (2003); member of a religious sect; promoter of Third World development; chairman of Barry Town FC (to August 2003)

Fashanu's stay at Villa was dogged by ill-luck. He was not quite match-fit when he arrived, struggled with an Achilles injury soon afterwards and then underwent dental work before suffering a career-threatening knee-ligament injury in a Premiership game against Manchester United, which saw him stretchered off. Although he didn't know it, Fashanu's playing days ended there. Capped twice by England, against Chile and Scotland in 1989, he had an exciting career as a robust, all-action, brave and determined striker. He appeared in 463 senior games and scored 162 goals. For Wimbledon alone he netted 132 times in 331 appearances and won an FA Cup-winner's medal in 1988 when the Dons beat Liverpool. In 1995 goalkeepers Bruce Grobbelaar and Hans Segers along with Fashanu (then of Villa) were charged with match-fixing. They appeared in court and were all found not guilty after a long-drawn-out trial.

Fashanu's elder brother, Justinus Soni, committed suicide in 1998. He, too, represented England at youth, Under-21 and 'B' team levels and scored over 80 goals in more than 275 matches while serving with 9 different clubs between 1978 and 1992.

FENCOTT, KENNETH SYDNEY
Forward: 5 apps
Born: Walsall, 27 December 1943
Career: Walsall Boys, Staffordshire and Birmingham County FA, VILLA (amateur, March 1959; professional, January 1961), Lincoln City (June 1964), Tamworth (August 1967), Blakenhall (1968–69); later ran a driving school in Birmingham

A reserve utility forward, Fencott made his League debut against Bolton in November 1961 at outside-left. He scored on his debut for Lincoln, for whom he played in all 5 forward-line positions, making 73 appearances and netting 13 goals before drifting into non-League soccer.

FENTON, GRAHAM ANTHONY
Forward: 18+21 apps, 3 goals
Born: Wallsend, 22 May 1974
Career: VILLA (YTS, June 1990; professional, February 1992), West Bromwich Albion (loan, January 1994), Blackburn Rovers (£1.5m, November 1995), Leicester City (£1.1m, August 1997), Walsall (free, March 2000), Stoke City (August–September 2000), St Mirren (October 2000), Blackpool (August 2001), Darlington (loan, September–October 2002), Blyth Spartans (season 2003–04)

A decidedly quick, all-purpose, right-sided utility forward, Fenton twice helped Villa win the League Cup (1994 and 1996), also gaining one England Under-21 cap. He found it hard-going following his transfer to Ewood Park but battled on well throughout his career.

FERGUSON, MICHAEL KEVIN
Midfield: 40 apps, 2 goals
Born: Burnley, 9 March 1943
Career: Burnley Schools, Plymouth Argyle (amateur, March 1959), Accrington Stanley (professional, June 1960), Blackburn Rovers (£1,500, March 1962), VILLA (£55,000, May 1968), Queens Park Rangers (£11,500, November 1969), Cambridge United (July 1973), Rochdale (July 1974), Los Angeles Aztecs/USA (April–August 1975), 1A Akranes/Iceland (player/coach, season 1975–76), Halifax Town (December 1976; retired May 1977); Rochdale (manager, September 1977–November 1978); thereafter coached around the world, mainly in the Middle East during the 1980s; Enfield (manager, 1989–90)

A well-built, strong-running player, who could also play at right-back and as an orthodox winger, Ferguson's registration papers became the property of the Football League when Accrington Stanley went bankrupt in 1962, and Blackburn had to pay the £1,500 transfer fee to the League for his services. He joined Villa for a record fee and during his time at the club scored only two goals – one after a superb fifty-yard dribble that took him past six players. He played his best football at Ewood Park (36 goals in 248 outings) and later helped 1A Akranes win the Icelandic League (1976). Ferguson was sacked as manager of Rochdale after a humiliating FA Cup defeat at the hands of non-League Droylsden. When he joined Blackburn, he was referred to as a 'flawed diamond' – the flaw, which frustrated fans and management alike, was a suspect temperament; he was sent off three times during his career – each for lashing out at an opponent.

FERRARESI, FABIO
Midfield: 0+1 app.
Born: Fano, Italy, 24 May 1979
Career: Fano FC/Italy (1996), Cosena/Italy (1997), VILLA (August 1998–July 1999), Cosena/Italy (July 1999)

Ferraresi failed to make an impression during his brief liaison with English football. His only game for Villa was as a substitute in the away leg of a UEFA Cup clash with Stromsgodset on 29 September 1998.

FINDLAY, JOHN WILLIAMSON
Goalkeeper: 17 apps
Born: Blairgowrie, Perthshire, 13 July 1954
Career: Perth Schools, VILLA (apprentice, July 1970; professional, June 1972), Luton Town (November 1978), Barnsley (loan, September 1983), Derby County (loan, January 1984), Swindon Town (July 1985), Portsmouth (January 1986), Coventry City (August, 1986; retired, injured, May 1989)

'Jake' Findlay, a Scottish youth international trialist, helped Villa's intermediate side win the FA Youth Cup in 1972 but was basically 'in reserve' and in 1978 moved to Kenilworth Road. He was forced to retire through injury, having played in 178 League games for Luton, gaining a Second Division championship medal in 1982. He failed to get a single first-team outing with either Pompey or the Sky Blues. Findlay, who weighed over 14 st. at his peak, was rewarded with a testimonial match in August 1989 when Coventry played West Bromwich Albion.

FISHER, ALBERT WILLIAM

Forward: 1 app.
Born: Birmingham, 2 February 1871 – *Died*: *circa* 1959
Career: Astbury Richmond/Handsworth (1900–01), Soho Caledonians (1901–02), VILLA (August 1902), Bristol City (August 1903), Brighton and Hove Albion (August 1905), Manchester City (June 1906), Bradford Park Avenue (June 1907), Coventry City (August 1908); Merthyr Town (secretary/manager, June 1909–May 1913), Notts County (secretary/manager, July 1913–May 1927); later a businessman
Fisher's only League game for Villa was as a stand-in centre-forward against Bolton in November 1902 (won 4–2). He was Bristol City's top marksman in 1904–05 with 13 goals but struggled at Manchester City (only 5 starts, 2 goals). Merthyr's first 'manager' after the Welsh club had become a limited company, he also became Notts County's first-ever manager and twice guided the Magpies to the Second Division title (1914, 1923) and the FA Cup semi-final (1922).

FISHER, JAMES ALBERT

Forward: 18 apps, 5 goals
Born: Denny, Scotland, 23 December 1876 – *Died*: 4 December 1937
Career: Vale of Forth, King's Park (February 1892), East Stirling (June 1895), St Bernard's (May 1896), VILLA (May 1897), Celtic (August 1898), Preston North End (on loan, January 1899), East Stirling (December 1899), Celtic (February 1900), Newton Heath (October 1900), King's Park (March 1902), Vale of Leven (December 1902), Fulham (August 1903; retired April 1904)
Fisher was a finely built outside- or inside-right, clever, with a good clean shot and 'plenty of pluck' near goal who partnered Jack Devey and Fred Wheldon in attack during his season with Villa. He served with the Royal Engineers in WW1. (There were two Fishers around at the same time and some reference books have their respective records mixed up.)

FLEMING, JAMES JOHN

Centre-forward: 4 apps, 2 goals
Born: Leith, Edinburgh, September 1864 – *Died*: Scotland, August 1934
Career: Vale of Leven, Army football with the 93rd Argyle and Sutherland Highlanders, Southampton St Mary's (October–December 1891), VILLA (May 1892), Lincoln City (October 1892), Larkhall Saints (May 1893)

An aggressive player, Fleming scored twice on his Villa debut in a 4–1 win over Everton in September 1892. He then 'fell out with the club' and joined Lincoln. He signed for Southampton after starring against them in an exhibition match while in the Army.

FOLLAN, EDWARD HARVEY

Forward: 36 apps, 7 goals
Born: Greenock, Scotland, 3 October 1929
Career: Renfrewshire Schools, Ardeer Recreation (Ayrshire League), Greenock Central, Prescot Cables, Army football, VILLA (professional, June 1952), Worcester City (May 1956), Hinckley Athletic (July 1961), Burton Albion (July 1963), Stourbridge (May 1965; retired, injured, May 1966)

Signed by Villa while serving in the Army, Follan underwent a cartilage operation in 1952 and had to wait until October 1954 before making his League debut in a 4–2 win at Manchester City. A talented inside-forward, he drifted into non-League football after four years with Villa.

FORD, TREFOR (TREVOR)

Centre-forward: 128 apps, 61 goals
Born: Swansea, 1 October 1923 – *Died*: Cardiff, June 2003
Career: Powys Avenue School, Swansea Boys, Tower United (Swansea), Swansea Town (juniors, May 1939; professional, May 1942), Army football (with Royal Artillery), Leyton Orient (WW2 guest), Swansea Town (August 1945), VILLA (£9,500, plus Tommy Dodds, January 1947), Sunderland (£30,000, October 1950), Cardiff City (£30,000, December 1953), PSV Eindhoven/Holland (£5,000, August 1956), Newport County (July 1960), Romford (1961; retired May 1962 but played in charity matches until 1976)

As a youngster, Ford was encouraged to play both cricket and football by his father. He started off on the soccer pitch as a full-back with his school team and took up the centre-forward position during WW2. He quickly made up for lost time by scoring 41 goals in the 1945–46 transitional season.

With his no-nonsense, hard-hitting, bustling style, Ford was capped by Wales in a Victory international against Northern Ireland – the first of many appearances for his country – and immediately became 'hot property', with Villa winning the race for his signature in 1947. He did exceedingly well at Villa Park, scoring a goal every two games, finishing as leading marksman three seasons running (1947–50), while also adding fourteen full caps to his collection of honours. However, Ford wanted a bigger stage, and after turning down offers from clubs in Colombia and Portugal, he joined Sunderland, Villa replacing him with Irishman Dave Walsh from WBA. He continued to find the net at Roker Park, notching 67 goals in 108 First Division matches alone. He then assisted Cardiff (signed instead of Tommy Taylor who went to Manchester United). He became a firm favourite with the fans as he hit 39 goals in less than 100 games for the Bluebirds. Sadly, it all turned sour for Ford in 1956. With Cardiff having a poor run, manager Trevor Morris asked him to play on the right-wing. A disagreement ensued and Ford's days at Ninian Park were numbered. His departure from Cardiff was escalated when he was handed a three-year ban from British football after he exposed 'under the counter' payments in his autobiography, *I Lead the Attack*.

Ford lodged an appeal and was subsequently reinstated only to be banned again after Football League secretary Alan Hardaker uncovered an illegal payment of £100, which had been made by Sunderland to Ford when he was at Roker Park. Undaunted, the Welsh goal-ace went abroad and spent three excellent years with the Dutch club PSV Eindhoven. He returned to the UK after his suspension was lifted but a knee injury hastened the end of a very fine career, Ford finishing with a League record of 178 goals in 348 appearances. He also notched 23 goals in 38 internationals for Wales.

People often wonder what sort of contribution Ford would have made in the 1958 World Cup finals in Sweden. His goalscoring record for his country (shared by Ivor Allchurch) remained intact for over 30 years until Ian Rush took over the mantle.

When he was scoring goals for Sunderland, Ford entered the motor trade and pursued a career in this field in South Wales after hanging up his boots.

In August 1968 Ford was a substitute fielder for Glamorgan at the St Helens ground, Swansea, when the West Indian Test cricketer, and world's greatest all-rounder, Garfield Sobers (playing for Notts) smashed six sixes in one over off the bowling of Malcolm Nash.

FOSTER, STEPHEN BRIAN
Centre-half: 17 apps, 3 goals
Born: Portsmouth, 24 September 1957
Career: Hampshire County Schools, Portsmouth (apprentice, June 1973; professional September 1975), Brighton and Hove Albion (£130,000, July 1979), VILLA (£150,000 plus Mark Jones, March 1984), Luton Town (£70,000, November 1984), Oxford United (free, July 1989), Brighton and Hove Albion (free, August 1992–May 1996)

A real hard-nut defender who was easily recognisable by his headband, Foster spent 21 years in the game as a professional, giving everything he had. His leadership qualities were second to none and at the end of the day he was rewarded with a well-deserved testimonial and benefit match at Brighton. He replaced Brendan Ormsby at the heart of the Villa defence but became unsettled, allowing Ormsby to regain his place. Foster then went south to Luton. He played in the 1983 FA Cup final replay for Brighton against Manchester United, having missed the first game through suspension. A League Cup winner with Luton (1988), he gained three England caps, played in one Under-21 international and made 804 appearances at club and international level (52 goals scored).

FRASER, JOHN CAMERON
Full-back: 40 apps, 1 goal
Born: Blackford, Perthshire, 24 May 1941
Career: Larbert Schools, Gairloch United, Dunfermline Athletic (August 1958), VILLA (£24,500, October 1962), Birmingham City (£9,000, May 1964), Crystal Palace (trial, September 1964), Falkirk (June 1966–May 1968)

A sturdy full-back, strong in the tackle, 'Cammy' Fraser won a Scottish Cup-winner's medal with Dunfermline a year before joining Villa. With Gordon Lee and Mick Wright fighting with him for a place in the first team, he had one decent season at Villa Park (his first) before moving to the Blues. He twice represented his country at Under-23 level (1961–62) and was a League Cup finalist with Villa against the Blues in 1963. He skippered Villa's reserve side when they won the Central League title in 1964 – his last mission before moving to St Andrew's. Fraser's father, Billy, played for Aldershot and Northampton.

FROGGATT, STEPHEN JUNIOR
Winger/left-back: 36+8 apps, 3 goals
Born: Lincoln, 9 March 1973
Career: VILLA (YTS, June 1989; professional, January 1991), Wolverhampton Wanderers (£1m, July 1994), Coventry City (£1.9m, October 1998; retired, injured, May 2001); later TV pundit

Froggatt completed his transition from outside-left to wing-back in 1996–97 when he regained his form and fitness after serious injury and illness problems following his transfer from Villa Park to Molineux. Capped twice by England at Under-21 level as a wide midfielder, occupying the left flank, 'Froggy' went on to earn selection to the PFA's First Division side in 1997 before returning to the Premiership with Coventry. In November 1999 he was named by England boss Kevin Keegan in the squad to play Scotland in the Euro 2000 play-offs against Scotland. He was in and out of the Sky Blues side before quitting the game through injury, aged 28.

GAGE, KEVIN WILLIAM
Full-back/midfield: 143+2 apps, 12 goals
Born: Chiswick, 21 April 1964
Career: Wimbledon (apprentice, June 1980; professional, January 1982), VILLA (£100,000, July 1987), Sheffield United (£150,000, November 1991), Preston North End (free, March 1996), Hull City (free, September 1997; retired May 1999 to concentrate on his pub/restaurant business in the Peak District)

The versatile Gage scored in all four divisions of the Football League. He did well with the Dons, for whom he accumulated 189 appearances. He took over from Gary Williams when he joined Villa and after leaving made over 130 appearances for the Blades before winding down his career in the lower divisions. A compact footballer, aggressive when he had to be, Gage won

England youth honours, helped the Dons win the Fourth Division title in 1983 and was in Villa's 1988 Second Division promotion side.

GALLACHER, BERNARD

Left-back: 69+3 apps, 1 goal

Born: Johnstone, Perthshire, 22 March 1967

Career: Perthshire County Schools, VILLA (apprentice, June 1983; professional, March 1985), Blackburn Rovers (loan, November 1990), Doncaster Rovers (non-contract, September–October 1991), Brighton and Hove Albion (October 1991–May 1993), Northampton Town (non-contract, January–May 1994), Bromsgrove Rovers (August 1994), Hong Kong football (from 1995)

A player who began his career on the left-wing, Gallacher developed into a very competent full-back, who did a useful job with Villa. He later had 50 outings for Brighton alongside another ex-Villa man, Steve Foster.

GARDNER, THOMAS

Wing-half: 79 apps, 1 goal

Born: Huyton, Lancashire, 28 May 1909 – *Died*: Chester, February 1970

Career: Orrell (May 1926), Liverpool (amateur, July 1928; professional, April 1929), Grimsby Town (June 1931), Hull City (May 1932), VILLA (£4,500, February 1934), Burnley (April 1938); guest for Preston North End (1941–42), Blackpool (March–April 1943), Southport (1943–44), Manchester United (April 1944), Blackburn Rovers (May 1945), Wrexham (December 1945); Wellington (August 1947), Oswestry Town (player/manager, June 1950, reverting to player/coach, January 1952), Saltney FC (August 1952), Chester (assistant trainer/groundsman, July 1954–May 1967, later steward for 12 months); then a hotelier in Wrexham

An enthusiastic footballer, the fair-haired Gardner (nicknamed 'Ghandi') had a fine career that spanned some 40 years. A constructive player, always wanting the ball, he suffered his fair share of injuries but always battled back. He had a decidedly long throw and won a *Daily Mail* competition in 1932 – wind-assisted, he could hurl a ball up to a distance of 40 yards! Capped twice by England, in 1934 against Czechoslovakia and 1935 against Holland, he played in an international trial (also in 1935), gained a Third Division (N) championship medal with Hull in 1933 and a WW2 League Cup (N) winner's medal as a guest with Blackpool in 1943. Gardner's only goal for Villa came in a 3–2 defeat at Fulham in January 1937.

GARFIELD, JAMES HENRY

Outside-right: 1 app.

Born: Finedon, Northamptonshire, July 1875 – *Died*: March 1949

Career: Wellingborough Town, Kettering Town, Gravesend United, VILLA (August 1899), Northampton Town (June 1900–May 1901), Kettering Town (1902–03)

Reserve initially to Charlie Athersmith, Garfield's only League game for Villa was against Stoke in November 1899. Deputising for Bobby Templeton, he scored in a 2–0 win.

GARRATT, GEORGE THOMAS

Outside-right: 17 apps, 1 goal

Born: Byker, County Durham, April 1884 – *Died*: Worcester, June 1926

Career: Rowley Regis School, Cradley St Luke's (1899), Brierley Hill Alliance (1902), Crewe Alexandra (1904), VILLA (March 1905), Southampton (briefly, February 1907), Plymouth Argyle (March 1907), West Bromwich Albion (May 1907), Crystal Palace (May 1908), Millwall (October 1913–April 1915), Kidderminster Harriers (1919–20)

Garratt moved to the Black Country with his family in 1892. He played soccer at school and then did well with a handful of local non-League clubs before joining Crewe. Well built, with no sight in one eye, he was basically an outside-right who was signed by Villa as cover for Billy Brawn. Garratt later did well with Crystal Palace, for whom he scored eight goals in 185 appearances.

GARRATY, WILLIAM

Centre-forward: 259 apps, 112 goals

Born: Saltley, Birmingham, 6 October 1878 – *Died*: Birmingham, 6 May 1931

Career: Church Road and Saltley St Saviour's Schools (Birmingham), Ashted Swifts, St Saviour's FC, Highfield Villa, Lozells FC, Aston Shakespeare, VILLA (professional, August 1897), Leicester Fosse (September 1908), West Bromwich Albion (£270, October 1908), Lincoln City (£100, November 1910; retired May 1911); VILLA (trainer, briefly, April–May 1913); seriously ill with pneumonia, April 1915; recovered and worked as a beer-delivery driver for Ansells Brewery until his death

An excellent marksman throughout his career, Garraty, with his dashing moustache, was top scorer in the whole country in 1899–1900 when his 27 goals (in 33 matches) helped Villa win the League title for the fifth time. He later added an FA Cup-winner's medal to his collection (1905) and also gained one England cap (against Wales in 1903). A positive forward, always looking to get in a shot on goal, he was part of Villa's brilliant attack in the late 1890s/early 1900s that included Charlie Athersmith, Jack Devey, Fred Wheldon and Steve Smith. He then partnered Jasper McLuckie and Joe Bache and later aided and abetted Harry Hampton, among others. He skippered WBA for whom he netted 22 goals in 59 appearances. Without doubt, Garraty was a very fine player.

His brother Frank played in Villa's second team in the late 1890s.

GARVEY, BATTY WALTER
Forward: 7 apps, 4 goals
Born: Aston, Birmingham 10 February 1894 – *Died*: Birmingham, 1963
Career: Aston Hall Swifts, Aston Shakespeare, VILLA (March 1888; retired, injured, May 1893)

Signed from a local junior club, 'Bat' Garvey made his debut for Villa in a friendly against Blackburn, coming into the side in place of Denny Hodgetts, who was on England duty against Scotland. Villa beat Rovers 6–4 and Garvey scored twice. At the start of the next season – September 1888 – he was inside-left in Villa's first League game against Wolves at Dudley Road. Recognised as a reserve 'forward', he was forced to retire at the age of 29 after struggling with injury for 3 years.

GAUDIE, RALPH
Forward: 5 apps, 1 goal
Born: Guisborough, February 1876 – *Died*: *circa* 1950
Career: Sheffield Saracens (briefly), South Bank, Sheffield United (professional, November 1897), VILLA (with John Cunningham, August 1898), South Bank (March 1899), VILLA (August 1899), Woolwich Arsenal (October 1899), Manchester United (August 1903; retired May 1904 after badly damaging his right ankle)

Reserve forward Gaudie scored on his League debut for Villa against Stoke in September 1898 when he deputised for Fred Wheldon.

GAVAN, JOHN THOMAS
Goalkeeper: 12 apps
Born: Walsall, 8 December 1939
Career: Hilary Street Old Boys, Staffordshire Youths, Walsall (amateur), Walsall Wood (April 1958), Blackpool (trial), VILLA (amateur, April 1962; professional, November 1962), Doncaster Rovers (July 1967–May 1968), Bilston Town (August 1968–May 1972), Dudley Town (briefly)

Gavan was a centre-forward at school, then an apprentice gas fitter before developing into a very useful goalkeeper. He made only 33 appearances during his senior career yet played in over 150 games at non-League level after leaving Doncaster.

GEDDIS, DAVID
Striker: 52+4 apps, 16 goals
Born: Carlisle, 12 March 1958
Career: Ipswich Town (junior, June 1973; professional, August 1975), Luton Town (loan), VILLA (£300,000, September 1979), Luton Town (loan, December 1982), Barnsley (£50,000, September 1983), Birmingham City (£50,000, December 1984), Brentford (loan, September 1986), Shrewsbury Town (£25,000, March 1987), Swindon Town (October 1988), Darlington

(March–May 1990); Middlesbrough (community officer, 1990s; later reserve-team coach, 2000–02)

As a raw 20-year-old striker, Geddis played superbly well for Ipswich in the 1978 FA Cup final against Arsenal, and was immediately marked up as a star of the future. He never quite made it to the top, although he did score plenty of goals – 77 coming in 264 League games up to 1991. Capped by England at youth and 'B'-team levels, Geddis won both the FA Youth Cup and FA Cup with Ipswich, and a European Cup medal with Villa as a non-playing substitute.

GEORGE, WILLIAM

Goalkeeper: 401 apps

Born: Shrewsbury, 29 June 1874 – *Died*: Birmingham, 4 December 1933

Career: Woolwich Ramblers, Army service with Royal Artillery (from October 1888), Trowbridge Town (when on leave, 1895–97), VILLA (£50, professional, October 1897), Birmingham (player/trainer, July 1911; retired as a player, May 1913); later worked at the Austin Rover plant, Longbridge, Birmingham; also played county cricket for Warwickshire (1901, 1902, 1907), Wiltshire and Shropshire

Said by some to have been one of the greatest – if not the greatest – goalkeepers in the history of the club, for many seasons George remained at the top of his form after making a splendid debut in the local derby for Villa against WBA in October 1897. A huge man (tipping the scales at 21st. 7lb), he held his position as first choice 'between the posts' right through until 1909, and only injuries, illness and international duties forced him to miss matches. He was quick on his feet, had a tremendous reach, was full of resource, punched the ball with great power and could kick like a mule! Described as 'a rare good man in the side and an ornament to the game', George starred in 358 First Division games for Villa. He won 3 England caps (1903) and was also taking part in the abandoned game against Scotland at Ibrox Park in 1902 when 26 people were killed as terraces collapsed at one end of the ground. He helped Villa win the League championship in 1899 and 1900 and also collected an FA Cup-winner's medal in 1905.

When George was 'signed' out of the Army in 1897, there was such a hullabaloo surrounding the transaction that two Villa committee members, George Ramsey and Fred Rinder, along with George himself, were suspended by the FA for a month!

GERRISH, WILLIAM WEBBER WALTER

Forward: 59 apps, 18 goals

Born: Bristol, December 1889 – *Died*: France, 1916

Career: Bristol Rovers, VILLA (£200, April 1909), Preston North End (August 1912), Chesterfield (November 1912–March 1914)

Able to play at inside-right or centre-forward, Gerrish averaged almost a goal every three games for Villa whom he served for over three years, gaining a

League championship medal in 1910. He netted 11 times in 49 games for Bristol Rovers. A fine positional player, never greedy, always alert and positive, Gerrish was sadly killed whilst on active service with the Middlesex Regiment (the Footballers' Battalion) in the attack on Guillemont in the Battle of the Somme in WW1.

GHRAYIB, NAJWAN

Left wing-back: 2+4 apps
Born: Israel, 30 January 1974
Career: Maccabi Haifa/Israel (April 1994), Maccabi Paetach/Israel (August 1995), Hapoel Haifa/Israel (August 1997), VILLA (£1m, August 1999), Hapoel Haifa/Israel (£150,000, February 2001)

When he joined Villa, Ghrayib was already an experienced player, having gained 16 caps for his country while also scoring 27 goals in 127 Israeli League matches. He found it difficult to dislodge Alan Wright from the left-back position and had to wait until April 2000 before starting his first Premiership match against Sunderland. He added two more caps to his tally at Villa Park but then struggled with his fitness in 2000–01 after fluid had built up in his legs, keeping him out of action for some ten weeks.

GIBSON, COLIN HAYWARD

Outside-right: 167 apps, 26 goals
Born: Normanby-on-Tees, near Middlesbrough, 16 September 1923 – *Died*: Stourbridge, 27 March 1992
Career: Penarth Pontoon, Cardiff City (£10, August 1942), Newcastle United (£15,000, July 1948), VILLA (£17,500, July 1949), Lincoln City (£6,000, January 1956), Stourbridge (July 1957), Cradley Heath (November 1958), Stourbridge (August 1959; retired May 1960); became landlord of the Spencer's Arms (Hagley)

An ex-Marine engineer on the dockside, Gibson earned his first wage at the age of fifteen, learning what made the giant eight-and-half-thousand-ton freight vessels tick! He gradually eased himself into professional football and became a dashing winger with great skill, expert control and a fine shot. Cardiff signed him on the recommendation of ex-Villa goalkeeper Cyril Spiers. But a year after helping the Ninian Park club win the Third Division (S) championship, Gibson was sold to Newcastle. He became a firm favourite with the Villa supporters, winning England 'B' honours against Holland and also representing the Football League. After losing his place to Tommy Southren and with Les Smith of Wolves also ready to move in, Gibson switched to Lincoln in 1956. Besides being a very fine footballer, he was also an accomplished pianist. A 1950 pen-picture described Gibson as a 'flank-turning, defence-undermining instrument' – an out-and-out winger really!

GIBSON, COLIN JOHN
Left-back/midfield: 233+5 apps, 17 goals
Born: Bridport, 6 April 1960
Career: Portsmouth Grammar School, West Sussex Schoolboys, Portsmouth (amateur), VILLA (YTS, July 1976; professional, April 1978), Manchester United (£275,000, November 1985), Port Vale (loan, September–October 1990), Leicester City (£100,000, December 1990), Blackpool (free, September 1994), Walsall (non-contract, May 1995–May 1996)

Gibson, who could play effectively at left-back and in midfield, had a fine career that spanned 20 years. He joined Villa at the age of 16 and was capped by England at youth, Under-21 and 'B' team levels. He gained a First Division championship medal in 1981, a European Cup medal as a non-playing substitute in 1982 and a European Super Cup prize in that year before switching to Old Trafford. After a little over five years with United (95 games played) and a loan spell at Vale Park, he linked up with ex-Villa man Brian Little at Leicester before winding down his career at Bloomfield Road and Walsall. Gibson appeared in 364 League games for his six clubs.

GIBSON, DAVID WEDDERBURN
Midfield: 21+3 apps, 1 goal
Born: Winchburgh, Scotland, 23 September 1938
Career: Livingston United (1953), Hibernian (£1,500, professional, September 1956), Leicester City (£25,000, January 1962), VILLA (free, September 1970), Exeter City (£3,500, January 1972; retired May 1974)

Gibson joined Villa soon after the team had started to play Third Division football for the first time in the club's history. A fine ball-player, his elegant control and visionary passing skills were a major factor in Leicester reaching two Wembley FA Cup finals (1963, 1969) and winning the League Cup (1964). He certainly played his best football at Filbert Street (339 games, 53 goals) but made only 24 appearances for Villa, being unable to adapt to a lower standard of football. He netted three times in seven internationals for Scotland and returned to Wembley as Villa's substitute in the 1971 League Cup final.

GIBSON, JAMES DAVIDSON
Half-back: 225 apps, 10 goals
Born: Larkhall, Lanarkshire, 12 June 1901 – *Died*: Erdington, 1 January 1978
Career: Glengowan School, Morning Star, Larkhall Thistle, Kirkintilloch Rob Roy (1917), Glasgow Ashfield, Partick Thistle (professional, April 1921), VILLA (£7,500, April 1927; retired May 1936); later worked as a welfare officer at ICI, Witton until 1962

Gibson was a wonderfully cultured half-back, able to occupy all three middle-line positions. Standing 6 ft 2 in. tall and weighing 12 st., he was a tireless performer with a terrific engine, always surging upfield to assist his forwards and then racing back to help out his defenders. He appeared in almost 200 competitive games for Partick before Villa brought his talents into the Football League in 1927. He remained for nine years, giving the club sterling service. Capped ten times by Scotland (1926–30), he twice represented the Football League and also played as a guest for an International XI against a District XI (1940). He was part of a brilliant Villa half-back line that comprised himself, Alec Talbot and Joe Tate (perhaps the best in the club's history). His son, Neil Gibson, played for Rangers, Partick and Scotland.

GIDMAN, JOHN
Right–back: 242+1 apps, 9 goals
Born: Liverpool, 10 January 1954
Career: Garston schoolboy football, Liverpool (apprentice, June 1969), VILLA (professional, August 1971), Everton (£650,000, October 1979), Manchester United (£450,000, August 1981), Manchester City (free, October 1986), Stoke City (August 1988), Darlington (player/assistant manager, February–May 1989), King's Lynn (manager, early 1990s); now runs a café/bar in Spain

An attack-minded full-back, Gidman had an excellent professional career. After failing to make the breakthrough at Anfield, he was snapped up by Villa scout Neville Briggs in 1971. He took time to establish himself in the first XI, but, once in, he stayed and amassed a fine record. He won England caps at full, 'B' and Under-23 levels, having earlier represented his country as a youth-team player. He helped Villa win the FA Youth Cup in 1972 and the League Cup in 1977 but missed the 1975 League Cup final win over Norwich after suffering an eye injury when a firework exploded in his face on Bonfire Night 1974, the year he won the club's 'Terrace Trophy' award. Gidman was sent off in the Nou Camp Stadium, playing for Villa against Barcelona in a UEFA Cup match in 1978. The ten men failed to hold on and lost 2–1. He later collected an FA Cup-winner's medal with Manchester United and ended his playing days with his former Villa team-mate Brian Little at Darlington. Gidman totalled 432 League appearances during his career.

GILLAN, JAMES STANLEY
Left–half: 3 apps
Born: Derby, December 1870 – *Died*: Ilkeston, 1944
Career: Burton United, Burton Swifts, VILLA (April 1893), Brierley Hill Alliance (September 1894), Cradley Heath (May 1895; retired, injured, April 1896)

Reserve to converted left-half Bob Chatt during his brief association with Villa, Gillan made three League appearances, lining up against Everton (his home debut), Nottingham Forest and Darwen in September–October 1893.

GILSON, THOMAS AUBREY

Full-back: 2 apps

Born: Lichfield, June 1879 – *Died*: Lichfield

Career: Whittington Royal, Burton Swifts (1898), VILLA (July 1900), Brentford (May 1901), Melksham FC (1902–03), Bristol City (August 1903), Clapton Orient (March–May 1906)

A solid full-back, Gilson deputised for Albert Evans in two away League games at Newcastle and Derby in April 1901.

GINOLA, DAVID DESIRÉ MARC

Midfield: 19+22 apps, 5 goals

Born: Gassin, near Toulon, France, 25 January 1967

Career: FC Toulon/France (1985), Racing Club de Paris/France (1988), Brest/France (1990), Paris St-Germain/France (1992), Newcastle United (£2.5m, July 1995), Tottenham Hotspur (£2m, July 1997), VILLA (£3m, August 2000), Everton (free, February 2002; retired May 2002); coaching in France (2002–03); also film star and TV personality (in France)

When he joined Villa in 2000, French international David Ginola immediately received wages of £40,000 per week, making him the highest-paid player in the club's history. In 1994 he had helped PSG win their first French League title in eight years and was also named both France's 'Player of the Year' and the 'Players' Player of the Year'.

After taking his tally of appearances in French football to well past the 200 mark (25 goals) and gaining international recognition, Ginola switched to England, signing for Newcastle. He netted 7 times in 76 outings for the Geordies and then appeared in 127 matches for Spurs (21 goals) before leaving in a blaze of publicity. A player with tremendous on-the-ball skill, he had a splendid body-swerve, stunning right-foot shot and a great deal of charisma. Voted both the Football Writers' and PFA 'Player of the Year' in 1999, he was also selected in the Premiership representative side, being regarded as the finest left-sided midfielder (winger) in the country. A celebrity both on and off the field, he unfortunately fell out with the management of the French national team in the mid-1990s and after attempting to settle his differences, failed to get a recall and subsequently missed out on his country's World Cup and European Championship triumphs. He won 17 caps, making his international debut in 1990 as a 'sub' against Albania in a European Championship qualifier. His last game for his country was in September 1995 against Azerbaijan. Ginola was injured during his first half-season with Villa and was surprisingly never a regular in the side, 22 of his appearances coming as a substitute. On the day manager John Gregory quit Villa Park, an unhappy Ginola was found guilty of misconduct by the FA, fined £22,000 and given a two-match suspension. Ginola's book *Le Magnifique* was a best-seller in the year 2000.

GITTINGS, ALFRED GEORGE

Forward: 1 app.

Born: Manchester, 3 July 1886 – *Died*: 1949

Career: Atherton Church House (1901), Adlington FC (1902), Bolton Wanderers (amateur, June 1903; professional, September 1903), Blackpool (briefly, 1905), Luton Town (May 1906), Queens Park Rangers (May 1907), VILLA (October 1908), Croydon Common (July 1909), Fulham (September 1910), Portsmouth (December 1910), Barrow (1911), Partick Thistle (May 1912), Dumbarton (May 1914)

A competent reserve at Villa Park, Gittings' only appearance came on Christmas Day 1908, when he deputised for George Reeves in the 1–1 home draw with Liverpool. He did very well in the Southern League.

GLOVER, DEAN VICTOR

Defender: 36+3 apps, 1 goal

Born: West Bromwich, 29 December 1963

Career: Kings Norton Schools, West Midlands Boys, VILLA (apprentice, June 1980; professional, December 1981), Sheffield United (loan, October 1986), Middlesbrough (June 1987), Port Vale (£200,000, February 1989; retired from League football, May 1998); Newcastle Town (manager), Port Vale (coach, then assistant manager, 2004)

Owing to an array of defenders at the club, the hard-tackling, wholehearted commitment of Glover secured fewer than 40 appearances for Villa. He made his debut in the FA Cup tie against Norwich in January 1984 and his only goal came in the 1–1 League Cup draw with Arsenal in January 1986. After more than 50 outings for Middlesbrough, Glover joined Port Vale for a record fee and over the next decade gave the Potteries' club sterling service, accumulating 430 appearances and 20 goals, helping Vale win the Sherpa Van Trophy in 1993 and gain promotion from Division Two the following season.

GODDARD, HOWARD VINCENT

Goalkeeper: 1 app.

Born: Warsop Vale, Mansfield, 24 January 1905 – *Died*: Shirebrook, 6 June 1966

Career: Warsop Rovers, Atwell Royal (briefly), Shirebrook Colliery (Notts), Shirebrook (June 1925), VILLA (April 1927), Mansfield Town (August 1928), Frickley Colliery (1929), Stockton (August 1930–May 1931)

Fourth-choice goalkeeper during his stay with Villa, Goddard's only senior outing came when he deputised for Tommy Jackson in a 3–1 defeat at Bolton in December 1927. An accomplished cricketer, he kept wicket for the Warsop Main and Shirebrook clubs.

GODFREY, BRIAN CAMERON

Midfielder: 156+4 apps, 25 goals

Born: Flint, North Wales, 1 May 1940

Career: Trialist with Wrexham, Chester and Tranmere Rovers; Flint Alexandra (August 1955), Everton (amateur, June 1957; professional, May 1958), Scunthorpe United (June 1960), Preston North End (October 1963), VILLA (September 1967), Bristol Rovers (in deal involving Ray Graydon, May 1971), Newport County (June 1973), Portland Timbers/NASL (summer 1975), Bath City (manager, August 1976–May 1978), Exeter City (January 1979–June 1983), Weymouth (August 1983–May 1987), Gloucester City (manager, June 1987–May 1989, February–May 1992); later Cinderford Town (manager, 1998–2000); played in charity matches until 1995

A Welsh international, capped three times at senior level and once by the Under-23s, Godfrey played for Villa in the 1971 League Cup final. Skippering the side on many occasions, he won the supporters' 'Terrace Trophy' award in 1968 and gained a full FA coaching badge. A gritty, hard-working, eager-beaver midfielder, he was bitterly disappointed to miss out on the 1964 FA Cup final with Preston. In a career spanning over 20 years, he amassed 605 appearances and scored 135 goals. As a manager, he guided Bath to the Southern League title in 1978 and Gloucester to the Southern League (Midland Division) crown in 1989. As boss of Cinderford, one of his first signings was ex-Villa star Chris Price.

GOFFIN, WILLIAM CHARLES

Forward: 173 apps, 42 goals

Born: Amington, Tamworth, 12 December 1920 – *Died*: 15 September 1987

Career: Tamworth schools football, Amington Village FC, Tamworth (August 1935), VILLA (amateur, August 1937; professional, December 1937); guest for Tamworth (December 1939), Birmingham (1942–43), Leicester City (1943–44, 1945–46), Nottingham Forest (1944–45), Swansea Town (1945–46); Walsall (August 1954), Tamworth (player/manager, August 1955; resigned as manager, February 1958; continued as player until May 1959)

'Cowboy' Goffin could play in any forward position, preferring to be in the centre. A dangerous little player with a powerful right-foot shot, he had the knack of arriving unexpectedly inside the penalty area and scored some marvellous goals with his quick and decisive reactions. He netted 45 times in WW2 for Villa and, coupled with his senior record for the club, his overall statistics made impressive reading. He helped Villa win the 1944 Wartime League Cup (N), playing in the first leg against Blackpool.

GOODALL, ARCHIBALD LEE

Utility: 14 apps, 7 goals

Born: Belfast, 19 June 1864 – *Died*: East Finchley, London, 29 November 1929

Career: St Jude's, Liverpool Stanley FC, Everton (August 1884), Preston North End (June 1888), VILLA (October 1888), Derby County (May 1889), Plymouth Argyle (May 1903), Glossop North End (January 1904; later player/manager), Wolverhampton Wanderers (October 1905; retired June 1906)

Inside-right-cum-centre-half, Goodall was forty-one years, five months and two days old when he made his last League appearance for Wolves in December 1905, making him the oldest player ever to play for that club. Raised in Scotland, Goodall played a couple of League games for Preston North End and after leaving Villa netted 52 times in 423 outings for Derby, making a club record of 151 consecutive League appearances between October 1892 and October 1897. He also helped the Rams reach two FA Cup finals (1898, 1903) and finish runners-up in the League. Capped eight times by Ireland (1898–1902), he was a real character, who, in 1898, caused some alarm when he tried to off-load his Cup final tickets to a spiv. He also refused to play an extra half-hour of the United Counties League Cup final against WBA in 1894 because he said his contract ended after 90 minutes! He once toured Europe and America with a strongman act, walking around with a massive metal hoop. A keen sportsman, he followed his country avidly at football, cricket and tennis, and in later life worked and lived in London. His brother, John, played for PNE, Glossop and Derby.

GOODE, BERTRAM JOHN

Forward: 7 apps, 3 goals

Born: Chester, 11 August 1886 – *Died*: Wrexham, 30 April 1955

Career: Old St Mary's, Hoole FC, Broughton Combination, Saltney FC, Chester (trial, 1906; professional, December 1907), Liverpool (May 1908), Wrexham (June 1910), VILLA (£250, April 1911), Hull City (£300, May 1912), Wrexham (May 1913); guest for Millwall (October 1917); guest for Southampton (1918–19); Rhos Athletic (August 1922), Chester (September 1922), Wrexham (August 1923; retired May 1926)

Following his move from Wrexham, Goode scored 46 goals for Villa's reserves as they won the Birmingham and District League championship in 1911–12. A good opportunist, unfortunately he made only a handful of first-team appearances before transferring to Hull, returning to Wrexham after becoming homesick! He won 6 Welsh Cup-winner's medals (1908–25), the first with Chester, then 5 with Wrexham, bagging 4 goals when the latter club beat Connah's Quay 6–0 in one final. Goode played in Wrexham's first-ever League game against Hartlepool in August 1921 and, despite missing the whole of 1922–23 and most of the 1923–24 and 1925–26 campaigns, he established quite a record with the club, securing 136 goals in 276 senior outings in two spells.

Regarded as one of Wrexham's greatest-ever players, he had a benefit match against a Liverpool XI in 1920.

GORDON, ROBERT

Centre-forward: 4 apps, 2 goals

Born: Leith, Edinburgh, 1873 – *Died*: Scotland, 1938

Career: Edinburgh Thistle (August 1888), Sheffield United (September 1889), Leith Rovers (October 1889), Leith Athletic, Heart of Midlothian (August 1890), Middlesbrough Ironopolis (September 1891), Heart of Midlothian (July 1893), VILLA (May 1894), Leicester Fosse (October 1894), Woolwich Arsenal (June 1895), Reading (August 1896), Forfar Athletic (1897), St Bernard's (May 1899; retired 1908)

Villa had high hopes of Gordon, a well-built, bustling striker who was described perhaps harshly by the *Daily Mail* as 'cumbrous'. He scored on his League debut against Small Heath but then lost his way and after netting past a Football League XI in William McGregor's benefit match, he moved to Leicester. He did well at Filbert Street (14 goals in 25 games) but failed to take his shooting boots to Plumstead! In 1897 Gordon scored twice for the Southern League against the London FA.

GOSS, FREDERICK CHARLES

Outside-right: 2 apps

Born: Shardlow, Derbyshire, 25 May 1914 – *Died*: Derby, 1983

Career: Ilkeston St Clare's, Ilkeston Town, VILLA (November 1936), Wrexham (September 1938), VILLA (January 1939), Stourbridge (March 1939; retired, injured, during WW2)

Signed as cover for Jackie Maund, Goss never threatened to win a first-team place with Villa and played in only two home League games, against Bury and West Ham in April 1937. He returned for a second spell with Villa as reserve to Frank Broome.

GRAHAM, GEORGE

Inside-forward: 10 apps, 2 goals

Born: Bargeddle, Lanark, 30 November 1944

Career: Coatbridge Schools, Swinton FC (West Scotland), Coatbridge Boys, VILLA (groundstaff, late 1959; professional, December 1961), Chelsea (£5,950, July 1964), Arsenal (£50,000, plus Tommy Baldwin, September 1966), Manchester United (£120,000, December 1972), Portsmouth (November 1974), Crystal Palace (November 1976), California Surf/NASL (loan, March–July 1978; retired as a player, May 1980); Crystal Palace (youth-team coach/assistant manager), Queens Park Rangers (coach, 1981), Millwall (manager, December 1982–May 1986), Arsenal (manager, May 1986–May 1995), Leeds United (manager, September 1996–September 1998), Tottenham Hotspur (manager, October 1998–April 2001)

Nicknamed 'Stroller', Graham never established himself at Villa Park although he did play in the 1963 League Cup final against the Blues. After leaving the club he went on to greater things, both as a player and a manager. He formed a terrific striking partnership at Chelsea with Barry Bridges, netting 46 goals in 102 appearances and gaining a League Cup-winner's medal in 1965. As a Gunner, he starred in 296 matches and hit 77 goals, collecting League championship and FA Cup-winning medals in 1971, a Fairs Cup-winner's medal (1970) and runner's-up awards in the FA Cup (1972) and League Cup (1968, 1969). Graham was the first player Tommy Docherty signed when he took over at Manchester United. He netted 2 goals in 46 appearances, captaining a struggling Reds side in 1973 and again the following year when they were relegated. He then struck 5 goals in 61 League games for Pompey as they dropped into Division Three before ending his playing days with a couple of strikes in 44 League outings for Palace, helping the Eagles win promotion to the Second Division in 1977. During his League career, Graham scored 95 goals in 455 appearances. Capped as a schoolboy and youth player by Scotland, he also represented his country twice at Under-23 level and in 12 full internationals. Moving into management with Millwall, his first success was to lead the Lions to victory in the final of the League Trophy in 1983, also guiding the Londoners to promotion from Division Three two years later. As boss of Arsenal, Graham won two League titles (1989, 1991) and the League Cup final (1987), and the team finished runners-up in the same competition (1988) before celebrating the double (1993). Graham guided Leeds into Europe in 1998 before taking charge of Spurs.

GRAHAM, JOHN

Forward: 20 apps, 7 goals

Born: Leyland, Lancashire, 12 April 1926

Career: Leyland Works FC, Blackburn Rovers (amateur 1944–45), VILLA (September 1945; professional, November 1946), Wrexham (June 1949), Wigan Athletic (July 1952), Rochdale (February 1953), Bradford City (July 1953–May 1954)

Utility forward Graham (a former draughtsman) was 'stand-in' for many talented players at Villa Park, including George Edwards, Trevor Ford and Billy Goffin. He promised so much at first but failed to produce the goods. He did have the pleasure of netting on both his League and FA Cup debuts – in a 5–2 home win over Brentford in September 1946 and a 5–1 defeat at Burnley in January 1947 respectively. He was transferred to Wrexham following the arrival of Colin Gibson and the emergence of Johnny Dixon.

GRAHAM, JOHN RICHMOND

Inside-forward: 11 apps, 4 goals

Born: Smethwick, August 1868 – *Died*: West Bromwich, 1932

Career: Smethwick Centaur, Oldbury Broadwell (1888), VILLA (August 1889), Brierley Hill Alliance (August 1893), Dudley Town (May 1895–April 1897)

An impish footballer, Graham had one good season with Villa when he appeared as Denny Hodgetts' left-wing partner in 1890–91.

GRAY, ANDREW ARTHUR

Midfield: 40+5 apps, 6 goals

Born: Lambeth, London, 22 February 1964

Career: Lambeth and London Borough Schools, Corinthian Casuals, Dulwich Hamlet, Crystal Palace (£2,000, professional, November 1984), VILLA (£150,000, November 1987), Queens Park Rangers (£425,000, February 1989), Crystal Palace (£500,000, August 1989), Tottenham Hotspur (£900,000, February 1992), Swindon Town (loan, December 1992–January 1993; quit League football, May 1994)

Gray was a forceful player, able to turn his hand to any request. Unfortunately, he failed to fit in with manager Graham Taylor's style or system and was subsequently transferred to QPR following the arrival of Nigel Callaghan and Ian Ormondroyd. Capped twice by England at Under-21 level, Gray gained one full cap and in 1991 helped Palace win the ZDS Cup. His career record was good – 335 appearances, 61 goals.

GRAY, ANDREW MULLEN

Striker: 206+4 apps, 78 goals

Born: Gorbals, Glasgow, 30 November 1955

Career: Clydebank Strollers, Dundee United (amateur, 1970; professional, May 1973), VILLA (£110,000, September 1975), Wolverhampton Wanderers (£1.15m, September 1979), Everton (£250,000, November 1983), VILLA (£150,000, July 1985), Notts County (loan, August 1987), West Bromwich Albion (£25,000, September 1987), Glasgow Rangers (September 1988), Cheltenham Town (August 1989), VILLA (assistant manager/coach, July 1991–June 1992); now a Sky Sports soccer analyst/pundit

Gray became the most expensive footballer in Britain when Wolves paid Villa £1.15m for his services in 1979, the transfer being completed on the Molineux pitch before the League game with Crystal Palace. A colourful figure wherever he played, Gray was brave, determined, totally committed and a tremendous header of the ball. He made almost 80 appearances for Dundee United, gaining a Scottish Cup runner's-up medal in 1974. Villa signed him for a club record fee of £110,000 and two years later he played in the two drawn games of the 1977 League Cup final and was voted 'Player of the Year' and 'Young Player of the Year' by the PFA.

After leaving Villa (the first time), Gray scored 45 goals in 162 appearances for Wolves, notching the winner against Nottingham Forest in the 1980 League Cup final. He then did the business with Everton (23 goals in 71 games) and during his time at Goodison Park collected winner's medals in three competitions: the FA Cup, Football League and European Cup-winner's Cup. As a stop-gap, Villa re-signed Gray in 1985 and after a loan spell with Notts

County he signed for WBA and then Glasgow Rangers, whom he helped win the League Cup and Premier League title, before returning to Villa in 1991 as assistant to Ron Atkinson. Gray was capped 20 times by Scotland, won Under-23, youth and schoolboy honours for his country and netted over 200 goals in more than 600 senior club matches.

He scored in three major finals – the FA Cup (1984), the League Cup (1980) and the European Cup-winners' Cup (1985) and appeared in a cup final with five different clubs.

GRAY, FRANKLIN JAMES SAMUEL
Forward: 2 apps
Born: Oldbury, September 1868 – *Died*: Birmingham, 1925
Career: Oldbury Richmond, Hockley Belmont, West Bromwich United, VILLA (July 1889), Birmingham St George's, Darlaston, Walsall Town Swifts (1892), Wednesbury Town (May 1893), Darlaston (1894–95)
A reserve with Villa, Gray's two outings for the club were both in the Football League, against Preston North End and West Brom in September 1889.

GRAY, JOSIAH ARTHUR
Wing-half: 7 apps
Born: Bristol, 1878 – *Died*: London, 1937
Career: Cambuslang, Clyde, Bristol Rovers (September 1902), VILLA (August 1904), Glasgow Rangers (April 1905), Tottenham Hotspur (briefly), Leyton (1908; retired May 1912)
Gray did well with Bristol Rovers before spending a season with Villa. He was a regular for Rangers for two years before having 24 games for Spurs, his debut coming against his old club, Bristol Rovers. Suspended by Spurs after a 'breach of club discipline' in 1907, Gray committed a further misdemeanour while suspended which led to an indefinite ban.

GRAY, STUART
Utility: 125+8 apps, 15 goals
Born: Withernsea, 19 April 1960
Career: Withernsea Youth Club, Nottingham Forest (apprentice, June 1976; professional, December 1980), Bolton Wanderers (loan, March–May 1983), Barnsley (£40,000, August 1983), VILLA (£150,000, November 1987), Southampton (£200,000, September 1991; retired as a player in 1993; later briefly on coaching staff at The Dell, then Saints' caretaker manager, March 2001; manager, July–October 2001), VILLA (coach, 2001–03), Wolverhampton Wanderers (assistant manager/coach, 2003–04)
Able to play as a centre-half, left-back and in midfield, Gray made over 50 appearances for Nottingham Forest and more than 125 for Barnsley before joining Villa. He spent four years at Villa Park, skippering the side on several occasions and helping the team gain promotion from the Second Division in

1988. Forced to quit first-class soccer through injury, he failed in his efforts as manager of Southampton.

GRAYDON, RAYMOND JACK

Outside-right: 226+5 apps, 81 goals

Born: Frenchay, Bristol, 21 July 1947

Career: Bristol Rovers (apprentice, July 1963; professional, September 1965), VILLA (£50,000, plus Brian Godfrey, June 1971), Coventry City (£50,000, July 1977), Washington Diplomats/NASL (summer, 1978), Oxford United (£35,000, November 1978; retired, May 1981; then coach); Watford (coach, 1988–90), Southampton (Youth team coach, early 1990s), Queens Park Rangers (coach, 1997), Port Vale (coach, March 1998); Walsall (manager, May 1998–January 2002), Bristol Rovers (manager, April 2002–04)

Graydon loved to hug the touchline. A speedy winger with good, close control, he could cross a ball with great precision and power, and possessed a strong right-foot shot. Capped by England at amateur and youth team levels, he netted 38 goals in 157 appearances for Bristol Rovers before moving to Villa – just in time to help his side win the Third Division title, missing only one League game and netting 14 goals. At Wembley in March 1975 he saw his late penalty against Norwich in the League Cup final saved by ex-Villa keeper Kevin Keelan. Graydon reacted quickest to net the rebound and earn his side a 1–0 victory. After scoring a goal every three games for Villa, Graydon moved to Coventry and ended his playing days with Oxford after a stint in the NASL. In all he appeared in 476 League and Cup matches (142 goals). As a manager, he guided the Saddlers to promotion from Division Two at the end of his first season, repeated the act in 2001 and then saved Bristol Rovers from demotion to the Conference.

GRAYSON, SIMON NICHOLAS

Utility: 43+21 apps, 2 goals

Born: 16 December 1969

Career: Leeds United (apprentice, June 1986; professional, June 1988), Leicester City (£50,000, March 1992), VILLA (£1.35m, July 1997), Blackburn Rovers (£750,000, July 1999), Sheffield Wednesday (loan, August–October 2000), Stockport County (loan, January–March 2001), Notts County (loan, September–October 2001), Bradford City (loan, February–April 2002), Blackpool (free, August 2002; caretaker manager, April–May 2004)

After making 229 appearances for Leicester, whom he helped win the League Cup in 1997, Grayson, a full-back-cum-midfielder, moved to Villa, signed by Brian Little, who had been his boss at Filbert Street. Having failed to establish himself at Elland Road, he did sterling work for the Foxes but struggled at times with Villa, and, indeed, for most of 1998–99 had to be content with a place on the subs' bench. Extremely versatile, he remained in the Premiership by joining Blackburn. He won the LDV Vans trophy with Blackpool in 2004.

GREEN, THOMAS CHARLES W.
Forward: 29 apps, 19 goals
Born: Worcester, 7 August 1863 – *Died*: Droitwich, December 1931
Career: St Peter's School, Dreadnought FC (Worcester), Mitchell St George's (1880), Small Heath (briefly), Mitchell St George's, Aston Unity (1883), Great Lever/Bolton (August 1883), Mitchell St George's (October 1883), Wolverhampton Wanderers (guest, 1885), Church FC (guest, 1885), West Bromwich Albion (August 1885), VILLA (June 1887), Kidderminster Harriers (August 1889), Worcester Rovers (September 1892; retired April 1901)

Father of Tommy Green, the WBA, West Ham and Coventry player of the 1930s, Green, an enthusiastic forward, had the pleasure of scoring Villa's first-ever League goal, against Wolves in September 1888. He had earlier appeared in both the 1886 and 1887 FA Cup finals for Albion, the latter against Villa.

GREENHALGH, BRIAN ARTHUR
Midfield: 39+3 apps, 12 goals
Born: Chesterfield, 20 February 1947
Career: Chesterfield and District Schools, Preston North End (apprentice, June 1963; professional, February 1965), VILLA (£35,000, September 1967), Leicester City (£15,000, February 1969), Huddersfield Town (June 1969), Cambridge United (July 1971), Bournemouth (February 1974), Torquay United (loan, July-October 1974), Watford (March 1975), Dartford (August 1976), Staines Town (1977–78); later Carshalton Athletic (player/manager), Wealdstone, Maidenhead United (coach), Chesham United (coach), Everton (chief scout, November 1990)

Greenhalgh played alongside Brian Godfrey at both Deepdale and Villa Park, later helping Huddersfield Town gain promotion. He netted 9 goals in his 19 League games for PNE, did very little at Filbert Street, played in the same forward-line as Frank Worthington at Huddersfield and scored over 50 times for Cambridge – his best return for any of his eight major clubs. His League record was 77 goals in 245 outings.

GREENHALGH, SAMUEL
Right-half: 48 apps, 2 goals
Born: Eagley, Lancashire, May 1882 – *Died*: Bolton, 1955
Career: Birtenshaw Wesleyans, Eagley United FC, Turton, Bolton Wanderers (May 1902), VILLA (January 1906), Bolton Wanderers (September 1907), Chorley (player/coach, August 1914–May 1916); later licensee of the Cheetham Arms, Dunscar (Bolton)

Greenhalgh made over 100 appearances and played in the 1904 FA Cup final for Bolton before moving to Villa. A powerful player, he continued to perform positively before returning to Burnden Park, taking his appearance tally to 278 (20 goals scored). He skippered the Trotters to the Second Division title in 1909 and led them to promotion two years later. Unfortunately, in 1912 he fell foul of the club after refusing to play on the wing in an emergency. He apologised and resumed playing after serving his suspension.

GREGORY, GORDON

Forward: 23+6 apps, 2 goals
Born: Hackney, London, 24 October 1943
Career: Daubeney Road and Lea Marsh Schools (Homerton), Hackney Boys, Leyton Orient (amateur, June 1959; professional, October 1961), Charlton Athletic (in exchange for John Sneddon and Cliff Holton, July 1966), VILLA (£7,777, October 1970), Hereford United (August 1972), Villa Old Stars (1975–80), Chelmsford United (September 1975), Maldon Town (player/manager, 1977–80), Bollingbroke and Wenley FC (1980; retired May 1982)

'Harry' Gregory won England youth honours and scored on his League debut for Orient against Ipswich in 1962. A versatile player with plenty of ability and effort, he netted 15 goals in 87 games for the 'O's' and 26 in 160 appearances for Charlton. Having skippered the Valiants, he did likewise at Villa and Hereford. Mainly an inside-forward, he appeared in 325 League matches for his 4 clubs (44 goals). Because of a poor disciplinary record (he was sent off five times), Gregory landed himself in trouble with the Essex FA after being dismissed playing for Bollingbroke and Wenley. He was handed a 56-day ban, fined £15 and given a final warning!

GREGORY, JOHN CHARLES

Midfield: 69+7 apps, 10 goals
Born: Scunthorpe, 11 May 1954
Career: Watford (trial), Northampton Town (apprentice, June 1969; professional, May 1973), VILLA (£40,000, June 1977), Brighton and Hove Albion (£250,000, July 1979), Queens Park Rangers (£300,000, June 1981), Derby County (£100,000, November 1985), Portsmouth (player/coach, August 1988; then manager January 1989–January 1990), Plymouth Argyle (non-contract player/caretaker manager, January 1990), Bolton Wanderers (non-contract, March 1990), Leicester City (coach, June 1991), football analyst on Sky TV (1991–92), VILLA (coach, seasons 1994–96), Wycombe Wanderers (manager, October 1996), VILLA (manager, February 1998–January 2002), Derby County (manager, January 2002); later, TV pundit

Having played with Brian Little at Villa and served as a coach under him at Filbert Street, Gregory took over as manager at Villa (from Little) and quickly settled in to his former home. He guided Villa to 6th, 6th and 8th places respectively in the Premiership in three seasons before resigning due to a lack of transfer funding (replaced by Graham Taylor) with the team lying 7th. He then took over the reins at his former club Derby but failed to pull up any trees and after some disturbing worries left Pride Park at the end of the season. Later he issued a writ against the club.

As a player, Gregory grafted hard and long in midfield (he actually fulfilled nine different outfield positions for Villa). He made 202 senior appearances for Northampton, starred in 82 matches for Brighton, 191 for QPR, 125 for the Rams, 3 for Plymouth and 7 for Bolton. Capped six times by England at senior level, he collected an FA Cup loser's medal with QPR (1982), won the Second Division championship with QPR in 1983 and Derby County in 1985 and gained promotion from the Third Division, also with the Rams (1986). Gregory's record at League level as manager of Villa was played 148, won 61, drawn 46 and lost 41. He spent £71.5m on new players but recouped only £46m in return.

GRIFFIN, HARRY GEORGE

Forward: 1 app.
Born: Dudley, September 1879 – *Died*: Wolverhampton, April 1946
Career: Lye Town, Dorset County, VILLA (July 1902), Dudley Town (October 1903), VILLA (August 1905), Cradley St Luke's (1906–07)

A reserve at Villa Park, Griffin's only appearance for the club was against Sunderland in October 1902 after George Johnson was injured.

GRIFFITHS, JEREMIAH ALBERT

Wing-half: 3 apps
Born: Aston, Birmingham, 12 September 1872 – *Died*: Hastings, September 1953
Career: St James FC/Aston (1887), Soho Villa, Halesowen (1890), VILLA (April 1895), Grimsby Town (May 1898), Wellingborough, Northampton Town (July 1903), St Leonard's United, Hastings and St Leonard's (July 1906); later ran a fish business in Hastings

Tough-tackling Griffiths, reserve to Jack Burton, Bob Chatt and Jimmy Crabtree, made three appearances for Villa in three years before helping Grimsby win the Second Division title in 1901. He had 84 outings for the Mariners in 5 seasons.

GRIFFITHS, JOHN

Centre-forward: 2+1 apps
Born: Oldbury, 16 June 1951
Career: Oldbury and West Smethwick Schools, VILLA (apprentice, October 1966; professional, November 1968), Stockport County (May 1970), Kidderminster Harriers (August 1975)

Griffiths, a useful centre-forward, was never given a chance by Villa, but later did a tremendous job at Edgeley Park, scoring 31 goals in 182 League games before moving to Kidderminster.

TOP LEFT: Charlie Athersmith — dashing England international winger

TOP RIGHT: John 'Baldy' Reynolds — dual international for England and Ireland

ABOVE LEFT: Andy Ducat — represented England at football and cricket

ABOVE RIGHT: Joe Bache — Villa captain, League and Cup winner

TOP LEFT: Albert Hall — box-of-tricks outside-left

TOP RIGHT: Charlie Wallace — missed a penalty in 1913 FA Cup final

ABOVE LEFT: Clem Stephenson — scorer of 96 goals in 216 appearances for Villa

ABOVE RIGHT: Harry Hampton — Villa's 242-goal marksman

ABOVE LEFT: Amos Moss, son of the 1920s captain of Villa and England

ABOVE RIGHT: Tom 'Pongo' Waring — scorer of a record 50 goals for Villa in 1930–31

FIRST RIGHT: Jimmy Allen — Villa's first five-figure signing

SECOND RIGHT: Tom Gardner — England international and long-throw expert

ABOVE: Tom Griffiths — winner of 21 Welsh caps

RIGHT: Alex Massie — Villa player and later manager

BELOW: Bob Iverson — tough-tackling defender; Jimmy Allen — ex-Portsmouth wing-half; George Cummings — Villa's block of granite full-back and Frank Broome — a Villa star before,

TOP LEFT: Harry Parkes — 16 years a Villa player, later club director

TOP RIGHT: Dave Walsh — prolific Irish international striker of the 1950s

ABOVE LEFT: Con Martin — Irish international defender and goalkeeper!

ABOVE RIGHT: Ken 'Shunter' Roberts — 1950s Villa reserve

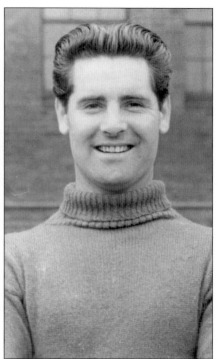

ABOVE: Trevor Ford — swashbuckling Welsh
international centre-forward

ABOVE RIGHT: Keith Jones — Welsh
international goalkeeper

RIGHT: Frank Moss, junior — followed his
father into the centre-half position

TOP LEFT: Johnny Dixon — Villa's FA Cup-winning captain

TOP RIGHT: Danny Blanchflower — Northern Ireland international wing-half

ABOVE LEFT: Peter Aldis — scored with a 35-yard header

ABOVE RIGHT: Tommy Thompson — played with Finney and Matthews at club level

ABOVE: Peter McParland —
dashing goalscoring left-winger

ABOVE RIGHT: Bobby Thomson
(in action v. Spurs) — twice a
League Cup winner

RIGHT: Geoff Sidebottom, Villa's
goalkeeper for four years
1961–65, dives at the feet of
Spurs' striker Bobby Smith

GRIFFITHS, THOMAS PERCIVAL

Centre-half. 67 apps, 1 goal

Born: Moss, near Wrexham, 21 February 1906 – *Died*: Moss, 25 December 1981

Career: Ffrith Valley FC (1919), Wrexham and District Schools, Wrexham Boys' Club, Wrexham (amateur, December 1922), Everton (£2,000, December 1926), Bolton Wanderers (December 1931), Middlesbrough (£6,500, March 1933), VILLA (£5,000, November 1935), Wrexham (player/coach, August 1938; retired February 1939, after losing his battle against rheumatism), VILLA (scout, 1938–39); played for RAF Bridgnorth (March 1941); Wrexham (two spells as coach (1945–46, 1948–49) before becoming a director of the club (from July 1950) while also acting as trainer to 1953); also Wales (trainer); later licensee of the Turf Hotel (Wrexham), the Hand Hotel and the Red Lion pub (Marchwiel); a cabinet-maker by trade, he was also a worthy cellist, performing in several concerts

Griffiths began as a centre-forward but much to his indignation was thrown in at centre-half when chosen to represent his local school. He did well but reverted back to leading his junior club's attack within a week. The former Wrexham and Wales full-back Tom Matthias saw Griffiths net eight goals in a match and immediately introduced him to Wrexham. He played as an amateur for a while and at 17 was offered professionalism by a number of clubs but refused. Asked to start a reserve game at right-half by Wrexham, halfway through he switched to centre-half, enjoyed it and stayed put. After winning inter-League and junior international caps for Wales and scoring twice in 36 games for Wrexham, he joined Everton, playing his first game for the Merseysiders behind Dixie Dean. The following Saturday he lined up for Wales in his first full international, his opponent, Dean of England! A stylish defender, Griffiths was a fine header of the ball and wasted very little time in clearing his lines. He took over as centre-half in the national side from Fred Keenor, the Cardiff skipper, and went on to lead his country, winning 21 caps, his last in 1937 against Northern Ireland. He made 76 League appearances for Everton and 48 for Bolton before moving to Villa in 1935. Unfortunately, he struggled with rheumatism over the next few years and eventually went back to Wrexham. Griffiths was at centre-half when Arsenal's Ted Drake slammed seven goals past Villa in a First Division game in 1935. Griffiths, who was a staunch teetotaller, had a cousin, Fred Smallwood, who played for Southampton.

GROVES, WILLIAM

Wing-half. 26 apps, 3 goals

Born: Leith, Edinburgh, 9 November 1869 – *Died*: Edinburgh, 13 February 1908

Career: Edinburgh Thistle, Leith Harp, Hibernian (1886), Celtic (August 1888), Everton (early 1889), Celtic (March 1889), West Bromwich Albion (October 1890), VILLA (£100, September 1893; retired November 1894);

returned with Hibernian (August 1895), Celtic (November 1896), Rushden (August 1898; retired May 1902)

Groves was a dashing centre-forward who developed into a stylish left-half. Swarthy, well-featured and well set-up, he had devastating speed and packed a thunderous shot. A player with masterly distribution qualities, he gained three full caps for Scotland (1888–89), represented the Football League and Edinburgh (in an Inter-City match), won a Scottish Cup-winner's medal with Hibs (1887) and collected runner's-up prizes in the same competition with Celtic (1889) and Hibs (1896). An FA Cup winner with WBA against Villa (1892), he then won a League championship with Villa (1894), did not play for Everton (leaving the club after a dispute regarding his registration) and hit 16 goals in 18 appearances in 3 spells with Celtic. Struck down with tuberculosis in 1894, Groves eventually died in utter penury.

GUDJONSSON, JOHANNES KARL
Midfield: 9+2 apps, 2 goals
Born: Akranes, Iceland, 25 May 1980
Career: 1A Akranes/Iceland (professional, July 1997), KRC Genk/Belgium (1998), MVV Maastricht/Holland (August 1999), RKC Waalwijk/Holland (July 2000), Real Betis/Spain (August 2001), VILLA (loan, January–May 2003), Wolverhampton Wanderers (September 2003), Real Betis/Spain (March 2004), Leicester City (August 2004)

An aggressive, 5 ft 8 in. eager-beaver midfielder who enjoys a challenge and a battle, Gudjonsson made 11 Premiership appearances for Villa in 2002–03, his first in the 5–2 win at Middlesbrough, and was sent off after scoring at Leeds on the final day. An Icelandic international with 6 youth, 10 Under-21 and 13 senior caps to his credit, he was not part of Villa boss David O'Leary's plans. Three of Gudjonsson's brothers are Iceland internationals.

GUTTRIDGE, RONALD
Full-back: 15 apps
Born: Widnes, 28 April 1916
Career: St Helens Schools, Liverpool (amateur), Stockport County (trial), Prescot Cables (January 1935), VILLA (March 1937); guest for Liverpool (1939–44), Notts County (1943–44), Nottingham Forest (1944–45); Brighton and Hove Albion (June 1948), Hastings United (May 1950); later ran his own wine and spirits business in Prescot

'Roy' Guttridge was reserve to Vic Potts and George Cummings during his time with Villa, his career being severely dented by WW2.

HADJI, MUSTAPHA
Midfield: 31+17 apps, 3 goals
Born: Ifrane, Morocco, 16 November 1971
Career: FC Nancy/France (1992–96), Sporting Lisbon/Portugal (August 1996),

Deportivo La Coruna/Spain (November 1997), Coventry City (£4m, August 1999), VILLA (£4.5m, July 2001), Hertha Berlin/Germany (trial, November 2003), Espanyol/Spain (2004)

Creative Moroccan international Hadji (63 full caps) could turn a game with a flick of the ball or an ingenious defence-splitting pass. Strong and powerful, he scored 31 goals in 139 games in France, followed up with 3 in 36 in Portugal and 2 in 31 in Spain. During his 2 seasons at Highfield Road he netted 12 times in 62 Premiership matches but left when the Sky Blues were relegated. His initial outings with Villa were restricted to a substitute role, but in September 2001 he established himself in the team and played well until a knee injury forced him onto the treatment table. He took time to regain full fitness and made only 11 appearances in the Premiership in 2002–03 as his form dipped.

HADLEY, GEORGE ANGUS

Half-back: 4 apps

Born: West Bromwich, 5 June 1893 – *Died*: Birmingham, April 1963

Career: West Bromwich Victoria (1909) Willenhall Swifts (August 1911), Southampton (July 1913); guest for Chesterfield Town (1916–17); VILLA (March 1919), Coventry City (July 1920; retired with broken collarbone, May 1922)

Stocky but steady, Hadley – a Scottish junior international as a teenager (his father worked north of the border) – made 62 appearances for Saints before WW1 interrupted his career. After the hostilities, he had just a handful of outings with Villa before starring in over 70 games for Coventry.

HADLEY, HARRY

Left-half: 11 apps

Born: Barrow-in-Furness, 26 October 1877 – *Died*: West Bromwich, 12 September 1942

Career: Cradley Heath and District Schools, Colley Gate United, Halesowen (1893–96), West Bromwich Albion (£100, February 1897), VILLA (£250, February 1905), Nottingham Forest (April 1906), Southampton (April 1907), Croydon Common (August 1908), Halesowen (February 1910), Merthyr Town (manager, May 1919–April 1922), Chesterfield (manager, April–August 1922), Merthyr Town (three spells as manager between 1923 and 1927), Aberdare Athletic (manager, November 1927–November 1928), Gillingham (manager, briefly in 1929–30), Aberdare Athletic (manager, April 1930–September 1931), Bangor City (manager, July 1935–April 1936)

Hadley, an industrious player, displayed a lot of composure. Capped by England against Ireland at Wolverhampton in 1905, he helped WBA win the Second Division title before joining Villa. He made over 180 appearances for the Baggies but managed less than a dozen for Villa before embarking on a very successful managerial career, leading Merthyr into the Football League in 1920. His brother, Ben Hadley, also played for WBA.

HAGGART, WILLIAM
Left-back: 2 apps
Born: Edinburgh, August 1874 – *Died*: Scotland, *circa* 1954
Career: Dairy Primrose (Edinburgh), Edinburgh Royal, VILLA (£40, April 1897), Partick Thistle (July 1900), Edinburgh Thistle (1901–02)
Highly rated north of the border, Haggart won junior international honours for Scotland before joining Villa. He never lived up to his reputation, despite being paid a seemingly massive wage of £6 per week for first-team games and £4 in the reserves! A heavy drinker, he appeared in court for assault in 1900.

HALE, ALFRED
Inside-forward: 7 apps, 2 goals
Born: Waterford, Ireland, 28 August 1939
Career: St Joseph's Juniors, Waterford (August 1957), VILLA (£4,500, June 1960), Doncaster Rovers (July 1962), Newport County (August 1965), Waterford (£3,000, July 1966), St Patrick's Athletic (1975)
Hale, a clever, scheming forward, represented the Republic of Ireland at both amateur and professional levels, winning 13 full caps. He didn't achieve much with Villa but later did well with Doncaster, netting 42 goals in 119 League games.

HALL, ALBERT EDWARD
Outside-left: 215 apps, 62 goals
Born: Wordsley, Stourbridge, 21 January 1882 – *Died*: Stourbridge, 17 October 1957
Career: Amblecote Council School, Brierley Hill Wanderers, Wall Heath, Stourbridge (August 1900), VILLA (July 1903), Millwall (December 1913), Stourbridge (September 1919; retired August 1916); later went into business in Stourbridge as an enamelware manufacturer
Hall was an exceptionally talented footballer, a goalscoring winger, a real box-of-tricks, who was lightning quick and possessed a cracking shot. He won an FA Cup-winner's medal with Villa in 1905 and a League championship medal five years later when he also earned his only England cap, partnering his club-mate Joe Bache against Ireland in Belfast. In 1909 he played for Birmingham against London and four years later moved to Millwall. Hall was also a fine cricketer and billiards player, representing Stourbridge CC in the Birmingham League and Amblecote Institute respectively.

HALSE, HAROLD JAMES
Centre-forward: 37 apps, 28 goals
Born: Stratford, east London, 1 January 1886 – *Died*: Colchester, Essex, 25 March 1949
Career: Park Road School (Wanstead), Newportians (Leyton), Wanstead, Barking Town (1904), Clapton Orient (amateur, August 1905), Southend United (June 1906), Manchester United (£350, March 1908), VILLA

(£1,200, July 1912), Chelsea (May 1913); guest for Clapton Orient (WW1); Charlton Athletic (July 1921; retired May 1923; scout until 1925); later ran a tobacconist shop at Walton-on-Naze

Halse, who scored over 200 goals in 2 seasons for Southend, netted just 45 seconds into his debut for Manchester United, the first of 50 goals in 124 appearances for the club. And when United beat Swindon 8–4 in the 1911 FA Charity Shield, Halse hit 6 goals. He gained an FA Cup-winner's medal with both United and Villa and collected a runner's-up medal in the same competition with Chelsea, a feat later equalled by Ernie Taylor, who did it with Newcastle, Blackpool and Manchester United in the 1950s. Not a player to catch the eye, Halse was, nevertheless, one of the finest marksmen of his day. Small, rather slight in build, he had the knack of snapping up the half-chance – a real top-class opportunist. Capped once by England, he also played for the Football League XI and won both First Division championship and runner's-up medals with United and Villa respectively, 1912 and 1913. Halse's goals-per-games record with Villa was tremendous – and his efforts included a five-timer against Derby in October 1912. He captained Charlton in their first season in the Football League (1921–22).

HAMILTON, IAN MICHAEL

Midfield: 234+19 apps, 48 goals

Born: Streatham, 31 October 1950

Career: Streatham and London Schools, Chelsea (juniors, 1965; professional, January 1968), Southend United (£5,000, September 1968), VILLA (£40,000, June 1969), Sheffield United (July 1976), Minnesota Kicks/USA (three summers: 1978, 1979, 1980), San Jose Earthquakes/USA (May–August 1982); later community officer at Rotherham United

An England youth international, 'Chico' Hamilton had a terrific left foot and did some sterling work for each of his four English clubs. He netted 65 goals in a total of 308 League games, played in two League Cup finals for Villa (1971 and 1975) and was the youngest player ever to appear in a First Division game for Chelsea, aged 16 years, 4 months, 18 days against Spurs in March 1967.

HAMILTON, WILLIAM MURDOCH

Inside-forward: 54 apps, 9 goals

Born: Airdrie, 16 February 1938 – *Died*: Canada, April 1976

Career: Drumpellier Amateurs (Coatbridge), Sheffield United (February 1956), Middlesbrough (£12,000, February 1961), Heart of Midlothian (£5,000, June 1962), VILLA (£25,000, August 1965), Hibernian (free, August 1967), South African football (August 1969–April 1970), Ross County (July 1970), Hamilton Academical (October 1970; retired May 1972)

In a career marred by illness and injury, ball-player Hamilton still performed well at both club and international level. Capped by Scotland against Finland in 1965, he played twice for the Scottish League and won a League Cup-winner's medal with Hearts in 1963. He netted 21 times in 79 League outings for Sheffield United and once in ten starts for 'Boro.

HAMPSON, JOHN
Defender: 15 apps
Born: Oswestry, 28 December 1887 – *Died*: Burslem, 3 December 1960
Career: Oswestry Town, Northampton Town (May 1910), Leeds City (August 1913), VILLA (£1,000, October 1919), Port Vale (£1,000, June 1921), Hanley Social Club (August 1924–April 1926); later ran own business in Oswestry
Efficient and hard-working, Hampson occupied six different positions during his time with Villa, including all five in defence. He later had over 100 outings for Port Vale before suffering a serious leg injury, which required two major operations.

HAMPTON, GEORGE HENRY
Full-back: 3 apps
Born: Wellington, Shropshire, 1890 – *Died*: Wellington, Shropshire, July 1956
Career: Wellington Council Schools, Wellington St George's, Glossop North End (August 1909), Bellis and Morcom (briefly), VILLA (£150, July 1914), Shrewsbury Town (May 1915), Willenhall (season 1919–20)
A wholehearted defender, signed as reserve to Bill Littlewood and Tom Lyons prior to the last season before WW1, Hampton appeared in 110 League games for Glossop. Brother of Harry (q.v.).

HAMPTON, JOSEPH HARRY
Centre-forward: 376 apps, 242 goals
Born: Wellington, Shropshire, 21 April 1885 – *Died*: Wrexham, 15 March 1963
Career: Wellington Council Schools, Potters Bank, Lilleshall Ironworks, Shifnal Juniors, Hadley FC (May 1903), Wellington Town (October 1903), VILLA (April 1904); guest for Bellis and Morcom, Birmingham, Blackpool, Derby County, Fulham, Nottingham Forest, Reading, Stoke (WW1); Birmingham (February 1920), Newport County (September 1922; retired May 1923); returned with Wellington Town (January 1924–May 1925), Preston North End (coach, June 1925–January 1926), Birmingham Works football (1926–28), Lilleshall Town (briefly), Birmingham (colts' coach, October 1934–May 1937); later ran the Carlton Café, Queen Street (Rhyl)
Elder brother of George (q.v), "Appy 'Arry 'Ampton' was a real terror to opposing goalkeepers and defenders. During the decade leading up to the outbreak of WW1, he was one of the finest goalscorers in Britain. Afraid of no one, his strong, forceful, determined style was admired and appreciated by plenty. The idol of the Villa Park faithful, Hampton was robust to the extreme. He often barged the goalkeeper, including the hefty 22 st. body-weight of 'Fatty' Foulke of Sheffield United fame, and the ball (if he had it in his possession) into the back of the net, sometimes taking a co-defender along for

good measure with one almighty shoulder-charge! With a devil-may-care attitude, his record as a marksman speaks for itself – it was quite brilliant. He rattled in goals galore for Villa – and after leaving the club continued to blast bullets into the netting a further 31 times in only 59 outings for neighbours Blues and claiming a few more for Newport.

Capped by England on four occasions (two goals scored), Hampton also represented the Football League three times, played for Birmingham against London in 1909, 1911 and 1913 and for England against South of England, also in 1913, having been an international trialist (Stripes against Whites) in 1911. He gained a League championship medal with Villa in 1910 and added two FA Cup-winner's medals to his collection in 1905 and 1913, scoring both goals in the 2–0 win over Newcastle in the former. He also featured in the losing final of 1920 and a year later helped the Blues win the Second Division title. Badly gassed during WW1, he recovered full fitness and health within two months. Hampton only discovered that his first name was Joseph late in life when there was a query about his date of birth. He went along to Somerset House in London and unearthed his own birth certificate that revealed that he was, and had been christened, Joseph Harry Hampton.

HANDLEY, BRIAN
Centre-forward: 3 apps
Born: Wakefield, 21 June 1936 – *Died*: 1982
Career: Goole Town, VILLA (September 1957), Torquay United (September 1960), Bridgwater Town (August 1964), Rochdale (February–May 1966); captained Paignton CC for five years (1961–66)
Handley never got an opportunity to show his worth with Villa owing to the presence of Gerry Hitchens. He did well with Torquay, scoring 33 goals in 80 League games.

HARDY, GEORGE CHARLES
Half-back: 6 apps, 1 goal
Born: Newbold Verdun, Derbyshire, 9 April 1912 – *Died*: *circa* 1990
Career: Newbold Victoria, Nuneaton Town (1932), VILLA (February 1934), Blackburn Rovers (August 1938), Nuneaton Town (1939–40); did not play after WW2
Younger brother of Sam (q.v.), Hardy was an attacking player, deputy to Messrs Gardner, Iverson and Massie at Villa, whose only goal came in the 2–1 home defeat by Nottingham Forest in March 1938.

HARDY, SAMUEL
Goalkeeper: 183 apps
Born: Newbold Verdun, Derbyshire, 26 August 1883 – *Died*: Chesterfield, 24 October 1966
Career: Newbold Church School, Newbold White Star (July 1900),

Chesterfield (professional, April 1903), Liverpool (£500, October 1905), VILLA (£600, May 1912); guest for Plymouth Argyle, Nottingham Forest and Royal Naval barracks (Plymouth) (WW1); Nottingham Forest (£1,000, August 1921; retired May 1925); later hotelier in Chesterfield; also ran his own billiard hall at Alfreton (Derbyshire)

'Chuffer Hardy was one of the greatest goalkeepers I ever played in front of,' said Jesse Pennington, the WBA and England full-back. Indeed, he was quite a player and during a splendid career amassed over 600 appearances for clubs and country. He made goalkeeping look easy and would have been considered a classic player in any era. He won 21 caps for England (1907–21), played in 3 Victory internationals, twice represented the Football League against the Scottish League, starred for Birmingham against London, for England against South of England in 1913 and for England against the North in 1914. He won a First Division championship medal with Liverpool (1906), a Second Division championship medal with Forest (1922) and collected two FA Cup-winner's medals with Villa (1913, 1920).

He joined Liverpool after playing tremendously well, despite conceding six goals for Chesterfield against the Merseysiders. He made 239 senior appearances for the Anfield club and after leaving Villa played in 109 games for Forest, having had over 70 outings for Chesterfield early in his career. During WW1 Hardy served in the Navy and escaped serious injury on two occasions. He also guested for Nottingham Forest in the 1919 championship play-off against Everton at Goodison Park (Forest won 1–0 after a 0–0 draw). His nephew, Ted Worrell, played for Aberdare, Fulham, New Brighton, Southport, Sheffield Wednesday and Watford.

HARE, CHARLES BOYD

Forward: 26 apps, 13 goals

Born: Yardley, Birmingham, June 1870 – *Died*: Erdington, Birmingham, 10 August 1947

Career: Warwick County, Birmingham United, VILLA (March 1891), Royal Arsenal (February 1896), Small Heath (November 1896), Watford (June 1898–May 1901), Plymouth Argyle (October 1903), Green Waves (September 1904–May 1905; then player/coach, May 1906–07); later served with the Warwickshire Yeomanry in the Boer War. On his return from South Africa he attempted to pick up his career in Devon non-League football but without success

One of a host of fine players produced by Warwick County, Hare was a talented forward who helped Villa win the League in 1894. A huge favourite with the fans, he later netted 14 times in 45 outings for the Blues.

HARKUS, GEORGE CECIL, MBE

Wing-half: 4 apps

Born: Newcastle-upon-Tyne, 25 September 1898 – *Died:* Southampton, 28 September 1950

Career: Nunsmoor, Edinburgh Emmett, Scotswood FC, VILLA (May 1921), Southampton (£250, May 1923), Olympique Lyonnais/France (1930), Oldham Athletic (trial, December 1930), New Milton (August 1931, after taking over the Wheatsheaf pub), Southampton (£250, February 1932), Southport (player/coach, September 1932–May 1933; retired as a player, October 1932, after suffering a serious injury during a game against Barrow's second XI); served in the RAF during WW2 as a flight lieutenant, receiving the MBE in the King's Honours List in 1949 'for keeping up morale in the forces while stationed in the Middle East'. A member of the RAF's soccer team, he was on the selection committee after the war, holding office until his death in 1950

An enthusiastic footballer, Harkus – reserve to George Blackburn and Frank Moss at Villa – became an inspirational captain of Southampton, for whom he made 220 appearances. In 1926 Harkus toured Canada with the FA, playing in 13 matches.

HARLEY, CHARLES CEDRIC

Outside-right: 1 app.

Born: Wednesbury, 7 March 1871 – *Died:* Wolverhampton, 1940

Career: Bloxwich Strollers, VILLA (April 1890), Notts County (September 1891–May 1892)

Small and compact, reserve to Albert Brown during his brief stay with Villa, Harley's only first-team outing for Villa was against Bolton (away) in October 1890 (lost 4–0).

HARPER, ROWLAND RICHARD GEORGE

Forward: 2 apps

Born: Lichfield, April 1881 – *Died:* Birmingham, August 1949

Career: Walsall Wood, Small Heath/Birmingham (April 1904), Burton United (£275, September 1906), VILLA (August 1907), Notts County (with J. Cantrell, March 1908), Mansfield Invicta (1910–11)

A temporary signing as cover for Charlie Wallace, Harper made two appearances for Villa. He had scored on his debut for Small Heath, for whom he made 29 appearances.

HARRIS, CECIL VERNON

Defender: 26 apps

Born: Grantham, 1 October 1898 – *Died:* 16 August 1976

Career: Billingborough School team, Billingborough Town, Black Watch (served in France, 1916–18), Black Watch War Ends FC, Billingborough

Town, Grantham (briefly), Cromwell Works (South Lincolnshire League), Llandrindod Wells (1921–22), VILLA (trial, July–August 1922; professional, September 1922), Grimsby Town (May 1926), Gainsborough Trinity (May 1929), Shillingthorpe (September 1930–May 1931)); later worked in Metherington (near Lincoln)

Harris, Eric Houghton's uncle, was a sound, two-footed defender who went on to make 47 League appearances for Grimsby.

HARRIS, GEORGE ABNER

Defender: 21 apps, 1 goal

Born: Halesowen, 1 January 1878 – *Died*: Brierly Hill, 10 June 1923.

Career: Gorsty Hill Council School, Haden Hill Rose, Halesowen (reserves), Coombs Wood (May 1895), Brierly Hill (April 1898), VILLA (June 1901), West Bromwich Albion (£400, January 1909), Wellington Town (June 1910), Coventry City (June 1912; retired, injured, May 1915); later licensee of the Sportsman Inn (Old Hill)

Twice selected as an England junior international (1905, 1906), Harris, of outstanding physique with great determination and a keen eye, was first reserve to Albert Leake, Joe Pearson and Joey Windmill at Villa. It would be 70 years before another player was transferred from Villa to Albion, John Deehan making the switch in 1979. Harris was tragically killed in a steelworks accident.

HARRIS, GEORGE EDWARD

Goalkeeper: 1 app.

Born: Redditch, July 1875 – *Died*: Headless Cross, Redditch, 27 June 1910

Career: Headless Cross, Redditch Excelsior, VILLA (May 1895), Wolverhampton Wanderers (July 1896), Grimsby Town (May 1900), Portsmouth (November 1901), Redditch Town (1906), Kidderminster Harriers (1907; retired 1908, after losing an eye in an air-gun accident)

Reserve to Tom Wilkes, Harris, splendidly built for his position, made one League appearance for Villa – a 2–2 home draw with Sheffield United in November 1895. He failed to make the first XI at Molineux but did well at both Grimsby and Pompey.

HARRIS, WALTER HENRY

Inside-forward: 20 apps, 4 goals

Born: Stonehouse, near Plymouth, 7 July 1904 – *Died*: Malvern

Career: Stonehouse Boys' School, Caulker Boys, Dockland United, Plymouth Ivanhoe, Torquay Town (1920), VILLA (August 1922), Bristol City (July 1929), Loughborough Corinthians (July 1930), Brierley Hill Alliance, Kidderminster Harriers (August 1931), FC Bruhl/Switzerland (coach, 1934–37); also briefly with Bath City (1934); after WW2, Malvern Link YC (coach), Barnards Green YC (coach), Malvern Town FC (trainer)

Short and stocky with a good technique, Harris scored a goal every 5 games for

Villa, claimed 15 in 26 games for Bristol City and netted 30 times for Bath before injury set in. He had earlier secured 110 goals in 2 seasons of schoolboy football in Devon.

HARRISON, JAMES CHARLES

Half-back: 8 apps, 1 goal
Born: Leicester, 12 February 1921
Career: Wellington Victoria, Leicester City (December 1940), Reading (WW2 guest), VILLA (£12,000, July 1949), Coventry City (July 1951), Corby Town (July 1953–55); served in the RAF in India and Burma and ran a successful haulage business, based at Wigmore (Leicester)

Harrison made his senior debut for Leicester as a centre-forward but developed into a fine full-back. He played 81 games for the Foxes including an appearance in the 1949 losing FA Cup final. He covered four different positions during his two seasons at Villa before joining a Coventry side with an average age of thirty-one.

HARRISON, THOMAS

Outside-left: 1 app.
Born: Birmingham, April 1867 – *Died*: 1942
Career: Aston Manor Council School, Coombs Wood, VILLA (August 1888), Halesowen (September 1889), Handsworth Richmond (May 1890–April 1892)

Reserve winger with a good turn of speed, Harrison's only League appearance for Villa saw him deputise for Denny Hodgetts in a 4–2 win at Notts County in December 1888.

HARROP, JAMES

Centre-half: 171 apps, 4 goals
Born: Heeley, Sheffield, 1884 – *Died*: 1958
Career: St Wilfred's and Heeley County Schools, Kent Road Mission (1898), Ronmoor Wesleyans (1900), Sheffield Wednesday (trialist, then amateur, 1903; professional, 1904), Denaby United (1906), Rotherham Town (1907), Liverpool (January 1908), VILLA (£600, June 1912); guest for Sheffield Wednesday (1915–19); Sheffield United (March 1921), Burton All Saints (August 1922–24)

The son of a Yorkshire farmer, Harrop signed for Villa a month after Sam Hardy had taken the same route. A cool, methodical defender, crafty at times with a clever brain, Harrop's presence at the heart of the defence went a long way to winning the FA Cup in 1913. He twice represented the Football League, appeared in two international trials, represented Birmingham against London (1913) and was reserve for England against Wales, also in 1913, but had the misfortune to miss Villa's 1920 FA Cup final triumph through injury. During WW1 Harrop worked as an agricultural implement manufacturer. He was known as 'Head Up' Harrop.

HARVEY, HAROLD
Forward: 11 apps, 3 goals
Born: Wednesbury, 5 April 1875 – *Died*: Birmingham, 1938
Career: Wolverhampton Road Council School (Wednesbury), Walsall Town Swifts (reserves), Small Heath (briefly), VILLA (September 1896), Burslem Port Vale (£50, June 1898), Manchester City (£180, January 1900), West Bromwich United (1900), Burton United (March 1901), Watford (August 1901–February 1903), Glentoran (August 1903), Darlaston (August 1903; retired May 1905)
After leaving Villa, where he had played as a reserve, inside- or centre-forward, Harvey netted 30 times in 65 matches for Port Vale, top-scoring for the Potteries' club in 1899–1900. He was sold to Manchester City because of Vale's increasing financial problems.

HARVEY, RICHARD ARNOLD
Full-back: 4 apps, 1 goal
Born: Nottingham, January 1860 – *Died*: Nottingham, December 1932
Career: Sandiacre Lime Firms, Notts Rangers, VILLA (April 1882), Normanton (October 1883), Repton School (August 1885; retired May 1892 after breaking his leg)
Harvey's only goal for Villa came from 'long distance' in the 4–1 home FA Cup win over Wednesbury Old Athletic in November 1882. He was a well-built, strong-tackling defender.

HARVEY, WALTER ALFRED
Versatile: 4 apps, 1 goal
Born: Derby, November 1856 – *Died*: Nottingham, *circa* 1940
Career: Derby St Luke's, Derby Midland, Wednesbury Strollers, VILLA (April 1882; retired with knee injury, May 1884); later lived in Newbold
Harvey, versatile and very talented, began as a left-winger, then starred as a full-back, playing in four FA Cup ties for Villa, his only goal coming against Wednesbury Old Athletic in November 1882.

HATELEY, ANTHONY
Striker: 148 apps, 86 goals
Born: Derby, 13 June 1941
Career: Schoolboy football, Normanton Sports Club, Derby County (schoolboy forms, 1955), Notts County (May 1956; professional, June 1958), VILLA (£20,000, August 1963), Chelsea (£100,000, October 1966), Liverpool (£100,000, July 1967), Coventry City (£80,000, September 1968), Birmingham City (£72,000, August 1969), Notts County (£20,000, November 1970), Oldham Athletic (£5,000, July 1972), Bromsgrove Rovers (May 1974), Prescot Town (July 1975), Keyworth United (December 1978; retired August 1979); later worked in Everton's lottery office, then employed by a brewery in Nottinghamshire

Hateley was a soccer nomad whose career realised 211 goals in 434 senior appearances. An out-and-out striker, he was tall and muscular and exceptionally strong in the air. He helped Notts County win the Third and Fourth Division championships in 1960 and 1971 and was an FA Cup finalist with Chelsea in 1967. Villa's top marksman three seasons running (1963–66), he is one of only 2 players to score 4 goals in a League Cup game for the club, doing so in the 7–1 home win over Bradford City in 1964. When he moved to Chelsea in 1966, Hateley became only the second £100,000 footballer in Britain (Alan Ball was the first). He is the father of striker Mark Hateley, who played for England during the 1980s.

HAYCOCK, FREDERICK JOSEPH

Forward: 110 apps, 33 goals

Born: Bootle, 19 April 1912 – *Died*: Great Barr, Birmingham, 10 April 1989

Career: Bootle Boys (June 1925), Liverpool and District Schools, Waterford (April 1928), Blackburn Rovers (September 1933), Prescot Cables (December 1933), VILLA (March 1934); guest for ICI Kynochs, Kidderminster Harriers, Leicester City, Liverpool, Nottingham Forest, Northampton Town, Notts County, Plymouth Argyle, Walsall and Wolves during WW2; Wrexham (December 1945), Stourbridge (July 1947), Sutton Coldfield Town (April 1953; manager, November 1956), Stourbridge (manager, October 1958), Sutton Town (manager, June 1959), Atherstone (manager, March 1962), Sutton Town (manager, February 1964); later managed two junior Sunday teams in Birmingham; also worked at ICI (Witton) for over 30 years

As a youngster, 'Schneider' Haycock played football on a Saturday morning and worked in his father's butcher's shop in the afternoon. After a useful spell in Ireland, he played for Prescot Cables before signing for Villa, with whom he spent 11 years, appearing in more than 100 first-class matches. He was chosen to play for Ireland in a representative match in 1934 – despite being a 'Scouser' – the Irish clearly remembering his skills when he was with Waterford! A grafter rather than a goalscorer, he was a key member of Villa's Second Division championship-winning side in 1938. He was a dedicated dahlia-grower.

HAYNES, ARTHUR EDWIN THOMAS

Forward: 4 apps

Born: Birmingham, 23 May 1924 – *Died*: 4 July 1990

Career: Schoolboy football; joined 70th Battalion Royal Warwickshire Regiment (1940); served in London Division of Black Watch; Paget Rangers, VILLA (amateur, August 1945; professional, January 1946), Walsall (June 1948), Weymouth (1949), Worcester City (June 1950), Bromsgrove Rovers (August 1960), Bulls Head FC (Stechford, 1957–58), Luton Town (Midland-based scout, 1959–60); later a scout for Leeds United (February 1972)

A well-built second-string forward who preferred the right-wing position, Haynes made four senior appearances for Villa before moving to Walsall.

HAZELDEN, WALTER
Inside-forward: 19 apps, 5 goals
Born: Ashton-in-Makerfield, 13 February 1941
Career: Wigan schoolboy football, VILLA (junior, June 1956; professional, February 1958), Wigan Athletic (July 1960), Rugby Town (August 1961), Ashton FC (July 1964; retired May 1968)
An England youth international (1957–58), Hazelden became the youngest player ever to appear in a Football League game for Villa when he scored on his debut against WBA in November 1957 at the age of 16 years, 257 days. Jimmy Brown took over the mantle in 1969. A skilful player, he did well after leaving Villa Park, although a badly damaged ankle kept him out of the game for quite a while.

HEARD, TIMOTHY PATRICK
Defender: 21+5 apps, 2 goals
Born: Hull, 17 March 1960
Career: Hull and Humberside District Schools, Everton (apprentice, June 1976; professional, March 1978), VILLA (£150,000 plus John Gidman, October 1979), Sheffield Wednesday (£60,000, January 1983), Newcastle United (September 1984), Middlesbrough (August 1985), Hull City (March 1986), Rotherham United (July 1988), Cardiff City (August 1989), Hull City (non-contract, August–October 1992)
An England youth international, Heard was a good 'stand-in' during Villa's League championship-winning season of 1980–81. A player with the 'right attitude', he collected an FA Youth Cup-winner's medal with Everton (1977) and during his career made over 300 appearances (293 in the Football League). He won a European Cup-winner's medal in 1982 as a non-playing substitute.

HEATH, ADRIAN PAUL
Forward: 9+3 apps
Born: Stoke-on-Trent, 17 January 1961
Career: Stoke City (apprentice, June 1977; professional, January 1979), Everton (£700,000, January 1982), Espanyol/Spain (August 1988–July 1989), VILLA (£360,000, August 1989), Manchester City (February 1990), Stoke City (March 1992), Burnley (August 1992), Sheffield United (December 1995), Burnley (non-contract, March 1996); later manager of Burnley (March 1996–97); Sheffield United (assistant manager/coach), Sunderland (coach/scout, seasons 2000–03)
Capped eight times by England at Under-21 level and once by the 'B' team, Heath was a sharp-shooting, nippy, all-action footballer with good close control who pounced on the half-chance in front of goal. He had a fine career, netting

120 goals in 525 League games in England alone (94 in 300 games for Everton). However, he never settled at Villa Park and failed to hit the target in his dozen outings. Heath won two League championship medals with Everton (1985, 1987), an FA Cup-winner's medal (1984) and a European Cup-winner's Cup medal (also in 1985), plus four FA Charity Shield triumphs. Unfortunately, he failed in his efforts as manager at Burnley.

HENDRIE, LEE ANDREW

Midfield: 206+50 apps, 26 goals
Born: Birmingham, 18 May 1977
Career: VILLA (YTS, June 1993; professional, May 1994)
Honoured by England at youth, Under-21 (13 times) and 'B' team levels, Hendrie also added one senior cap to his collection when he represented his country against Czechoslovakia in November 1998. He shared the Midland Football Writers' 'Young Player of the Year' award with Robbie Keane of Wolves in 1998–99 after playing in his 50th League game for the club. A purposeful competitor with a powerful right-foot shot, Hendrie has suffered his fair share of injury problems over the years. He can also be a little hot-headed at times. His father, Paul, played for the Blues, while cousin John starred for Coventry, Hereford, Bradford City, Newcastle, Leeds, Barnsley and Middlesbrough.

HENSHALL, HORACE VINCENT

Inside-forward: 50 apps, 11 goals
Born: Hednesford, 14 June 1887 – *Died*: Hednesford, 7 December 1951
Career: Bridgetown Amateurs (Walsall League), VILLA (amateur, May 1905; professional, May 1906), Notts County (November 1912), Barnsley (WW1 guest), Sheffield Wednesday (player/reserve-team coach, June 1922), Chesterfield (August 1923–May 1924), Lincoln City (manager, May 1924–June 1927), Notts County (manager, June 1927–May 1934, then secretary at Meadow Lane, retiring in April 1935); later licensee of the Navigation Inn, Nottingham (from October 1935)
Henshall played for England in a junior international against Scotland in April 1908 and for Birmingham FA against Scotland Juniors a year later. A hard-running, enthusiastic inside-forward with a powerful right-foot shot, he scored 27 goals in 164 League outings for Notts County after leaving Villa. He was a very popular figure at Meadow Lane and when he returned there as manager the fans took to him deeply as he guided the Magpies to the Third Division (S) title in 1931. Engaged with the Air Service of the Royal Navy during WW1, he also enjoyed photography.

HICKMAN, JOSEPH

Goalkeeper: 2 apps
Born: County Durham, August 1901 – *Died*: 1980
Career: Lintz Colliery, Hartlepool United (January 1927), VILLA (December

1927), Hartlepool United (June 1928), Scarborough (June 1929), Durham City (August 1930), Spennymoor United, Clapton Orient (briefly), Horden Colliery Welfare (1931), Ashington (October 1936), Connah's Quay (retired April 1937)

Hickman was reserve to Tommy Jackson and Ben Olney during his time with Villa. He conceded 9 goals in his 2 games – a 5–4 home win over Sheffield Wednesday and a 5–0 defeat at Derby, either side of Christmas 1927. His brother, George Hickman, played for WBA.

HICKSON, DAVID

Centre-forward: 12 apps, 1 goal

Born: Ellesmere Port, Cheshire, 30 October 1929

Career: Ellesmere Port FC (1944), Everton (amateur, 1947; professional, May 1949), VILLA (£17,500, September 1955), Huddersfield Town (£16,000, November 1955), Everton (£6,500, July 1957), Liverpool (£10,500, November 1959), Cambridge City (July 1961), Bury (£1,000 paid to Liverpool, January 1962), Tranmere Rovers (July 1962, two-month trial; signed permanently, September 1962), Ballymena (player/manager, July 1964), Ellesmere Port (February 1965; player/manager, March 1965), Northwich Victoria (1966), Winsford United (September 1967), Fleetwood Town, Ellesmere Port Town (manager again, season 1973–74); later worked as a Liverpool bookmaker; now employed by Everton as stadium guide and matchday host

Hickson, a dashing centre-forward who excelled in the air, was always hitting the headlines, more often than not due to brushes with authority, yet he was a quiet, unassuming man off the field, some would even say shy! He scored 71 goals in almost 150 games for Everton before moving to Villa as a replacement (or so it seemed) for Dave Walsh. He failed to settle down and was transferred to Huddersfield, Villa losing £1,500 in the process. Hickson later returned to Goodison where he took his goal-tally up to 111 in 243 games. He then claimed another 37 in 60 outings for Liverpool and when he quit soccer in 1964, he had bagged well over 200 goals in almost 450 games.

HICKTON, ARTHUR JOSEPH

Utility: 1 app.

Born: Birmingham, June 1867 – *Died*: Warwick, 1940

Career: Birmingham Waterworks FC (1886), VILLA (July 1889), Rugby Wanderers (November 1890), Coventry Standard FC, Nuneaton Welfare (1901; retired 1902)

Tall, strong and versatile, able to play at centre-half or centre-forward, Hickton's only League appearance for Villa was against Accrington in September 1889, when he deputised for Archie Hunter.

HINCHCLIFFE, JOHN

Outside-right: 2 apps
Born: Tillicoultry, Scotland, 4 June 1938
Career: Alva Academy School (Glasgow), Menstria Vics, L. Pieter's Boys' Club (Glasgow), trials with Sheffield United, Chelsea and Preston North End as a 15-year-old; VILLA (amateur, early September 1956; part-time professional, late September 1956), Workington (June 1958), Hartlepool United (October 1961), Weymouth (briefly), Durham City (August 1964; retired 1969)

A Scottish schoolboy international, Hinchcliffe spent two years with Villa, playing in two away League games in 1957–58, at Manchester United and Chelsea. He was unfortunate to have had Les Smith and Tommy Southren to contest a place with, but later did well in the lower divisions, making over 120 appearances for Workington and 95 for Hartlepool.

HINCHLEY, ALBERT AUDLEY

Goalkeeper: 11 apps
Born: Warwick, 7 August 1869 – *Died:* Birmingham, June 1922
Career: Warwick County (1888), VILLA (September 1890), Cape Hill FC /Smethwick (August 1892)

Hinchley provided adequate cover for Jack Warner during Villa's FA Cup final season of 1891–92, making all his League appearances in succession.

HINDLE, JOHN

Goalkeeper: 15 apps
Born: Preston, 10 November 1921 – *Died:* 1987
Career: Clifton Boys' Club, Preston North End (professional, November 1946), Barrow (May 1948), VILLA (June 1950), Barrow (August 1951; retired, injured, July 1956)

Hindle made only one League appearance for Preston before establishing himself between the posts at Barrow. He performed with confidence and diligence at Holker Street, attracting the attention of several big-named clubs with Villa signing him in 1950, as cover for Joe Rutherford and Keith Jones. He returned to Barrow after one season in the First Division and took his League appearance-tally with the Cumbrians to 266.

HISBENT, JOSEPH SAMUEL

Defender: 2 apps
Born: Plymouth, May 1884 – *Died:* Devon, 1949
Career: Green Waves FC (1903), VILLA (August 1905), Portsmouth (September 1906), Brentford (August 1908), Middlesbrough (May 1911–May 1915); did not play after WW1

Strongly built, very alert and reserve to Albert Evans, Harry Hadley and Joey Windmill, Hisbent made his Villa debut at left-back against Sunderland in February 1906. He made 30 Southern League appearances for the Bees.

HISLOP, PERCY DAVID

Inside-forward: 7 apps, 3 goals

Born: Glasgow, 12 September 1870 – *Died*: Scotland 1929

Career: Glasgow Royal (1888–89), VILLA (May 1891), Forfar Athletic (September 1892), Perth FC (1894–95)

A squarely built player with good skills, Hislop never settled down at Villa despite doing well in the handful of games he played, scoring a goal on his debut in a 5–1 home win over Blackburn in September 1891 when he partnered Denny Hodgetts on the left-wing.

HITCHENS, GERALD ARCHIBALD

Centre-forward: 160 apps, 96 goals

Born: Rawnsley, Staffordshire, 8 October 1934 – *Died*: North Wales, April 1983

Career: Highley Council School, Highley Youth Club, Highley Village Boys, Highley Miners' Welfare FC, Kidderminster Harriers (August 1953), Cardiff City (£1,500, January 1955), VILLA (£22,500, December 1957), Inter Milan/Italy (£60,000, June 1961), Torino/Italy (£50,000, November 1962), Atalanta/Bergamo/Italy (£25,000, June 1965), Cagliari of Sardinia/Italy (£5,000, June 1967), Worcester City (November 1969), Merthyr Tydfil (September 1971; retired May 1972); went into business in Pontypridd

Two years after playing in a local cup final in Highley, Hitchens scored a dramatic goal on his League debut for Cardiff against Wolves to earn his side a crucial victory which kept them in the First Division. Forming a tremendous partnership with ex-Villa star Trevor Ford, he top-scored for Cardiff in two successive seasons, going on to net 40 goals in 95 League appearances for the Welsh club. He also fired in 18 goals in 12 Test matches when touring South Africa with the FA in 1956. After moving to Villa, Hitchens continued his magnificent strike-record and was leading marksman three seasons running (1958–61), going on to claim almost 100 goals, including a 5-timer when Charlton were hammered 11–1 in November 1959. He helped Villa win the Second Division championship that season and reach the League Cup final the following year. A swashbuckling, all-action centre-forward, fearsome and deadly, Hitchens starred for England at Under-23 level and won the first of 7 full caps in an 8–0 win over Mexico at Wembley in 1961. He then spent 6 years playing in Italy's Serie 'A' and 'B', netting a further 75 goals before winding down his career in non-League football. He died from a heart attack playing in a charity match in North Wales. Hitchens was an uncut diamond before being polished into a precious jewel.

HITZLSPERGER, THOMAS

Midfield: 65+19 apps, 10 goals

Born: Munich, Germany, 5 April 1982

Career: Bayern Munich/Germany (May 1998), VILLA (free, August 2000), Chesterfield (loan, October–November 2001)

Capped by his country at youth and Under-21 levels (12 appearances made in the latter category), Hitzlsperger – who failed to make Bayern's first team – packs a stunning right-foot shot and has already scored 3 cracking goals from distance. A classy footballer with a terrific engine, he made 13 appearances for Villa and 6 for Chesterfield during his first 2 seasons in English football, but in 2002–03 he came into his own by scoring twice in 26 Premiership matches. He added to Germany's senior squad in 2004.

HOBSON, CHARLES SIDNEY HERBERT

Goalkeeper: 2 apps
Born: Walsall, November 1861 – *Died:* 1927
Career: Walsall MW, Walsall Swifts (1882), VILLA (August 1884), Bilston (September 1887), Darlaston (1888–89)
Hobson, a very lean, wiry goalkeeper, 6 ft 4 in. tall, was first choice for Villa in 1885–86.

HOCKEY, TREVOR

Midfield: 24 apps, 1 goal
Born: Keighley, Yorkshire, 1 May 1943 – *Died:* Keighley, 1 April 1987
Career: Yorkshire Schools, West Riding Under-19s, Keighley Central Youth Club, Bradford City (amateur, June 1958; professional May 1960), Nottingham Forest (£15,000, November 1961), Newcastle United (£25,000, November 1963), Birmingham City (£22,500, November 1965), Sheffield United (£35,000, January 1971), Norwich City (£30,000, plus Jim Bone, February 1973), VILLA (£38,000, June 1973), Bradford City (June 1974), Athlone Town (player/manager, March 1976), San Diego Jaws/USA (April–August 1976), San Jose Earthquakes/USA (April–May 1977), Los Angeles Quicksilvers/USA (June–July 1977), Stalybridge Celtic (manager, August 1977); later coached the British Army of the Rhine soldiers' children's soccer team and attempted to start a soccer school at Keighley rugby club (1980)
One of football's great journeymen, Hockey's professional career spanned almost 16 years. In that time he amassed over 600 appearances, and in 1968 (aged 25) became the youngest player ever to appear on all 92 League grounds. He starred at Rugby League and Rugby Union before signing for Bradford City. After that, Hockey toured the whole of England, literally! Nicknamed 'Dai Fungus' (because of his thick beard), he won nine caps for Wales (via parentage qualification), his first in 1972 against Finland, making him the first 'Anglo' to play for Wales, and his last as a Villa player against Poland in Katowice in 1974, when he was sent off. He gained a Second Division championship medal with Newcastle in 1965 and helped Sheffield United win promotion to the First Division in 1971. A gritty performer, full of drive and endeavour, Hockey died of a heart attack when taking part in a five-a-side tournament.

HODGE, STEPHEN BRIAN

Midfield: 69 apps, 16 goals

Born: Nottingham, 25 October 1962

Career: Notts Schools, Nottinghamshire Boys, Nottingham Forest (apprentice, May 1978; professional, October 1980), VILLA (£450,000, August 1985), Tottenham Hotspur (£650,000, December 1986), Nottingham Forest (£575,000, August 1988), Leeds United (£900,000, July 1991), Derby County (loan, August 1994), Queens Park Rangers (£300,000, October 1994), Watford (free, February 1995), Hong Kong football (January 1996), Leyton Orient (August 1997; retired May 1998)

Exceptionally skilful and hard-working, Hodge had a fine career, spanning 20 years. He amassed over 500 appearances and scored more than 100 goals. Capped 24 times by England – first in 1986 against USSR – he also played in 2 'B' and 8 Under-21 internationals and was twice a League Cup winner during his second spell with Forest (1989 and 1990). He also gained a Simod Cup-winner's medal (1989), played in two FA Cup finals (a loser in 1987 and a winner in 1991) and in 1992 helped Leeds win the last League championship before the Premiership. Accompanying Paul Birch and Mark Walters in Villa's midfield, Hodge had a fine 1985–86 season, but then Spurs' boss David Pleat lured him to White Hart Lane. He was sent off in new manager Terry Venables' opening match in charge of the London club and after that Hodge's career was on the line. He suffered with injuries but still produced some useful performances.

HODGETTS, DENNIS

Outside-left: 215 apps, 91 goals

Born: Birmingham, 28 November 1863 – *Died*: Birmingham, 25 March 1945

Career: The Dreadnought, Birmingham St George's (August 1879), Great Lever (August 1880), Birmingham St George's (1882), VILLA (February 1886), Small Heath (August 1896; retired August 1898); VILLA (coach, 1899–1900); later licensee of the Salutation Inn, Summer Lane, Aston; elected as vice president of VILLA (June 1910), a position he held until his death at the age of 81

Hodgetts was a born footballer, very powerful, who could also play both inside- and outside-left, but preferring the latter. With his immaculately waxed moustache and parted hair, he was a star performer, adored by the fans. Strong, decisive, clever with many original ideas, he could use both feet, was difficult to dispossess and could unleash a terrific shot. His ball distribution was exceptional and altogether he was an uncommonly fine goalscoring forward who became an admirably fine coach, helping develop several future players for the club. During his years with Villa, Hodgetts scored well over 100 goals (all matches). He won two League championship medals (1894, 1896), appeared in three FA Cup finals, gaining winner's medals in two (1887, 1895) and a loser's in 1892, and starred in six internationals for England (1888–94). A fine billiards player, he won a major national tournament in 1899.

HODGSON, GORDON

Inside-forward: 28 apps, 11 goals

Born: Johannesburg, 16 April 1904 – *Died*: Stoke-on-Trent, 14 June 1951

Career: (initially in South Africa) Benoni FC, Rustenberg FC (1921), Pretoria
(1922–23), Transvaal (1924–25); Liverpool (December 1925), VILLA
(£3,000, January 1936), Leeds United (£1,500, March 1937; player/youth-
team coach, August 1942), Hartlepool United (WW2 guest), Port Vale
(manager, October 1946 to his death); played cricket for Spen Victoria and
Transvaal, Lancashire (56 matches between 1928 and 1932) and Forfarshire
(1934–36); also excelled at baseball

Born of English parents, Hodgson scored 240 goals in 378 games for
Liverpool before joining Villa. He won three England caps and also played
twice for the Football League. The only player to have scored five goals in a
League game for Leeds (against Leicester in October 1938), he first came to
the UK with the South African touring party in 1924 and after some
impressive displays signed for Liverpool. He actually held the aggregate
scoring record for the Merseysiders, which was eventually beaten by Roger
Hunt. He bagged 32 goals in 1928–29 and 36 in 1930–31. During his time
with Villa he partnered Eric Houghton on the left-wing between tedious
injury problems. Taking in all types of games, Hodgson scored 304 goals
during his career. He was in charge of Port Vale when they moved to their
present ground in 1950 and his death came as a great shock to everyone
associated with the Potteries club.

HOGG, ANTHONY RAYMOND

Defender: 21 apps

Born: Lowick, Northumberland, 11 December 1929

Career: Lowick WMC (August 1945), Berwick Rangers (June 1950), VILLA
(March 1955), Mansfield Town (July 1958), Peterborough United (August
1960; retired, injured, June 1961); later became a bookmaker, based in Lozells
and Handsworth (Birmingham)

One-time shoe manufacturer in the north of England, Hogg skippered Berwick
Rangers for three seasons before moving to Villa. A useful full-back or wing-
half, as hard as nails, quick in recovery, he covered for Stan Lynn and Vic Crowe.

HOLE, BARRINGTON GERARD

Wing-half/inside-forward: 53 apps, 9 goals

Born: Swansea, 16 September 1942

Career: Swansea and District Schools, Swansea Town (trial), Cardiff City
(juniors, June 1958; professional, February 1960), Blackburn Rovers
(£45,000, June 1966), VILLA (£60,000, September 1968), Swansea Town
(£20,000, July 1970–May 1972); became a greengrocer in Swansea, like his
father before him, and played intermediate Sunday League football until
1978

A frail-looking player, confident on the ball, Hole made over 300 appearances for Cardiff and Blackburn before moving to Villa. A Welsh schoolboy international, he joined the playing staff at Ninian Park in preference to his hometown. He made his League debut at the age of 17 and became a permanent fixture in the Bluebirds' side in 1960, showing great maturity way beyond his years. While at Cardiff, he won 5 Welsh Under-23 caps and made the first of his 30 full international appearances. After more than 50 first-team games for Villa, he caused a sensation by walking out on the club after a disagreement with caretaker manager Arthur Cox in 1970 – a year after being voted the supporters' 'Terrace Trophy'-winner. His brothers Alan and Colin also played for Swansea in 1953–54.

HOPKINS, ROBERT ARTHUR
Utility: 1+2 apps, 1 goal
Born: Hall Green, Birmingham, 25 October 1961
Career: South Birmingham Schools, West Midland County Boys, VILLA (apprentice, June 1977; professional, July 1979), Birmingham City (deal involving Alan Curbishley, March 1983), Manchester City (£130,000, September 1986), West Bromwich Albion (£60,000, plus Imre Varadi, October 1986), Birmingham City (£25,000, March 1989), Shrewsbury Town (July 1991), South China/Hong Kong (1992), Instant Dictionary FC/Hong Kong (May–December 1992), Solihull Borough (January 1993), Colchester United (non-contract, February 1993), Solihull Borough (July 1993–May 1994); later Bromsgrove Rovers (1999–2000), Paget Rangers (season 2000–01), Pelsall (coach, October 2003)

Hopkins' early career was littered with disciplinary problems, but he always gave total commitment whether playing wide on the right of midfield, in a central midfield position or even as a full-back. An FA Youth Cup winner, he had the pleasure of scoring with his first kick in League football, as a substitute for Villa against Norwich in March 1980. He helped the Blues win promotion to the First Division in 1985 and was a non-playing 'sub' when they lifted the Leyland DAF Trophy at Wembley in 1991. He appeared in 307 League games for his 6 major clubs in England (46 goals).

HORNE, STANLEY FREDERICK
Utility: 6 apps
Born: Clanfield, near Witney, Oxfordshire, 17 December 1944
Career: Bampton Youth Club (1959), VILLA (amateur, August 1960; professional, December 1961), Manchester City (September 1965), Fulham (£18,000, February 1969), Chester City (£2,000, August 1973), Rochdale (December 1973–May 1975)

The versatile, hard-working Horne was advised to give up playing football while at Villa Park. After just half-a-dozen outings covering a variety of positions, he chose to defy doctors' orders and went on to amass over 200 appearances for his next four clubs! Basically a reserve at Villa Park, he settled down as Manchester City's left-back and later starred in 80 games as Fulham's right-half, skippering the Cottagers on several occasions.

HORTON, THOMAS ALBERT

Forward: 1 app.
Born: Dudley Port, Tipton, April 1859 – *Died*: West Bromwich, May 1921
Career: Tipton BCT, VILLA (September 1880), Walsall Town Swifts (August 1882), Dudley Royal Exchange, Swan Village FC (West Bromwich)

A lively reserve to Ollie Whateley and Howard Vaughton, Horton made one appearance for Villa, in a 4–2 FA Cup defeat by Wednesbury Old Athletic in January 1882.

HOUGHTON, RAYMOND JAMES

Midfield: 105+16 apps, 11 goals
Born: Glasgow, 9 January 1962
Career: London junior football, West Ham United (junior, June 1977; professional, July 1979), Fulham (free, July 1982), Oxford United (£147,000, September 1985), Liverpool (£825,000, October 1987), VILLA (£900,000, July 1992), Crystal Palace (£300,000, March 1995), Reading (free, July 1997; retired June 1999)

After a hesitant start (he made just one substitute appearance for the Hammers), Houghton's career blossomed at Fulham. He played in 145 matches for the Cottagers before transferring to Oxford. The son of an Irish farmer, he added 105 first-team appearances to his tally with the 'U's', helping them win the League Cup in 1986. He then did exceedingly well at Anfield, fitting in nicely behind his former Oxford colleague John Aldridge. More prizes came along – two League championship medals (1988 and 1990), Charity Shield successes in the same two years and two FA Cup-winner's medals (1989, 1992). He netted 38 goals in 202 outings for the Merseysiders and eventually won 73 caps for the Republic of Ireland, playing splendidly in both the European championships and World Cup competitions for manager Jack Charlton. A player able to unlock the tightest of defences, Houghton collected a second League Cup-winner's medal in 1994 before losing his place following the arrival of new boss Brian Little. He arrived too late to save Palace from relegation but was instrumental in getting the Eagles into the 1996 First Division play-off final, where they lost to Leicester. That disappointment was quickly forgotten, however, as Palace went one better the following year and beat Sheffield United to regain their Premiership status. When Houghton retired, his record stood at 716 League and Cup appearances and 93 goals.

HOUGHTON, WILLIAM ERIC

Winger: 392 apps, 170 goals

Born: Billingborough, Lincolnshire, 29 June 1910 – *Died*: Lincolnshire, May 1996

Career: Billingborough Council School, Donnington School, Boston Town (1915), Billingborough Rovers (1919), Billingborough FC, VILLA (trial, professional, August 1927); guest for Brentford, Coventry City, Hereford United, Kidderminster Harriers, Leicester City, Nottingham Forest and Notts County during WW2; Notts County (December 1946; manager, April 1949–August 1953), VILLA (manager, September 1953–November 1958), Nottingham Forest (chief scout, July 1959; resigned November 1960), Rugby Town (secretary/manager, February 1961; resigned March 1964), VILLA (scout, October 1964), Walsall (scout, late 1965, then director), VILLA (coach and assistant to Youth Development Department, 1970; director, September 1972–December 1979; thereafter senior vice president from January 1983 until his death in 1996); played cricket for Lincolnshire and Warwickshire's second XI

'Coog' Houghton played his first football as a pupil at Donnington School which, in itself, holds a unique place in football history, being one of the 15 entries for the very first FA (English) Cup competition of 1871–72. After assisting two local teams, he was all set to join Boston United before his uncle and ex-Villa player 'Cec' Harris persuaded him to have trials at Villa Park. Houghton came through with flying colours, gave up his baker's job and signed professional forms, earning £3 per week with a further 50 shillings (£2.50) when he got into the reserve side. As a direct left-winger, he developed quickly in the Central League side before making his bow in the First Division in January 1930 against Leeds. Villa lost the game 4–3 and Houghton missed a penalty! But he never let that affect his progress and was a regular in the side within 12 months (after Arthur Dorrell had moved on). He starred in the attack-minded forward-line of 1930–31 when Villa netted 128 goals in 42 League matches, Houghton scoring 30 himself. Two-footed, fast, strong, stylish in full stride and totally committed, he was a highly consistent performer who possessed a cracking shot, often sending free-kicks and spot-kicks towards goal with tremendous force.

Besides his first-class achievements, he scored 87 goals in 151 WW2 games, and in first team, reserves and other competitive matches for Villa, cracked in no fewer than 345 goals, 79 of them penalties, missing only 7 times from the spot in more than 700 outings. The fifth-highest scorer in the club's history, he struck one of the greatest goals ever seen at Villa Park – a cracking 40-yard free-kick against Derby in December 1931. He helped Villa regain their First Division status (1938) and gained a Wartime League Cup (N)-winner's medal in 1944. Capped seven times by England at full international level, Houghton also represented the Football League on four occasions, was an England trialist, played for the Birmingham County FA Juniors against Scotland in 1928 and had several games for the RAF and the RAF XI. He actually scored a penalty on his last appearance for Villa against Huddersfield reserves on Boxing Day 1946 (won 4–1). As boss of Notts County, he guided them to the Third Division (S) championship in 1950 and seven years later proudly led Villa to FA Cup glory over Manchester United. After five years in charge, Houghton was dismissed as the team began to struggle. He led his team in 223 League games – 78 ended in wins, 54 were drawn and 91 lost.

He then teamed up (as scout) with his former colleague Billy Walker at Nottingham Forest and in 1972 returned to Villa Park as a director. When he died (aged 86), he had been associated with Villa for 46 years. His brother, Ron, played for Notts County. Houghton made his first-class cricket debut for Warwickshire against India at Edgbaston in August 1946, just as he began his 18th season as a Villa professional.

HOWARTH, SYDNEY
Forward: 9 apps, 2 goals
Born: Bristol, 28 June 1923 – *Died*: Cardiff, 11 January 2004
Career: Bristol schoolboy football, Bury (amateur), Bristol City (trial), Notts County (trial), Arsenal (trial), Barry Town (1939–40), Aberaman (1945), Merthyr Tydfil (1946), VILLA (£6,500, June 1948), Swansea Town (September 1950), Walsall (September 1952), Merthyr Tydfil (August 1953; retired May 1955)
Son of a former Bristol City player, Howarth was a tough character with a terrific right-foot shot. He was reliable cover for George Edwards and Trevor Ford and therefore his first-team opportunities were limited. He netted 7 times in 39 League games for the Swans. He joined Villa for a record fee for a non-League player.

HUGHES, DAVID THOMAS
Midfield: 4+1 apps, 1 goal
Born: Birmingham, 19 March 1958
Career: Birmingham Parks football, VILLA (apprentice, June 1974; professional, February 1976), Lincoln City (£20,000, April 1977), Scunthorpe United (June 1981), Lincoln City (March–April 1982), Worcester City (January 1983)
Hughes did very well at Sincil Bank after leaving Villa Park where he was reserve to Des Bremner, Gordon Cowans and Dennis Mortimer, among others. He made over 60 appearances for the Imps and more than 20 for Scunthorpe.

HUGHES, ROBERT DAVID
Defender: 4+3 apps
Born: Wrexham, 1 February 1978
Career: VILLA (YTS, June 1994; professional, July 1996), Carlisle United (March–May 1998), non-League football (from August 1998)

An efficient reserve defender, Hughes spent four years with Villa before moving down the ladder to Carlisle.

HUGHES, THOMAS ALEXANDER

Goalkeeper: 23 apps
Born: Dalmuir, Scotland, 11 July 1947
Career: Clydebank (juniors, 1963), Chelsea (July 1965), VILLA (£12,500, June 1971), Brighton and Hove Albion (loan, February–March 1973), Hereford United (£15,000, August 1973; retired October 1982; then manager to March 1983)

Hughes was the unfortunate understudy to Peter Bonetti at Chelsea and made only 11 appearances for the London club, despite winning 2 Scottish Under-23 caps. After breaking a leg, he was subsequently replaced by Villa's John Phillips and, ironically after recovering from that setback, was then transferred to Villa Park! He struggled to hold down a first-team place and after a loan spell at Brighton moved to Edgar Street. He went on to amass more than 250 appearances for Hereford, helping the Bulls win the Third Division title in 1976. However, after suffering relegation immediately, Hughes the manager then saw his team successfully gain re-election to the Football League at the end of the 1979–80 season. But things didn't improve all that much on the pitch and he found himself out of a job when the curtain came down on the 1982–83 campaign.

HUMPHRIES, HOWARD

Forward: 21 apps, 2 goals
Born: Aston, Birmingham, 7 February 1894 – *Died*: 1960
Career: Handsworth Grammar School, Handsworth Amateurs (May 1911), VILLA (professional, July 1913); guest for Kynochs (1917–18) and Crystal Palace (1918–19); Southend United (December 1921), Rotherham County (March 1922–April 1923)

Nurtured initially as cover for Clem Stephenson, Humphries developed into a very useful utility player, who occupied four different positions during his time at Villa Park. He scored six times in ten WW1 games.

HUNT, DAVID

Midfield: 14+1 apps
Born: Leicester, 17 April 1959
Career: Derby County (apprentice, June 1975; professional, February 1977), Notts County (March 1978), VILLA (June 1987), Mansfield Town (June 1989), Burton Albion (August 1991), Leicester United (September 1991)

When Hunt arrived to bolster up Villa's midfield, he had already appeared in over 350 games for his previous two clubs, the majority with the Magpies. However, owing to some frustrating injuries, a couple of suspensions and a lack of form, he never really settled down with any authority at Villa despite a handful of very competitive displays.

HUNT, STEPHEN KENNETH

Midfield: 76+5 apps, 9 goals

Born: Perry Barr, Birmingham, 4 August 1956

Career: Yew Tree Infants and Junior Schools, Aston and Witton Boys, Warwickshire Schoolboys, Stanley Star, VILLA (apprentice, July 1972; professional, January 1974), New York Cosmos/USA (£50,000, February 1977), Coventry City (£40,000, August 1978), New York Cosmos/USA (loan, May 1982), West Bromwich Albion (£80,000, March 1984), VILLA (£90,000, plus Darren Bradley, March 1986; retired May 1988), Willenhall Town (manager, June 1988), Port Vale (youth-team coach, July 1989; then community officer, June 1990), Leicester City (youth coach, 1991–92), VS Rugby Town (manager, 1994–95), AP Leamington (manager, 1996–97), Hinckley Town (coach, 1997–99), Bembridge FC/Isle of Wight (coach, 2003–04)

An energetic, hard-working, purposeful footballer with a fine left foot, Hunt gave his three Midland clubs excellent service. After scoring once in 8 first XI outings for Villa, he played in the NASL, returning to England to sign for Coventry, for whom he made 216 appearances (34 goals). A further spell with the Cosmos preceded his transfer to WBA and after winning two England caps, he returned to Villa for what was to be his last season in League football. He had the misfortune to play in successive relegation teams – with WBA (1986) and Villa (1988). In his first spell in the NASL, Hunt, playing with Pele and Franz Beckenbauer, helped Cosmos win two Super Bowl titles (1977, 1978) and was voted 'The Most Valuable Player' in the first year.

HUNTER, ANDREW

Forward: 10 apps, 5 goals

Born: Joppa, Ayrshire, August 1864 – *Died*: Australia, 12 June 1888

Career: Ayr Thistle, Third Lanark, Vale of Leven FC, VILLA (August 1879; retired May 1884 with a thigh injury); emigrated to Australia, October 1884

Brother of Archie (q.v.), Hunter had tremendous all-round ability. A strong, well-built forward, he could take out three players with one hefty challenge. His career ended abruptly, and so did his life when he suffered a fatal heart attack at the age of 23.

HUNTER, ARCHIBALD

Centre-forward: 73 apps, 42 goals

Born: Joppa, Ayrshire, 23 September 1859 – *Died*: Birmingham, 29 November 1894

Career: Third Lanark, Ayr Thistle, VILLA (August 1878 to his death)

There is no doubt that the auburn-haired Hunter was a great player – one of the best footballers of the 1880s and '90s. He was an individualist with a commanding personality; he was robust yet decidedly fair and never committed a foul in anger.

Known as 'The Old Warhorse', he was a mixture of toughness and cleverness, a player who often ran down the touchline, pulling defenders all over the field.

He was such an important member of the Villa side that in 1889 he was transported to an away game against Notts County in a specially chartered train!

A business engagement brought him down south to Birmingham in 1878. He enquired as to the whereabouts of Calthorpe FC, which had earlier toured Scotland and played a game in Ayr, near to where he lived. Instead, fate led him to Villa. He never looked back.

It was Villa's George Ramsay who took Hunter under his wing. He looked after the Scot during his early days in Birmingham and initially played Hunter under a different name to hide his true identity – so that other clubs (mainly from Scotland) didn't get to know of his whereabouts!

Hunter appeared in only 73 first-class matches for Villa, but claimed 42 goals, 33 of which came in the FA Cup – a club record that still stands today. Hunter, in fact, was the first player to score in every round of the FA Cup competition – for Villa in 1886–87 when he skippered the side to a 2–0 victory over WBA in the final at The Oval.

A Scottish gentleman and a thoroughbred among sportsmen, Hunter collapsed of a heart attack while playing for Villa against Everton on Merseyside on 4 January 1890. Medical advice stated that he should never play again. Sadly he didn't – and after struggling with his health, he died peacefully in a Birmingham hospital four years later at the age of 35.

HUNTER, GEORGE

Half-back: 98 apps, 1 goal

Born: Peshawar, India, 16 August 1886 – *Died*: London, February 1934

Career: Peshawar junior football/the Army, Maidstone, Croydon Common (August 1907), VILLA (February 1908), Oldham Athletic (£1,200, January 1912), Chelsea (£1,000, March 1913), Manchester United (£1,300, March 1914–May 1915); guest for Belfast Celtic, Croydon Common, Birmingham, Sunderland and Brentford during WW1; Portsmouth (August 1919; retired 1922)

A well-built, powerful player, noted for his tough and vigorous tackling, 'Cocky' Hunter – the comedian in the camp – was rather reckless at times and often conceded free-kicks in dangerous positions while also giving away his fair share of penalties. Nevertheless, he was always a very competitive footballer with a fiery temper. He made almost 100 appearances for Villa, with whom he won a League championship medal in 1910 and twice represented the Football League in 1911, also playing for Birmingham County FA against London in 1909. He made only two appearances for Chelsea before being released – his manager and colleagues being unable to control him.

Hunter went on to skipper Manchester United and played behind the great Billy Meredith during his time at Old Trafford. He was in trouble with United's directorate in January 1915 and was suspended *sine die* for failing to comply with training regulations, and as the club captain it was thought he should have set a better example. Hailing from a military background (born ten miles from the Khyber Pass), Hunter saw active service in France and Gallipoli during WW1 when he served as a company sergeant-major.

INGLIS, JOHN FRANCIS

Forward: 2 apps, 1 goal
Born: Leven, Fife, Scotland, 19 May 1947
Career: Leven Schools, Glenrothes FC, VILLA (professional, September 1965), Crewe Alexandra (July 1968–May 1970), Hereford United (March 1971), Worcester City (February 1972; retired April 1977); later a building society manager in Leicestershire

A reliable reserve at Villa Park, Inglis went on to do reasonably well at Gresty Road, netting 10 goals in 47 League appearances for the 'Alex'.

IVERSON, ROBERT THOMAS JAMES

Left-half: 153 apps, 12 goals
Born: Folkestone, 17 October 1910 – *Died*: Birmingham, 19 June 1953
Career: Folkestone County School, Kent Boys, Folkestone FC (August 1926), Tottenham Hotspur (August 1932), Northfleet (season 1932–33), Ramsgate Press Wanderers (June 1933), Lincoln City (September 1934), Wolverhampton Wanderers (March 1935), VILLA (December 1936; retired May 1948; then reserve/youth-team coach, first-team coach, August 1949; later coach to fourth team until July 1952); guest for Birmingham, Bournemouth, Kidderminster Harriers, Leicester City, Northampton Town, Notts County, Nottingham Forest and Sutton Town during WW2

Iverson was an honest competitor, big and strong, with a receding hairline (he was almost bald when he retired). Noted as a wing-half (and occasionally as an inside-forward), he wasn't given much of a chance at Molineux to show off his skills but after joining Villa he became a firm favourite with the home fans and made over 325 appearances in the claret and blue strip (153 in League and Cup and 173 in WW2 – 55 goals). He helped Villa win the Second Division title in 1938 and the Wartime League Cup (N) in 1944. He also claimed the fastest-ever goal by a Villa player, finding the Charlton net after just 9.3 seconds from the start of a League game in December 1938. Amazingly he repeated that feat on Christmas Day 1947 when he scored just as quickly in a reserve game against Everton. A keen angler and self-taught pianist, Iverson revelled in jazz.

JACKSON, DENNIS LEONARD

Defender: 8 apps
Born: Birmingham, 8 March 1932
Career: Birmingham and District Schools, West Bromwich Albion (amateur, August 1949), Army football (1952–54), Hednesford Town (July 1954), VILLA (trial, June 1954; professional, October 1954), Millwall (May 1959),

Rugby Town (August 1961; retired May 1966); became a bookmaker before working in a bakery in the 1970s

Jackson spent three years as an amateur with WBA before going into the Army. Had a cartilage operation in 1953 and joined Hednesford on his demob, signing professional forms for Villa, aged 22. A competitive performer, he appeared in over 80 games for Millwall.

JACKSON, THOMAS

Goalkeeper: 186 apps

Born: Benwell, Newcastle-upon-Tyne, 16 March 1898 – *Died*: Sheldon, Birmingham, 1975

Career: South Benwell School (two years), Rutherford College/Newcastle, Rutherford College Old Boys, Rutherford Juniors, Benwell Colliery, Benwell Athletic, Northumberland Fusiliers (served in Belgium and France, WW1, from 1914), Durham University (1918), VILLA (amateur, August 1919; professional, July 1920), Kidderminster Harriers (May 1930; retired May 1931); became a part-time teacher; also worked for Lucas (Birmingham)

Jackson qualified to become a teacher at Durham University before embarking on a successful footballing career. A very useful keeper, he was approached one evening during an after-match tea at Newcastle's Station Hotel by Villa's scout Billy Wright, who had been chatting with Norman Anderson, one of the best goalkeepers in the League. He asked Jackson if he would like to play for the Villa. At first Jackson thought it was Bolden Villa (a town side). 'No,' said Wright. *'Villa* in Birmingham.'

After discussing it with his family, Jackson accepted the offer and moved to Villa Park, initially as an amateur before signing as a professional in 1920. As cover for Cyril Spiers and Sam Hardy, he made his League debut against Sunderland in February 1921 and he did well. Then, following Hardy's departure in the August, Jackson established himself in the first team, although he was under pressure at times from Spiers. He went on to amass almost 190 appearances for the club and played in the 1924 FA Cup final defeat by Newcastle. He was one of four 'Tommys' on Villa's books in 1920–21, the others being Smart, Boyman and Weston. Another Tommy (Mort) arrived the following season.

JAKEMAN, GEORGE JOHN WILLIAM

Defender: 8 apps

Born: Small Heath, Birmingham, 19 April 1899 – *Died*: Hall Green, Birmingham, 1970

Career: Yardley Road School, Wolseley Motor Works, Small Heath Boys' Club (1913), Wellington Town (junior), Metro Carriage Works FC (Smethwick), VILLA (amateur, 1916; professional, May 1922), Notts County (August 1929), Kidderminster Harriers (August 1933), Kirkby FC (retired May 1936); later worked for S.U. Carburettors Co. Ltd and was in charge of Birmingham's youngsters (St Andrew's Athletic); played second XI cricket for Warwickshire; cricket and football coach at Rugby Public School; also FA soccer coach in Warwickshire

An England junior international against Scotland (1917), Jakeman was an amateur with Villa during WW1 but had to wait until February 1925 before making his League debut at WBA. With several other quality defenders at the club, he found it difficult to make headway and moved to Notts County, for whom he appeared in 75 games. He played with Len Capewell (q.v.) at Wellington. His son, George, was also a footballer.

JAMES, DAVID BENJAMIN

Goalkeeper: 85 apps

Born: Welwyn Garden City, 1 August 1970

Career: Watford (YTS, June 1986; professional, July 1988), Liverpool (£1m, July 1992), VILLA (£1.8m, June 1999), West Ham United (£3.5m, July 2002), Manchester City (£2m, January 2004)

James, recruited by Villa boss John Gregory to replace Mark Bosnich, was already established as one of the country's leading goalkeepers with 98 appearances for Watford and 277 for Liverpool behind him. He had also won his first full cap for England after representing his country at youth, Under-21 (ten games) and 'B' team levels. An FA Youth Cup winner with Watford (1989), he added a League Cup-winner's medal to his collection (1995) and during his first season with Villa (when he suffered with a knee injury) his form got him into Kevin Keegan's squad for Euro 2000. He helped Villa reach the 2000 FA Cup final after some brilliant penalty saves in the semi-final shoot-out with Bolton. A big, powerful fellow, who dominates his area well, James is likely to have a momentary lapse in concentration, and that has led to goals being conceded. He retained his England position despite dropping out of the Premiership with the Hammers in 2003. He re-entered the top flight early in 2004 when he replaced David Seaman between the posts at Manchester City. He now has almost 30 full caps to his name and played in Euro 2004.

JASZCZUN, ANTONY JOHN

Defender: 0+1 app.

Born: Kettering, 16 September 1977

Career: VILLA (YTS, June 1994; professional, July 1996), Blackpool (£30,000, January 2000), Northampton Town (June 2004)

After making one substitute appearance for Villa in an away League Cup tie against Chelsea in October 1998, 'Tommy' Jaszczun quickly established himself in the Seasiders' side, scoring on his debut against Stoke in an AWS match.

JEFFRIES, RONALD JOHN

Centre-forward: 2 apps

Born: Hall Green, Birmingham, 24 March 1930

Career: Moor Green, Birmingham City (trial, 1948–49), VILLA (professional,

December 1950), Walsall (November 1953), Tonbridge (February 1954), Kettering Town (June–October 1954), Stourbridge (August 1955–57); later ran an ironmonger's shop near St Andrew's

On 17 February 1951, just two months after joining Villa and a week after playing in a first-team friendly against Luton, Jeffries made his League debut in place of Dave Walsh at Tottenham. A big, strong, thrustful player, he did well in a 3–2 defeat and was called on to deputise for the Irishman a fortnight later at Arsenal. Those were his only senior outings for the club. He was a reserve for the next two years before being sold to Walsall.

JENKINS, LEE ROBERT
Midfield: 0+3 apps
Born: West Bromwich, 17 March 1961
Career: Barr Beacon School, Villa Boys, Dunlop Terriers (Under-14s), VILLA (apprentice, June 1977; professional, January 1979), Port Vale (November 1980), Rovenaniemi Palloseura ROPS/Finland (August 1981), Birmingham City (October 1985), Fannairin Palloilijat (FinnaPa FC)/Finland (1986–88)

An attacking midfielder, England youth international Jenkins gained an FA Youth Cup-winner's medal and had three outings in the first XI before leaving for Port Vale, where he struggled. He later did very well in Finland, but failed to finish his only game for the Blues (injured against WBA).

JOACHIM, JULIAN KEVIN
Striker: 114+59 apps, 45 goals
Born: Boston, Lincs, 20 September 1974
Career: Leicester City (YTS, June 1990; professional, September 1992), VILLA (£1.5m, February 1996), Coventry City (player-exchange deal involving Mustapha Hadji, July 2001), Leeds United (free, June 2004)

Joachim represented England at youth-team level, won 9 Under-21 caps and scored 31 goals in 119 first-team outings for Leicester before Brian Little signed him for Villa. After a slow start when he had Tommy Johnson, Savo Milosevic and Dwight Yorke to contest with for a place in the side, he did much better in 1997–98 and became a hit with the fans. He strove on manfully, scored some excellent goals and generally gave a good account of himself, despite suffering niggling injuries and losing his form and appetite at times. A dashing player with plenty of speed, Joachim unfortunately lost his place following an abortive attempt to play for St Vincent in the World Cup qualifying competition during 1999–2000. He flew to the Caribbean only to be told that the games he had played for England at Under-21 level some years earlier ruled him out of contention. He holds the record for most 'sub' appearances for Villa (59).

JOHNSEN, JEAN RONNY

Defender: 51+4 apps, 1 goal

Born: Sandefjord, Norway, 10 June 1969

Career: FC Stokke/Norway (1987), IF EIK-Tonsberg/Norway (1988), Lyn Oslo/Norway (1992), Lillestrom/Norway (1994), Besiktas/Turkey (1995), Manchester United (£1.2m, July 1996), VILLA (free, August 2002; released May 2004), Southampton (trial, August 2004)

During his time at Old Trafford, Johnsen was used occasionally as an emergency midfielder. He was already an experienced international when he joined Manchester United, for whom he added a further 150 appearances. A treble winner with the Reds in 1999, he also starred in the Premiership triumphs of 1997 and 2001 and collected an FA Charity Shield prize in 1997. He has played in 48 full internationals for Norway and gave Villa good service for 2 seasons.

JOHNSON, GEORGE EDWARD

Forward: 110 apps, 47 goals

Born: West Bromwich, 11 November 1871 – *Died:* Walsall, May 1934

Career: West Bromwich Baptist and Beeches Road Schools, West Bromwich Sandwell, West Bromwich Baptist FC, Wrockwardine Wood (May 1892), West Bromwich Albion (professional, May 1895), Walsall (September 1896), VILLA (£300, April 1898; retired, injured, December 1904)

Johnson was a thoughtful and aggressive player who was restricted to just two games with WBA but struck 26 goals in 59 outings for Walsall before moving to Villa. Initially 'strike' partner to Jack Devey and Fred Wheldon, then to Devey and Bill Garraty and finally to Garraty and Joe Bache (among others), Johnson won a League championship medal in 1899 and helped Villa retain the trophy the following season (nine appearances).

JOHNSON, THOMAS

Striker: 49+22 apps, 17 goals

Born: Newcastle, 15 January 1971

Career: Notts County (apprentice, June 1987; professional, January 1989), Derby County (£1.3m, March 1992), VILLA (£1.45m, January 1995), Celtic (£2.4m, March 1997), Everton (loan, September–October 1999), Sheffield Wednesday (free, September 2001), Kilmarnock (free, December 2001), Gillingham (free, August 2002)

Johnson scored 57 goals in 149 games during his time at Meadow Lane and followed up with 41 in 129 outings for the Rams. He continued to find the net with Villa before losing his way under Brian Little, eventually moving to Celtic. Capped seven times by England at Under-21 level, Johnson suffered a serious knee injury at Parkhead that sidelined him for six months in 1999. He regained match fitness at Goodison Park and then returned to have a useful spell back at Celtic under Martin O'Neill, helping the Bhoys win the Scottish League Cup in 2000 and later adding the Premier League and Cup double in 2001. He was a League Cup winner with Villa in 1996.

JOHNSON, WILLIAM WALTER FRANCIS
Goalkeeper: 4 apps
Born: Bradeley, Smallthorne, Staffordshire, 29 August 1902 – *Died*: 1967
Career: Bradeley Juniors, Bradeley United, Ravensdale Mission, Leek Alexandra, West Bromwich Albion (amateur, 1924), Buxton (briefly), VILLA (January 1926), Charlton Athletic (May 1928), Yeovil and Peters United (May 1929; retired May 1931)
Johnson, the son of a coalminer, covered for Tommy Jackson during his Villa days and was on the winning side in three of his four outings. Standing 6 ft tall and weighing 13 st., he was signed by ex-player, then manager of Charlton, Albert Lindon in 1928. He helped the Addicks win the Third Division (S) title in his only season with the club.

JOHNSTONE, CHARLES SAMUEL
Forward: 2 apps
Born: Aston, Birmingham, 30 September 1856 – *Died*: Conobie, Dumfriesshire, Scotland, 30 September 1941
Career: Saltley College, VILLA (August 1878), Lozells British Constitutionals FC (May 1882; retired May 1884 to concentrate on teaching); later headmaster at both Jenkins Street and Burbury Street Schools, Lozells, Birmingham; joined the VILLA board of directors in 1896; became a vice president of the club in the 1920s with another former player, Tom Pank
The son of Fergus Johnstone, vice president of Villa in the late 1870s, Johnstone was a fast-raiding forward who always wore a red skull cap, to distinguish him from all the other players on the field! A grand little footballer, he made two FA Cup appearances for Villa and played in scores of friendly matches and other local competitions.

JOHNSTONE, JOHN CHARLES
Half-back: 115 apps, 1 goal
Born: Dundee, 7 April 1896 – *Died*: Erdington, Birmingham, 1952
Career: High School (Dundee), Dundee schoolboy football, Royal Flying Corps (demobbed, 1919), Montrose (juniors, then professional), Dundee Harp, Dundee, VILLA (February 1922), Reading (July 1928; retired, injured, May 1929); later licensee of the Red Lion (Erdington) and the Holly Bush Inn (Cradley Heath)
Johnstone was a cheerful, well-built half-back, whose speed in recovery was second to none. Injuries prevented him from being one of the great Villa stars of the 1920s, his best season coming in 1925–26 when he appeared in 38 matches. His only goal came in a 2–0 home League win over Leicester in April 1927. He was a very accomplished pianist.

JONES, ALLAN RAYMOND

Outside-left: 1 app.

Born: Winshall, near Burton-on-Trent, 3 November 1941

Career: Hillside Secondary Modern School (Burton), Burton and South Derbyshire Boys' County team, VILLA (amateur, July 1957; professional, November 1958), Nuneaton Borough (loan, January 1962; signed February 1962; retired, injured, May 1963)

Founder member of the Bilston Table Tennis Association, Jones' career was plagued by injuries, his only appearance for Villa coming in a 3–1 defeat at Fulham in October 1961 when he deputised for Harry Burrows.

JONES, JAMES WALTER EDMUND

Centre-forward: 2 apps, 1 goal

Born: Wellington, Salop, 2 April 1890 – *Died*: Bristol, September 1951

Career: Wellington Schools, Wellington Ravenhurst FC, Old Hill Red Rose FC, Shrewsbury Town (August 1909), VILLA (July 1910), Walsall, Bristol Rovers (May 1919; retired April 1924); later reported on Central League matches for the *Sports Argus*

Jones was a 'galloping' centre-forward, who scored once against Bradford City in his 2 First Division games for Villa before netting 12 times in 38 Southern League matches for Bristol Rovers, whom he joined in exchange for Ben Anstey.

JONES, KEITH

Goalkeeper: 199 apps

Born: Nantyglo, Monmouthshire, 23 October 1928

Career: Stourport Swifts (1943–44), West Bromwich Albion (amateur, 1944–45), Kidderminster Harriers (August 1945–April 1946), VILLA (professional, May 1946), Port Vale (July 1957), Crewe Alexandra (April 1959), Southport (July 1960–May 1961)

After doing exceedingly well with the Harriers, Jones took over between the posts at Villa Park during the second half of the 1947–48 season when Joe Rutherford was injured. His debut at Wolves on Christmas Eve drew a crowd of 50,000. Two years later (November 1949), Jones was capped by Wales against Scotland and although on the losing side, the selectors were satisfied with his performance and chose him for the next international against Belgium. Unfortunately, 72 hours before the game he cried off injured and never got another chance. Replaced by Nigel Sims, he later played 64 League games for Port Vale and 46 for Crewe but was a reserve at Southport.

JONES, LESLIE CLIFFORD

Full-back: 5 apps

Born: Mountain Ash, Wales, 1 January 1930

Career: West Park School, Craigath Juniors, Bedfordshire Boys; served and played in the Army (1948–50); Luton Town (professional, October 1950), VILLA (January 1958), Worcester City (July 1959–May 1960)

A well-built defender, Jones made over 100 first-team appearances for Luton before moving to Villa, primarily as cover for Stan Lynn and Peter Aldis. He made his debut in February 1958 against Blackpool when he marked Stanley Matthews.

JONES, MARK ANTHONY WALDRON

Full-back: 33 apps

Born: Warley, West Midlands, 22 October 1961

Career: Warley Schools, VILLA (apprentice, June 1977; professional, July 1979), Brighton and Hove Albion (£50,000, March 1984), Birmingham City (player-exchange deal involving Mick Ferguson, October 1984), Shrewsbury Town (loan, February 1987; signed March 1987), Hereford United (June 1987), Worcester City (May 1991–May 1992), Hednesford Town (on loan, player/coach), Redditch United, Merthyr Tydfil

A tidy, efficient defender, never overawed, Jones gained FA Youth Cup and Southern Floodlit Cup-winner's medals in 1980. He later added a European Super Cup-winner's medal to his collection and also played in the World Club Championship game for Villa against Penarol in 1982. His career at St Andrew's was hampered by injury and he made 40 appearances for the Blues, having played in 9 matches for Brighton.

JONES, PERCY OSWALD

Defender: 15 apps

Born: Aston, Birmingham, 1899 – *Died*: Birmingham, *circa* 1960

Career: Ellisons Works FC, Birmingham University Old Boys, VILLA (September 1919), Cradley Heath (August 1924; retired May 1925)

Tough-nut defender, deputy to George Blackburn, Tommy Smart and Tommy Weston, 'Post Office' Jones was forced to retire with a knee injury at the age of 26.

JONES, THOMAS WILLIAM

Half-back: 5 apps

Born: Edgbaston, Birmingham, June 1905 – *Deceased*

Career: Birmingham St George's, Oakengates Town (August 1921), VILLA (professional, July 1922), Burnley (briefly, August–December 1928)

Jones spent almost three seasons in Villa's reserve team before making his League debut against Arsenal in April 1925. An attacking player, he enthused over attempting long shots at goal and once netted with a 45-yard toe-ender in a second-team game.

JONES, WALTER ARCHIBALD
Centre-forward: 2 apps
Born: Wednesfield, 25 January 1861 – *Died*: Wolverhampton, 1940
Career: Walsall Young Baptists, Walsall Town Swifts, VILLA (April 1885; retired, injured, May 1886)
Slightly built, awkward looking in style, Jones played in two FA Cup games for Villa before fracturing his right leg in a Birmingham Senior Cup tie.

KACHLOUL, HASSAN
Midfield: 25+12 apps, 2 goals
Born: Agadir, Morocco, 19 February 1973
Career: Nimes/France (July 1992), Dunkerque/France (August 1995), FC Metz/France (July 1996), St Etienne/France (July 1997), Southampton (£250,000, October 1998), VILLA (free, July 2001), Wolverhampton Wanderers (loan, September–October 2003; again on loan, January–May 2004); released by VILLA (May 2004)
Villa's second Moroccan international (35 caps), Hassan Kachloul scored 32 goals in 137 League games in France before joining Saints after a successful World Cup campaign. A hard-working midfielder, he signed for Villa on a 'Bosman free' and was a regular in the side for four months before a hamstring injury put him out of action. Thereafter he struggled to regain his place.

KAPENGWE, EMMENT
Forward: 3 apps
Born: Zambia, 27 March 1943
Career: Zambia national football, Atlanta Chiefs/NASL (1967), VILLA (September 1969), Atlanta Chiefs/NASL (May 1970–October 1972)
Zambian international Kapengwe was recommended to Villa, with his colleague Freddie Mwila, by ex-player Phil Woosnam. Unfortunately he failed to live up to expectations and returned to the NASL after just eight months in England. Kapengwe made his League debut against Carlisle in November 1969.

KEARNS, JOHN HENRY
Left-back: 40 apps
Born: Nuneaton, April 1880 – *Died*: Walsall, January 1949
Career: Lichfield City (September 1896), Hartshill Unity (August 1898), Coventry City (May 1903), Birmingham (£100, April 1906), VILLA (player-exchange deal, February 1909), Bristol City (April 1912); signed for West Ham United (briefly) while serving as a private in the Army (1917); did not play after WW1
Kearns, a wonderfully composed player whose attitude and biting tackle were allied to a clean-kicking technique, gave nothing away. Very positive, he had a useful career, and was stand-in for Tommy Smart and Alf Miles at Villa. He

made 64 appearances for the Blues and 93 for Bristol City, but failed to make the first XI at Coventry.

KEELAN, KEVIN DAMIEN, MBE

Goalkeeper: 5 apps

Born: Calcutta, India, 5 January 1941

Career: St Ambrose Roman Catholic School, Worcestershire County Schools, Carpet Traders FC (Kidderminster and District League), Kidderminster Harriers (trial, 1956), VILLA (junior, July 1957; professional, July 1958), Stockport County (April 1961), Kidderminster Harriers (August 1961), Wrexham (November 1961), Norwich City (£7,000, July 1963–February 1980); three spells with the New England Teamen (1978–80); Tampa Bay Rowdies (May-September 1981); voted NASL's 'top goalkeeper' (1978); later a director of the Teamen; also goalkeeping coach to Tampa Bay Mutiny (1996–97); now runs a construction company in Florida with ex-League goalkeeper Peter Mellor

Keelan left Villa Park in 1961 after failing to displace Nigel Sims. At this point his career took off. He had 3 games for Stockport, played in over 70 matches for Wrexham and amassed a club record 673 appearances for Norwich – after his boss at Carrow Road, Ron Ashman, had called his signing the 'bargain of the century'. An ever-present for five seasons, including three in succession (1971–74), he was the last line of the Norwich defence when the Division Two title was won in 1972. He gained promotion a second time in 1975 and played in two losing League Cup finals: against Spurs (1973) and against Villa (1975). A flawless keeper, with a massive pair of hands, Keelan was a spectacular, extrovert showman who overcame early hot-headedness and rashness to continually turn in 'blinding displays' for City. He was acrobatic when he had to be, shrewd in judgement and a tremendous club man to Norwich – although he did become the first goalkeeper in the Norfolk club's history to be sent off in a major game! He also saw the framework of the goal fall on top of him during one game, and faced four penalties, in normal time, in another. He was awarded the MBE for services to football (Norwich in particular).

KENNING, MICHAEL JOHN

Outside-right: 3 apps

Born: Erdington, Birmingham, 18 August 1940

Career: Slade Road School (Erdington), Erdington Boys, Birmingham and District Schools, Brookhill (Sunday League), VILLA (amateur, June 1957; part-time professional while working as an apprentice-welder; full-time professional, October 1959), Shrewsbury Town (£2,000, May 1961), Charlton Athletic (£10,500, November 1962), Norwich City (£27,000, December 1966), Wolverhampton Wanderers (£35,000, January 1968), Charlton Athletic (£20,000, March 1969), Queens Park Rangers (guest, May 1971), Watford (£9,000, December 1971), Germiston Callies/South Africa

(1973–74), Atherstone United (briefly, 1974–75), Germiston Callies (player/manager, May 1975), Durban United (manager, 1979–80), Witts University/South Africa (part-time manager, 1980–81); now works in South Africa for a safety equipment company

Kenning's career in England spanned 14 years, during which time he appeared in over 500 matches and scored more than 100 goals, 59 coming in 238 outings in his two spells at The Valley. An out-and-out winger with good pace and a strong shot, he failed to make headway at Villa Park. He later became a well-respected manager in South Africa.

While with Charlton, he had a lucky escape in August 1970 when his car was involved in a head-on collision on the M1.

KEOWN, MARTIN RAYMOND
Defender: 129+3 apps, 3 goals
Born: Oxford, 24 July 1966
Career: Arsenal (apprentice, June 1982; professional, February 1984), Brighton and Hove Albion (loan, February 1985), VILLA (£200,000, June 1986), Everton (£750,000, August 1989), Arsenal (£2m, February 1993–May 2004), Leicester City (July 2004)

Villa did good business in the transfer market when they sold Keown to Everton, making a profit of more than half-a-million pounds – but should they have let him go? When he joined the club in 1986, he had already made over 50 first-class appearances. He played alongside Paul Elliott, Steve Sims and Allan Evans, plus a few others at Villa, being strong in the tackle, dominant in the air – a defender of the highest quality who went on to greater things. He starred in 126 games for Everton and after returning to Highbury he became an established England defender, adding 43 full caps to those he won at youth (4), Under-21 (8) and 'B' team levels. Alongside Tony Adams, Sol Campbell and occasionally Steve Bould, he formed a wonderful defensive partnership. He gained three Premiership, three FA Cup and three Charity Shield-winner's medals with Arsenal, completing the double in 1998. When released by the Gunners in 2004 (after his testimonial), his record with Arsenal was most impressive: 450 appearances, and his overall career appearance-tally (at club and international level) stood at over 780 (14 goals).

KERR, ALBERT WIGHAM
Outside-left: 29 apps, 4 goals
Born: Lanchester, County Durham, 11 August 1917 – *Died*: Birmingham, March 1979
Career: Lanchester Rovers, Gateshead Colts, Medomsley Juniors (July 1935), VILLA (professional, July 1936; retired, May 1948, having had a steel plate inserted in his hip following a footballing injury); guest for Charlton Athletic, Luton Town, Northampton Town, Plymouth Argyle, Portsmouth

and Solihull Town during WW2; served with the Police Reserve, played for the Royal Navy and for a Malta Select XI; also had a spell with Lovells Athletic; later ran a grocery shop in Aston

Always willing, Kerr was an inspirational player at times. Unfortunately, his career was dogged by injury and illness. However, he did help Villa win the Second Division title in 1938. His brother, Bob, had a trial at Villa Park.

KERR, PAUL ANDREW

Forward: 23+12 apps, 6 goals
Born: Portsmouth, 9 June 1964
Career: VILLA (apprentice, June 1980; professional, May 1982), Middlesbrough (January 1987), Millwall (March 1991), Port Vale (£140,000, July 1992), Leicester City (loan, March 1994), Portsmouth (on trial, August 1994), Port Vale (September 1994), West Bromwich Albion (trial), Wycombe Wanderers (non-contract, October 1995), Waterlooville, Whitby Town (player/coach, season 1997–98)

A consistent marksman in Villa's intermediate and reserve sides, Kerr won a Birmingham Senior Cup-winner's medal before transferring to Middlesbrough, for whom he scored 13 goals in 125 League games. He later netted 14 times in 44 games for Millwall, 20 in 84 for Port Vale (whom he helped win promotion from Division Two in 1994) and ended his career with 62 goals in 339 club matches.

KIMBERLEY, WALTER JOHN

Defender: 7 apps
Born: Aston, Birmingham, May 1886 – *Died*: France, May 1918
Career: Gower Street School, Gravelly Hill, Tower Unity, Selly Oak St Mary's, Coldstream Guards (three years), Aston Manor, VILLA (professional, July 1907), Coventry City (August 1912), Walsall (1914, until his death)

A hard-tackling defender, reserve to Alf Miles and George Tranter, Kimberley was wounded during the Battle of Marne (held POW, October 1914). He died of tuberculosis, due to lack of treatment in an Army hospital.

KING, PHILIP GEOFFREY

Left-back: 20+3 apps
Born: Bristol, 28 December 1967
Career: Exeter City (apprentice, January 1984; professional, January 1985), Torquay United (£3,000, July 1986), Swindon Town (£155,000, February 1987), Sheffield Wednesday (£400,000, November 1989), Notts County (loan, October 1993), VILLA (£250,000, August 1994), West Bromwich Albion (loan, November 1995), Swindon Town (free, March 1997; later appointed player/coach), Brighton and Hove Albion (1998), Chester City (trial, April 1998), Kidderminster Harriers (May 1999–April 2001), Bath City (2001–02)

A competent, attacking full-back, King accumulated almost 150 appearances for Swindon during his first spell at the club. He spent two and a half years with Villa and it was his vital spot-kick in the penalty shoot-out against Inter Milan that took his side through to the second round of the UEFA Cup in September 1994. He then became a 'forgotten player' and subsequently returned to his former club. Capped once by England 'B', King gained a League Cup-winner's medal with Wednesday in 1991.

KINGABY, HERBERT CHARLES LAWRENCE JAMES

Outside-right: 4 apps

Born: London, August 1880 – *Died*: London, *circa* 1957

Career: Middlesex, Clapton, West Hampstead FC, Clapton Orient (August 1903), VILLA (£400, March 1906), Fulham (September 1906), Leyton (May 1907), Peterborough City (October 1910), Croydon Common (August 1913; retired 1919); served with the Royal Flying Corps during WW1

Nicknamed 'Rabbit' because of his speed, Kingaby scored Clapton Orient's first-ever League goal in September 1905. He stayed with Villa for barely two months, replacing George Garratt in each of his senior games. He made almost 200 competitive appearances during a chequered career. In 1912, a legal test case was heard in the King's Bench Division: *Villa v. H.C.L.J. Kingaby*. Kingaby stated that six years earlier (in 1906) he believed he was entitled to a percentage of a transfer fee. The hearing lasted half a day. However, the judgment went against the player: Villa won the case and subsequently were awarded costs as well!

KINGDON, WILLIAM ISSACHER GARFIELD

Wing-half: 241 apps, 5 goals

Born: Barbourne, Worcester, 25 June 1907 – *Died*: Weymouth, 18 March 1977

Career: St Stephen's School (Worcester), Worcestershire Schools, Kepex FC/Worcester (1920), Kidderminster Harriers (1922), Kepex (1924), Kidderminster Harriers (May 1925), VILLA (initially as an amateur; professional, March 1926), Southampton (June 1936), Yeovil and Petters United (player/manager, February 1938; retired as a player in WW2; remained as manager until May 1946), Weymouth (manager, August 1947–May 1960); also ran the Fountain Hotel (Weymouth)

An England junior international, capped against Scotland in April 1926, 'Gypo' Kingdon was a small, compact player who wore his heart on his chest! Very forceful, recommended to the club by Joe Windmill, he was a great asset to the team after taking over from Charlie Johnstone on a regular basis in 1926–27. After appearing in 49 games for Saints, Kingdon, a carpenter by trade, did well as manager of Weymouth, being instrumental in forming the Dorset club.

KINSELLA, MARK ANTHONY

Midfielder: 20+6 apps

Born: Dublin, 12 August 1972

Career: Home Farm (1990), Colchester United (August 1998), Charlton Athletic (£150,000, September 1996), VILLA (£750,000, August 2002), West Bromwich Albion (January–May 2004), Walsall (July 2004)

A Republic of Ireland international with 5 youth, one 'B', 8 Under-21 and over 40 full caps to his credit, Kinsella, an excellent passer of the ball with a terrific shot, had amassed more than 430 appearances and scored 58 goals before signing for Villa. Unfortunately, he failed to get regular first-team football and played in only 19 Premiership games before helping WBA regain their Premiership status in 2004.

KINSEY, GEORGE

Left-half: 3 apps

Born: Burton-on-Trent, 20 June 1866 – *Died*: 10 January 1911

Career: Burton Crusaders (1883), Burton Swifts (1885), Mitchell St George's (1888), Wolverhampton Wanderers (professional, July 1891), VILLA (£500, June 1894), Derby County (May 1895), Notts County (March 1897), Eastville (Bristol) Rovers (July 1897), Burton Swifts (1902–04), Burton Early Closing FC (August 1904, reinstated as an amateur; retired May 1906); later a publican in Burton

Kinsey produced his best football with Wolves, gaining an FA Cup-winner's medal and playing twice for England. A dominating figure, he had a magnificent game for Wolves in the 1893 FA Cup final against Everton before joining Villa the following year. Unfortunately, and perhaps surprisingly, the move from Molineux did not work out for Kinsey and after just three appearances (all in place of George Russell) he switched to Derby. An ever-present in his first season with the Rams, who were also enjoying their first campaign at the Baseball Ground, he gained a League championship runner's-up medal in 1896 and played twice more for England while also helping establish Bristol Rovers (then Eastville Rovers) in the Southern League.

KIRTON, WILLIAM JOHN

Inside-forward: 261 apps, 59 goals

Born: Newcastle, 2 December 1896 – *Died*: Sutton Coldfield, 27 September 1970

Career: Todd's Nook School (North Shields), Pandon Temperance FC (1917), Leeds City (May 1919), VILLA (£500, October 1919), Coventry City (September 1928), Kidderminster Harriers (September and October 1930), Leamington Town (November 1930; retired July 1931); later ran a newsagent's shop in Kingstanding (Birmingham)

Kirton was a strongly built, gifted player who was at his best when going full tilt at defenders, running with the ball close to his feet. It took an awful lot to dispossess him when in sight of goal. He teamed up superbly well with Clem Stephenson and Billy Walker and then with Billy Dickson and Walker and later with Len Capewell and Dicky York. During 1926–27 he lost his place in the team and a year later moved to Coventry. An FA Cup winner in 1920 and loser in 1924, he scored in his only international for England against Ireland in October 1921. A teetotaller and non-smoker, he was also a very fine golfer and had a handicap of eight.

KUBICKI, DARIUSZ

Right-back: 31+2 apps
Born: Warsaw, Poland, 6 June 1963
Career: Mielec FC/Poland (1985), Zastra FC/Poland (1987), Legia Warsaw/Poland (August 1988), VILLA (£200,000, August 1991), Sunderland (£100,000, March 1994), Wolverhampton Wanderers (August 1997–May 1998), Tranmere Rovers (loan, March 1998), Carlisle United (free, July 1998), Darlington (October 1998); returned to Poland, December 1999, after finishing his studies at Sunderland University

Kubicki was one of Ron Atkinson's first signings as manager of Villa in 1991. Already an established and experienced Polish international, Kubicki was fast approaching the personal milestone of 50 full caps for his country and was relishing the thought of performing in the top flight of British football. He had an excellent first season with Villa, appearing in 31 games before losing his place (late on) to Earl Barrett. After failing to regain the right-back berth, he switched to Roker Park where he did very well, amassing over 150 senior appearances and helping Sunderland reach the Premiership. Released after relegation in 1997, he moved to Molineux but never really settled with Wolves and after a loan spell with Tranmere was released in 1998. Ending his career at Darlington, he appeared in 218 matches during his 9 years in England.

KYLE, PETER

Centre-forward: 5 apps
Born: Calder, Lanarkshire, 21 December 1878 – *Died*: Glasgow, 19 January 1957
Career: Glasgow and District Schools, Glasgow Parkhead (June 1896), Partick Thistle, Clyde (October 1898), Liverpool (May 1899), Leicester Fosse (May 1900), West Ham United (September 1901), Kettering Town (December 1901), Wellingborough (briefly), Aberdeen (September 1902), Cowdenbeath (January 1903), Heart of Midlothian (August 1903), Leicester Fosse (October 1903), Port Glasgow Athletic (April 1904), Royal Albert/Scotland (June 1904), Partick Thistle (April 1905), Royal Albert (May 1905), Tottenham Hotspur (May 1905), Woolwich Arsenal (April 1906), VILLA (March 1908), Sheffield United (£1,100, October 1908, with Robert Evans), Royal Albert (July 1909), Watford (November 1909), Royal Albert (season 1910–11)

Kyle, with his waxed moustache and jet-black hair, was a dangerous centre-forward with an eye for goal. In a nomadic career he travelled all over Britain, assisting 17 different clubs, making over 200 appearances and scoring more than

40 goals. He could be temperamental at times and was suspended by Spurs for a breach of club rules in March 1906 (he never played for the London club again). A Scottish international trialist, his last game for Arsenal was against Villa – the following month he moved to Villa Park! He scored 19 goals in 41 games for Spurs, 22 in 60 for Arsenal.

LAIDLAW, JOHN WALLACE

Forward: 2 apps
Born: Muirkirk, Kilmarnock, December 1891 – *Died*: Scotland, July 1954
Career: Muirkirk Athletic, Kilmarnock (briefly), South Shields (October 1913), VILLA (December 1913), Kilmarnock (June 1914–May 1915), Chesterfield (briefly after WW1)
A nippy little player, able to perform in all three inner forward positions, Laidlaw made an impressive League debut for Villa against Derby on Christmas Day 1913, but unfortunately failed to settle in Birmingham.

LAMPTEY, NII ODARTEY

Striker: 3+6 apps, 3 goals
Born: Accra, Ghana, 10 December 1974
Career: Accra Union/Ghana, PSV Eindhoven/Netherlands, RSC Anderlecht/ Belgium (January 1991), VILLA (£1m, August 1994), Coventry City (August 1995; left club May 1997 after failing to obtain a work permit due to insufficient games at competitive level)
A striker, rarely given a chance by Villa, Lamptey's three goals for Villa all came in the League Cup and when he left the club he had 21 international caps to his credit. A member of the Ghanaian team that competed in the African Nations Cup in 1996, he was sent off in the semi-final. Before he was 16, Lamptey had already made a sensational start to his League career in Belgium, scoring in each of his 4 games. In a UEFA Cup-tie in March 1991, his 82nd-minute goal for Anderlecht against AS Roma made him the youngest scorer in any major European cup competition.

LAW, SAMUEL RICHARD

Half-back: 10 apps, 1 goal
Born: Handsworth, Birmingham, 2 January 1850 – *Died*: Birmingham, 22 August 1920
Career: Aston Hall School, Aston Unity (1873), VILLA (August 1878; retired, injured, May 1882)
Brother of Tom Law (a Villa reserve) and nephew of Alfred Law, the 1890s Warwickshire cricketer, Samuel was nicknamed 'Mutton Chops' because of his heavy, drooping moustache and long side-burns. A tough-tackling defender, his only goal for Villa came in a 3–2 FA Cup first-round replay win over Stafford Road in January 1880. He also played cricket for the Warwickshire club and ground.

LAWRENCE, JAMES

Defender: 14 apps

Born: Earlstown, June 1892 – *Died*: Nuneaton, April 1937

Career: Earlstown Boys' Club, Earlstown FC; served in Army during WW1 (from 1914), VILLA (WW1 guest, then professional, May 1918), Coventry City (June 1920; retired, injured, June 1925)

Hardy defender Lawrence deputised for Tommy Weston during the 1919–20 season and was named among the reserves for the FA Cup final before his departure to Highfield Road. He made 136 appearances for Coventry (2 goals).

LAYTON, ARTHUR EDMUND DAVID

Full-back: 17 apps

Born: Durham, 7 February 1885 – *Died*: Durham, 1959

Career: Durham and District Schools, Royston United, Sheffield United (trial), South Kirby (1905), Rotherham Town (1906), VILLA (January 1908, with Ben Jones), Middlesbrough (September 1911), Whitby Town (briefly); to Australia with brother for two years, playing in Queensland; Cardiff City (£250, June 1914); guest for Barnsley (1915–17); Stockport County (player/manager, December 1920; retired April 1923)

A former Durham miner, Layton was a worthy competitor who possessed a hefty challenge and acted as a diligent deputy for Tommy Lyons. He became surplus to requirements when Tom Weston joined Lyons and Alf Miles to contest the full-back position. Layton was with Cardiff when the Welsh club gained entry into the Football League in 1919. He made over 60 appearances for both the Bluebirds and Stockport, gaining a Third Division (N) championship medal with the latter club in 1922. When in Australia he helped New South Wales defeat Queensland in the annual Shield final.

LEACH, JAMES MAXWELL

Wing-half: 78 apps, 3 goals

Born: Spennymoor, County Durham, 10 July 1890 – *Died*: 1951

Career: Durham and District Schools, Newcastle St Wilfred's (1908), Spennymoor United (1910), Spen Black and White (1911), VILLA (August 1912), Queens Park Rangers (July 1922; retired May 1923)

An elegant player, Leach was also brainy, witty and confident on the ball, always having plenty of time to assess the situation before him. After gaining an FA Cup-winner's medal and a First Division runner's-up prize with Villa in 1913, injury forced Leach to miss the whole of the first season after WW1. Consequently he had to sit and watch Villa record another FA Cup final victory over Huddersfield in 1920.

LEAKE, ALEXANDER

Defender: 141 apps, 9 goals

Born: Small Heath, Birmingham, 11 July 1871 – *Died*: Birmingham, 29 March 1938

Career: Jenkins Street and Little Green Lane Schools (Bordesley Green), Hoskins and Sewell FC, Kings Heath Albion, Saltley Gas Works FC, Singers, Hoskins and Sewell, Old Hill Wanderers, Small Heath Alliance (July 1894), VILLA (June 1902), Burnley (December 1907–May 1910), Wednesbury Old Athletic (July 1910; retired May 1912), Crystal Palace (trainer/coach, July 1912–May 1915), Merthyr Town (trainer/coach, October 1919–July 1920), Walsall (trainer, September 1932–May 1933)

Football to Leake was a pleasure! He often cracked a joke with an opponent while robbing him of the ball and regularly burst out laughing just before a corner-kick was being taken. He was a genuine 'Brummagem Button', a good-humoured, easy-going defender whose temperament was second to none. A determined, honest worker, tireless to the extreme, his stamina was unsurpassed. He never played to the gallery, always battling for his team; he never shirked a tackle and gave nothing less than 100 per cent every time he took the field. He was as safe as houses, never dallied on the ball and often came out best in the 50–50 challenges.

He scored 23 goals in 221 games in the 8 years from 1894 (the last 6 as captain) before leaving Muntz Street for Villa Park – 3 years later he starred for Villa when they won the FA Cup. During his two and a half years with Burnley, he played in ninety matches, most of them as skipper. He quit competitive soccer in 1910, having scored 34 goals in 464 appearances. After WW1, Leake attempted to pass on some of his vast knowledge of football by coaching at several council schools and colleges in the Birmingham area.

With his dapper moustache and well-groomed hair, he won five full caps for England and also represented the Football League. He was chosen as a 'stand-by' reserve for his country in 1912 when coaching at Palace. He was nearing his 41st birthday at the time.

Besides being a fine footballer, Leake was also a competent swimmer and often dived to the bottom of the brine baths at Droitwich to retrieve a coin! He was very useful on the athletics track as well, specialising in the 400 yards and hurdles events. He was also a keen gardener, despite being a blacksmith by trade. The original 'Clown Prince of Soccer', Alec Leake was the humorist in the dressing-room.

His cousin, Jimmy Windridge, also played for Birmingham and ex-Villa player Charlie Johnstone was headmaster of Jenkins Street School when Leake was a pupil there in 1880.

LEE, EDWARD BOTTERILL

Half-back: 11 apps

Born: Harborne, Birmingham, April 1857 – *Died*: South Africa, August 1903

Career: Lordswood Council and Aston Manor Schools, VILLA (1874–75 season; founder member; retired, due to ill-health, April 1883); emigrated to South Africa in the late 1880s

Lee was a smart player, hard but fair, who lined up in most of Villa's early FA Cup games while also playing regularly in friendly and other local competitions.

LEE, GORDON FRANCIS

Defender: 142 apps, 2 goals

Born: Pye Green, near Hednesford, 13 July 1934

Career: Littleworth School, Girton Road Gasworks FC, Hednesford Town (1951), National Service in the RAF, VILLA (professional, October 1955), Shrewsbury Town (player/coach, July 1966), Port Vale (manager, May 1968–January 1974), Blackburn Rovers (manager, January 1974–June 1975), Newcastle United (manager, June 1975–February 1977), Everton (manager, February 1977–May 1981), Preston North End (manager, December 1981–December 1983), KR Reykjavik/Iceland (manager/coach, mid-1980s); coached in Saudi Arabia (1985–87), Leicester City (coach, January 1988, then assistant manager at Filbert Street and later caretaker manager, January–May 1991); thereafter acted as a scout for several League clubs

Lee was a resourceful footballer, able to play in a variety of defensive positions. He was recommended to Villa by Hednesford manager Jackie Martin, who, in fact, had been Lee's schoolteacher some years earlier and had himself starred for Villa as a forward. Lee played for Villa in both the 1961 and 1963 League Cup finals, collecting a winner's prize in the former. After surveying the scene as coach under Arthur Rowley at Shrewsbury, Lee hit the rocky road of club management in the Potteries. He won a hard-earned reputation as a soccer trouble-shooter at Vale Park and Ewood Park before being enticed by bigger clubs in the First Division. He never paid more than £5,000 for a player before guiding Port Vale to the Fourth Division championship in 1970. He then led Blackburn to Third Division glory in 1975 and over the next two years saw both Newcastle and Everton lose League Cup finals, the latter to his former club Villa in 1977. He was on £20,000 per annum at Goodison Park (big money for a boss in those days), but he found it difficult to handle certain players on Merseyside and with the board of directors continually at his throat, he was sacked in 1981. He had some success as a coach in Iceland and the Middle East before finally working for Leicester. He kept them out of the Second Division as caretaker boss in 1991 but lost his job for his efforts! Such is football. Lee now resides in Lytham St Anne's.

LEE, JAMES THOMAS
Goalkeeper: 18 apps
Born: Audley, Staffs, 12 April 1892 – *Died:* Dudley, *circa* 1955
Career: Audley Welfare Commission, Wulfrunians (1915), Army service with Grenadier Guards, VILLA (March 1919), West Ham United (briefly), Stoke (£750, August 1921), Macclesfield Town (July 1923; retired May 1924), Burton All Saints

Sam Hardy's deputy during his short stay at Villa Park, Lee (an ex-Grenadier Guardsman and former policeman) often relied on his long legs stopping the ball rather than using his hands. He went on to make 24 appearances for Stoke.

LEIGH, WALTER HERBERT
Centre-forward: 1 app.
Born: Yardley, Birmingham, 12 November 1874 – *Died:* 1938
Career: Hall Green School, Bournville FC (Birmingham), Cadishead Amateurs, VILLA (August 1898–April 1899), Altrincham (July 1899), Grimsby Town (June 1900), Bristol City (May 1902), New Brompton (July 1903), Clapton Orient (1905–06), Hastings St Leonard's (1906–07), Clapton Orient (July 1907), Kettering Town (August 1908), Runcorn (season 1909–10)

Well-built amateur 'Swappy' Leigh's only game for Villa was in the 1–1 draw at Everton in April 1899, when he deputised for Jack Devey. He helped Grimsby win the Second Division title (1901) and netted 28 goals in 119 League games during his career.

LEONARD, KEITH ANDREW
Striker: 45+2 apps, 17 goals
Born: Birmingham, 10 November 1950
Career: West Bromwich Albion (trial, 1965), Kidderminster Harriers (1966), Darlaston (1967), Highgate United (1968), VILLA (trial, March 1972; professional April 1972), Port Vale (loan, November 1979–February 1974); forced to retire at the age of 24 through injury, suffered initially when playing for Villa against Arsenal, September 1975; later became coach at Villa Park (1975–77), Birmingham City (1982–86) and West Bromwich Albion (1986–87), while also acting as assistant manager to Ron Saunders at both St Andrew's and The Hawthorns; was rewarded with a testimonial (by Villa); ran a post office in Shirley, Birmingham

Leonard was a burly striker who acted as the perfect foil to Brian Little after taking over from Sammy Morgan as leader of the attack. An uncompromising player, he helped Villa win the League Cup and promotion from the Second Division in 1975, and prior to his career-ending injury against the Gunners, he had suffered a double fracture of the same leg in a road accident in December 1972. He now lives in Solihull.

LEONHARDSEN, OYVIND

Midfielder: 19 apps, 3 goals

Born: Kristiansund, Norway, 17 August 1970

Career: Clausenengen/Norway (August 1987), Molde/Norway (June 1989), Rosenborg/Norway (August 1992), Wimbledon (£660,000, November 1994), Liverpool (£3.5m, June 1997), Tottenham Hotspur (£3m, August 1999), VILLA (August 2002; released June 2003)

Oyvind Leonhardsen, scorer of 19 goals in 86 full internationals, also represented his country in 14 Under-21 and 3 youth internationals. He netted 29 goals in 107 Norwegian League games before moving to England, where he continued to find the target, scoring 16 times in 102 outings for the Dons, 7 in 48 games for Liverpool and 11 in 72 appearances for Spurs. A plucky, chunky-looking player, he suffered with injuries during his last season at White Hart Lane but recovered sufficiently well to serve Villa for a season.

LESCOTT, AARON ANTHONY

Midfielder: 0+1 app.

Born: Birmingham, 2 December 1978

Career: VILLA (YTS, June 1995; professional, July 1996), Lincoln City (loan, March–April 2000), Sheffield Wednesday (£100,000, October 2000), Stockport County (£75,000, November 2001)

A wholehearted player, Lescott failed to gain a first-team place at Villa Park, making only one substitute appearance in the home FA Cup tie against Hull in January 1999. He made a bright start with the Owls but then lost his way and after 43 games moved to Stockport. His brother, Joleon Lescott, played for Wolves.

LILLIS, MARK ANTHONY

Striker: 37+1 apps, 4 goals

Born: Manchester, 17 January 1960

Career: Manchester and District Schools, Lancashire County Youths, Manchester City (juniors, 1976–77), Huddersfield Town (professional, July 1978), Manchester City (£150,000, June 1985), Derby County (£100,000, plus player, August 1986), VILLA (£130,000, September 1987), Scunthorpe United (£40,000, September 1989), Stockport County (September 1991–May 1992); various coaching positions (1993–98), Halifax Town (manager, June 1999–September 2000)

An attacking player, strong and willing, Lillis was a prolific marksman who scored 63 goals in 242 outings for Huddersfield before netting 15 times in 51 appearances for Manchester City. He failed to impress at Derby but did well at Villa, helping them gain promotion from the Second Division in 1988. He had earlier been a key member in two Huddersfield sides that climbed out of the Fourth and Third Divisions in 1980 and 1983 respectively. However, he didn't have much success as manager at The Shay.

LINDON, ALBERT EDWARD

Goalkeeper. 1 app.

Born: Aston, 24 January 1891 – *Died*: Dowlais, Wales, 1 October 1976

Career: Aston Hall Schools, Vaughan United, Delta Metal Works FC, Birmingham Fruiterers FC (1905–06), Delta Metals Works FC (1907), Birmingham (June 1910), VILLA (£750, August 1911), Barnsley (May 1912); guest for Huddersfield Town (1915–16), Birmingham (1916–17), Lincoln City (1917), Harborne Linwood (1917), Coventry City (March 1918; signed for £1,000, May 1919), Merthyr Town (August 1920; then player/manager, August 1924–January 1928), Charlton Athletic (player, December 1927; player/manager, January–May 1928; player/coach and assistant manager, June 1928–December 1932; retired as a player 1931; caretaker manager, December 1932–May 1933; assistant manager again, May 1933–March 1934), Arsenal (scout, September 1947–December 1949), Cardiff City (scout, January 1950, later assistant manager), Merthyr Tydfil (manager, June 1957–May 1959, August–November 1959), Swindon Town (scout, July 1960), Newport County (chief scout, October 1961, until his death in 1976)

Lindon's footballing career spanned 66 years (1910–76). Competent and agile, he gained a Welsh Cup runner's-up medal with Merthyr in 1924, a Third Division (S) championship medal with Charlton in 1929 and Birmingham Senior Cup and League medals with Villa. He was selected for the Welsh League XI against the Irish League in 1927, but his club (Merthyr) would not release him! His only first-team outing for Villa was against Tottenham Hotspur in March 1912 and before retiring he appeared in a further 325 senior games for his other main clubs (234 for Merthyr). Well-respected, Lindon was an excellent judge of a player and it was he who 'found' Dai Astley (for Charlton). He was manager of Merthyr when they twice had to seek re-election to the Football League. He is also in the record books as being one of the heaviest players ever to assist Villa (16 st.).

LINTON, IVOR

Midfield: 17+13 apps

Born: West Bromwich, 20 November 1959

Career: West Bromwich and District Schools, South Staffordshire Boys, VILLA (trial, apprentice, June 1976; professional, September 1977), Peterborough United (August 1982), Birmingham City (December 1983–February 1984), Bilston Town, IF Kasko and IF Kraft Naipes/Finland (1984–89)

Linton was rated very highly as a teenager by Villa, gaining an FA Youth Cup runner's-up medal in 1978, but unfortunately he failed to maintain his early promise, although he did well in Finland after being converted into a striker.

LITTLE, ALAN

Inside-forward: 4+1 apps, 1 goal

Born: Horden, County Durham, 5 February 1955

Career: Horden Schools, Durham County Boys, VILLA (apprentice, June 1971; professional, January 1973), Southend United (£10,000, December 1974), Barnsley (£6,000, August 1977), Doncaster Rovers (£30,000, December 1979), Torquay United (October 1982), Halifax Town (November 1983), Hartlepool United (July 1985; retired as a player to become coach, May 1986), York City (assistant manager/coach, then manager, March 1993–February 1999), Southend United (manager, March 1999–October 2000)

Little fought hard to establish himself as a player with Villa, but after leaving the club he amassed a career record of over 450 League and Cup appearances before hanging up his boots to become a coach and later manager. As a player he won both FA Youth Cup and Southern Junior Cup-winner's medals with Villa and helped Doncaster gain promotion from Division Four in 1981. Then, as a manager, he successfully guided York to promotion from Division Three in 1993.

In November 1998, for the first time since 1974, two brothers – Alan of York and Brian (q.v.) of Stoke – were in charge of their respective League clubs when they met at the Britannia Stadium in a Division Two game.

LITTLE, BRIAN

Forward: 295+7 apps, 82 goals

Born: Peterlee, County Durham, 25 November 1953

Career: County Durham Schools, East Durham Boys, East Durham Senior Schools, Durham County Youths; trials with Burnley, Leeds United, Manchester City, Newcastle United, Stoke City, Sunderland and West Bromwich Albion (August 1968–May 1969); VILLA (trial, then apprentice, July 1969; professional, June 1971; retired May 1982 after working briefly in the offices of the club's Development Association Department); VILLA (coach, season 1985–86), Wolverhampton Wanderers (coach, January 1986; caretaker manager, August–October 1986), Middlesbrough (coach), Darlington (manager, February 1989–May 1991), Leicester City (manager, May 1991–November 1994), VILLA (manager, November 1994–February 1998), Stoke City (manager, February 1998–August 1999), West Bromwich Albion (manager, September 1999–March 2000), Hull City (manager, August 2000–February 2002); Sky Sports soccer reporter and summariser (season 2002–03); Tranmere Rovers (manager, October 2003)

Little was a star performer with Villa during the 1970s. He won just one England cap, as a late substitute for Mick Channon against Wales at Wembley in May 1975. He was an inspirational, all-action, goal-seeking (and scoring) forward with pace, skill and splendid shot. With his long hair (and good looks), he was a huge favourite with the fans, and top-scored for Villa in their successful

1976–77 League Cup campaign with ten goals, including two in the second replay of the final against Everton at Old Trafford. He played exceptionally well off Andy Gray and John Deehan and had his best season in 1976–77 when he netted 26 times in 56 outings. An FA Youth Cup-winner with Villa in 1972 (against Liverpool), he also helped the team gain promotion from Division Two in 1975 before a proposed £600,000 transfer from Villa Park to Birmingham City in 1979 collapsed on medical grounds. After guiding Darlington back into the Football League in 1990 as Conference champions, he then lifted the 'Quakers' out of the Fourth Division the following season before taking over at Filbert Street. Little returned to Villa Park as manager in place of Ron Atkinson, but in 1998, almost two years after Villa had recorded an excellent 3–0 League Cup final victory over Leeds at Wembley, he was replaced by another ex-Villa player, John Gregory. Little's League record as Villa's boss was moderate: 130 games played, 51 won, 36 drawn and 43 lost.

LITTLEWOOD, WILLIAM ARTHUR

Defender: 51 apps
Born: Aston, Birmingham, December 1892 – *Died*: Shrewsbury, 1949
Career: Verity Works FC, Worcester City (1908), VILLA (June 1910); guest for Bellis and Morcom (1915–16), Bilston United (1915–16), Halesowen Town (1916–18), Ward End Works (1917–18), Coventry City (1918–19), Wellington Town (August 1920), GKN Sankeys (August 1923), Brierley Hill Alliance (August 1925), Worcester City (August 1927)

Littlewood was able to play at full-back or centre-half. A strong, clean striker of the ball, he gained a regular place in the side in 1914 before WW1 disrupted his progress.

LLOYD, FRANK

Outside-right: 7 apps, 1 goal
Born: London, 18 September 1876 – *Died*: 1945
Career: Islington Schools, Finsbury Park, Wednesbury Old Athletic, Woolwich Arsenal (May 1899), VILLA (May 1900), Dundee (October 1901), Dudley Town (August 1905)

A winger of no mean skill, Lloyd was being watched by several Midland clubs before Arsenal swooped to take him to London in 1899. After scoring three goals in nineteen League and FA Cup games for Arsenal, he couldn't establish himself at Villa owing to the form of Charlie Athersmith.

LOACH, ARTHUR ALBERT

Forward: 3 apps, 4 goals
Born: West Bromwich, November 1863 – *Died*: Rhyl, February 1958
Career: Christ Church School, George Salter Works (1878), West Bromwich Albion (August 1882), VILLA (May 1886), Rhyl (1888; retired April 1890 through injury).

Speedy player and a useful goalscorer, Loach played for WBA against Villa in the 1886 FA Cup final. The following season he struck 4 goals in only 3 senior outings for Villa, including a brace on his debut against Wednesbury Old Athletic in a 13–0 FA Cup win.

LOCHHEAD, ANDREW LORIMAR

Striker: 150+4 apps, 44 goals

Born: Lenzie, near Milngavie, 9 March 1941

Career: Renfrew Juniors, Burnley (December 1958), Leicester City (£80,000, October 1968), VILLA (£30,000, February 1970), Oldham Athletic (August 1973), Denver Dynamo/NASL (loan, April–June 1974), Oldham Athletic (coach, 1974–75), Padiham (manager, 1975–76); scouted for several Lancashire clubs (including Burnley) during the 1980s when he also ran a pub; later steward of the Ightenmount bowling club (Burnley)

Described in Paul Taylor's book *Fossils and Foxes* as a six-foot, bullet-domed central striker, Lochhead won one Under-23 cap for Scotland and scored 128 goals in 266 games for Burnley before going on to net 19 times in 63 outings for Leicester, collecting an FA Cup runner's-up medal in 1969. Powerful in the air, he was brave and determined and could take the heftiest of challenges without batting an eyelid. He was leading marksman with 25 goals when Villa won the Third Division championship in 1972, and was also voted 'Midland Footballer of the Year' and the supporters' 'Terrace Trophy' winner that same season. It is said that he was the player who got Villa going and he formed a fine striking partnership with Geoff Vowden.

LOCKETT, ARTHUR HENRY

Outside-left: 41 apps, 5 goals

Born: Alsager Bank, near Stoke-on-Trent, August 1875 – *Died*: Crewe, 1957

Career: Crewe Alexandra, Stoke (May 1900), VILLA (April 1903), Preston North End (September 1905), Watford (July 1908–May 1912); returned to North Staffs, then non-League football; retired in 1915

A very swift and talented winger, Lockett's only fault was that he held on to the ball a fraction too long at times. Nevertheless, he had an excellent career, amassed more than 350 appearances and scored over 25 goals. Capped by England in February 1903 in a 4–0 win over Ireland, he also represented the Football League.

LOCKHART, NORMAN

Outside-left: 85 apps, 12 goals

Born: Belfast, 4 March 1924

Career: Springfield Road School, Windsor Star, Distillery (1940), Linfield (£225, August 1942), Swansea Town (£2,500, October 1946), Coventry City (£7,000, October 1947), VILLA (£15,500, September 1952), Bury (£2,000, November 1956–May 1958)

Initially a fast raiding winger, Lockhart could cross a ball splendidly on the run. He played in the same Linfield forward-line as another future Villa player, Dave Walsh, and they helped that club win two Irish Cup finals (1945 and 1946) as well as gaining a runner's-up medal in the same competition in 1944. Lockhart then did exceptionally well during his 5 years at Coventry, netting 44 goals in 189 appearances for the Sky Blues, despite suffering with injuries, including a broken ankle. He replaced Billy Goffin on the left-wing at Villa Park and after fellow Irishman Peter McParland had taken over the number 11 shirt, Lockhart had a few outings on the opposite flank. Lockhart, who made in excess of 500 appearances during his career (in Ireland and the Football League) gained eight senior caps for Northern Ireland (four as a Villa player). He also toured Canada with the Irish FA in 1953, appearing in seven of the ten games.

LOGAN, ALEC

Centre-forward: 25 apps, 12 goals
Born: Barrhead, Glasgow, February 1880 – *Died*: Scotland, 1938
Career: Barrhead Veronese, Hibernian (August 1901), Arthurlie (1905), Falkirk (August 1906), VILLA (March 1907), Falkirk (July 1909–May 1910), Bristol City (1910–11)

An old-fashioned centre-forward, rough and ready, who deputised several times for Harry Hampton in Villa's attack, Logan won a Scottish Cup-winner's medal with Hibs (1902) and he did well during his two seasons with Villa. He was the brother of James Lochhead Logan (q.v.).

LOGAN, JAMES

Centre-forward: 15 apps, 8 goals
Born: Troon, Ayrshire, 24 June 1870 – *Died*: Loughborough, 25 May 1896
Career: Ayr United, Sunderland (August 1891), Ayr United, VILLA (July 1892), Notts County (October 1893), Dundee, Newcastle United (August 1895), Loughborough Town (March 1896)

Capped by Scotland in 1891, Logan won an FA Cup-winner's medal with Notts County three years later, scoring a hat-trick against Bolton (a joint record to this day). Stocky and weighty, he was a prolific and cunning marksman who was always a danger in front of goal. He made over 200 appearances north and south of the border and claimed more than sixty goals, averaging one for every two games played for Villa. He died at age 25, after a short illness.

LOGAN, JAMES LOCHHEAD

Defender: 157 apps, 4 goals
Born: Barrhead, 8 August 1885 – *Died*: Worcester, 1958
Career: Barrhead Veronese (1900), Queens Park (August 1902), VILLA (July 1905), Glasgow Rangers (September 1912–May 1917); landlord of the Witton Arms Hotel for many years

Logan was a magnificent all-round defender, strong-shouldered, beefy around the thighs and a player who was both fearless and resolute. During his career he amassed in excess of 250 League and Cup games north and south of the border (118 for Rangers). Known as 'White Head' and 'Gentleman Jim', he partnered Alf Miles at full-back at Villa Park before taking over the centre-half berth from Chris Buckley, later switching to wing-half on Buckley's return to the side. Logan played for Birmingham against London in October 1909 – his only representative honour.

LOWE, EDWARD

Defender: 117 apps, 3 goals

Born: Halesowen, 11 July 1925

Career: Halesowen and Stourbridge Schools, Goshill and Chambers FC, Napier Aircraft Co. (Finchley), Millwall (amateur, 1940), Finchley, Kynoch Works XI, VILLA (May 1945), Fulham (£15,000, with brother, Reg, May 1950), Notts County (player/manager, July 1963; retired April 1965); became a purchasing manager for a Nottingham boiler and central heating company; worked down the pit as a Bevin Boy during WW2 (1942–45)

'Sticks' Lowe was a player who thrived on hard work, being first out onto the training pitch no matter what the weather! He was a solid defender, able to occupy several positions. He was tenacious in the tackle and could mark the best inside-forwards out of a game. His leggy stride and balding head were prominent all over the country as he amassed a splendid career record of almost 650 club appearances for Villa, Fulham and Notts County over a period of 21 years. After leaving Villa he made 511 appearances for Fulham (10 goals) and added another 9 to his tally while at Meadow Lane. Lowe, under the tuition of manager Alex Massie, became Villa's first post-war international, capped by England against France, Switzerland and Portugal in 1947, starring in a 10–0 win over the latter country in Lisbon. He was placed fourth in the 'Footballer of the Year' awards in 1963.

LYNCH, BARRIE JOHN

Full-back: 3 apps

Born: Northfield, Birmingham, 8 June 1951

Career: Rubery Hill School, Cross Castle, VILLA (apprentice, June 1967; professional, January 1969), Oldham Athletic (loan, September 1969), Atlanta Chiefs/NASL (June 1971), Grimsby Town (September 1972), Scunthorpe United (July 1973), Portland Timbers/USA (May 1975), Torquay United (September 1975–May 1977), Portland Timbers/USA (1977–81), Halesowen Town (manager, early 1980s), Stratford Town (manager, 1986–87), Redditch United (manager, November 1988–May 1989)

A busy, biting player, Lynch made over 150 League appearances after leaving Villa Park, having failed to dislodge Charlie Aitken.

LYNN, STANLEY

Right-back: 324 apps, 38 goals

Born: Bolton, 18 June 1928 – *Died*: Birmingham, 28 April 2002

Career: Devonshire Road School, Whitworths FC, Accrington Stanley (professional, July 1947), VILLA (£10,000, March 1950), Birmingham City (October 1961), Stourbridge (August 1966–May 1968), Kingsbury United (1969–70)

Rock-hard with a kick like a mule, Lynn – nicknamed 'Stan the Wham' and 'Lynn the Lash' – was an outstanding defender, always totally committed, who was recruited by Villa as cover for Harry Parkes and Peter Aldis (he eventually became a terrific partner to the latter). But surprisingly during his early days with Villa, Lynn played as an emergency centre-forward, scoring from that position against Derby in December 1950 and Fulham in November 1951.

Lynn himself said: 'I wasn't worth £10,000,' but during his 11 years with Villa he repaid that money three or four times over by appearing in over 320 games and netting almost 40 goals, including a host of penalties. He bagged a hat-trick in a League game against Sunderland in January 1958 to become the first full-back to achieve this feat in a Division One game. Lynn won an FA Cup-winner's medal in 1957 and collected a Second Division championship medal in 1960. He also starred in the first leg of the 1961 League Cup final before leaving Villa Park for neighbouring St Andrew's in 1961. Two years later he gained his second League Cup-winner's prize when the Blues defeated his former club Villa in the two-legged final of 1963. Lynn, who quit League football in 1966 after almost 150 games for the Blues, was a keen golfer who later worked in the stores at Lucas.

LYONS, ALFRED THOMAS

Full-back: 238 apps

Born: Littleworth, Hednesford, 5 July 1885 – *Died*: Hednesford, October 1938

Career: Hazelslade School (Hednesford), Heath Hayes Boys, Hednesford Town, Hednesford Victoria (1904), Bridgetown Amateurs (1905), VILLA (trial, January 1907; professional, April 1907), Port Vale (WW1 guest, January 1917; signed August 1919), Walsall (player/coach, July 1922–May 1923)

Lyons was a fearless tackler, a defender with an astute footballing brain who invariably played with his head bowed forward. In his younger days he was a determined centre-half but was groomed into a classy full-back at Villa Park, teaming up splendidly with Alf Miles. Lyons gained a League championship medal in 1910 and an FA Cup-winner's medal in 1913. He later added 66 appearances to his tally with Port Vale.

His brother, Bert Lyons, played for Clapton Orient and Spurs in the 1930s.

MacEWAN, JAMES

Outside-right: 181+1 apps, 32 goals

Born: Dundee, 22 March 1929

Career: Arbroath (amateur, April 1945; professional, April 1946), Raith Rovers

(June 1950), VILLA (£8,000, July 1959), Walsall (player, August 1966–May 1968; then trainer, 1968–75); South Africa (coaching, 1975–77); later worked at Ansells Brewery and for the Social Services Department in Handsworth; now lives in Castle Bromwich

A fragile-looking winger but nevertheless a very competent one, MacEwan had been a regular marksman in Scottish football during the late 1950s, being Raith Rovers' top scorer in 1956–57, 1957–58 and 1958–59, when he totalled 54 goals in 209 appearances, also gaining a Scottish 'B' cap. During his seven seasons at Villa Park he did sterling work in the claret and blue strip, helping the team win the Second Division title in 1960 and the League Cup the following year while accumulating a fine set of statistics himself.

MACKAY, NORMAN
Forward: 2 apps
Born: Edinburgh, 26 May 1902 – *Deceased*
Career: Leith Amateurs, Gala Fairydean, Hibernian (September 1920), St Bernard's (1921), Edinburgh Royal, Lochgelly United (July 1922), Broxburn (August 1923), Blackburn Rovers (trial), VILLA (December 1923), Clydebank (trial, June 1925), Yoker Athletic, Bathgate (September 1925), Broxburn (January 1926), Lovells Athletic (briefly), Bournemouth (trial, December 1927–January 1928), Lovells Athletic, Plymouth Argyle (£200, January 1928), Southend United (December 1934), Clydebank (July 1935), Cork (August 1938), Llanelli (player/coach, September 1938–August 1939), Tottenham Hotspur (scout, October 1939); later worked as a civil servant in Edinburgh

Mackay made only two League appearances for Villa – against Sheffield United and Huddersfield, both away, in 1923–24. With so much competition for places he drifted into the Welsh League with Lovells and was combining playing football with a job as a rep selling toffees to shops when Plymouth moved in and enticed him back into League action. He did splendidly at Home Park, netting a hat-trick against Coventry on his Pilgrims' debut. He was eventually switched to a wing-half position and went on to claim 14 goals in 241 first-class matches before joining Southend, later signing for Clydebank in 1935, 9 years after the Scottish club had rejected him following a fortnight's trial! Described as a 'hard nut, small but tough', Mackay was certainly a player allowed to 'get away' by Villa.

Mackay was a fine musician who could play the banjo, ukelele, violin, mandolin and the bagpipes. He also loved boxing and owned a large collection of football photographs.

His brother, Donald Morgan Mackay, also played football in Scotland.

MacLEOD, JOHN MURDOCK

Winger: 137+2 apps, 18 goals

Born: Edinburgh, 23 November 1938

Career: Edinburgh junior football, Edinburgh Thistle, Armadale (1955), Hibernian (August 1957), Arsenal (£40,000, July 1961), VILLA (£35,000, September 1964), KV Mechelen/Belgium (July 1968), Raith Rovers (August 1971), Newtonrange Star (April 1972; retired May 1975)

A darting little winger, able to occupy both flanks, MacLeod was capped by Scotland at Under-23 level before going on to play in four full internationals as well as representing the Scottish League. He scored 28 goals in 112 senior games for the Gunners before linking up with a variety of inside partners, including Ron Wylie, Willie Hamilton, Phil Woosnam and Peter Broadbent during his 4 years with Villa, eventually being replaced by Mike Ferguson.

MAGGS, PERCY

Goalkeeper: 14 apps

Born: Clutton, near Bristol, February 1905 – *Died*: Griffithstown, 19 December 1985

Career: Bath City (1925), VILLA (May 1928), Blackpool (August 1931), Torquay United (June 1932–September 1939); did not play after WW2

A giant of a man, Maggs had his best season with Villa in 1930–31, when, fighting for a place with Fred Biddlestone and Reg Miles, he had an unbroken run of 11 appearances, being on the losing side just twice. After leaving Villa, he had 24 League outings for Blackpool and 206 for Torquay.

MAIDEN, WALTER HENRY

Full-back: 1 app.

Born: Kidderminster, August 1896 – *Died*: 1955

Career: Worcester Road School, Sutton Swifts, Kidderminster Harriers (August 1914), VILLA (March 1915); served with the RAF in Italy and played unit football during WW1; Stourbridge (September 1920; retired May 1922), Hednesford Town (1924).

A steady, safe-kicking reserve full-back, Maiden's only League outing for Villa came when he partnered Jimmy Lawrence in a 6–1 defeat at Bradford in September 1919.

MANDLEY, JOHN

Winger: 112 apps, 26 goals

Born: Hanley, Stoke-on-Trent, 2 February 1909 – *Died*: Bucknall, Stoke-on-Trent, 18 December 1988

Career: Hanley Roman Catholic School, Cross Street Mission (North Staffs Sunday League football), Boothen Vics (1925), Port Vale (amateur, August 1926; professional, February 1928), VILLA (£7,000, March 1930), Altrincham (August 1934); later worked down the pit

Tricky and elusive with good pace and a strong shot, 'Potter' Mandley could deliver the perfect cross, given the chance. He worked as a haulage hand at the Cobridge coal-pit before joining Port Vale. After 51 outings for the Valiants (6 goals scored), he took over the right-wing berth at Villa from Dicky York, but then lost his place following the arrival of Arthur Cunliffe as Eric Houghton switched wings.

MANN, CHRISTOPHER JAMES

Defender: 11 apps
Born: Guisborough, January 1877 – *Died*: Birmingham, 15 July 1934
Career: Mount Pleasant, Guisborough, Middlesbrough, West Bromwich Albion (amateur), VILLA (March 1897), Burton United (September 1901), Gresley Rovers (1905; retired 1907)
Strong and positive, Mann replaced James Cowan in each of his senior games for the club, and after leaving Villa, he captained Burton in over 120 matches.

MANN, FRANK DRURY

Outside-right: 1 app.
Born: Newark, 17 March 1891 – *Died*: Nottingham, February 1959
Career: Newark Castle United, Newark Castle Rovers, Newark Town, Leeds City (amateur, February 1909), Lincoln City (amateur, March 1909), VILLA (amateur, December 1909; professional, May 1911), Huddersfield Town (£1,000, July 1912), Manchester United (£1,750, March 1923), Mossley (August 1930), Meltham Mills FC (reinstated as an amateur, October 1931; retired May 1932)
Signed as an orthodox winger, Mann made one appearance for Villa, against Blackburn in March 1912 as a replacement for Charlie Wallace. He topped Huddersfield's scoring charts in his first two seasons at Leeds Road and in 1919–20 netted 18 times in 43 games when the Terriers came close to winning the double, finishing runners-up in both the First Division and FA Cup final, the latter against Villa. An FA Cup winner in 1922, a year later, after netting 75 goals in 226 outings for Huddersfield, he was transferred to Manchester United. He played splendidly for the Reds after switching to wing-half and starred in their Second Division promotion-winning side of 1925, being the important link between defence and attack. Nimble, fleet-footed, quick-thinking and remarkably consistent, Mann made 197 appearances for United (5 goals) before drifting into non-League football.

After leaving Villa, he scored 80 goals in 423 appearances – certainly one who got away!

MARRIOTT, WILLIAM WALLACE

Winger: 8 apps
Born: Northampton, April 1877 – *Died*: Cambridge, January 1944
Career: Wellingborough All Saints (school team), Wellingborough Montrose,

Wellingborough (August 1897), VILLA (£300, April 1901), Bristol Rovers (August 1902), Northampton Town (August 1904), New Brompton (July 1905–May 1908)

Energetic and pacy, Marriott had a brief run in Villa's first team when injuries were causing a problem during 1901–02. He netted 6 times in 56 outings for Bristol Rovers and later did well with the Cobblers and New Brompton, scoring 14 goals in 80 Southern League encounters for the latter club.

MARSHALL, FREDERICK ARNOLD

Winger: 3 apps

Born: Walsall, 1 August 1870 – *Died*: Wednesbury, 1941

Career: Broadway Council School (Walsall), Birmingham St George's, Wednesbury Old Athletic, VILLA (April 1890), Birmingham St George's (October 1890), Nechells (September 1891), Walsall Town Swifts (1892–93), Bordesley Green Victoria (August 1893–May 1896)

Determined and able to play on both flanks, Marshall spent only four months with Villa.

MARTIN, CORNELIUS JOSEPH

Centre-half/goalkeeper: 213 apps, 1 goal

Born: Dublin, 20 March 1923

Career: Drumcondra (1939), Glentoran (1940), Leeds United (£8,000, December 1946), VILLA (September 1948), Waterford (player/manager, July 1956; retired May 1964); assisted Cork Hibernians (briefly) when working as an insurance agent in Dublin

'A broth of a Bhoy', Martin, 6 ft 1 in. tall and 13 st. in weight, was a wonderfully versatile footballer who could play anywhere and often did! Under manager Frank Buckley, he had appeared in 49 League and FA Cup games for Leeds United as a left-back, centre-half, left-half and inside-forward, before moving to Villa to become the only Irishman at the club. He was immediately installed in the centre-half position but during his first season played a few games at right-back. He missed only two games in 1949–50 and was a permanent fixture in defence for two-thirds of the following campaign before injury sidelined him for two months. Then, having shown what his capabilities were, he became Villa's first-choice goalkeeper at the start of the 1951–52 campaign, taking over between the posts from Joe Rutherford. Martin had started the campaign at left-back with Rutherford in goal, but once he took the green jersey he played very well, making twenty-seven appearances as the last line of defence in two spells, split when John Cordell stepped in for three games and Rutherford returned for his last outing for the club in October. Martin eventually reverted back to the centre-half position following the emergence of Keith Jones and remained in Villa's defence (injuries and international duties apart) until December 1955, when Jimmy Dugdale was signed from West Bromwich Albion.

Martin scored once for Villa – a penalty in a 4–1 League win at Charlton in April 1950. He represented both Northern Ireland and the Republic of Ireland at international level, winning 36 caps between 1946 and 1956 (30 for the FAI and 6 for IFA). He was rated one of the best three centre-halves in European football in 1949–50 after helping Eire to that historic and record-breaking 2–0 victory over England at Goodison Park on 29 September 1949.

So keen and determined to play football, Martin was Villa's centre-half against Stoke on 10 April 1948 and 24 hours later lined up for Eire against Belgium in Dublin. One interesting statistical fact is that more than one million spectators attended the 27 League games Martin kept goal in for Villa – and 56,177 were present for the Cup tie at St James' Park. Martin's son, Mick, played for Manchester United, WBA, Newcastle and the Republic of Ireland.

MARTIN, JOHN

Winger: 1 app.

Born: Ashington, 4 December 1946

Career: Ashington and County Durham Schools, VILLA (apprentice, July 1962; professional, July 1964), Colchester United (May 1966), Workington (July 1969), Southport (August 1974–May 1976), Torquay United (August–September 1976)

Martin was a useful footballer, neat and tidy, whose only first-team game for Villa was at Blackpool in September 1964 when he occupied the left-wing berth, allowing Harry Burrows to move inside. After leaving Villa, he scored 11 goals in 78 League appearances for Colchester, 32 in 207 for Workington and 7 in 63 for Southport.

MARTIN, JOHN ROWLAND

Forward: 53 apps, 22 goals

Born: Hamstead, Birmingham, 5 August 1914 – *Died*: 1996

Career: West Hill Boys' School, Hednesford and Rugeley Grammar School, St Mark's and St John's College (London), London Combined Colleges (1932–33), Hednesford Town (amateur, October 1934), VILLA (part-time professional, January 1935; retired May 1949); served in Army during WW2; guest for Birmingham (1939–40), Nottingham Forest (1939–40), Wrexham (1939–40), Wellington Town (1941), Aldershot (1941–42), Portsmouth (1941–42), Tottenham Hotspur (1942–45); later headmaster of Lilleworth Secondary Modern School (Hednesford); Hednesford Town (manager, June 1950)

Martin, a 'Corinthian-type' forward, big and strong, won international honours during WW2 for England against Wales and Scotland. He also represented the Football League (against an All British XI, March 1940), the FA XI (against the Army, March 1942), an All-British XI, the Combined Services and Birmingham County FA (against Scottish Juniors in April 1935 and March 1936 and the Irish Free State in April 1936 respectively). Although the hostilities certainly disrupted his career, he nevertheless played in 48 WW2 games for Villa and scored 14 goals (besides his senior statistics).

MARTIN, LIONEL JOHN
Forward: 44+13 apps, 9 goals
Born: Ludlow, 15 May 1947
Career: Cleobury Mortimer and Clee Hill Schools, Shropshire Boys, Clee Hill Boys, VILLA (apprentice, July 1962; professional, July 1964), Doncaster Rovers (loan, March–April 1971), Worcester City (£2,500, July 1972–May 1980), Dudley Town (assistant manager), Tamworth (assistant manager); also earned a living as a stores manager for the Birmingham Parks Department (Erdington) and as a garage manager
A clever, hard-working inside-forward, Martin made only one appearance, as a substitute, in Villa's 1971–72 Third Division championship-winning season. He later helped Worcester win the Southern League Premier title (1979).

MASEFIELD, KEITH LEONARD
Full-back: 3 apps
Born: Birmingham, 26 February 1957
Career: Warwickshire and District Schools, VILLA (apprentice, June 1972; professional, October 1974–August 1977), FC Haarlem/Holland (September 1977–May 1979)
Having done very well at intermediate- and reserve-team levels, Masefield made his League debut for Villa as a substitute for Ray Graydon in a 2–0 home win over Manchester United in February 1975. After his contract was cancelled by mutual consent in August 1977, he did reasonably well in Dutch football.

MASON, THOMAS WALTER
Goalkeeper: 3 apps
Born: Burton-on-Trent, April 1858 – *Died*: Derby, 14 January 1945
Career: Burton Alsopp's (May 1880), VILLA (July 1882), Burton (August 1883), Derby St Luke's (1885–86); later appointed vice president and then president of the VILLA Shareholders' Association
Reliable and safe, Mason weighed 14 st. in his prime. Villa's first-choice keeper during 1882–83, he was 86 when he died. He was the brother of William Bernard Mason (q.v.).

MASON, WILLIAM BERNARD
Forward: 2 apps, 2 goals
Born: Birmingham, February 1885 – *Died*: Birmingham, September 1922
Career: Moseley Grasshoppers (1872), VILLA (player, March 1874; player/secretary from May 1874), Wednesbury Town (August 1880)
Founder member of Villa and the club's first honorary secretary, Mason, tall and

well built, enjoyed dribbling with the ball – to the annoyance of his colleagues! He played in Villa's first two FA Cup games against Stafford Road (Wolverhampton), scoring twice in the 3–2 replay win.

MASSIE, ALEXANDER C.

Wing-half: 152 apps, 5 goals

Born: Possilpark, Glasgow, 13 March 1906 – *Died*: Welwyn Garden City, 20 September 1977

Career: Shawfield Juniors, Partick Thistle, Petershill FC/Glasgow, Glasgow Juniors, Glasgow Benburb, Glasgow Ashfield, Ayr United, Bury (£1,750, January 1927), Bethlehem Steel Corporation FC/USA (August 1928), Dublin Dolphin (August 1930), Heart of Midlothian (£900, October 1930), VILLA (£6,000, December 1935); guest for Birmingham (1939–40), Nottingham Forest (1939–40), Solihull Town (1939–40), Notts County (1940–41), Heart of Midlothian (August 1943); VILLA (manager, August 1945–August 1950), Torquay United (manager, November 1950–September 1951), Hereford United (manager, October 1951–November 1952); thereafter coached local amateur sides in Welwyn Garden City

A Scottish international (18 caps), Massie also represented the Scottish League on 6 occasions, played for an International XI against a District XI in 1940 and helped Villa win the Second Division title in 1938 and the Wartime League Cup (N) in 1944. After failing to impress at Gigg Lane, he went to America to work and play football, returning with an appetite for the game that he never lost. A player who always wore an odd-sized pair of boots every time he took the field, Massie was successfully converted from an inside-forward into a wing-half at Tynecastle. He was a methodical footballer with poise, skill and commitment. He had remarkable positional sense and drove his team-mates on with unstinting determination. He made well over 350 senior appearances either side of the border before the outbreak of WW2, and besides his Villa peacetime record of over 150 games, Massie added 131 to his tally during the hostilities before retiring to become manager. Barracked by a small minority of Villa supporters after failing to bring success on the field, he bossed the team in 168 League matches, winning 68 and drawing 40.

MATTHEWS, WILLIAM

Centre-forward: 25 apps, 12 goals

Born: Mansfield, July 1880 – *Died*: 1916

Career: Ripley Athletic, VILLA (October 1903), Nottingham Forest (reserves, briefly), Notts County (December 1906), Derby County (July 1912), Newport County (August 1912 until his death)

Matthews – aggressive and full of enterprise – scored a goal every two games for Villa. He went on to net 36 times in 177 League starts for Notts County and is one of only a handful of players to have served with 3 different clubs named County.

MAUND, JOHN HENRY
Winger: 48 apps, 8 goals
Born: Hednesford, 5 January 1914 – *Died*: Hednesford, 1994
Career: Cannock Boys, Hednesford Town (1932), VILLA (October 1934), Nottingham Forest (July 1939); guest for Hednesford Town (1940–42), Notts County (1943–44), Northampton Town (1943–44), Walsall (1943–44), Port Vale (1944–45); Walsall (signed October 1946–April 1948; assistant trainer at Fellows Park, August 1948; head trainer, August 1950–January 1958), Hednesford Town (manager, August 1961–63)

Short and stocky (5 ft 4 in. tall and barely 11 st. in weight), Maund's best season with Villa was in 1936–37 when he made 30 League appearances. His career was severely disrupted by WW2 but after the war he netted 7 times in 32 Third Division (S) games for the Saddlers. He died from a heart attack.

McAULEY, WILLIAM
Inside-forward: 6 apps
Born: Glasgow, 1 November 1879 – *Died*: Scotland, *circa* 1950
Career: Glasgow and District Schools, Cambuslang Hibernian, Celtic (April 1898), Sheffield Wednesday (October 1898), Dundee (February 1899), Walsall Town Swifts (May 1899), VILLA (August 1900), Portsmouth (May 1901), Middlesbrough (July 1902), Aberdeen (July 1903), Falkirk (May 1906), Hibernian (May 1907), Alloa Athletic (May 1909; retired April 1913)

An orthodox forward, McAuley deputised for Jack Devey in Villa's first team in 1900–01. He made 28 appearances for Walsall, 21 for Middlesbrough and 11 in the Southern League with Pompey.

McAVENNIE, FRANK
Striker: 0+3 apps
Born: Glasgow, 22 November 1959
Career: St Johnstone Boys' club (1978), St Mirren (March 1980), West Ham United (£340,000, June 1985), Celtic (£800,000, October 1987), West Ham United (£1.25m, March 1989), VILLA (on trial, August–September 1992), Celtic (January 1993–June 1994), Swindon Town (loan, February 1994)

After doing well north of the border with St Mirren (50 goals in 135 League games), McAvennie made a massive impact in the Football League with West Ham. Teaming up with Tony Cottee, he netted 39 times in less than 100 appearances for the Hammers in his first 2 seasons at Upton Park. After returning to Scotland, he notched 35 goals in 70 appearances for Celtic before having a second spell at West Ham. Manager Ron Atkinson enticed him to Villa Park early in the 1992–93 season, but he failed to meet the required standards and left without ever starting a game. An international youth-team player, McAvennie was voted Scotland's 'Young Player of the Year' in 1982. He won five Under-21 caps with St Mirren and later added five full caps to his tally with West Ham and Celtic and also helped the Bhoys complete the double in 1988.

McCANN, GAVIN PETER

Midfield: 35 apps, 2 goals

Born: Blackpool, 10 January 1978

Career: Everton (apprentice, June 1992; professional, July 1995), Sunderland (£500,000, November 1998), VILLA (£2.25m, July 2003)

An England international (capped once against Spain in 2001), McCann was manager David O'Leary's first major signing for Villa, after appearing in 134 competitive matches for Sunderland. An industrious player, a real all-rounder with a great engine, he is also aggressive and over the years has picked up a fair amount of yellow cards. He made his Villa debut against Portsmouth in August 2003.

McCLURE, ALEXANDER

Defender: 7 apps

Born: Workington, 3 April 1892 – *Died*: Birmingham, August 1973

Career: Grangemouth Juniors (Cumbria), South Bank, Grangetown Juniors, Birmingham (August 1911); guest for Bellis and Morcom (1916); VILLA (December 1923), Stoke (October 1924), Coventry City (May 1926), Walsall (March-May 1928), Luton Town (coach, briefly), Birmingham City (coach, August 1928; assistant manager, 1929–32); played for Market Harborough Town (August 1929–May 1931) when registered at St Andrew's; Bromsgrove Rovers (coach), Market Harborough (coach); later worked for Rudge Motor Cycles and ran a haulage business in Small Heath

McClure was a solid defender with superb positional sense who served with five different Midland clubs (1911–28). He became the fulcrum of the defence at St Andrew's and for almost 12 seasons was like a rock, accumulating a fine record of 198 senior appearances and scoring 4 goals. He spent just ten months at Villa Park, deputising for both George Blackburn and Vic Milne. A sailor during WW1, McClure participated in the Zeebrugge Affair (one of the great military actions) and after the war he returned to St Andrew's and helped the Blues win the Second Division championship (1921). In May 1923, when on tour with the Blues in Spain, he was sent off against Real Madrid for telling his goalkeeper, Dan Tremelling, where to stand (by an upright) when facing a penalty kick! His brother, Sammy, played for Blackburn, and his nephew, Joe, played for Everton.

McDONALD, ROBERT WOOD

Midfield/left-back: 40+6 apps, 5 goals

Born: Aberdeen, 13 April 1955

Career: Aberdeen schoolboy football, King Street Sports Club (Aberdeen), VILLA (apprentice, June 1971; professional, September 1972), Coventry City (£45,000, August 1976), Manchester City (October 1980), Oxford United (September 1983), Leeds United (£25,000, February 1987), Wolverhampton Wanderers (loan, February–March 1988), VS Rugby (July

1988), Burton Albion (1990), Redditch United (1991), Armitage (1991–92), Burton Albion (1992–93)

Efficient and hard-working, McDonald had a fine career as a professional footballer, amassing well over 500 appearances for 6 different clubs with his best set of statistics coming at Highfield Road: 15 goals in 180 outings. Capped by Scotland at schoolboy level, he also played for his country's youth team. He made almost 50 appearances for Villa, gained both Junior Floodlit League Cup and FA Youth Cup-winner's medals in 1971–72, received a League Cup-winner's tankard in 1975 and helped Villa win promotion from the Second Division that same year. He was one of John Bond's first signings for Manchester City.

McELENY, CHARLES RICHARD
Right-half: 1 app.
Born: Glasgow, 6 February 1872 – *Died:* Scotland, 1 August 1908
Career: Greenock Volunteers, Abercorn, Celtic (November 1893), Burnley (November 1895), Celtic (May 1896), New Brighton (August 1897), VILLA (May 1899), Swindon Town (May 1900), Brentford (August 1901), Morton (August 1902), Edinburgh Thistle (season 1903–04)

With a never-tiring thirst for work, McEleny was a forceful player who made well over 100 senior appearances during his career. He was given just one first-team outing by Villa, taking over from Tommy Bowman at Preston in December 1899 when he had a hand in two of the goals in a 5–0 win. Unfortunately, he seemed to have a lukewarm approach to training.

McGRATH, JOHN
Midfield: 0+3 apps
Born: Limerick, Ireland 27 March 1980
Career: Irish junior football, Belvedere FC (1996), VILLA (professional, March 1998), Dagenham and Redbridge (briefly), Doncaster Rovers (free, August 2003)

An aggressive Republic of Ireland Under-21 international, McGrath made his Premiership debut for Villa as a second-half substitute for Steve Staunton in the game at Chelsea on New Year's Day 2001. He had just two more outings before being released.

McGRATH, PAUL
Defender: 315+8 apps, 10 goals
Born: Ealing, London, 4 December 1959
Career: St Patrick's Athletic (Dublin), Manchester United (£30,000, April 1982), VILLA (£450,000, August 1989), Derby County (£100,000, October 1996), Sheffield United (free, August 1997; retired May 1998)

McGrath was 22 when Ron Atkinson signed him for Manchester United. A tall, commanding centre-back, well-built, he was cool, controlled and steady under pressure and went on to play in almost 200 first-class games during his

7 years at Old Trafford (16 goals), gaining an FA Cup-winner's medal in 1985. Despite his dodgy knees, McGrath continued to do the business for Villa and he certainly paid back the near half-a-million pound transfer fee (with interest)! He helped Villa beat his old club United in the 1994 League Cup final and added a second League Cup medal to his collection in 1996 (against Leeds). As his career continued, so his performances got better and better. He went on to win 83 full international caps for the Republic of Ireland before moving to Derby in 1996. He ended his career with 648 senior appearances under his belt. In May 1995 over 12,000 fans paid £98,900 to see Villa beat the Blues 2–0 in McGrath's testimonial match.

McINALLY, ALAN BRUCE

Striker: 63+9 apps, 28 goals
Born: Ayr, Ayrshire, 10 February 1963
Career: Ayrshire and District Schools, Ayr United (1979–80), Celtic (£110,000, August 1985), VILLA (£225,000, July 1987), Bayern Munich/Germany (£1m, July 1989; retired May 1992); later a journalist, working for the *Sunday Mercury* newspaper and soccer analyst on TV programmes, including Sky Sports

McInally had a rather disappointing first season in English football, scoring just six goals in thirty-one games for Villa. But then he netted in each of his first four League matches at the start of 1988–89 and went on to finish with an excellent record before his move over to the Bundesliga. A member of the Scottish 1990 World Cup squad, McInally, strong and powerful, went on to gain eight full caps for his country. He helped Celtic win the Scottish Premiership in 1985 and 1986 and was a member of Villa's Second Division promotion-winning side in 1988. He hit 35 goals in 200 games for Ayr, notched 22 in 86 outings for Celtic and went on to average a goal every 3 games with Bayern.

McKENZIE, JOHN WILSON

Right-back: 5 apps
Born: Montrose, September 1875 – *Died*: Scotland, 1943
Career: Montrose (1902–04), Dundee (August 1904), VILLA (April 1908), Bristol Rovers (July 1909; retired, with back injury, May 1914)

Well-built with a strong kick, McKenzie made well over one hundred appearances for Dundee before moving to Villa, where he spent just the one season, deputising in five games for the injured Tommy Lyons.

McKNIGHT, THOMAS VICTOR

Inside-forward: 10 apps, 3 goals
Born: Lichfield, April 1868 – *Died*: Birmingham, 1930
Career: Lichfield St Paul's, Burton Swifts (August 1889), VILLA (May 1890), Leek Alexandra (September 1891–May 1893)

Of medium height but weighty, McKnight was a plucky competitor who struggled with injuries throughout his career. He was sent off, along with Welsh international Caesar Jenkyns, for fighting in a 'friendly' encounter against Small Heath in February 1891.

McLACHLAN, ALBERT JAMES

Left-half: 3 apps

Born: Kirkcudbright, 18 February 1892 – *Died*: Edinburgh, 1956

Career: St Cuthbert Wanderers, VILLA (September 1913), Aberdeen (July 1914), Dundee (briefly); served in the Military (1916–19); guest for Leeds City (1918–19); re-engaged by Aberdeen (August 1919), Heart of Midlothian (September 1927; retired, with a persistent groin injury, May 1928)

Younger brother of John (q.v.), McLachlan was a tigerish competitor who tackled strongly. He also had the positional know-how but never settled in Birmingham and made only 3 appearances for Villa before going on to amass 358 for Aberdeen (16 goals). The first player to receive two benefits from the Dons, McLachlan represented the Scottish League in 1920.

McLACHLAN, JOHN ANDREW

Inside-forward: 17 apps, 3 goals

Born: Dumfries, July 1888 – *Died*: Glasgow, January 1944

Career: St Catherine's Boys' Club, Partick Thistle (1907), Dundee (1909), VILLA (August 1912), Dundee (August 1915); guest for Leicester Fosse (1916–17); did not figure after WW1

A player with boundless energy, McLachlan had done well with Dundee before trying his luck with Villa. After languishing in the reserves for long periods, he returned to Dens Park, where he ended his career. He was the brother of Albert McLachlan (q.v.).

McLAVERTY, JOHN GEORGE

Centre-half: 2 apps

Born: South Shields, 14 October 1892 – *Died*: Durham, 1957

Career: Chester Moor, Sacriston United (1910–12), Birtley Colliery, VILLA (February 1913), Chesterfield (£25, May 1914), South Shields (loan, August–September 1914), served in WW1; Wallsend FC (November 1919), Shildon Athletic (August 1921), West Stanley (July 1922–April 1923)

A well-built defender, McLaverty was reserve to Jimmy Harrop at Villa and consequently found it difficult to gain a place in the side. He made his League debut on Christmas Day 1913, in a 2–0 win at Derby.

McLOUGHLIN, ALAN FRANCIS

Midfield: 1 app.

Born: Manchester, 20 April 1967

Career: Manchester United (YTS, June 1983; professional, April 1985), Swindon Town (free, August 1986), Torquay United (loan, March 1987), Southampton (£1m, December 1990), VILLA (loan, September 1991),

Portsmouth (£400,000, February 1992), Wigan Athletic (£250,000, December 1999), Rochdale (free, December 2001–May 2002)

McLoughlin, capped 42 times by the Republic of Ireland and once by his country's 'B' team, appeared in over 600 senior games as a professional, having failed to make the first XI at Old Trafford!

McLUCKIE, JAMES SIME

Left-half/inside-left: 15 apps, 1 goal

Born: Stonehouse, Lanarkshire, 2 April 1908 – *Died*: Edinburgh, November 1986

Career: Hamilton Acciesy, Tranent Juniors, Hamilton Academical (July 1928), Manchester City (February 1933), VILLA (£6,500, December 1934), Ipswich Town (July 1936); guest for Hamilton Academical (1939–40), Norwich City (1939–40), Southend United (1940–41), Leyton Orient (1942–44), Queens Park Rangers (1943–44); Clacton Town (player, coach/manager, July 1947; retired as a player, June 1949)

A brilliant ball-artist and inspiring captain, McLuckie was capped by Scotland against Wales in 1934. He made over 50 appearances for Hamilton and 37 for Manchester City before joining Villa. He served Ipswich superbly for 3 years, being the first player to sign professional forms for the Portman Road club, for whom he netted 12 goals in 124 games, skippering them in their first season of League football (1938–39).

McLUCKIE, JASPER

Forward: 62 apps, 45 goals

Born: Lancashire, 1 January 1878 – *Died*: Scotland, 1924

Career: Glasgow Perthshire (trial, July 1895; signed December 1895), Accrington Fereday, Pine Villa Colts, Darwen (trial), Jordanhill FC (1896), Bury (1898), VILLA (September 1901), Plymouth Argyle (May 1904), Dundee (April 1905), Third Lanark (season 1906–07)

Described as being a 'grand goalscoring forward', McLuckie was sharp and incisive inside the penalty area, a real terrier whose career record was outstanding. After striking 31 goals for Bury, and doing the business for Villa, he added 6 more goals to his tally with Plymouth. Unfortunately, a knee injury cut short his career.

McMAHON, PATRICK

Midfield/forward: 141+9 apps, 30 goals

Born: Croy, near Kilsyth, Scotland, 19 September 1945

Career: Glasgow and Kilsyth District Schools, Inverness Colts, Kilsyth Rangers (1965–67), Dumbarton (trial), Chelsea (trial), Celtic (August 1967), VILLA (free, June 1969), Portland Timbers/NASL (March 1976), Caribous/Colorado, NASL (1977), Atlanta Chiefs/NASL (assistant manager/coach, 1978; retired 1980); continued to live in USA; formed his own company, supplying aluminium to the industry; later a copywriter for an agency in Portland, Oregon (USA)

'Mahogany' McMahon was a skilful ball-player, fast, alert with good heading ability and a powerful right-foot shot. He scored Villa's winning goal in the 1970–71 League Cup semi-final second-leg victory over Manchester United, only to receive a loser's medal when Spurs triumphed at Wembley. He helped Villa win the Third Division title the following season, having been a Scottish Junior Cup winner with Kilsyth Rangers in 1967.

McMAHON, STEPHEN

Midfield: 90+1 apps, 7 goals
Born: Liverpool, 20 August 1961
Career: Everton (apprentice, June 1977; professional, August 1979), VILLA (£300,000, May 1983), Liverpool (£350,000, September 1985), Manchester City (December 1991), Swindon Town (player/manager, November 1994–October 1999), Blackpool (manager, January 2000–May 2004)

An aggressive, hard-tackling, totally committed footballer, McMahon gained medals galore at Anfield – three League championships (1986, 1988, 1990), two for winning the FA Cup (1988, 1989), a European Super Cup-winning trophy (1989) and three FA Charity Shield prizes (1986, 1988, 1989). He won seventeen caps for England, played in six Under-21 and two 'B' internationals and was in his country's 1990 World Cup squad. McMahon made 120 appearances for Everton (14 goals scored), starred in 277 matches for Liverpool (50 goals), netted once in 90 outings for Manchester City and made 51 appearances for Swindon. He battled well at Villa Park, manning midfield with Dennis Mortimer, Alan Curbishley and also Gordon Cowans. McMahon's son, Stephen junior, joined Blackpool as a professional in 2002.

McMORRAN, JAMES WILSON

Midfield: 12 apps
Born: Muirkirk, Ayrshire, 29 October 1942
Career: VILLA (junior, July 1958; professional, October 1959), Falkirk (trial, January 1963), Third Lanark (February 1963), Walsall (£6,000, November 1964), Swansea City (June 1968), Walsall (November 1968), Notts County (July 1969), Halifax Town (August 1970), Worcester City (July 1971), Hednesford Town (briefly), Blakenhall (1973), Redditch United (August 1974), Rushall Olympic (April 1979); Villa Old Stars

McMorran won Scottish schoolboy honours as a teenager but failed to make an impact at Villa Park. He did well in Scotland and made over 100 appearancees for Walsall.

McMULLAN, JAMES

Half-back: no apps
Born: Denny, Stirlingshire, 26 March 1895 – *Died*: Sheffield, 28 November 1964
Career: Denny Hibernians, Third Lanark (1911–12), Partick Thistle (November

1913), Maidstone United (player/manager, July 1921), Partick Thistle (August 1923), Manchester City (£4,700, February 1926; retired May 1933), Oldham Athletic (manager, May 1933–May 1934), VILLA (manager, May 1934–October 1936), Notts County (manager, November 1936–December 1937), Sheffield Wednesday (manager, December 1937–April 1942); not involved in football after WW2

Capped sixteen times by Scotland, McMullan also appeared in four Victory internationals and represented the Scottish League on four occasions. He helped Manchester City win the Second Division title in 1928 and reach the 1926 and 1933 FA Cup finals, receiving a runner's-up medal each time. He missed the Scottish Cup final with Partick in 1921 through injury. A fine captain for both club and country, McMullan led the famous Wembley Wizards to that emphatic 5–1 victory over England at Wembley on 31 March 1928. In the early 1920s he turned down a £5,000 transfer to Newcastle, preferring to stay in Scottish football, but later came south and played in 242 matches for Manchester City. As a manager he took Villa into the Second Division after spending well over £30,000 on new players! However, he steered Sheffield Wednesday clear of relegation to Division Three, before missing promotion to the First Division by just a point in 1938–39.

As manager of Villa, McMullan saw the team play 53 League games, winning 17 and drawing 15.

McNAUGHT, KENNETH

Centre-half: 260 apps, 13 goals

Born: Kirkcaldy, Fife, 17 January 1955

Career: Everton (apprentice, July 1971; professional, May 1972), VILLA (£200,000, July 1977), West Bromwich Albion (£125,000, August 1983), Manchester City (loan, December 1984–January 1985), Sheffield United (£10,000, July 1985; retired May 1986), Dunfermline Athletic (coach), Swansea City (assistant manager), Vale of Earn/Scotland (manager); now working at the Pro's Shop on the Scottish golf course at Gleneagles

McNaught gained youth and amateur honours for Scotland. After more than 65 outings for Everton, he became the backbone of Villa's defence, winning League championship, European Cup and Super Cup-winner's medals. Commanding in the air, positive and sure in the tackle, he was a true professional. He made his debut for WBA in a 4–3 defeat at Villa Park and played over 100 games for the Baggies before switching to Bramall Lane after a loan spell at Maine Road. His father, Willie, was a Scottish international.

McPARLAND, PETER JAMES

Outside-left/centre-forward: 341 apps, 120 goals

Born: Newry, County Down, Northern Ireland, 25 April 1934

Career: Newry schoolboy football, Dundalk Juniors (1950), Dundalk United (April 1952), VILLA (£3,880, August 1952), Wolverhampton Wanderers

(£35,000, January 1962), Plymouth Argyle (£30,000, January 1963), Worcester City (July 1964), Peterborough United (August 1966), Atlanta Chiefs/NASL (October 1966–November 1968), Glentoran (player/manager, December 1968–71), Chelsea (scout, February 1972); coached in Kuwait (Quadsiai), Libya and Hong Kong (five months); No. 1 Club/Kuwait (coach/manager, 1979–80); after returning from the Far East, ran a property business with his son in Bournemouth for many years

'Packy' McParland, who played mainly as a left-winger but could also perform at centre-forward, was fast, direct with a terrific shot. In 1952, while he was serving his apprenticeship as a coppersmith and having been watched several times, George Martin, the Villa manager, signed him for less than £4,000. What a buy – over the next ten years McParland gave his all for the club, scoring several vital goals including when Villa beat Manchester United 2–1 in the 1957 FA Cup final. He also gained a Second Division championship medal in 1960 and then collected a League Cup-winner's tankard in 1961 when he became the first player to score in the final of that competition and also in an FA Cup final. In between times McParland represented the Football League XI and won 34 full caps for Northern Ireland (33 with Villa), playing for his country in the 1958 World Cup finals. He now lives in Dorset.

MELLBERG, ERIK OLOF
Defender: 119 apps, 2 goals
Born: Amncharad, Sweden, 3 September 1977
Career: FC Gullspang/Sweden (April 1994), Degerfors/Sweden (August 1996), AIK Stockholm/Sweden (February 1998), Racing Santander/Spain (August 1998), VILLA (£5m, July 2001)

Swedish international Mellberg, who has over 30 full caps under his belt, made 64 League appearances in his homeland and almost 100 in Spain before being signed to partner Ozalan Alpay at the heart of the Villa defence. A rock-solid performer, strong and decisive in the tackle and a powerful header of the ball, he enjoyed a very successful first season in the English Premiership, making 36 appearances despite suffering damaged ankle ligaments. An ever-present in 2002–03, he missed very few games the following season and despite having had six different partners at the heart of Villa's defence, he still comes up with the goods. He played in Euro 2004.

MERSON, PAUL CHARLES
Midfield: 126+19 apps, 19 goals
Born: Harlesden, London, 20 March 1968
Career: Harlesden junior football, Brent and Ealing District Boys, Middlesex Schools, Forest United; trials with Chelsea, QPR and Watford (1981–82); Arsenal (schoolboy forms April 1982; apprentice, July 1984; professional, December 1985), Brentford (loan, January–February 1987), Middlesbrough (£4.5m, July 1997), VILLA (£6.75m, September 1998), Portsmouth (free,

July 2002), Walsall (free, July 2003; caretaker manager, March 2004; player/manager, May 2004)

By the time he joined Villa, shortly after the start of the 1998–99 season, Merson had already appeared in over 500 matches for clubs and country and scored almost 120 goals. A powerfully built player, able to adapt to whatever his manager/coach required, whether as a creative midfielder or as an all-out attacker, he had also gained twenty-one full caps for England, plus four with the 'B' team, four at Under-21 level and a handful as a youth-team player. In fact, he had been a surprise choice for the France '98 World Cup finals after successfully overcoming a well-publicised personal drug-addiction problem that required lengthy hospital treatment. He returned to action a much leaner, more positive player and consequently became a top-line performer, hence his big-money (and surprise) transfer to Middlesbrough, whom he helped reach the Premiership in his first season – and then did likewise with Portsmouth. Voted PFA 'Young Player of the Year' in 1989, Merson helped Arsenal win two League championships (1989, 1991), the FA Cup and League Cup double (1993) and the European Cup-winner's Cup (1994). He scored for the Gunners in their 1993 League Cup final win over Sheffield Wednesday. A crowd-pleaser, his talent, workrate, endeavour and undoubted ability are certainly recognised by his fellow professionals. He had a few problems at Villa Park (on and off the field) but always gave 100 per cent on the field. A season after leaving the club he was voted into the PFA's First Division team for the 2002–03 season as Portsmouth gained promotion to the Premiership. As caretaker manager, he failed to keep Walsall in the First Division.

Merson's autobiography, *Rock Bottom*, was published in 1995 and he followed up with *Hero and Villain* in 2000.

MILES, ALFRED

Full-back: 270 apps

Born: Aston, January 1884 – *Died*: Wylde Green, Sutton Coldfield, 8 February 1926

Career: Heath Villa, Aston St Mary's (1900), VILLA (July 1902; retired May 1914); served in Army during WW1, hospitalised in France; VILLA (trainer, January 1919–August 1925); later worked at Kynochs

Miles, the doyen of the Villa side, was skipper several times, especially in seasons 1910–12. A sportsman through and through and admired by the fans, he played for Birmingham Juniors against the Scottish Juniors in April 1902 and three years later gained an FA Cup-winner's medal. He missed the 1913 final after being dislodged by Tom Weston. A great striker of the ball (left-footed), he was the embodiment of pluck and determination, possessed a never-say-die attitude but was not too strong constitutionally. Miles was Villa's spongeman at Wembley for the 1924 FA Cup final.

MILES, REGINALD

Goalkeeper: 16 apps

Born: Enfield, Middlesex, 8 July 1905 – *Died*: Enfield, Middlesex, 1978

Career: Enfield Schools, Enfield Town (August 1921), Dulwich Hamlet, British Army, Enfield, VILLA (amateur, November 1930; contract cancelled September 1931), Dulwich Hamlet (September–October 1931), Millwall (October 1931), Catford Wanderers (August 1932), Millwall (September 1933), Dulwich Hamlet (season 1934–35)

Miles was a London stockbroker who caught Villa's eye when playing Army football. Reliable rather than spectacular, he was first choice between the posts (ahead of Fred Biddlestone and Percy Maggs) during the second half of the 1930–31 season. He left the club following the emergence of Harry Morton.

MILLER, ARCHIBALD THEODORE

Wing-half: 10 apps

Born: Rossie Island, Montrose, 26 January 1877 – *Died*: Sussex, *circa* 1929

Career: Montrose (August 1893), Millwall Athletic (August 1896), VILLA (£200, April 1901), Millwall Athletic (loan, February 1903; signed May 1903), Brighton and Hove Albion (May 1904–May 1905); later returned to Scotland

Miller made over 100 Southern League appearances for Millwall before joining Villa. For a brief period he showed all the capabilities of competing at the highest level but failed to establish himself in the side, returning to Millwall in 1903.

MILLINGTON, CHARLES JOHN HENRY

Outside-right: 38 apps, 14 goals

Born: Lincoln, 25 April 1884 – *Died*: Lincoln, 13 June 1955

Career: Grantham Park Avenue, Grantham, Ripley Athletic (January 1905), VILLA (September 1905), Fulham (£400, October 1907), Birmingham (£100, August 1909), Wellington Town (August 1912), Brierley Hill Alliance (March 1913), Stourbridge (April 1914); guest for Leicester Fosse (1917–18); Ward Ends Works FC (1919), Wellington Town (August 1919), Oakengates (player/manager, August 1922), Wellington Town (August 1924; retired May 1925); returned to Lincoln to work in the iron industry; was also a prominent all-rounder with Lincolnshire cricket club

'Nut' Millington was a strong, purposeful winger, quick and cunning with plenty of willpower who notched up a good scoring record with Villa. He later netted 21 times in 63 outings for Fulham and claimed 13 goals in 87 appearances for the Blues.

His son, George, played for Shrewsbury, Port Vale, Northampton, Halifax, Bristol Rovers and Arsenal.

MILNE, DR VICTOR EDWARD

Centre-half: 175 apps, 1 goal

Born: Aberdeen, 22 June 1897 – *Died:* Little Aston, Sutton Coldfield, 6 September 1971

Career: Boys' Brigade football, Aberdeen City Boys, Robert Gordon's College, Aberdeen University (1915), Royal Engineers (1916–18), Aberdeen (August 1919), VILLA (amateur, August 1923; retired May 1929 to concentrate on his profession as doctor); VILLA (club doctor, 1930–33); general practitioner and medical officer of health for Aldridge (1929–69); served with the Royal Engineers in France during WW1 (recruited because of his chemistry knowledge)

An 'Apollo-sized' defender, Milne took over the centre-half mantle from murder-victim Tommy Ball in 1923 and was Villa's first-choice pivot for six years (medical duties permitting). Powerfully built, he gained an FA Cup-winner's medal in 1924, when he also became the first doctor to play at Wembley and, indeed, was the first Scotsman to appear in a final for Villa since 1897. His only goal for Villa was the winner against Notts County (2–1) in September 1925.

While studying to become a doctor at Aberdeen University, he gained both soccer and cricket blues and also competed on the athletics track. Having graduated in 1921, he gained a Diploma in Health two years later. He took over from Dr Jessop as the Villa doctor in 1930. His father was chairman of Aberdeen FC.

MILOSEVIC, SAVO

Striker: 110+7 apps, 32 goals

Born: Bijelina, Yugoslavia, 2 September 1973

Career: Partizan Belgrade/Yugoslavia (professional, 1990), VILLA (£3.5m, July 1995), Real Zaragoza/Spain (£3.7m, June 1999), Parma/Italy (£16m, July 2000), Celta Vigo/Spain (seasons 2002–04)

Many eyebrows were raised when Milosevic (6 ft 2 in. tall) joined Villa after manager Brian Little had watched and assessed him on video only! However, such scepticism seemed well founded when, after being substituted on his Premiership debut against Manchester United, Milosevic failed to score until December, whereupon he bagged a hat-trick against Coventry to silence his critics. A strong, powerful player with heaps of talent, he tended to drift in and out of the game – but he did score some cracking goals, including a beauty in Villa's 3–0 League Cup final win over Leeds in 1996. A proposed move to the Italian club Perugia fell through before he got back to business in the Premiership. He eventually took his goal-tally to 32 before quitting the British soccer scene to join Real Zaragoza, later switching to Parma after a very successful European championship campaign, when he finished up as the tournament's joint top scorer with five goals. Milosevic, capped almost 50 times by Yugoslavia, helped Celta Vigo qualify for the European Champions League as they finished fourth in Spain's La Liga in 2003.

MITCHINSON, THOMAS WILLIAM

Inside-forward: 52 apps, 9 goals
Born: Sunderland, 24 February 1943 – *Died*: 2002
Career: Sunderland and Wearside schoolboy football, Sunderland (apprentice, July 1958; professional, December 1960), Mansfield Town (January 1966), VILLA (£18,000, August 1967), Torquay United (£8,000, May 1969), Bournemouth (£2,000, December 1971; retired, injured, May 1973)

A steady, probing player with a good eye, Mitchinson was the first signing (with his Mansfield colleague Dick Edwards) by Tommy Cummings when he took over as Villa manager. During his career, Mitchinson amassed more than 300 appearances and scored almost 50 goals.

MOORE, ISAAC GEORGE

Inside-forward: 6 apps
Born: Tipton, December 1867 – *Died*: West Bromwich, September 1948
Career: St Stephen's FC, VILLA (July 1889), Dudley Town (August 1890), Netherton Saints (1892–94)

Muscular, hardy and mobile, Moore made six appearances for Villa, plus more than twenty in other matches during his only season at the club.

MOORE, LUKE

Midfield: 0+7 apps
Born: Birmingham, 13 February 1986
Career: VILLA (YTS, April 2002; professional, February 2004)

An England schoolboy and youth international, Moore was a 2002 FA Youth Cup winner with Villa and made his Premiership debut in the local derby with Birmingham City in February 2004.

MOORE, STEFAN

Utility: 11+18 apps, 2 goals
Born: Birmingham 28 September 1983
Career: VILLA (YTS, April 2000; professional, October 2001), Chesterfield (loan, October–November 2001), Millwall (loan, June 2004)

England youth international Moore broke into Villa's first team in the Premiership during 2002–03, making 13 appearances and scoring one goal. A hard-working, hard-running, pacy player who can occupy several positions including the right-wing berth, he has bigger and better things ahead of him. He skippered Villa's youngsters as they lifted the 2002 FA Youth Cup, Moore himself scoring twice in the first-leg victory over Everton at Goodison Park.

MOORE, THOMAS D.

Outside-left: 1 app., 1 goal
Born: Dudley Port, Tipton, 27 April 1910 – *Deceased*
Career: Dudley Welfare, Tipton All Souls, Stourbridge (1930), VILLA

(February 1932), Bournemouth and Boscombe Athletic (August 1934), Stourbridge (April 1935), Dudley Town, Birmingham (briefly, 1935), Swansea Town (1936), Stourbridge (1937), Vono Sports (1939), Dudley Town (1946; retired 1949)

A smart, tricky winger, Moore played for Birmingham Juniors against the Scottish Juniors at Edinburgh in April 1932 but eight months later broke his right leg during a reserve-team game and was out of action until August 1933. Unfortunately, he never recovered from that setback and left the Villa after one League game against Huddersfield in April 1932, when he scored in a 2–1 victory. He was the grandson of Isaac Moore (q.v.).

MORALEE, MATTHEW

Inside-forward: 12 apps, 1 goal

Born: Mexborough, 21 February 1912 – *Died*: Doncaster, September 1991

Career: Ormsby United, Denaby United (April 1929), Gainsborough Trinity (May 1930), Grimsby Town (February 1931), VILLA (October 1936), Leicester City (November 1937), Shrewsbury Town (July 1939); guest for Grimsby Town (1939–43), Doncaster Rovers (1940–41), Bradford City (1942–43), Rotherham United (1942–45); Denaby United (season 1946–47); later a licensee in Oldham

An intelligent, prompting schemer, Moralee never quite bore out his early promise. He scored 5 times in 27 outings for Grimsby and claimed 6 goals in 43 games for Leicester – this despite a 12-month suspension for various problems at Filbert Street.

MORBY, JOHN HENRY

Defender: 3 apps

Born: Wednesfield, August 1920

Career: Wolverhampton Wanderers (trial, 1936), Hednesford Town (1938), VILLA (December 1943); guest for Blakenhall St Luke's (1940–41), Leicester City (1944–45); Worcester City (July 1948), Kidderminster Harriers (August 1950), Lye Town (August 1951–May 1952); later resided in Essington (Wolverhampton)

A WW2 signing, Morby was a strapping defender able to occupy a variety of positions but preferred the centre-half berth. He played in thirty-two WW2 games for Villa plus three FA Cup matches in 1945–46, two against Chelsea when the aggregate attendance was 116,000.

MORGAN, SAMUEL JOHN

Striker: 51 apps, 15 goals

Born: Belfast, 3 December 1946

Career: Gorleston and Norfolk Schools, Gorleston (amateur), Port Vale (trial, January 1970; professional, July 1970), VILLA (£22,222, August 1973, with £5,400 to follow later), Brighton and Hove Albion (£10,000, December

1975), Cambridge United (August 1977), Sparta Rotterdam/Holland (1978), Groningen/Holland (1979–80), Gorleston (player August 1980, later manager); then Great Yarmouth Schools FC (manager, secretary and chairman, in that order); USA (coaching); Norwich City (junior coach, later director of the Football Academy, 2000–01)

A tall, aggressive striker, capped 18 times by Northern Ireland (1972–78), Morgan was Port Vale's 'Player of the Year' in 1972 and top scorer for the Potteries club the following season. He ended up with 27 goals in 126 outings for the Valiants before moving to Villa on a detailed payment scheme. He battled hard and long during his time before switching to Brighton. In a 20-year career (in England and Holland) Morgan netted 65 goals in over 300 appearances.

MORLEY, WILLIAM ANTHONY

Outside-left: 170+10 apps, 34 goals

Born: Ormskirk, 26 August 1954

Career: Ormskirk and District Schools, Preston North End (apprentice, July 1969; professional, August 1972), Burnley (£100,000, February 1976), VILLA (£200,000, June 1979), West Bromwich Albion (£75,000, December 1983), Birmingham City (loan, November–December 1984), FC Seiko/Japan (August 1985), FC Den Haag/Holland (July 1986), Walsall (trial, June 1987), Notts County (trial, July 1987), West Bromwich Albion (August 1987), Burnley (loan, October–November 1988), Tampa Bay Rowdies/USA (March 1989), Hamrun Spartans/Malta (April 1990), New Zealand football (season 1990–91), Sutton Coldfield Town (1992), Bromsgrove Rovers (player/coach, January 1995), Stratford Town (player, March 1995); also coach in Australia and Hong Kong; assisted both VILLA and WBA Old Stars (1990s)

A fast-raiding winger, Morley could deliver pin-point crosses on the run, drive in some powerful shots with both feet, and score some stunning goals – his effort at Goodison Park in a League game against Everton in February 1981 was voted 'Goal of the Season'.

Morley became a vital cog in the Villa machine, helping them win the Football League title, the European Cup and European Super Cup in double-quick time in the early 1980s. Halfway through the 1983–84 season he left Villa for neighbours West Brom and did well at The Hawthorns before trying his luck in Japan, having had a loan spell at St Andrew's late in 1984. Capped six times by England at senior level, Morley played for his country's youth team on seven occasions and also won one 'B' and one Under-23 cap. During his career in England he amassed in excess of 450 appearances and scored over 65 goals. He helped Den Haag win promotion to the Dutch First Division, gaining a Cup runner's-up medal in his only season in Holland (1986–87).

MORRALL, TERENCE STEPHEN

Defender: 9 apps

Born: Smethwick, 24 November 1938

Career: Holly Lodge Grammar School, Birmingham County Boys, Church Rovers, VILLA (juniors, 1953; professional, November 1955), Shrewsbury Town (April 1961), Wrexham (July 1963), Southport (July 1965), Stourbridge (player/manager, November 1966; retired as player, January 1967); Warley Borough (manager, May 1968–70); played football in Cyprus and Jordan during his National Service (1958–59)

Like his uncle, George 'Lofty' Morrall (ex-Birmingham player), Morrall was also a stern, rugged defender whose chances at Villa Park were restricted owing to the presence and form of so many other fine full-backs and centre-halves. He made 31 League appearances for Shrewsbury, 42 for Wrexham and one for Southport before moving down the ladder. He now lives in Wall Heath, Dudley.

MORRIS, WILLIAM

Defender: 53 apps, 1 goal

Born: Danesmoor, 12 February 1888 – *Died*: Birmingham, 1949

Career: Clay Cross, Derby County (September 1907), Clay Cross (December 1907); to America for two years; Clay Cross, Alfreton (August 1910), Chesterfield (July 1911), VILLA (March 1912–May 1915), guest for Notts County (1919); Alfreton Town (1919–20)

Tall with all the physical requirements required to be a defender, centre-half Morris was a regular in Villa's League side during the first half of 1912–13 before losing his place. Never a regular after that, he ended his days at Villa Park with just one goal to his name, scoring in a 5–0 FA Cup win over West Ham in February 1913. He had started out as a centre-forward with Clay Cross.

MORT, THOMAS

Full-back: 368 apps, 2 goals

Born: Kearsley, near Bolton, 1 December 1897 – *Died*: Wigan, 6 June 1967

Career: Farnworth Council School, Kearsley St Stephen's, Newton Lads' Club, Lancashire Fusiliers, Altrincham (December 1918), Rochdale (professional, June 1921), VILLA (April 1922; retired May 1935); later a businessman in Wigan

Mort was a marvellous partner to Tommy Smart, the pair being known affectionately as 'Death and Glory' as they defended magnificently week after week. Mort, who took over from Tommy Weston, was a great exponent of the sliding tackle, especially on the heavy grounds. He won 3 England caps in the mid-1920s, appeared in the 1924 FA Cup final and made almost 370 appearances for Villa in 13 years. He skippered the side after Jimmy Gibson. Mort's cousin, Enoch Mort, played for Cardiff.

MORTIMER, DENNIS GEORGE
Midfield: 405+1 apps, 36 goals
Born: Liverpool, 5 April 1952
Career: Kirby Boys, Coventry City (apprentice, July 1967; professional, September 1969), VILLA (£175,000, December 1975), Sheffield United (loan, December 1984), Brighton and Hove Albion (August 1985), Birmingham City (August 1986), Kettering Town (July 1987), Redditch United (player/manager, November 1987–October 1988), West Bromwich Albion (football in the community officer, August 1989, later reserve-team player/coach), VILLA (junior coach)

An excellent player, full of drive, determination, passion and loads of skill, Mortimer had a will to win. He first shot to prominence with Coventry when his hair was so long that the fans called him Doris! He made 215 appearances and scored 10 goals for the Sky Blues before transferring to Villa, signed by Ron Saunders. With Des Bremner and Gordon Cowans either side of him, he became a vital cog in the engine-room as Villa stormed to victory in the League Cup final of 1977, won the Football League championship in 1981 and carried off both the European and Super Cups in 1982, skippering the side in each of the last three triumphs. He was capped by England six times as a youth-team player, starred in three 'B' and six Under-23 internationals and in 1971 toured Australia with the FA. As a teenager with Kirby Boys, Mortimer played alongside his future Villa colleague Kenny Swain.

MORTIMER, PAUL HENRY
Utility: 12+2 apps, 1 goal
Born: Kensington, London, 8 May 1968
Career: Henry Compton Secondary School and West London Schools, Fulham (junior, 1984–86), Farnborough Town, Charlton Athletic (trial, July 1987; professional, September 1987), VILLA (£350,000, July 1991), Crystal Palace (£500,000, October 1991), Brentford (loan, January–February 1993), Charlton Athletic (£200,000, July 1994), Bristol City (free, August 1999; retired May 2000)

Able to play as a full-back, central defender, in midfield or as a stand-in striker, Mortimer, a former bookshop assistant in Fleet Street, spent barely three months at Villa Park. Seemingly destined to play his football in London, he had already starred in over 120 games for Charlton and after leaving he appeared in 160 matches for Palace, Brentford, Charlton and Bristol City. Capped twice by England at Under-21 level, he was troubled with a hamstring injury in the late 1990s, which eventually led to his retirement.

MORTON, HAROLD
Goalkeeper: 207 apps
Born: Oldham, 7 January 1909 – *Died*: *circa* 1975
Career: St Luke's School (1919–23), Chadderton Sunday School, Oldham Boys,

Platt Brothers Ironworks FC, Middleton Road Primitives (1925–27), Bury (trial, 1927), Bolton Wanderers (trial, 1928), Royal Welsh Fusiliers (Army service, 1928–30), Southampton (trial, September 1930), VILLA (trial, October 1930; signed, November 1930), Everton (March 1937), Burnley (May 1939; retired during WW2)

Morton, a former fireman and Rugby League full-back, was spotted by Villa playing for the Royal Welsh Fusiliers and, after his demob, was invited down by Villa for a trial. After successfully completing his trial period, he was offered a professional contract within a week. He made his League debut in unusual circumstances at Manchester City in November 1930. He was sitting in the stand waiting for the kick-off when he was called down to the dressing-room after Fred Biddlestone had been injured in the pre-match warm-up. He never looked back and served Villa admirably until leaving for Everton in 1937. One of the smallest keepers in the game, he commanded his area well, being both brave and darting. Unfortunately, Morton was between the posts when Ted Drake of Arsenal put seven goals past him in a First Division match in 1935. Played in one game as Ted Sagar's deputy when Everton won the League title in 1939.

MOSELEY, GRAHAM

Goalkeeper: 3 apps
Born: Manchester, 16 November 1953
Career: Blackburn Rovers (apprentice, July 1969; professional, September 1971), Derby County (September 1972), VILLA (loan, August–September 1974), Walsall (loan, October 1977), Brighton and Hove Albion (November 1977), Ipswich Town (loan, March 1984), Cardiff City (August 1986–May 1988)

Moseley was the second player who was signed on loan by Villa after Jim Cumbes had been injured. An England youth international, he played for the Rams in the 1976 FA Cup semi-final and helped Brighton twice win promotion, from Division Three in 1977 and into the First Division in 1979, also playing in the 1983 FA Cup final defeat by Manchester United. An agile six-footer, he made 265 League appearances during his career, 189 with Brighton.

MOSS, AMOS

Wing-half: 110 apps, 5 goals
Born: Aston, Birmingham, 28 August 1921 – *Died*: Birmingham, 8 April 2004
Career: Birmingham Boys' Club, VILLA (amateur, May 1937; professional, May 1939); guest for Leeds United (1942–43), Wrexham (1944–45), Clapton Orient (1945–46); Kettering Town (June 1956), Wisbech Town (May 1957), Kidderminster Harriers (player/coach, August 1959), Rugby Town (August 1961; then reserve-team player/coach, September 1962; retired May 1963)

The blond-haired Moss, 6 ft 1 in. tall, was a teak-tough defender, younger brother of Frank (q.v.), who did artful work in Villa's reserve side before making headway in the first XI. He was also able to fill in as an inside-forward.

MOSS, ARTHUR JAMES
Wing-half: 5 apps
Born: Crewe, 14 November 1887 – *Died*: 1930
Career: Crewe Central, Willaston White Star, Crewe Alexandra, Whitchurch, VILLA (£250, September 1908), Bristol City (August 1912–April 1915), Army service during WW1; Runcorn (1918), Eccles United, Crewe Alexandra (May 1921; retired May 1924)

Initially introduced to first-team action in place of the injured Chris Buckley in 1908, Moss starred resolutely in over 100 second- and third-team games for Villa. He went on to make 85 League appearances for Bristol City before WW1 and 136 for Crewe afterwards. He was awarded the Military Cross during WW1.

MOSS, FRANK (SENIOR)
Centre-half: 283 apps, 9 goals
Born: Aston, Birmingham, 17 April 1895 – *Died*: Worcester, 15 September 1965
Career: Burlington Street School (Aston), Aston Manor, Walsall (August 1911), VILLA (February 1914), guest for Bellis and Morcom (1916); Aston Park Rangers (1919), Smethwick Carriage Works FC (1919), Bradford City (1919), Cardiff City (£2,500, January 1929), Oldham Athletic (July 1929), Bromsgrove Rovers (player/manager, September 1929), Worcester City (1932; retired May 1934); licensee of the Grosvenor Arms, Worcester (1930–65)

Father of Amos (q.v.) and Frank junior (q.v.), Moss senior was, like his two sons, blond-haired, strong and resilient. Nicknamed 'Snowy', he captained both his club (Villa) in the FA Cup final against Newcastle United and his country (England) against Scotland on successive Saturdays at Wembley in April 1924. Four years earlier (1920) he replaced the injured Jimmy Harrop at the eleventh hour prior to the FA Cup final against Huddersfield Town and played a 'blinder' in Villa's 1–0 win. The athlete at the heart of the Villa defence, strong, dominant, quick in recovery and excellent in the air, he won five caps and represented the Football League twice before moving to Cardiff in 1929 – just after the Welsh club had been hammered 6–1 by Villa in an FA Cup tie! He was seriously injured during WW1 while serving as a corporal with the 4th Lincolnshire Regiment at Bouchezvenes, France. He returned to England as a PT instructor.

MOSS, FRANK (JUNIOR)
Centre-half: 313 apps, 3 goals
Born: Aston, Birmingham, September 1917 – *Died*: Looe, Cornwall, 5 May 1997
Career: Cowper Street and Ryland Road Schools (Birmingham), St Clement's School (Worcester), Worcester Nondescripts FC (1930), Worcester City

(August 1933), Sheffield Wednesday (trial, 1934), Wolverhampton Wanderers (professional, August 1937), VILLA (£2,000, May 1938); guest for Birmingham (1939–40), Northampton Town (1939–40), Stourbridge (1940), Worcester City (1940), Wrexham (1939–40), Southampton (1944–45), Watford (1945–46); retired, injured, June 1955; VILLA (coaching staff, 1955–56); later ran a newsagent's business in Kingstanding, Birmingham, which he started in 1940; in 1969 moved to the Cornish seaside resort of Looe, where he remained until his death

Moss was a born fighter for club (at football) and country (at war). A resourceful defender who had the habit of subduing the best centre-forwards and inside men in the country. Played in the North against South schools trial match in February 1932 and was selected for the final of the English Schools Trophy that season. Wolves admitted they made a mistake in releasing him (likewise Wednesday). He finally established himself in the Villa side in 1946–47 and was a regular in the side over the next 8 years, accumulating well over 300 senior appearances. During WW2 he served in the Royal Navy, operating on gunboats and destroyers in the Middle East. He could have signed for Middlesbrough, Leicester, Portsmouth or Blackburn but chose Villa in the end.

MOUNTFIELD, DEREK
Defender: 118+2 apps, 17 goals
Born: Liverpool, 2 November 1962
Career: Tranmere Rovers (juniors, June 1978; professional, November 1980), Everton (£30,000, June 1982), VILLA (£450,000, June 1988), Wolverhampton Wanderers (£150,000, November 1991), Carlisle United (free, May 1994), Northampton Town (loan, October 1995), Walsall (November 1995, player–coach July 1997), Bromsgrove Rovers (September 1998), Ballymena (manager, briefly), Scarborough (caretaker manager, January–April 1999), Workington (player/coach, 1999–2000)

Full-back or centre-half Mountfield made 29 appearances for Tranmere before moving into the First Division with Everton. It was a good move for player and club as Mountfield went on to make 154 appearances for the Merseysiders, scoring 25 goals and helping them twice win the Football League championship (1985, 1987), capture the FA Cup (1984) and the European Cup-winners' Cup (1985). He also played in two losing FA Cup finals (1985, 1986) and represented England at Under-21 and 'B' team levels. Mountfield partnered Allan Evans and then Paul McGrath in Villa's defence. He later passed the 600 mark in club appearances.

MULDOON, THOMAS PATRICK
Half-back: 34 apps
Born: Granard, Athlone, Ireland, February 1901 – *Deceased*
Career: Deer Park National School (Athlone), St Mary's Intermediate School (1912–14); Army service with Leicester Regiment; Athlone Town (1919–20), VILLA (October 1924), Tottenham Hotspur (September 1927),

Walsall (July 1929–May 1931); later employed at the local labour exchange Muldoon occupied the left-half position in the main during his three-year stay with Villa. He failed to make the first XI with Spurs but appeared in over 50 League games for the Saddlers. He also gained one cap for Ireland and served in India during WW1.

MULRANEY, AMBROSE
Winger: 12 apps, 2 goals
Born: Wishaw, near Motherwell, 18 May 1916 – *Died*: Kinver, summer 2001
Career: Wishaw White Rose (1929), Carluke Rovers (1930), trials with Heart
   of Midlothian, Celtic, Hamilton Academical, Blackpool, Sligo Rovers, and
   Clapton Orient; Dartford (August 1935), Ipswich Town (1938–39); guest
   for Birmingham, Blackburn Rovers, Brentford, Charlton Athletic, Chelsea,
   Hibernian, Leicester City, Manchester City, Millwall, Third Lanark and
   Wolverhampton Wanderers during WW2; Birmingham City (£3,750,
   October 1945), Shrewsbury Town (July 1947), Kidderminster Harriers (July
   1948), VILLA (September 1948), Cradley Heath (player/manager, August
   1949), Brierley Hill Alliance (manager, July 1952; retired from football, May
   1954); worked as a carpenter in Kinver; recovered from a heart attack in
   1968

Mulraney was a fast-raiding winger able to occupy both flanks. A Scottish schoolboy international trialist, he represented the Scottish Alliance XI and had the pleasure of claiming Ipswich's first League hat-trick against Bristol City in April 1939. He scored 57 goals in 159 games for the Blues during and immediately after WW2, helping them win the Football League (S) title and reach the FA Cup semi-final in 1946. After spells with Shrewsbury and Kidderminster he returned to League action with Villa, spending the remainder of the 1948–49 season with the club before becoming player–manager of Cradley Heath. During WW2 Mulraney served in the RAF, attaining the rank of flight sergeant, PT instructor.

MURRAY, JAMES ARTHUR
Forward: 2 apps
Born: Benwhat, Ayrshire, 9 June 1880 – *Died*: Glasgow, 29 October 1933
Career: St Augustine's, Benwhat Hathertwell, Ayr United (1897), VILLA
   (March 1901), Small Heath (November 1901), Watford (June 1902),
   Kettering Town (May 1903), Wellingborough (November 1903)
A stocky reserve utility forward, Scottish junior international Murray's capabilities were somewhat limited, failing to shine with either Villa or the Blues. He had 24 Southern League outings with Watford.

MURRAY, SCOTT GEORGE

Midfield: 4 apps

Born: Aberdeen, 26 May 1974

Career: Fraserburgh FC, VILLA (£35,000, professional, March 1994), Bristol City (£150,000, December 1997), Reading (July 2003)

A right-sided midfield player, Scottish 'B' international Murray tasted Premiership football with Villa before becoming a folk hero at Ashton Gate, scoring 61 goals in 271 games for Bristol City. Totally committed, he has pace and strength and shoots on sight!

MWILA, FREDERICK

Forward: 1 app.

Born: Zambia, 6 July 1946

Career: Rokana United/Zambia, Atlanta Chiefs/NASL (1967), VILLA (September 1969), Atlanta Chiefs/NASL (May 1970); coached in Germany (1976, 1981), Brazil (1985), Power Dynamoes FC/Botswana (1981), Township Rollers/Botswana (manager, mid-1980s), Botswana (national team manager/coach, late 1980s), Zambia (national coach, early 1990s)

Mwila joined Villa with fellow countryman Emment Kapwenge (q.v.) but failed to make any impression in English football. He had just one League game – in the 0–0 home draw with Blackpool in November 1969. In his first season with the Chiefs he struck 12 goals and was a star performer for 7 years, netting 25 goals in 1975, his best return.

MYERSCOUGH, WILLIAM HENRY

Forward: 74 apps, 17 goals

Born: Farnworth, Bolton, 22 June 1930 – *Died*: Manchester, March 1977

Career: Manchester County FA, Manchester City (amateur), Ashfield FC, Walsall (professional, June 1954), VILLA (in exchange for Dave Walsh, July 1955), Rotherham United (July 1959), Coventry City (July 1960), Chester (March 1962), Wrexham (July 1963), Macclesfield Town (May 1964), Manchester Meat Traders (reinstated as amateur, October 1967; retired May 1968)

Myerscough was a wholehearted footballer, able to occupy any forward position, who contested the number 9 shirt with Derek Pace at Villa. He had the pleasure of scoring the winning goal against WBA in the 1957 FA Cup semi-final replay and then starred at Wembley when Manchester United were defeated 2–1 in the final.

NASH, HAROLD EDWARD

Inside-left: 12 apps, 5 goals

Born: Fishponds, Bristol, 10 April 1892 – *Died*: Fishponds, 1970

Career: Brislington United, Mardy, Aberdare (May 1910), Abertillery (May

1913), Treharris (briefly), Pontypridd (August 1914), VILLA (February 1915); guest for Bellis and Morcom (1915), Lincoln City (1917); Coventry City (August 1920), Cardiff City (February 1921), Merthyr Town (May 1923), Bargoed (July 1925), Ystrad-Mynach (briefly), Bargoed Athletic (manager, August 1926–May 1929)

Deputising for Joe Bache, Nash made a terrific start to his League career, scoring a hat-trick on his debut for Villa against Liverpool in April 1915 (won 6–3). He netted twice more before the end of that season but did little after that. He later gave Cardiff good service.

NEAL, JOHN
Full-back: 114 apps
Born: Silksworth, County Durham, 3 April 1932
Career: Seaham Harbour Schools, Silksworth Colliery Welfare Juniors, RAF (clerk), Hull City (professional, August 1949), King's Lynn (July 1956), Swindon Town (July 1957), VILLA (£6,000, July 1959), Southend United (November 1962; retired June 1967); worked at Fords of Dagenham (1967–68), Wrexham (coach, then manager, September 1968–May 1977), Middlesbrough (manager, May 1977–May 1981), Chelsea (manager, May 1981–June 1985, then advisor at Stamford Bridge to 1987)

A junior sprint champion as a teenager, Neal was a keen, tackling full-back, quick in recovery who made 60 League appearances for Hull and 91 as Swindon's captain before joining Villa to replace Doug Winton. He helped Villa win the Second Division title and League Cup in successive seasons (1960, 1961) before making over 100 appearances for the Shrimpers, quitting the game with 416 games under his belt, having represented the Third Division South against the North as a Swindon player. He enjoyed success as manager of Wrexham, leading them to promotion from the Fourth to the Third Division in 1970 and to victory in the 1972 and 1975 Welsh Cup finals, thus gaining entry into the European Cup-winner's Cup. As boss of Middlesbrough, he sold some star players, including Graeme Souness to Liverpool and David Mills to WBA. He left Ayresome Park after transferring Craig Johnston to Anfield. Neal also took Chelsea to the Second Division title in 1984.

NELSON, FERNANDO
Right-back: 65+8 apps
Born: Portugal, 5 November 1971.
Career: SC Salgueiros/Portugal (professional, 1988), Sporting Lisbon/Portugal (£240,000, August 1991), VILLA (£1.75m, July 1996), FC Porto/Portugal (£1.1m, August 1998)

Nelson represented Portugal in the Under-14 championships before becoming a professional with Salgueiros, with whom he won a Portuguese Second Division championship medal. Following his transfer to Sporting Lisbon, he appeared in four domestic Cup finals, being on the winning side twice, including the Super Cup. On the international front, he added four Under-21 caps to his tally and collected a runner's-up medal in the European Under-21 championships. He went on to play in 23 intermediate fixtures and made his full international debut before moving to Villa. Nelson, the only Premiership player in Portugal's Euro '96 squad, played in midfield after Gary Charles had arrived, and made 39 appearances in his first season while taking his total of international caps to 6 before returning to Portugal.

NIBLO, THOMAS BRUCE D.

Forward: 51 apps, 9 goals

Born: Dunfermline, 24 September 1877 – *Died*: Newcastle, December 1929

Career: Dunfermline schools football, Calgrow Oak, Hamilton Academical (amateur), Linthouse FC/Glasgow (August 1896), Newcastle United (£90, April 1898), Middlesbrough (loan, April 1900), VILLA (January 1902), Nottingham Forest (April 1904), Watford (May 1906), Newcastle United (August 1907; coach to juniors, January–May 1908), Hebburn Argyle (player/manager, July 1908), Aberdeen (December 1908), Raith Rovers (August 1909–October 1910), Cardiff City (December 1910), Blyth Spartans (April 1911–May 1913); guest for Fulham (1915–16), Crystal Palace (1916–17); then a publican on Tyneside, having taken a pub initially in 1907

A tall, well-built Scottish international (one cap gained against England in 1904), Niblo was a 'capital' player, full of dash from start to finish, a real forceful player who was an out-and-out trier but lacked cohesion and was prone to being rather greedy – to the annoyance of his colleagues. He partnered Joe Bache on the left-wing for most of his Villa days, although he did appear at centre-forward. He made over 250 appearances at club level and lined up for the Anglo Scots against Home Scots in March 1904. He served as a corporal in the Army (1914–18). His son, Alan, was on Newcastle's books and his grandson, Alan junior, captained Wolves' reserve side.

NIBLOE, JOSEPH

Full-back: 52 apps

Born: Corkerhill, Renfrewshire, 23 November 1903 – *Died*: Doncaster, October 1976

Career: Kirkdonald School, Shawfield Juniors (Glasgow), Rutherglen Glencairn, Glencairn Green, Kilmarnock (professional, June 1924), VILLA (£1,875, September 1932), Sheffield Wednesday (August 1934, in exchange for George Beeson; retired May 1938), Sheffield Wednesday (part-time coach, 1939–46); also worked at the Sheffield steelworks of Samuel Fox

Nibloe, one-time brass moulder, began as a centre-forward and had a few games as a wing-half before establishing himself as a strong and resilient full-back who cleared his lines with alacrity. He gained 11 full caps for Scotland (1929–32) and twice represented the Scottish League. He won a Scottish Cup-winner's medal with Kilmarnock in 1929, followed by a runner's-up prize three years later and in 1935 was an FA Cup winner with Sheffield Wednesday when former Villa star Billy Walker was the Owls' manager. Nibloe, who partnered Danny Blair at Villa, amassed 128 appearances in his 5 years at Hillsborough.

NICHOLL, CHRISTOPHER JOHN

Centre-half: 251 apps, 20 goals

Born: Wilmslow, Cheshire, 12 October 1946

Career: Macclesfield Schools, Burnley (apprentice, June 1963; professional, April 1965), Witton Albion (August 1966), Halifax Town (£1,000, June 1968), Luton Town (£30,000, August 1969), VILLA (£90,000, March 1972), Southampton (£90,000, June 1977), Grimsby Town (player/assistant manager, August 1983; retired as a player, July 1985), Southampton (manager, July 1985–May 1991), Wigan Athletic (scout, 1991–93), Walsall (manager, September 1994–June 1997)

A natural central defender, capped 51 times by Northern Ireland, Nicholl made over 800 appearances in his 22-year playing career (647 in the Football League). He joined Luton for a record fee and quickly became the cornerstone of the Hatters' defence. Honest, efficient, strong in the air, he was sold to Villa to help balance the books at Kenilworth Road and was a star in the claret and blue strip, especially after cracking home a stunning goal in the 1977 League Cup final, second replay, against Everton, which set Villa up for a 3–2 victory at Old Trafford. He had earlier helped Villa win the Third Division title (1972), and gain promotion and lift the League Cup in 1975. He continued to perform superbly at The Dell, helping Saints reach the 1979 League Cup final and then, as Southampton's manager, he took them into second spot in the First Division – the highest placing in the club's history. Nicholl later became Walsall's 25th manager. He now lives in Southampton.

● Statistically unique, Nicholl is the only player (so far) who, in the same match, has scored two goals (all from open play) for both sides. The dubious and unlikely feat occurred in the 2–2 League draw between Villa and Leicester City at Filbert Street in March 1976.

NICHOLSON, JOSEPH ROBINSON

Utility: 1 app.

Born: Ryhope, near Sunderland, 4 June 1898 – *Died:* Durham, 1974

Career: Ryhope Council School, Ryhope Villa, Army football, Ryhope Comrades (January 1919), Clapton Orient (July 1919), Cardiff City (August 1924), VILLA (June 1926, in exchange for George Blackburn), Spennymoor United (August 1927), Shildon (October 1929), Muirton Miners' Welfare (July 1930), Easington Colliery (December 1931; retired May 1932)

Able to play at wing-half or centre-forward, Nicholson was a regular in the Orient side for 4 years, making 147 appearances. He netted 12 goals in 46 outings for Cardiff but never fitted in with Villa's plans and made just one

League appearance – at centre-forward in a 4–0 defeat at Newcastle on the opening day of the 1926–27 season. His brother, Joe, played for Nottingham Forest.

NIELSEN, KENT

Defender: 96+6 apps, 5 goals
Born: Brondby, Denmark, 28 December 1961
Career: Bronshoj FC/Denmark (junior member, 1976; part-time professional, August 1978), IF Brondby/Denmark (professional, August 1986), VILLA (£500,000, July 1989), Aarhus FC/Denmark (February 1992)

Nielsen became a laboratory assistant on leaving school but quickly took up serious football and developed into a solid, uncompromising defender who was signed by Villa boss Graham Taylor as a straight replacement for Martin Keown. Nielsen had already won 29 full caps for Denmark and during his time in the Football League added another 11 to that total as well as appearing in over a century of games for Villa.

NILIS, LUC

Striker: 5 apps, 2 goals
Born: Hasselt, Belgium, 25 May 1967
Career: RSC Anderlecht/Belgium (1988), PSV Eindhoven/Holland (1993), VILLA (July 2000; retired, injured, January 2001)

Experienced Belgian international Nilis (54 caps won) scored on his Villa debut – in the second leg of the InterToto Cup clash with Marila Pribram. But then soon afterwards, in a Premiership game at Ipswich, he suffered a horrific double fracture of the right leg in a clash with keeper Richard Wright. He never recovered full fitness and retired in 2001. In November 2000, Nilis admitted in a Birmingham newspaper that he came mighty close to having part of his right leg amputated. A prolific marksman in both Belgian and Dutch football as well as on the international scene, Nilis had scored 67 goals in 109 first-class matches for PSV and Anderlecht before arriving at Villa Park.

NOON, MICHAEL THOMAS

Defender: 82 apps, 1 goal
Born: Burton-on-Trent, June 1876 – *Died*: Leicester, 4 February 1939
Career: Burton Schools, Coalville Town, Burton Swifts (March 1898), VILLA (March 1899), Plymouth Argyle (May 1906; retired May 1907; appointed trainer until 1908), Coalville Town (season 1908–09); later licensee of the Rose and Crown public house, Whitwick, Leicestershire; also coalminer at Whitwick; stood for Coalville at the Urban Council elections (lost)

A stylish defender who could occupy most positions satisfactorily, Noon was never a first-team regular during his seven years with Villa, having his best season in 1902–03 when he played in sixteen matches as the team finished runners-up in the First Division. He scored his only goal against Everton (won

2–1) in October 1902. At the start of his career he played in 35 League matches for Burton and ended by having 30 outings for Plymouth.

NORRIS, FRANK HAROLD
Forward: 9 apps, 2 goals
Born: Aston, Birmingham, 14 August 1907 – *Died*: 1980
Career: Adelaide FC (Birmingham Victoria League, 1920–22), Halesowen Town (August 1922), VILLA (February 1926), West Ham United (June 1928), Crystal Palace (June 1933–December 1934), French League football (August 1934–April 1935), Shirley Town (August 1935; retired May 1936)
A sprightly footballer, a man of many parts, Norris had to wait until April 1926 before making his debut for Villa (against Arsenal). He later did well (as a right-half) with West Ham, for whom he netted 6 times in 65 appearances, including a hat-trick as a stand-in centre-forward against Oldham in October 1932.

NORTON, DAVID WAYNE
Defender: 54+2 apps, 2 goals
Born: Cannock, 3 March 1965
Career: VILLA (apprentice, June 1981; professional, March 1983), Notts County (August 1988), Rochdale (loan, October 1990), Hull City (loan, January 1991; signed August 1991), Northampton Town (August 1994), Hereford United (August 1996), Cheltenham Town (August 1998), Yeovil Town (1999), Forest Green Rovers (joint manager, August 2000), Tamworth (July 2001), Gainsborough Trinity (player/manager, November 2001), Tamworth (May 2002)
England youth international Norton graduated through the ranks at Villa Park and developed into a very competent defender before transferring to Notts County. During the next 8 years he made over 350 appearances prior to dropping into the Conference with Hereford, managed by former Villa boss Graham Turner. He later linked up with two other ex-Villa players, Nigel Spink and Tony Daley, at Forest Green.

OAKES, MICHAEL CHRISTIAN
Goalkeeper: 59+2 apps
Born: Northfield, Birmingham, 30 October 1973
Career: VILLA (apprentice, July 1989; professional, July 1991), Scarborough (loan, September 1993), Bromsgrove Rovers (loan), Gloucester City (loan), Wolverhampton Wanderers (£400,000, October 1999)
After becoming third choice at Villa Park behind David James and Peter Enckelman, Oakes had no hesitation in moving to Wolves. Capped six times by England at Under-21 level, Oakes – an excellent shot-stopper – was rated as one of the best keepers in the First Division in 2000–01. However, he lost his place in the Wolves side to Matt Murray in 2002–03 when promotion was gained to the Premiership. His father, Alan, appeared in 669 games for Manchester City.

O'CONNOR, JAMES

Utility: 4 apps

Born: Greenock, 7 January 1867 – *Died*: Birmingham, 1929

Career: Vale of Leven, Hibernian, Celtic (August 1888), Glasgow Hibernians (September 1889), Renton (October 1889), Warwick County (December 1889), VILLA (January 1890), Burslem Port Vale (trial, August 1891), Celtic (March 1892), Nottingham Forest (April 1892; retired, injured, April 1893)

O'Connor, a reserve wing-half or centre-forward, made his Villa debut in a 2–1 home defeat by Bolton in January 1890 when deputising for Harry Devey. He was 26 when he retired.

O'DONNELL, FRANCIS JOSEPH

Forward: 31 apps, 14 goals

Born: Buckhaven, Fife, 31 August 1911 – *Died*: Macclesfield, 4 September 1952

Career: Scottish schoolboy football, Wellesley Juniors, Celtic (September 1930), Preston North End (£5,000, plus brother Hugh O'Donnell, May 1935), Blackpool (£8,000, plus two players, November 1937), VILLA (£10,500, November 1938); guest for Blackpool (1939–40, 1944–45), Heart of Midlothian (1939–40), Wolverhampton Wanderers (1940–41), RAF Cosford (1940–41), Brighton and Hove Albion (1941–42, 1944–46), Fulham (1942–43), Brentford (1942–43), York City (1942–43), Tottenham Hotspur (1944–45), Nottingham Forest (1945–46; signed free, March 1947), Buxton (player/manager, December 1948–May 1952)

A big, strong, thrustful and brainy inside- or centre-forward, O'Donnell scored in every round of Preston's 1937 FA Cup run, netting the only goal in the final defeat by Sunderland – one of 42 he claimed in his 100 appearances for the Deepdale club. Full of fighting spirit, and capped 6 times by Scotland (1936–38), he went on to net 17 times in his 30 League outings for Blackpool before fellow Scot Alex Massie lured him to Villa Park. He did well with Villa, playing between Freddie Haycock and Ronnie Starling before serving in the RAF during WW2.

OLNEY, BENJAMIN ALBERT

Goalkeeper: 97 apps

Born: Holborn, London, 15 March 1899 – *Died*: Derby, 23 September 1943

Career: Farley's Athletic, Aston Park Rangers, Brierley Hill Alliance, Stourbridge (August 1919), Derby County (£800, April 1921), VILLA (December 1927), Bilston United (player/manager, July 1930), Walsall (August 1931), Shrewsbury Town (August 1932), Moor Green (reinstated as an amateur, August 1934–April 1935); later licensee of the Horse and Jockey, Bilston; then employed at the Rolls Royce factory (Derby)

Olney was capped twice by England, against France and Belgium in 1928. He also played in two unofficial Test matches against South Africa in 1929 and in one junior international. He made 240 appearances for Derby before moving to

Villa Park – a week or so after the Rams had completed the double over Villa in the First Division. Olney missed only 11 games, all through injury and illness, during his 5 years at the Baseball Ground and his impressive appearance record stood for over 40 years until beaten by Reg Matthews in 1968. After helping the Rams win promotion from Division Two in 1926, he quickly bedded himself in at Villa, playing very efficiently after replacing Tommy Jackson. Known as 'Big Ben', he gave way to Fred Biddlestone in 1930. His brother, Wal Olney, was a boxer and his son a junior footballer with Birmingham.

OLNEY, IAN DOUGLAS
Striker: 83+31 apps, 21 goals
Born: Luton, 17 December 1969
Career: Gloucestershire Schools, Ebley FC, VILLA (YTS, June 1986; professional, July 1988), Oldham Athletic (£700,000, July 1992; retired May 1998); returned briefly with Halesowen Town (January–May 2000)
A very useful 6 ft 1 in. striker, strong and mobile, Olney made the breakthrough at Villa Park in 1988–89 after two excellent scoring campaigns in the reserve and intermediate sides. He netted on his senior debut against Birmingham in the League Cup in October 1988 and went on to make well over 100 appearances while gaining 10 England Under-21 caps. He had a good first season with the Latics (13 goals in 39 games) but then suffered injury problems which led to him quitting top-class soccer in 1998.

O'NEILL, ALAN
Inside-forward: 36 apps, 14 goals
Born: Deptford, Sunderland, 13 November 1937
Career: Deptford Council School, Sunderland and District Schools, Sunderland (juniors, July 1953; professional February 1956), VILLA (£9,000, October 1960), Plymouth Argyle (November 1962), Bournemouth (February 1964–May 1965)
Five days after his transfer from Roker Park, O'Neill scored with his first kick (after 25 seconds) for Villa against Birmingham in October 1960, and later added a second goal in a 6–2 win. A workmanlike player, he did well at Sunderland (27 goals in 74 League games) and Plymouth (14 goals in 40 appearances) while netting 8 times in 37 starts for Bournemouth. Christened Alan Hope, he changed his name to O'Neill in 1956 after his mother had remarried. He now lives in Bournemouth.

ORMONDROYD, IAN
Forward: 56+18 apps, 10 goals
Born: Bradford, 22 September 1964
Career: Thackley FC, Bradford City (professional, September 1985), Oldham Athletic (loan, March 1987), VILLA (£650,000, February 1989), Derby County (£350,000, September 1991), Leicester City (March 1992), Hull

220

City (loan, January 1995), Bradford City (£75,000, July 1995), Oldham Athletic (free, September 1996), Scunthorpe United (£25,000, September 1997–May 1998)

A record signing in 1989, 'Sticks' or 'Legs' Ormondroyd, 6 ft 4 in. tall and 13 st. 6 lb in weight, spent two and a half years at Villa Park, during which time he scored some important goals. Good in the air, able and generally useful on the ground, his 13 years of competitive football produced good figures: 451 appearances and 83 goals. A niggling ankle injury eventually resulted in him leaving the League stage.

ORMSBY, BRENDAN THOMAS CHRISTOPHER

Defender: 136+4 apps, 7 goals
Born: Edgbaston, Birmingham, 1 October 1960
Career: Ladywood Comprehensive School (Birmingham), VILLA (apprentice, March 1976; professional, October 1978), Leeds United (£65,000, February 1986), Shrewsbury Town (loan, January 1990), Doncaster Rovers (July 1990), Scarborough (August 1992), Waterford United (1993–94), Wigan Athletic (non-contract, August–September 1994)

A ginger-haired centre-half, strong and reliable, totally committed, Ormsby came through the junior ranks at Villa Park to earn England youth honours. Injured, he lost his place in the side to Paul Elliott, but recovered and went on to add a further 150-plus outings to his career statistics.

OVERTON, JOHN

Defender: 3 apps
Born: Rotherham, 2 May 1956
Career: Yorkshire Schools, VILLA (apprentice, June 1972; professional, January 1974), Halifax Town (loan, March 1976), Gillingham (June 1976–May 1981); played non-League football (1981–88)

Overton was a reserve at Villa Park, playing in three senior games, all in February 1976. He made 178 League appearances in 5 seasons at the Priestfield Stadium (10 goals).

PACE, DEREK JOHN

Centre-forward: 107 apps, 42 goals
Born: Essington near Wolverhampton, 17 March 1932 – *Died*: 1989
Career: Bloxwich Strollers, VILLA (professional, September 1949), Sheffield United (£12,000, December 1957), Notts County (December 1964), Walsall (July 1966; retired May 1967), Walsall Wood (manager, July 1968–May 1970)

'Doc' Pace scored over 40 goals for Bloxwich Strollers before becoming a 'pro' with Villa. Discovered by former defender George Cummings, he went on to amass a fine record during his time at Villa Park, averaging a goal in every 229 minutes before transferring to Bramall Lane on Boxing Day 1957, signed by future Villa boss Joe Mercer. Pace spent 7 years with the Blades, adding 140 goals to his tally (in 253 games). After assisting Notts County, injuries annoyed him considerably at Walsall, which resulted in his retirement in 1967. He represented the Army against Ireland during his National Service in the RAMC and helped Sheffield United gain promotion to the First Division in 1959.

PALETHORPE, JOHN THOMAS

Centre-forward: 6 apps, 2 goals
Born: Leicester, 23 November 1909 – *Died*: May 1984
Career: Maidenhead United (1927), Crystal Palace (professional, August 1929), Reading (March 1931), Stoke City (March, 1933), Preston North End (December 1933), Sheffield Wednesday (December 1934), VILLA (November 1935), Crystal Palace (October 1936), Chelmsford City (August 1938), Shorts Sports (August 1939), Colchester United (briefly; retired 1946)

'SOS' Palethorpe was a big, bustling centre-forward, who won promotion from the Second Division in successive seasons with Stoke (1933) and Preston (1934) and then gained an FA Cup-winner's medal with Sheffield Wednesday (1935). After being relegated from the First Division with Villa in 1936, he moved on soon afterwards. He was always cracking jokes and was the life and soul of the party. Palethorpe gave up his job as a shoe-manufacturer to become a professional footballer in 1929. He had a fine career, netting 107 goals in 177 League appearances over a period of 8 years (1930–38). His nephew, Chris Palethorpe, played for Reading.

PANK, THOMAS

Defender: 10 apps
Born: Aston, Birmingham, January 1853 – *Died*: Oxford, August 1929
Career: Birmingham Excelsior FC, VILLA (August 1875; retired, injured, May 1883); went into business in Oxford, where he lived until his death; was a VILLA vice president in the 1920s

With his heavy moustache and long stride, Pank was a true Victorian footballer, as hard as nails, rough and ready but very competitive. He would play anywhere in defence as long as he could get a game! He was a member of Villa's first-ever FA Cup side against Stafford Road FC in December 1879 and, all told, appeared in ten senior matches for the club as well as starring in scores of friendlies and local cup games. Pank was an outstanding athlete and founder member of the Birchfield Harriers Athletic Club before he took up football. His manly physique was considered to be so well nigh perfect that the statue on the lid of the Lord Mayor of Birmingham Charity Cup was a model of Pank in action. He was killed in a road accident.

PARK, ROBERT CLYDESDALE
Utility: 71+15 apps, 10 goals
Born: Edinburgh, 3 July 1946
Career: Peterlee Schools, East Durham Boys, Middlesbrough (schoolboy forms, then amateur, May 1961), Paton and Baldwins Works XI, Darlington Wool Firms FC (Sunday side), VILLA (apprentice, September 1961; professional, July 1963), Wrexham (May 1969), Peterborough United (June 1972), Northampton Town (February 1973), Hartlepool United (July 1974), Easington Coalminers' Welfare (May 1975; retired as player, May 1980), Peterlee Newtown (assistant manager, seasons 1980–82)

A ball-playing wing-half or inside-forward, Park, who lined up in the same Durham Boys' team as Colin Bell, signed for Villa after scoring a hat-trick for Darlington Wool Firms FC in a Sunday morning game. He quickly made an impression at Villa Park with some useful Central League displays but after turning professional had to fight for a first-team place with Alan Deakin, Brian Godfrey, Willie Hamilton, Dave Pountney, Mike Tindall and Ron Wylie during his eight years at the club. Nevertheless, he persevered before becoming a casualty of Tommy Docherty's axe! Then, with former Villa full-back John Neal as his manager, he starred in 125 matches for Wrexham (8 goals), collecting a Welsh Cup runner's-up medal in 1971.

PARKER, GARRY STUART
Midfield: 113+6 apps, 114 goals
Born: Oxford, 7 September 1965
Career: Luton Town (apprentice, June 1981; professional, May 1983), Hull City (£72,000, February 1986), Nottingham Forest (£260,000, March 1988), VILLA (£650,000, November 1991), Leicester City (£300,000, February 1995; retired as a player, June 1999; then coach)

Regarded as one of the finest right-sided midfielders in League football during the early 1990s, Parker had already established himself firmly in the game by the time he joined Villa in 1991. He had made 54 appearances for the Hatters, 95 for Hull and 151 for Forest, whom he helped win the European Super Cup in 1989 and register 2 successive League Cup final victories (1989, 1990). Capped by England at youth, 'B' and Under-21 levels (six caps gained in the latter category), he added another League Cup triumph to his collection in 1997 and was in the Leicester side that gained promotion to the Premiership that same year. Parker made close on 150 appearances for the Foxes before taking up coaching duties at Filbert Street.

PARKER, GRAHAM SYDNEY
Midfield: 20+1 apps, 1 goal
Born: Coventry, 23 May 1946
Career: Coventry and Warwickshire Schools, VILLA (apprentice, July 1961; professional, May 1963), Rotherham United (£6,000, December 1967),

Lincoln City (£2,500, July 1968), Exeter City (March 1969), Torquay United (May 1974–May 1975); retired, May 1977, after playing in charity matches for two years

A player allowed to slip away, Parker – nicknamed 'Fezz' – made 250 appearances after leaving Villa Park, released by manager Tommy Cummings. A neat, compact player, Parker won six schoolboy caps for England.

PARKES, HENRY ARTHUR

Full-back: 345 apps, 4 goals

Born: Erdington, Birmingham, 4 January 1920

Career: Slade Road School (Erdington), GEC Works team (Witton), VILLA (trial, April–May 1935), Boldmere St Michael's (1937), VILLA (amateur, April 1939; professional, August 1939); guest for Northampton Town and West Bromwich Albion during WW2; retired, June 1955, to concentrate on his thriving sports outfitter's shop in Corporation Street, Birmingham, which he ran for 40 years; later served as a director at both Villa Park and Birmingham City

Parkes played for Villa in ten different positions. A tremendously versatile footballer, he was a 'hard-boiled' Brummie, the joker in the pack, who possessed a biting tackle, was quick in recovery, cleared his lines diligently without any fuss or bother, was utterly reliable and never complained! A wonderful professional, he preferred the right-back position, where he partnered George Cummings, Dicky Dorsett and Peter Aldis to great effect before handing over to Stan Lynn. Besides his senior record with Villa, Parkes also appeared in 134 WW2 fixtures, scored 41 goals and gained a Wartime League Cup (N)-winner's medal in 1944. He was in line for an England cap in 1946 but had the misfortune to damage an arm at Derby, an injury that not only cost him his place in the Villa side but also an international outing.

PARSONS, DENNIS RONALD

Goalkeeper: 41 apps

Born: Birmingham, 29 May 1925 – *Died*: 1980

Career: BSA Cycle Works, Wolverhampton Wanderers (February 1944), Hereford United (1951), VILLA (August 1952), Kidderminster Harriers (August 1956), Wellington Town (August 1957), Hereford United (April 1959; retired, injured, May 1960)

Parsons, sound and safe, was reserve to England's Bert Williams at Molineux and then understudied Welsh international Keith Jones at Villa Park. With WW2 still in progress, the luckless Parsons had to wait three years before making his League debut, ironically against the team he was to join, Villa.

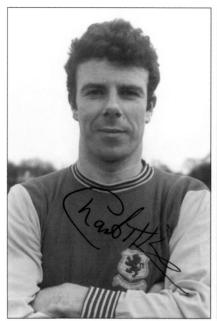

TOP LEFT: Charlie Aitken — record appearance-maker and long-serving left-back

TOP RIGHT: Bruce Rioch — attacking Scottish international midfielder

ABOVE: Jim Cumbes — goalkeeping-cricketer (with Welsh international Trevor Hockey)

ABOVE: John Burridge —
nomadic goalkeeper

TOP: Chris Nicholl (on extreme left)
made over 250 appearances for Villa at
centre-half

RIGHT: Trevor Hockey, Welsh
international midfielder

TOP LEFT: Brian Little — Villa player and later manager

TOP RIGHT: John Gidman — Youth Cup- and League Cup-winning right-back

ABOVE LEFT: John Deehan — England Under-21 striker

ABOVE RIGHT: Andy Gray — aggressive Scottish international striker

TOP LEFT: Des Bremner — midfielder in Villa's League and European Cup wins

TOP RIGHT: Jimmy Rimmer — member of two European Cup-final squads

ABOVE LEFT: Ken McNaught — League and European Cup winner with Villa

ABOVE RIGHT: Dennis Mortimer — League and European Cup-winning skipper

TOP LEFT: Gary Shaw — 1980s strike-partner to Peter Withe

TOP RIGHT: Gary Williams — Able-bodied defender or midfielder

LEFT: Peter Withe (with opposing goalkeeper Barry Siddall) scorer of Villa's European Cup-winning goal in 1982

TOP LEFT: Colin Gibson — versatile star of the 1980s

TOP RIGHT: Neale Cooper — tough-tackling Scotsman

RIGHT: David Platt — goalscoring midfielder with Villa and England

TOP LEFT: Nigel Sims — 1957 FA Cup-winning goalkeeper

TOP RIGHT: Sasa Curcic — Yugoslavian midfielder

ABOVE LEFT: Paul McGrath — Villa's masterful Republic of Ireland defender

ABOVE RIGHT: Cyrille Regis — striker who served with four Midlands clubs

ABOVE LEFT: Dean Saunders — Welsh
international goalscorer

ABOVE RIGHT: Steve Staunton —
Republic of Ireland full-back,
ex-Liverpool

RIGHT: Ron Saunders — managed
Villa to their first League title in 71
years

PATON, DANIEL THOMAS
Inside-forward: 1 app.
Born: Birmingham, 1870 – *Died*: Birmingham, 1938
Career: Bordesley Green Baptists, Aston Royal, VILLA (September 1892), Birmingham Excelsior (December 1892–April 1894)
Paton, an amateur, spent barely four months with Villa, for whom he made one appearance, in a 6–1 home League defeat by Sunderland two weeks after joining.

PATON, JAMES JABEZ
Centre-forward: 3 apps, 1 goal
Born: Glasgow, 1 July 1855 – *Died*: Scotland, *circa* 1924
Career: Vale of Leven (1884), VILLA (July 1889), Dundee Harp (September 1891–May 1892), VILLA (August 1892–March 1893)
Paton was 34 when he joined Villa as a reserve to Archie Hunter and Albert Allen. He failed to impress and was subsequently released.

PEARSON, JOSEPH FRANK
Wing-half: 118 apps, 7 goals
Born: Brierley Hill, 19 September 1877 – *Died*: Birmingham, 1946
Career: Saltley College (1895), VILLA (August 1900; retired May 1908); became headmaster at both Pensnett Junior and Wollaston Church of England Schools; also qualified as a linesman, running the line in the England–Scotland international at Villa Park in 1922; later mayor of Stourbridge for two years (1941–42)
Pearson was an orthodox footballer, sharp and incisive, who was an FA Cup winner in 1905 before giving up the game after failing to overcome a niggling knee injury that had troubled him for two years.

PEJIC, MICHAEL
Full-back: 12 apps
Born: Chesterton, Staffordshire, 25 January 1950
Career: Chesterton and North Staffs Schools, Corona Drinks FC, Stoke City (apprentice, June 1966; professional, January 1968), Everton (£135,000, February 1977), VILLA (£225,000, September 1979; retired May 1980 with groin injury, suffered against Liverpool, December 1979); became a farmer (unsuccessfully); then Leek Town (manager, 1981–82), Northwich Victoria (manager, 1982–83), Port Vale (youth coach, July 1986; senior coach, December 1987–March 1992), FA coach and player development officer; Kuwait (coach), Chester City (manager, 1994–95), Stoke City (Youth coach, 1995–99)
Son of a Yugoslav miner, Pejic was a thoughtful player who covered well, tackled aggressively and cleared his lines effectively. During a fine career, he won four full England caps and appeared in eight Under-23 internationals as well as helping Stoke win the League Cup in 1972. He made 89 appearances for Everton and over 300 for the Potters.

His brother, Mel, also played for Stoke and made over 400 League appearances for Hereford and 100-plus for Wrexham (1979–95).

PENDLETON, JOHN JAMES

Half-back: 6 apps
Born: Liverpool, August 1896 – *Died*: Lancaster, 1955
Career: Served in King's Liverpool Regiment; South Liverpool (1915), VILLA (January 1920), Wigan Borough (August 1921), Walsall (August 1924–April 1925), Mold (season 1925–26)

Able to occupy any half-back position, Pendleton was signed by Villa on the say-so of Frank Barson. Strong and well-built, he was perhaps a shade out of his depth in the First Division.

PENRICE, GARY KENNETH

Midfield: 14+6 apps, 1 goal
Born: Bristol, 23 March 1964
Career: Mangotsfield (1982), Bristol Rovers (professional, November 1984), Watford (£500,000, November 1989), VILLA (£1m, March 1991), Queens Park Rangers (£625,000, October 1991), Watford (£300,000, November 1995), Bristol Rovers (player/coach, September 1997; retired as a player, May 2000)

An exceptionally fine footballer, able to play as an out-and-out striker if required, Penrice did far better at a lower level than he did in the top flight. Good on the ball, he was able to hold play up and bring his fellow attackers into the game with a positive pass or movement. He failed to hit it off with Villa, but his career record was superb: 119 goals in 518 appearances, 74 coming in 311 outings for Bristol Rovers.

PERRY, THOMAS

Wing-half: 29 apps, 1 goal
Born: West Bromwich, 12 August 1871 – *Died*: West Bromwich, July 1927
Career: Christ Church School (West Bromwich), Christ Church FC, West Bromwich Baptists, Stourbridge (1889), West Bromwich Albion (July 1890), VILLA (£50, October 1901; retired January 1903 through injury); later worked with one of his three brothers in West Bromwich

Although only 30, England international Perry was past his best when he joined Villa from WBA. He remained at the club for a year, scoring his only goal in a 3–2 win over Derby in February 1902. Earlier he had been a stalwart performer for Albion, amassing 277 appearances. He won one England cap (1898), played three times for the Football League XI (mid-1890s) and also starred for a Division One Select XI against Villa (1894). He lined up for Albion against Villa in the 1895 FA Cup final and played regularly for the Throstles during their first season at the Hawthorns (1900–01). He had two other brothers – Walter and Charlie – who both played for Albion.

PHILLIPS, CUTHBERT

Outside-right: 25 apps, 5 goals

Born: Victoria, Monmouthshire, 23 June 1910 – *Died*: Lichfield, 21 October 1969

Career: Ebbw Vale (August 1924), Merthyr Town, Plymouth Argyle (trial), Torquay United (trial), Ebbw Vale, Wolverhampton Wanderers (professional, August 1929), VILLA (£9,000, January 1936), Birmingham (March 1938), Chelmsford City (August 1939; retired May 1945); later licensee of Butters Arms, Bushbury, and also in Lichfield

Phillips – known as Charlie – won Welsh schoolboy honours while working as a boilerman and playing for Ebbw Vale in 1924–25. Several clubs wanted to sign him and he had offers from Plymouth Argyle, Torquay and Cardiff before signing for Wolves in 1929. A speedy forward, mostly at home on the right wing, he made 202 appearances during his Molineux days (65 goals scored), was capped 10 times by Wales and gained a Second Division championship in 1932, netting 18 important goals that season. He also scored on his international debut against Northern Ireland at Wrexham in 1931. He went on to captain his country on six occasions. At Christmas 1935, as skipper of Wolves he was sent off against Bolton and a month later was transferred to Villa, having made over 200 appearances during his time at Molineux. Capped three more times as a Villa player, he scored on his debut in a 3–1 win at Derby but unfortunately could not prevent relegation and when Villa returned as Second Division champions he managed only a handful of games. After a little over a season at St Andrew's, Phillips went into non-League football, retiring in 1945. A fine all-round sportsman, he also excelled at cricket, golf, tennis, Rugby Union and various athletics events.

PHILLIPS, LEIGHTON

Defender: 168+7 apps, 4 goals

Born: Briton Ferry, near Swansea, 25 September 1949

Career: Bryn Hyfred Junior and Cort Sart Secondary Schools (Briton Ferry), Neath Area Schools, Neath Under-12s, Cardiff City (apprentice, June 1965; professional, April 1967), VILLA (£100,000, September 1974), Swansea City (£70,000, November 1978), Charlton Athletic (£25,000, August 1981; player/coach, June 1982), Exeter City (free, March–May 1983), Llanelli (player/manager, August 1984; retired as player, May 1985)

Phillips represented Wales at schoolboy, Under-21, Under-23 and senior levels (58 full caps, a record haul for a defender in Welsh football at that time). A fine player, not the flashy type, just a good, honest performer, giving nothing away, he scored on his senior debut for Cardiff and after being successfully converted into a defender went on to appear in 180 League games for the Ninian Park club before moving to Villa. Already cup-tied, he missed Villa's 1975 League Cup final win over Norwich but did help steer the side to promotion from Division Two that season and then made up for his earlier disappointment by gaining a

League Cup-winner's medal himself in 1977 (against Everton). Phillips later starred in two more promotion campaigns with Swansea (1979, 1981). A superb 'reader' of the game, he was nicknamed 'Brodwein' and made 472 League appearances during his career. He now lives in Neath, South Wales, and works as Senior Life underwriter for the Confederation Life Insurance Co.

PHILLIPS, THOMAS JOHN SEYMOUR
Goalkeeper: 17 apps
Born: Shrewsbury, 7 July 1951
Career: Shropshire County Boys, Shrewsbury Town (apprentice, July 1966; professional, November 1968), VILLA (£35,000, October 1969), Chelsea (£30,000, August 1970), Swansea City (loan, March 1979), Crewe Alexandra (loan, August–September 1979), Brighton and Hove Albion (£15,000, March 1980), Charlton Athletic (free, July 1981), Crystal Palace (free, January 1983); to Hong Kong; then Crystal Palace (reserves, 1984; retired May 1985)

Phillips was a fine, agile goalkeeper but was inconsistent. Nevertheless, he won four caps at both Under-23 and senior levels for Wales. He made over 50 appearances for the 'Shrews' and despite understudying Peter Bonetti at Chelsea, still played in 150 games for the London club, helping them reach the 1971 European Cup-winner's Cup final. He was signed by Chelsea after future Villa keeper Tommy Hughes had broken his leg and was Alan Mullery's first capture when he took over as Charlton manager.

PHOENIX, ARTHUR
Centre-forward: 4 apps, 3 goals
Born: Patricroft near Manchester, 5 March 1902 – *Died*: 1979
Career: Urmston Council School, Hadfield, Glossop North End (1922), Birmingham (May 1923), VILLA (May 1924), Barnsley (September 1925), Exeter City (July 1926), Wigan Borough (July 1929), Bath City (early November 1930), Torquay United (November 1930), Mansfield Town (July 1931), Racing Club de Paris/France (August 1932), Sandbach Ramblers (October 1933), Dublin Shelbourne (January 1934), Ballymena (August 1935), Mossley (briefly), Nelson (November 1935; retired April 1937)

A very efficient, hard-working player, Phoenix was certainly a soccer nomad who served with no fewer than 15 clubs. He never really settled down anywhere and had his best days at Exeter, for whom he netted 9 times in 52 League outings.

PIMBLETT, FRANCIS ROY
Midfield: 11 apps
Born: Liverpool, 12 March 1957
Career: Liverpool and Merseyside District Schools, VILLA (apprentice, June 1973; professional, October 1974), Newport County (loan, March 1976),

Stockport County (July 1976), Brisbane City/Australia (May 1979), Hartlepool United (March–April 1980)

An efficient footballer, Pimblett won eight England schoolboy caps and was also a youth international trialist before struggling for three years at Villa Park, having his contract cancelled by mutual consent. He only made 20 League appearances during his career.

PINNER, MICHAEL JOHN

Goalkeeper: 4 apps

Born: Boston, Lincolnshire, 16 February 1934

Career: Boston Grammar School, Wyberton Rangers, Notts County (junior, October 1948), Cambridge University (1950), Hendon (1951), Pegasus (1952), VILLA (three spells: May 1954, February 1956 and April 1957), Arsenal (October 1957), Sheffield Wednesday (December 1957), Queens Park Rangers (July 1959), Manchester United (February 1961), Middlesex Wanderers, Hendon (briefly), Chelsea Casuals, Chelsea (October 1961), Arsenal (December 1961), Swansea Town (August 1962), Leyton Orient (October 1962; professional, October 1963), Belfast Distillery (July 1965; retired May 1967); became a prominent solicitor

Pinner decided to turn professional at the age of 29, having appeared in more than 250 competitive games as an amateur and winning over 50 caps for his country at that level. He played in two Olympic Games soccer tournaments – Melbourne (1956) and Rome (1960) – and was reserve in Tokyo (1964). He represented the RAF (he was an officer in the education department) and played in four Varsity matches against Oxford University. Daring, agile and a fine shot-stopper, Pinner made his debut for Villa in a 3–3 draw at Bolton in September 1954 and during his career he played in 32 different countries with the FA, Middlesex Wanderers, Great Britain and the England amateur side.

PLATT, DAVID ANDREW

Forward/midfield: 155 apps, 68 goals

Born: Oldham, 10 June 1966

Career: Chadderton, Manchester United (apprentice, June 1982; professional, July 1984), Crewe Alexandra (free, February 1985), VILLA (£200,000, February 1988), Bari/Italy (£5.5m, July 1991), Juventus/Italy (£6.5m, June 1992), Sampdoria/Italy (£5.25m, August 1993), Arsenal (£4.75m, July 1995), Sampdoria/Italy (free transfer, player/coach/manager, August–November 1998), Nottingham Forest (player/manager, August 1999; retired July 2001), England Under-21 (coach/manager 2001–May 2004)

An attacking midfielder with flair, drive and an excellent scoring record, Platt was 'given away' by Manchester United without ever appearing in the first team. Nurtured at Gresty Road, he netted 60 goals in 152 games for the 'Alex' before making his mark with Villa, and then progressing in Italy and later at Arsenal. He helped Villa win promotion to the First Division in his first season and did his bit in ensuring the team held their position in the top flight. But the lure of the Italian lira saw him enter Serie 'A', where he spent 4 seasons, playing in over 100 matches (at various levels) and scoring 30 times. With 27 goals in 62 appearances, Platt is 8th in the list of England's top 10 marksmen and he notched England's only goal in Euro' 92. He also appeared in three 'B' and three Under-21 matches and gained both Premiership and FA Cup-winner's medals with Arsenal in 1998. When he retired, Platt's club career was excellent – 585 appearances, 201 goals. He didn't achieve much as England Under-21 boss and is now a racehorse owner.

PODMORE, WILLIAM HORACE

Inside-right: 1 app.
Born: Derby, 22 July 1872 – *Died*: Nottingham, August 1940
Career: Derby Council Schools, Burton United, VILLA (August 1894), Derby Midland (April 1896), Great Lever (August 1896–May 1897)
Podmore, a long-striding winger, spent one season with Villa, appearing in the FA Cup tie against Derby in February 1895 (won 2–1).

POOLE, KEVIN

Goalkeeper: 32 apps
Born: Bromsgrove, 21 July 1963
Career: VILLA (apprentice, June 1979; professional, June 1981), Northampton Town (loan, November 1984), Middlesbrough (August 1987), Hartlepool United (loan, March 1991), Leicester City (£40,000, July 1991), Birmingham City (free, August 1997), Bolton Wanderers (free, October 2001; released May 2004)
Owing to the form of Jimmy Rimmer, Nigel Spink and to a certain extent Mervyn Day, Poole was never a regular at Villa. However, after leaving the club he made over 250 senior appearances with other clubs and was a League Cup winner in 1997 with Leicester. Sound on crosses and a specialist penalty-saver, he has saved over a dozen spot-kicks in regular time.

POSTMA, STEFAN

Goalkeeper: 8+3 apps
Born: Utrecht, Holland, 10 June 1976
Career: FC Utrecht/Holland, De Graaschap/Holland, VILLA (£1.5m, May 2002)
Signed initially as cover for Peter Enckelman, Postma, 6 ft 6 in. tall and probably the joint tallest player ever to appear for Villa, made just nine appearances in his first season and then had two 'sub' outings in 2003–04 when playing second fiddle to Thomas Sorensen.

POTTER, FREDERICK

Goalkeeper: 7 apps

Born: Cradley Heath, 29 November 1940

Career: Homer Street School (Cradley), Cradley Heath Juniors, North Worcester Boys, Halesowen Town (reserves), Codsall Villa, VILLA (amateur, June 1956; professional, July 1959), Swindon Town (trial, November 1961), Doncaster Rovers (July 1962), Burton Albion (May 1966), Hereford United (July 1970; retired May 1974 after failing to recover from a cartilage operation)

As a youngster, Potter was an outfield player occupying four or five different positions before becoming a goalkeeper with Cradley Heath Juniors. He was in line as a possible replacement for Nigel Sims but chose to leave Villa to join Doncaster Rovers, for whom he appeared in more than 125 games. Once at inside-forward, he helped Hereford gain entry into the Football League in 1972.

POTTS, VICTOR ERNEST

Full-back: 72 apps

Born: Aston, Birmingham, 20 August 1915 – *Died*: Sutton Coldfield, 22 October 1996

Career: Birchfield Road Schools, Metro Welfare FC, Tottenham Hotspur (amateur, August 1933), Northfleet United (July 1934), Tottenham Hotspur (part-time professional, August 1937), Doncaster Rovers (£3,000, August 1938), VILLA (guest, October 1940; signed permanently, August 1945; retired May 1949), Notts County (reserve-team trainer, June 1949), Wolseley Athletic FC (part-time player, 1951–52), Southend United (trainer, August 1954), Notts County (head trainer, August 1955), Walsall (trainer, May 1957–April 1963), Tottenham Hotspur (scout, mid-1960s); later worked for British Leyland

Potts slipped the eye of Villa by joining Spurs at the age of 18. He played for the London club's nursery side (Northfleet), brushing shoulders with some of the finest players in the game who later became great managers, namely Bill Nicholson, Vic Buckingham and Freddie Cox. Cartilage trouble affected his progress and he underwent surgery twice inside three years. Having lost so much playing time, he was eventually given a free transfer from White Hart Lane and with both Barnsley and Doncaster seeking his services, he chose the latter club, joining in 1938. The outbreak of WW2 brought Potts back to his native Birmingham to work on aircraft generators. Here he bumped into Norman Smith, who had been closely associated with the Birchfield Road School side, and after a brief chat, Potts agreed to guest for Villa during the hostilities. He played over 200 games for the club between 1941 and 1945, and was signed on a permanent basis at the start of the 1945–46 transitional season by his former playing colleague Alex Massie. An exceptionally fine player, very consistent and seemingly always at ease, Potts never looked flustered as he went on to appear in over 70 post-war games for Villa before retiring in 1949. He teamed up with his old buddy Eric Houghton at Meadow Lane and later came out of retirement to assist Wolseley Athletic.

POUNTNEY, DAVID HAROLD
Wing-half/inside-left: 126+2 apps, 7 goals
Born: Baschurch, Salop, 12 October 1939
Career: Baschurch County School, Shropshire and District Boys, Myddle Youth Club, Shrewsbury Town (professional, September 1957), VILLA (£20,000, October 1963), Shrewsbury Town (£10,000, February 1968), Chester City (June 1970), Oswestry Town (player/manager, July 1973; retired August 1976); later ran a sports shop in Church Stretton

Pountney, a powerfully built player, happy to play on either side of the pitch, made over 500 senior appearances during his career. With Villa, he performed in midfield with Alan Deakin, Ron Wylie, Mike Tindall and Phil Woosnam and defended resolutely alongside John Sleeuwenhoek.

POWELL, IVOR VERDUN
Left-half: 86 apps, 5 goals
Born: Gillach, near Bargoed, Glamorgan, 5 July 1916
Career: Bargoed, Queens Park Rangers (trial, November 1936), Barnet, Queens Park Rangers (professional, September 1937); guest for Bradford City and Blackpool during WW2; VILLA (£17,500, December 1948), Port Vale (player/manager, July–November 1951), Barry Town (December 1951), Bradford City (May 1952; player/manager, May–November 1954; manager to February 1955), Leeds United (trainer/coach, July 1956), Carlisle United (manager, May 1960–May 1963), Bath City (manager, June 1964–August 1965), PAOK Salonika/Greece (coach), head football coach at the University of Bath (late 1960s/1970s)

Powell was an attacking player, solid, industrious, totally committed with an exceptionally long throw who gained eight caps for Wales between 1946 and 1951 (four with Villa) plus four more in WW2 and Victory internationals. A chance conversation on a bowling green between a South Wales football enthusiast and a director of QPR led to Powell being invited along to Loftus Road for a trial. His performances were not fully appreciated at first and he went off to assist Barnet before Rangers took another look at him, and this time offered him a contract. During WW2 he served in the Reserve Police and in the RAF in India before becoming a PT instructor in Blackpool. While there, Powell struck up a great friendship with Stanley Matthews who subsequently became his best man at his wedding. When he joined Villa, after having gained a Third Division (S) championship medal with QPR, the fee involved was a record for both clubs and also a record for a half-back at that time. During his association with Villa, Powell underwent two cartilage operations from which he never fully recovered. After forming a fine middle-line with Frank Moss and

Con Martin, he moved to Port Vale. Unfortunately he was not well liked by the players, whom he tried 'to rule by fear', and, as a result, with the Potteries' club bottom of the Third Division (S), his contract was cancelled after four months. He also had his contract cancelled by Carlisle following relegation in 1963 – 12 months after winning promotion from Division Four! In between his service at Bradford and his appointment at Leeds, Powell was a publican in Manningham.

PRICE, CHRISTOPHER JOHN
Right-back: 141+3 apps, 2 goals
Born: Hereford, 30 March 1960
Career: Hereford schoolboy football, Hereford Schools Select, Hereford United (junior, June 1976; professional, January 1978), Blackburn Rovers (£25,000, July 1986), VILLA (£125,000, May 1988), Blackburn Rovers (£150,000, February 1992), Portsmouth (£50,000, January 1993), Hereford United (1994); spell in USA; Sutton Town (February 1995), Newport County (manager, 1996–97), Cinderford Town (player/manager, August 1998–May 2000), Cheltenham Town (assistant manager, 2001–02)
Price had appeared in 373 games for Hereford and over 90 for Blackburn before joining Villa. A 1977 England youth international trialist, he gained an FMC-winner's medal with Blackburn in 1987 and two years later helped Villa finish runners-up in the First Division. A fine, determined defender, quick in responding to a fast, direct winger, Price was exceptionally good at overlapping, possessed natural ability and a strong kick. He partnered Derek Mountfield, Kevin Gage and Stuart Gray (among others) at full-back before returning to Ewood Park. He later joined ex-Villa manager Graham Turner at Hereford, and then teamed up with another former Villa player, Brian Godfrey, at Cinderford Town. Price held the appearance record for Hereford until it was beaten by Mel Pejic in 1991.

PRICE, LLEWELLYN PERCY
Winger: 10 apps
Born: Caersws, near Newtown, 12 August 1896 – *Died*: 1969
Career: Barmouth (briefly), Hampstead Town, Mansfield Town (July 1920), VILLA (March 1921), Notts County (June 1922), Queens Park Rangers (May 1928), Grantham Town (February 1929–May 1930)
Able to play on both flanks, Price deputised for the injured Arthur Dorrell at the end of 1920–21. After Dorrell had regained full fitness, he became surplus to requirements and was allowed to leave the club in 1922.

PRICE, ROBERT OSCAR
Defender: 8 apps
Born: Hereford, February 1860 – *Died*: Worcester, 1921
Career: Hereford Thistle, Worcester Rovers, VILLA (April 1884; retired June 1887)

A muscular, rugged defender, Price served the club admirably for three years before retiring, aged 27, after dislocating his hip.

PRITCHARD, ROY THOMAS
Full-back: 3 apps
Born: Dawley, Shropshire, 9 May 1925 – *Died*: Willenhall, January 1993
Career: Dawley Council School, Dawley and District Schools, Wolverhampton
  Wanderers (junior, 1941; professional, August 1945); guest for Mansfield
  Town, Notts County, Swindon Town and Walsall during WW2; VILLA
  (February 1956), Notts County (November 1957), Port Vale (August 1958),
  GKN Sankeys/Wellington Town (August 1960), Banbury Spencer (August
  1961; retired June 1964); participated in various charity matches until 1990
Former Bevin Boy, Pritchard was a strong tackler who gained experience by guesting for League clubs during WW2. He made his League debut in the first post-war season with Wolves and established himself in the team the following season. In 1949 he gained an FA Cup-winner's medal and five years later added a League championship medal to his collection. After more than 220 appearances for Wolves, he moved to Villa but had the misfortune to break his jaw in his first game against Arsenal. That proved to be his only appearance of the season. In the 1990s Wolves introduced the Roy Pritchard Trophy, presented to the club's 'Young Player of the Year'.

PRITTY, GEORGE JOSEPH
Wing-half: 4 apps
Born: Nechells, Birmingham, 4 March 1915 – *Died*: 1996
Career: Tottenham Hotspur (amateur, April 1930), Metro Old Boys, Newport
  County (May 1933), VILLA (May 1935), Nottingham Forest (December
  1938); guest for Solihull Town (1939–40) and Wrexham (1941–42);
  Cheltenham Town (June 1948); later a spot welder at Fisher and Ludlow
Hardy and resolute, Pritty played for Birmingham County FA against the Scottish Juniors in March 1935 and against the Irish Free State the following year. During his three and a half years at Villa he deputised mainly for Bob Iverson and after leaving appeared in 54 games for Forest. A fine all-round sportsman, he enjoyed cricket, bowls and tennis.

PROUDLER, ARTHUR
Half-back: 1 app.
Born: Kingswinford, near Dudley, 3 October 1929
Career: Brierley Hill Schools, Halesowen Town (1945), VILLA (professional,
  December 1947), Crystal Palace (June 1956), Dorchester Town
  (player/manager, May 1959), Stourbridge (player/coach, August 1960),
  Stafford Rangers (January 1961), Bristol City (coach, 1964–65), Everton
  (youth-team coach, July 1966–May 1970), Blackburn Rovers (coach,
  1971–72); later ran a mail-order firm in Liverpool

Proudler ('Atlas' to his friends) played just 20 minutes of first-team football for Villa before leaving the pitch with a nasty gash above his eye on his debut against Leicester in November 1953. An expert with penalty kicks, he did very well in reserve and intermediate competitions before making 26 appearances for Palace.

PURSLOW, THOMAS

Forward: 1 app., 1 goal

Born: Perry Barr, Birmingham, June 1870 – *Died*: Birmingham, November 1937

Career: Nechells Old Boys, VILLA (August 1894), Walsall Town Swifts (September 1895), Darlaston (1897), Willenhall Pickwick (1899; retired, May 1903)

Reserve to Denny Hodgetts during his time with Villa, Purslow scored on his debut against WBA in November 1894 and hit three hat-tricks for the reserves in 1894–95.

RACHEL, ADAM

Goalkeeper: 0+1 app.

Born: Birmingham, 10 December 1976

Career: VILLA (YTS, June 1993; professional, May 1995), Blackpool (free, September 1999), Moor Green (July 2001)

An agile shot-stopper, Rachel made one substitute appearance for Villa, in a Premiership game at Blackburn on Boxing Day 1998, taking the place of Michael Oakes, who was sent off. Although Mark Bosnich was out injured, he found himself third choice behind Oakes and Peter Enckelman and subsequently joined Blackpool on a two-year contract.

RALPHS, ALBERT

Outside-right: 1 app.

Born: Nantwich, Cheshire, 10 February 1892 – *Died*: Chester, November 1964

Career: Nantwich FC (1907), Burnell's Ironworks FC (1908), Whitchurch (1909), VILLA (November 1911), Chester (June 1912), Mold FC (1914–15); did not figure after WW1

A short, stocky winger, Ralphs stood in for Charlie Wallace against Notts County in March 1912, his only game for Villa.

RAMSAY, GEORGE BURRELL

Forward: no senior apps

Born: Glasgow, 3 March 1855 – *Died*: Llandrindod Wells, October 1935

Career: Cathcart schoolboy football (Glasgow), Oxford FC/Glasgow, Glasgow Rangers (trial, 1875), VILLA (August 1876; retired as a player through injury, June 1882; remained at club, appointed club secretary in 1884, serving in that capacity until 1926; later honorary advisor and vice president at Villa Park)

One of the great dribblers of the 'early' game, a master of close control, George

Ramsay captained Villa for four years from 1876. He was the central figure of a grand trio of pioneers of the club, William McGregor (founder of the Football League) and Fred Rinder being the other two. It is said that Ramsay was the last player to kick a ball at Villa's Perry Barr Ground and the first to kick one at Villa Park – but surprisingly he never appeared in a first-class game for the club. He was, however, a key member of the team that won the Birmingham Senior Cup in 1880 (Villa's first trophy success). He always wore a smart polo-cap and long shorts, a star the crowds loved to watch.

With Rinder, Ramsay, who received two Football League Service Award medals in 1909 and 1927, negotiated the lease of Villa Park after earlier 'finding' the Perry Barr ground.

RAMSEY, JOHN
Left-back: 4 apps
Born: Bordesley Green, Birmingham, 11 September 1870 – *Died*: Birmingham, December 1942
Career: Church FC (Birmingham), Aston Unity (briefly), VILLA (August 1892), Ward End FC (June 1893–May 1894)
Big, brave and brawny, Ramsey's temper let him down on many occasions and this resulted in him leaving the club! He was always in trouble with referees and lost his temper far too easily. A rough and ready player.

RANDLE, WALTER WILLIAM
Outside-right: 1 app.
Born: Aston, Birmingham, 21 August 1870 – *Died*: January 1931
Career: Aston Hall School, Aston Unity, VILLA (May 1893), Leek (September 1894), Aston Victoria (1896; retired May 1903); returned to Aston to work in the licensing trade
Randle was a determined winger who had very little chance of regular first-team football owing to the prolonged form of Charlie Wallace. His only senior outing was against Sunderland in November 1893.

REEVES, GEORGE
Forward: 36 apps, 11 goals
Born: Huthwaite, Hucknall, July 1884 – *Died*: Yorkshire, September 1954
Career: Sutton-in-Ashfield FC, Ripley Athletic, Sutton Town, Barnsley (December 1906), VILLA (£1,000, November 1907), Bradford Park Avenue (November 1909), Blackpool (1912), Hucknall Colliery (1914); did not figure after WW1
Described as a 'strong, nifty forward', Reeves had good technique and a big heart. He netted 15 goals in 30 League games for Barnsley and 17 in 59 League appearances for Bradford. He helped Villa to runner's-up spot in the First Division in 1908 when deputising for Charlie Wallace on the wing, and after a serious knee injury in March 1909 he was always 'in reserve'.

REGIS, CYRILLE

Striker: 54+9 apps, 12 goals

Born: Maripasoula, French Guiana, 9 February 1958

Career: Kensal Rise and Cardinal Hinsley RC Schools (Harlesden, London), Borough of Brent Boys, Oxford and Kilburn Boys, Ryder Brent Valley, Molesey FC, Hayes (July 1976), West Bromwich Albion (£5,000, May 1977), Coventry City (£250,000, October 1984), VILLA (July 1991), Wolverhampton Wanderers (free, August 1993), Wycombe Wanderers (free, August 1994), Chester City (August 1995; retired May 1996), West Bromwich Albion (reserve-team coach, July 1997–February 2000); played as a guest for Happy Valley FC/Hong Kong (1978–79); now a football agent living in Sutton Coldfield

One of the great goalscorers of the late 1970s and 1980s, 'Smokin' Joe' Regis made a rapid rise from non-League football with Hayes to reach the FA Cup semi-final with WBA in just eight months. He cost Albion 'peanuts', having been spotted by the club's former player Ronnie Allen. He scored on his Central League, Football League, FA Cup and League Cup debuts for the Baggies, for whom he netted 112 goals in 302 appearances. Capped five times at full international level by England, Regis also appeared in three 'B' and six Under-21 matches, was voted PFA 'Young Footballer of the Year' in 1979, taking the runner's-up spot behind Steve Perryman (Spurs) in the 1982 'Footballer of the Year' poll. He helped Coventry win the FA Cup in 1987 and scored 62 goals in over 280 outings for the Sky Blues before joining Villa, where he did well before switching to Wolves, mainly as a squad player. Ending his playing career in 1996 after brief spells with Wycombe and Chester, Regis scored over 200 goals in top-class football and became the first player, at senior level, to represent Albion, Coventry, Villa and Wolves.

RENNEVILLE, WILLIAM THOMAS JAMES

Centre-forward: 2 apps, 1 goal

Born: Mullingar, near Dublin, May 1898 – *Died*: Ireland, 1948

Career: Irish schoolboy football, London Colleges, Leyton (1908), VILLA (May 1910; retired April 1912); returned with Walsall (August 1912), Worcester City (October 1914; retired, injured, May 1915); Walsall (August 1919–May 1920)

A footballer with dash and determination, Renneville (5 ft 6 in. tall) could battle it out fairly and squarely with the toughest defenders around. Capped four times by Ireland (1910–12), he had just two outings for Villa before injuring himself in a reserve game.

REYNOLDS, JOHN

Right-half: 110 apps, 17 goals

Born: Blackburn, 21 February 1869 – *Died*: Sheffield, 12 March 1917

Career: Portglenone and Ballymena Schools (County Antrim, Ireland), Park

Road FC (Blackburn), Witton, Blackburn Rovers (reserves, 1884–85), Park Road FC (1886), East Lancashire Regiment (December 1886, posted to Ireland), Distillery (1888), Ulster (June 1890), West Bromwich Albion (March 1891), Droitwich Town (on loan, 1892), VILLA (£50, April 1892), Celtic (May 1897), Southampton St Mary's (January 1898), Bristol St George's (July 1898), Royston FC/Yorkshire (September 1899), Grafton FC/New Zealand (coach, season 1902–03), Stockport County (player, August–October 1903), Willesden Town (January 1904; retired April 1905), Cardiff City (coach, season 1907–08); subsequently became a miner near Sheffield

A stumpy wee man, 'Baldy' Reynolds had played five times for Ireland before his Lancashire birth was discovered. He went on to win a further eight English caps as well as three League championship medals and two more FA Cup-winner's medals with Villa in 1895 and 1897, having gained his first with WBA (against Villa) in 1892 when he scored in a 3–0 victory. He also represented the Football League on three occasions and featured in an England trial match in 1894. A marvellously competitive player, Reynolds mastered every trick in the book and, aided by some remarkable ball skills, his footwork was, at times, exceptionally brilliant. After leaving Villa with a lot of happy memories, he won a Scottish League championship medal with Celtic in 1898, thus completing a hat-trick of Cup triumphs, having collected an Irish winner's prize with Ulster in 1891. He left Albion after falling out with the committee!

RICHARDS, LEONARD JOSEPH

Goalkeeper: 7 apps
Born: Woodsetton, near Dudley, 23 October 1892 – *Died*: Wednesbury, 1954
Career: Dudley College, Hurst Hill Wesleyans, Stourbridge (1908), VILLA (March 1911), Stourbridge (1913–14), Bilston (April 1915), Willenhall (1920)

An amateur who chose to quit playing football to concentrate on his teaching profession, Richards made seven appearances for Villa, six at the end of 1911–12 as deputy for Brendal Anstey. A good handler of the ball, he saved two penalties in those initial games against Preston and Oldham.

RICHARDSON, KEVIN

Midfield: 171+1 apps, 16 goals
Born: Newcastle-upon-Tyne, 4 December 1962
Career: Everton (apprentice, June 1978; professional, December 1980), Watford (£225,000, September 1986), Arsenal (£200,000, August 1987), Real Sociedad/Spain (£750,000, July 1990), VILLA (£450,000, August 1991), Coventry City (£300,000, February 1995), Southampton (£150,000, September 1997), Barnsley (£300,000, July 1998), Blackpool (loan, January–February 1999; retired May 2000), Stockport County (assistant manager/coach, 2002–03)

Richardson was a consistent performer over the years, working tirelessly for every club he served. He played in over 140 games for Everton before transferring to Watford and then starred in over 120 matches for Arsenal. He moved to Villa Park after a spell with Real Sociedad and played very well during his three and a half years with the club, skippering the side to victory over Manchester United in the 1994 League Cup final. He called it a day in 2000 after assisting four other League clubs. Capped once by England, Richardson gained winner's medals with Everton in the FA Cup (1984), European Cup-winner's Cup (1985) and League championship (1985) and followed up by collecting a second League championship medal with Arsenal in 1989. He also played in Everton's Charity Shield-winning team of 1984.

RIDDELL, THOMAS CYRIL

Full-back: 10 apps
Born: Handsworth, Birmingham, 20 March 1858 – *Died*: Birmingham, 1934
Career: Excelsior FC, VILLA (August 1882; retired, knee injury, May 1887)
Riddell, 6 ft 4 in. tall, 15 st. in weight, was extremely strong, could kick a ball up to 100 yards from a standing position but was described as a 'bit of a plodder'. His ten games for Villa were in the FA Cup.

RIDEOUT, PAUL DAVID

Striker: 56+7 apps, 22 goals
Born: Bournemouth, 14 August 1964
Career: Priestlands School, Southampton and Hampshire Schools, Lawrence
  Boys' Club, Lymington, Southampton (schoolboy forms, 1979–80), Swindon
  Town (apprentice, June 1980; professional, August 1981), VILLA (£250,000,
  June 1983), Bari/Italy (£400,000, July 1985), Southampton (£430,000, July
  1988), Swindon Town (loan, March–April 1991), Notts County (£250,000,
  September 1991), Glasgow Rangers (£500,000, January 1992), Everton
  (£500,000, August 1992), Red Star/France (August 1998), Tranmere Rovers
  (free, August 2000; retired May 2002)
Rideout achieved fame playing for England schoolboys when he netted a stunning goal in a televised game against Scotland at Wembley. He was on Southampton's books at the time, but was allowed to join Swindon as a 17-year-old. He returned to The Dell, signed by ex-Villa defender Chris Nicholl in 1988, having by then scored 75 goals in some 250 competitive matches. He'd also added eight England youth caps and five more at Under-21 level to those he had gained as a schoolboy. Rideout – a record 'sale' by Swindon to Villa in 1983 – played very well alongside Peter Withe and Gary Shaw, and in a fine career claimed more than 150 goals in almost 550 first-class appearances, collecting an FA Cup-winner's medal in 1995 when his goal gave Everton a 1–0 win over Manchester United. When he made his League debut in November 1980 against Hull, he became Swindon's youngest-ever player at the age of 16 years, 107 days.

RIDGEWELL, LIAM MATTHEW
Defender: 5+9 apps
Born: London, 21 July 1984
Career: West Ham United (schoolboy), VILLA (junior, 1998; apprentice, July 2000; professional, July 2001), Bournemouth (loan, October–November 2002)

An FA Youth Cup winner with Villa in 2002, England youth international Ridgewell made his first senior appearance as a 'sub' against Blackburn in the FA Cup in January 2003. He was named in the England Under-21 squad later that same year.

RILEY, THOMAS
Full-back: 16 apps
Born: Blackburn, March 1882 – *Died:* Southampton, 1939
Career: Lancaster Council School, Chorley, Blackburn Rovers (April 1902), Brentford (August 1905), VILLA (April 1906), Brentwood (June 1908), Southampton (July 1909; retired, injured, June 1912)

Riley was a lightweight player who could use both feet to good effect but was 'slow in recovery'. Prior to joining Villa, he appeared in 29 Southern League games for Brentford and 25 for Blackburn in the First Division. He didn't make a senior appearance for Saints.

RIMMER, JOHN JAMES
Goalkeeper: 287 apps
Born: Southport, 10 February 1948
Career: Southport and Merseyside Schoolboys, Manchester United (amateur, May 1963; apprentice, September 1963; professional, May 1965), Swansea City (loan, October 1973–February 1974), Arsenal (£40,000, February 1974), VILLA (£65,000, August 1977), Swansea City (August 1983), Hamrun Spartans/Malta (August 1986); Swansea City (coach, July 1987–May 1988); quit football to run a golf centre in Swansea

After making his League debut for Manchester United in April 1968, the following month Rimmer was on the subs' bench for the Reds against Benfica in the European Cup final. He went on to make 46 appearances during his time at Old Trafford (plus 17 on loan with Swansea) before transferring to Arsenal. Agile and positive, he did not command his area with the sort of authority a manager would have liked – that finally arrived with experience some ten years after his United debut! And as a result – after gaining a full England cap against Italy in Milan in 1976 to go with the two he had already won at Under-23 level – he went on to give Villa excellent service during his six years at the club. Rimmer amassed almost 290 appearances, helping Villa win the League title in 1981, the European Cup (although he was only on the field for a few minutes before going off with a back injury) and the Super Cup in 1982. He was an ever-present for four seasons between the posts. A fitness fanatic, always on the bounce, he was voted Villa's Jubilee Club's 'Player of the Year' in 1978 and in his professional career (1965–87) he accumulated over 550 appearances at senior level (470 in the Football League).

RIOCH, BRUCE DAVID
Midfield: 171+5 apps, 37 goals
Born: Aldershot, 6 September 1947
Career: Romsey Junior School (Cambridge), Cambridge and District Schools, Dynamo Boys' Club, Luton Town (apprentice, September 1962; professional, September 1964), VILLA (£100,000, with brother Neil (q.v.), July 1969), Derby County (£200,000, February 1974), Everton (£180,000, December 1976), Derby County (£150,000, November 1977), Birmingham City (loan, December 1978), Sheffield United (loan, March 1979), Torquay United (player/coach, October 1980), Seattle Sounders/USA (loan, March–June 1981), Torquay United (player–manager, July 1982–January 1984), Seattle Sounders/USA (coach, July 1985–January 1986), Middlesbrough (assistant manager, January 1986; manager, March 1986–March 1990), Millwall (manager, April 1990–March 1992), Bolton Wanderers (manager, May 1992–May 1995), Arsenal (manager, June 1995–August 1996), Norwich City (manager, June 1998–April 2000), Wigan Athletic (manager, July 2000–May 2001)

Rioch was the first English-born player ever to captain Scotland (1978) and the first £100,000 footballer in the Third Division (with Villa, 1970). The son of a Scottish sergeant major, he was an all-action, hard-shooting midfielder who gained 24 full caps and accumulated over 600 appearances at club level. He played brilliantly during his time with Villa, helping them win the Third Division title in 1972. He later added to his appearance-tally significantly before taking his first steps in management with Torquay. Rioch helped Derby win the First Division title (1975) and then guided Middlesbrough to promotion from Division Three to Division One in successive seasons (1987–88) and took Bolton from Division Two into the Premiership in two years (1993).

RIOCH, DANIEL GORDON (NEIL)
Defender: 19+6 apps, 3 goals
Born: Paddington, London, 13 April 1951
Career: Paddington and Central London Schools, Luton Town (apprentice, June 1966; professional, July 1968), VILLA (with brother Bruce, September 1969), Portland Timbers/USA (1971), York City (loan, February 1972), Northampton Town (loan, March 1972), Plymouth Argyle (May 1975), Atlanta Chiefs/NASL (1976–77), Toronto Blizzard/Canada (1978), Southend United (briefly, 1978–79); Midlands non-League football (1979–90); manager of the Villa Old Stars; also a fine club cricketer

Rioch, overshadowed throughout his career by his brother Bruce (q.v.), defended well when given the opportunity. He made more of an impact in the NASL than he did in the Football League.

RITCHIE, STUART ARTHUR
Midfield: 0+1 app.
Born: Southampton, 20 May 1968
Career: Hampshire County Schools, VILLA (apprentice, June 1984; professional, May 1986), Crewe Alexandra (June 1987–May 1988), Waterford, Bashley, Newport/Isle of Wight

Ritchie had the briefest of professional careers with Villa, making just one substitute appearance against Manchester United in May 1987 when he replaced Andy Gray in front of 35,000 fans. He had 18 League outings with the 'Alex'.

ROBERTS, DAVID
Wing-forward: 18+1 apps, 2 goals
Born: Erdington, Birmingham, 21 December 1946
Career: Marsh Hill School, Birmingham Works Under-12s, Lucas Eagle FC, VILLA (junior, 1962; professional, December 1963), Shrewsbury Town (£5,000, March 1968), Swansea Town (May 1974), Worcester City (August 1975–May 1979), Shrewsbury Town (player–coach, 1979–80), Highton United (coach, 1980s)

An honest worker, Roberts was a reserve with Villa before going on to net 21 times in 230 League games for Shrewsbury. Always alert, he had the ability to do the unexpected.

ROBERTS, KENNETH
Forward: 46 apps, 7 goals
Born: Crewe, 10 March 1931
Career: Crewe Villa, Cardiff City (amateur, 1949), VILLA (amateur, June 1951; professional, August 1951), Sutton Town, Wellington Town (July 1958–April 1960), Stourbridge (July 1962–December 1964), Redditch United, Bedworth Town, Kynochs (1969–71); also played for the Kynoch's, Dunlop and Lea Marston cricket clubs

A former driver in the RASC and one-time railway porter at Crewe station (so you know where his nickname came from!), 'Shunter' Roberts was recommended to Villa while on military service. A tough, thoughtful utility player with strength and mobility, he scored seven goals for Villa before injury cut short a promising career. He once hit a century in less than an hour for Kynoch's CC.

ROBERTS, KENNETH OWEN
Outside-right: 38 apps, 3 goals
Born: Rhosmedre Cefn Mawr, near Wrexham, 27 March 1936
Career: Maelor Youth Club, Wrexham (junior, 1950; amateur, May 1951), VILLA

(May 1953), Boston United (on loan, October–November 1953); retired May 1958 with knee injury; Oswestry (trainer/coach, July 1958), Wrexham (trainer/coach, May 1961; later assistant manager, February 1965; coach and chief scout, January 1966–April 1967), Bradford Park Avenue (assistant manager, April 1967–April 1968), Chester (manager, March 1968–September 1976; general manager to 1979; then administration at Sealand Road), Wrexham (chief scout and youth development officer to 1982), Cefn Druids (manager), Chester City (youth development officer, 1995)

Roberts shares the record with Everton's Albert Geldard as the youngest-ever Football League debutant – 15 years, 158 days old when he appeared for Wrexham against Bradford in September 1951. Capped by Wales at youth-team level, Roberts had pace, ample skill and a penchant for hard work when injury forced him into an early retirement. He was only 32 when appointed manager of Chester and in 1974–75 guided the Sealand Road club to promotion from Division Four. In that same season he came within a whisker of taking Chester to Wembley, but his dream was shattered when they lost 5–4 on aggregate to his former club Villa in the League Cup semi-final. He did gain some consolation, though, with a Welsh Cup final victory.

ROBERTS, ROBERT JOHN

Goalkeeper: 4 apps
Born: West Bromwich, April 1859 – *Died*: Byker, Newcastle, 26 October 1929
Career: Christ Church School, Salter's Works, West Bromwich Albion (amateur, 1879; professional, August 1885), Sunderland Albion (May 1890), West Bromwich Albion (May 1891), VILLA (May 1892; retired June 1893)

Roberts was the first WBA player to be capped, for England against Scotland in 1887. A fine figure of a man, 6 ft 4 in. tall and weighing over 13 st., he wore a size 13 boot and started off as a forward before establishing himself as the 'last line of defence'. He appeared in more than 400 games for Albion (at various levels) and won 3 full caps. He played for the Football Alliance (with Sunderland Albion), starred in three international trials and in three FA Cup finals, for WBA against Blackburn (1886), Villa (1887) and Preston (1888), gaining a winner's medal in the latter. He also played in Albion's first-ever FA Cup tie, against Wednesbury Town in November 1883, and the club's first Football League game, against Stoke in September 1888. He was well past his best when he joined Villa (as cover for Bill Dunning).

ROBERTS, WALTER DAVID

Forward: 5 apps, 1 goal
Born: Stourbridge, July 1859 – *Died*: 1914
Career: Norton FC (Stourbridge), VILLA (May 1882), Church FC (September 1884), Stourbridge (September 1886–May 1888)

An ambling type of player with a strong right-foot shot, Roberts' only goal for Villa was against Walsall Swifts in November 1883 (won 5–1).

ROBERTSON, RICHARD REX
Centre-half: 3 apps
Born: Hockley, Birmingham, December 1860 – *Died:* Birmingham, 1921
Career: Excelsior, VILLA (August 1884), Stourbridge (September 1887), Halesowen, Coombs Wood, Netherton St Luke's (1893; retired May 1895 through injury)
Robertson was a tough competitor who made three FA Cup appearances for Villa, the first against Wednesbury Town in 1884.

ROBEY, JAMES HENRY
Defender: 3 apps
Born: Ratcliffe, January 1911
Career: Stalybridge Celtic, VILLA (May 1935), Aberdeen (February 1938), Wigan Athletic (July 1939; retired during WW2)
Another tough competitor, able to take the strongest of challenges, Robey played in three League games for Villa and four for the Dons.

ROBINSON, PHILIP JOHN
Utility: 2+1 apps, 1 goal
Born: Stafford, 6 January 1967
Career: Stafford and District Schools, VILLA (groundstaff, aged 14; apprentice, June 1983; professional, January 1985), Wolverhampton Wanderers (£5,000, June 1987), Notts County (£67,500, August 1989), Birmingham City (loan, March 1991), Huddersfield Town (£50,000, September 1992), Northampton Town (loan, September 1994), Chesterfield (£15,000, December 1994), Notts County (£80,000, August 1996), Stoke City (free, June 1998), Hereford United (player/coach, August 2000), Stafford Rangers (manager, May 2002).
Equally adept in defence or midfield, red-haired Robinson always gave a good account of himself. After failing to consolidate with Villa, he joined Wolves and went on to play in 90 first-team games for the Molineux club (9 goals), helping them win both the Fourth and Third Division titles and SVT. He was a key member of Notts County's Third Division promotion-winning side in 1990 and helped the Blues lift the Leyland DAF Cup a year later. Robinson ventured into physiotherapy while playing for Hereford United. He appeared in 534 games at competitive level and scored 51 goals.

ROBSON, JOHN DIXON
Full-back: 173+5 apps, 1 goal
Born: Consett, 15 July 1950 – *Died:* Sutton Coldfield, 12 May 2004
Career: Durham Schools, Birtley Youth Club, Derby County (junior, July 1966; professional, October 1967), VILLA (£90,000, October 1972; contract cancelled, November 1978, after being forced to quit football with multiple sclerosis); awarded a testimonial match in October 1978

Robson collected both First and Second Division championship medals and made 211 appearances (5 goals scored) for Derby before moving to Villa. Capped seven times by England at Under-23 level, he starred in Villa's promotion-winning side of 1975 and gained two League Cup-winner's medals, against Norwich (1975) and against Everton (1977). The sure-footed Robson was a valuable member of the defence and occasionally filled in as an extra centre-half. He teamed up superbly well with Charlie Aitken and John Gidman. He sadly died after a hard battle against multiple sclerosis.

ROOSE, LEIGH RICHMOND

Goalkeeper: 10 apps

Born: Holt, near Wrexham, 27 November 1877 – *Died*: France, 7 October 1916

Career: Holt Academy, University of Wales (Aberystwyth), Aberystwyth Town (1898), Ruabon Druids (August 1900), London Welsh (soccer), Stoke (amateur, October 1901), Everton (November 1904), Stoke (August 1905), Sunderland (January 1908), Huddersfield Town (April 1911), VILLA (August 1911), Woolwich Arsenal (December 1911), Llandudno Town (1912–14); joined the 9th Battalion Royal Fusiliers as a lance corporal at the outbreak of WW1 (1914)

The son of a Presbyterian minister, Roose was taught for a short time by H.G. Wells, gaining a science degree at university. He was a Welsh Cup winner with the Druids in 1900 before training in bacteriology at King's College Hospital, London. He failed to qualify, and, as a result, joined Stoke.

H. Catton ('Tityrus' of the *Athletic News*) described Roose as 'dexterous though daring, valiant though volatile'. Another writer was more expansive, stating: 'Few men exhibit their personality so vividly in their play as L.R. Roose. You cannot spend five minutes in his company without being impressed by his vivacity, his boldness, his knowledge of men and things – a clever man undoubtedly, but one entirely unrestrained in word or action. On the field his whole attention is centred on the game, he rarely stands listlessly by the goalpost even when the ball is at the other end of the enclosure, but is ever following the game keenly and closely.'

A great character, he was also a very wealthy man as well as being a superb keeper, who thought nothing of charging some 15–20 yards away from his goal to clear the ball. Unorthodox in style when dealing with shots hit straight at him, he often double-punched the ball away or even headed it clear! After leaving Stoke, he replaced Billy Scott at Everton and then helped save Sunderland from relegation during his time on Wearside, being presented with an illuminated address by the mayor for his efforts. An inveterate practical joker, Roose was also an erratic genius, and he never took the field wearing a clean pair of shorts. His boots lasted him for years and generally he had a scruffy appearance about him – but what a star!

Roose, who won 24 senior caps for Wales plus a handful as an amateur, was recruited by Villa to fill in for Brendel Anstey. He played in only 10 League games before joining Arsenal, and during his career made over 300 appearances in club and international football – and one suspects that he would have carried on longer, had he lived! He was killed in action during WW1, aged 38.

ROSS, IAN
Defender: 205 apps, 3 goals
Born: Glasgow, 26 January 1947
Career: Glasgow and District Schools, Liverpool (apprentice, June 1963; professional, August 1965), VILLA (£70,000, February 1972), Notts County (loan, October 1976), Northampton Town (loan, November 1976), Peterborough United (December 1976), Santa Barbara FC/USA (May 1978), Wolverhampton Wanderers (player/coach, August 1979), Hereford United (non-contract, player/coach, October 1982), Wolverhampton Wanderers (coach, early 1983), Oman (coach, June 1983), Birmingham City (reserve-team coach), FC Valur/Iceland (manager/coach, August 1984–June 1988), coached in South Africa and Australia (1988–late 1991), Huddersfield Town (manager, March 1992–May 1993); later licensee of the Gardeners Arms, Timperley (near Altrincham)

Ross was a fine professional, a trier who simply loved football, battling through every game he played no matter what the circumstances. Mainly a reserve at Anfield, where he was a useful squad player, he became a firm favourite with the Villa fans. Nicknamed 'Roscoe', he helped Villa clinch the Third Division title in 1972 and then led the side to victory in the 1975 League Cup final and to promotion from Division Two that same season. He played in over 100 games for Peterborough and by the time he went into management in Iceland he was already an experienced coach. He guided FC Valur to their domestic League championship in 1985 and after coaching in South Africa and Australia, he accepted his first and only managerial post in England with Huddersfield, steering the Terriers into the promotion play-offs in 1992 and then lifting them clear of relegation the following season. As a player, Ross appeared in more than 400 club matches (356 in the League) and in 1976 had the 'distinction' of playing for 4 different clubs in 4 months!

ROWAN, BRIAN
Left-back: 1 app.
Born: Glasgow, 28 June 1948
Career: Glasgow Schools, Ballieston Juniors, VILLA (amateur, April 1969; professional, May 1969), Watford (October 1971–May 1972)

Rowan, a one-time heating engineer from Glasgow, was almost 21 when he arrived at Villa Park. It was hoped he might follow in the footsteps of Charlie Aitken, but he failed to make the grade and his only League appearance, in September 1969, was against his future club, Watford. As a 16 year old, Rowan was forced to pull out of a Scottish junior international against Wales through injury. His father was a professional footballer in Scotland.

ROXBURGH, JOHN ALEXANDER

Outside-left: 12 apps, 3 goals

Born: Granton, Edinburgh, 10 November 1901 – *Died*: 1965

Career: Edinburgh Emmett, Rugby Town, Leicester City (June 1920), VILLA (October 1922), Stoke (February 1924), Sheffield United (August 1925), Sheffield FC (1927–28)

Roxburgh was selected for an England amateur international before his birthplace was confirmed! A winger, full of vim and vigour, he made his League debut for Leicester at the age of 18 (against West Ham) and went on to score 3 goals in 50 senior games for the Foxes before moving to Villa. He had a useful 'half-season' with Villa, replacing Billy Kirton in the main and scored twice on his debut against his future club Stoke. He later played in 14 League games for the Potters and 5 for the Blades. His brother, Andrew, played for Leicester (1920–21) and a third Roxburgh sibling, Walter, had trials with Leicester (1921).

RUDGE, DAVID HARRY

Winger: 53+7 apps, 10 goals

Born: Wolverhampton, 21 January 1948

Career: Wolverhampton and District Boys, VILLA (apprentice, June 1964; professional, May 1965), Hereford United (£5,000, August 1972), Torquay United (December 1975), Kingsbury United (May 1978–May 1981); later associated with various non-League clubs in south Devon, including Newton Abbot (coach, 2002–04)

A go-ahead winger, good on the ball, Rudge was Villa's 'Terrace Trophy Player of the Year' in 1970. He made an impressive debut for the club at Arsenal in August 1966 and went on to play in 82 League games for Hereford and 64 for Torquay.

RUSSELL, GEORGE QUENTIN

Left-half: 37 apps, 3 goals

Born: Ayrshire, 21 August 1869 – *Died*: Glasgow, 1930

Career: Ayr FC, VILLA (April 1892), Glasgow United (May 1895; retired, injured, April 1897)

A player with boundless energy, Russell was always eager to get forward and assist the front men – thus his positional sense left a lot to be desired.

RUTHERFORD, JOSEPH HENRY HAMILTON

Goalkeeper: 156 apps

Born: Fatfield, near Chester-le-Street, County Durham, 20 September 1914 – *Died*: Sutton Coldfield, 27 December 1994

Career: Chester-le-Street Schools, Chester-le-Street Juniors, West Ham United (trial, 1928), Reading (trial), Fatfield Juniors, Chester Moor Temperance, Ferryhill, Blyth Spartans, Chester-le-Street, Birtley Colliery, Southport (amateur, June 1931; professional, August 1936), VILLA (£2,500, February 1939); served in the RAF during WW2; guest for Solihull Town (1939–40), Nottingham Forest (1941–42), Lincoln City (1943–44), Mansfield Town (1943–44); Bilston United (September 1952; retired in October 1953); later ran a road haulage company and was clerk for Bryant's Builders as well as working behind the scenes at Villa Park, including a spell in the pools office; engaged also as ground assistant at the club's Bodymoor Heath complex

By the time he joined Southport in 1931, Rutherford had already been playing football for nine years. He made almost 100 appearances for Southport before moving to Villa. A brave and fearless keeper, he slowly bedded himself in and eventually took over the green jersey from Fred Biddlestone towards the end of 1938–39. He played quite a few games for Villa during WW2 and was an ever-present in the League side in 1946–47, one of his best performances coming at Everton when he twice saved a retaken penalty. He was between the posts when Charlie Mitten fired a hat-trick of spot-kicks past him in Manchester United's 7–0 League victory at Old Trafford in March 1950. Rutherford handed over his duties indirectly to Con Martin, the centre-half he had played behind in more than 75 matches prior to 1951. He represented the Army against Birmingham in December 1941 and attained the rank of sergeant major during WW2, serving with the RASC.

SABIN, ARTHUR HENRY

Goalkeeper: 2 apps

Born: Kingstanding, Birmingham, 25 January 1939 – *Died*: Birmingham, March, 1958

Career: Kingstanding Schools, Aston Boys, Birmingham County FA, VILLA (juniors, June 1955; professional, January 1957 until his death)

Sabin chipped a bone in his neck during his second game for Villa, a home draw with Spurs in November 1957. Sadly that injury caused problems and four months later he died, aged nineteen.

SAMUEL, JLLOYD

Left-back: 113+20 apps, 3 goals

Born: Trinidad, 29 March 1981

Career: Charlton Athletic (YTS, April 1997), VILLA (YTS, April 1998; professional, February 1999), Gillingham (loan, October–November 2001)

Capped seven times by England at Under-18 level, having earlier gained youth-team honours, Samuel made his anticipated breakthrough with Villa in 1999–2000 when he played in ten senior matches, five as a substitute. He also sat on the bench for the last FA Cup final at Wembley but was not called into action. A footballer with a lot to offer, he scored his first goal (a gem) in the 3–1 Premiership win over Charlton in September 2003.

SAUNDERS, DEAN

Striker: 143+1 app., 49 goals

Born: Swansea, 21 June 1964

Career: Swansea City (apprentice, July 1980; professional, June 1982), Cardiff City (loan, March 1985), Brighton and Hove Albion (free, August 1985), Oxford United (£60,000, March 1987), Derby County (£1m, October 1988), Liverpool (£2.9m, July 1991), VILLA (£2.3m, September 1992), Galatasaray/Turkey (£2.35m, July 1995), Nottingham Forest (£1.5m, July 1996), Sheffield United (free, December 1997), Benfica/Portugal (£500,000, December 1998), Bradford City (free, August 1999; retired July 2001), Blackburn Rovers (coach)

One of the game's most prolific marksmen, Saunders hit his first League goal for Swansea against Oldham in March 1984 and his last 17 years later for Bradford City. A positive, all-action, unselfish striker, he simply knew where the goal was, and when he hung up his boots at the end of 2000–01, his impressive career record read: 805 appearances and 276 goals. Saunders also held (since beaten) the Welsh international record for being the most honoured outfield player with 73 caps to his credit.

Surprisingly he only gained two club medals, the first with Liverpool as FA Cup-winners (1992) and his second with Villa as League Cup victors (1994), when he scored twice in the 3–1 win over Manchester United. His best performances on the whole came with Derby (131 senior appearances, 57 goals) and certainly with Villa, but wherever he played he gave his all and the fans certainly enjoyed what they saw from a top-class striker.

In 1994, a case began at the High Court (London) involving former Villa defender Paul Elliott (Chelsea) and Saunders (Villa). It revolved around a tackle by Saunders (playing for Liverpool) on Elliott that effectively ended the latter's career. Elliott lost the case and was faced with a legal bill of £500,000.

SAWARD, PATRICK

Left-half: 170 apps, 2 goals

Born: Cobh, County Cork, 17 August 1928 – *Died:* Newmarket, 20 September 2002

Career: Cork and Cobh County Schools, Beckenham FC (1945), Crystal Palace (amateur trialist), Millwall (professional, July 1951), VILLA (£7,000, August 1955), Huddersfield Town (March 1961), Coventry City (October 1963; then player/coach, later assistant manager, July 1967), Brighton and Hove Albion (manager, July 1970–October 1973), NASR Al/Saudi Arabia (general manager/coach, 1973–75); thereafter ran a café/bar on the island of Menorca before his death from Alzheimer's disease

Saward, a tough competitor, was best as a wing-half, although he occasionally occupied an inside-forward berth. A valuable member of Villa's 1957 FA Cup-winning and 1960 Second Division championship-winning sides, he won 18 caps for the Republic of Ireland. As a manager, Saward was an extrovert, his good humour creating a happy feeling in the dressing-room. He had a good eye for a player (he 'found' Willie Carr and Dennis Mortimer) and was very successful as a coach at Coventry, leading the youngsters to the FA Youth Cup final. The Sky Blues also enjoyed European experience when he was right-hand man to boss Noel Cantwell. Saward guided Brighton to promotion from Division Three in 1972. His Army service took him to Singapore and Malta.

SCHMEICHEL, PETER BOLESLAW, MBE

Goalkeeper: 36 apps, 1 goal
Born: Gladsaxe, Denmark, 18 November 1963
Career: Hvidore FC/Denmark (August 1984), Brondby IF/Denmark (July 1987), Manchester United (£550,000, August 1991), Sporting Lisbon/Portugal (June 1999), VILLA (free, July 2001), Manchester City (free, August 2002; retired May 2003)

Schmeichel is said to have been Manchester United's greatest-ever goalkeeper. He made 398 appearances for the Reds – his last as skipper in the final of the 1999 Champions League against Bayern Munich when the treble was clinched. With his massive frame, he helped the Reds win five Premiership titles, having tasted League success with Brondby IF. He later gained a seventh League championship medal with Sporting Lisbon. He was also successful in two Danish Cup finals with Brondby and in three FA Cup finals, a League Cup final, European Cup final, European Super Cup and four FA Charity Shield matches with Manchester United, while winning a European championship-winner's medal with Denmark in 1992. A highly influential figure, he had a great presence, was a tremendous shot-stopper, possessed exceptional aerial ability and was supremely confident in distribution with hand or foot. In his one season at Villa Park he gave the fans something to remember him by with some brilliant saves during his outings – and he scored in the Premiership game against Everton at Goodison Park, thus becoming the first Villa keeper to achieve this feat in open play. Indeed, he netted a dozen or so goals in competitive football. His frequent forays upfield for set pieces always excited the crowd and, in fact, he was also the first keeper to represent both Manchester clubs in competitive football. Capped a record 129 times by his country (one goal scored), he was voted Danish 'Footballer of the Year' in 1990 and was voted best goalkeeper in Europe in 1998. Awarded the MBE (for services to football – and perhaps especially Manchester United) in December 2001, during his 19-year professional career Schmeichel amassed 888 appearances at club and international level.

SCIMECA, RICARDO

Defender: 68+29 apps, 2 goals
Born: Leamington Spa, 13 June 1975
Career: VILLA (YTS, June 1991; professional, July 1993), Nottingham Forest (£3m, July 1999), Leicester City (July 2003), West Bromwich Albion (£100,000, May 2004)

After eight years with Villa, Scimeca – David Platt's first signing as manager of Forest – was appointed captain in his first season at the club. Honoured by England at 'B' and Under-21 levels (nine caps won for the latter), he had two long-term injuries with Villa and never really commanded a regular place in the side. He has excellent skills, good control and an appetite for hard work. He stayed in the Premiership with WBA in 2004.

SCOTT, ANTHONY JAMES ERNEST

Outside-left: 54+3 apps, 5 goals

Born: St Neots, Cambridgeshire, 1 April 1941

Career: Huntingdon Boys, St Neots Town, West Ham United (juniors, June 1957; professional, May 1958), VILLA (£25,000, October 1965), Torquay United (£5,000, September 1967), Bournemouth (July 1970), Exeter City (June 1972; retired, injured, May 1974), Manchester City (youth coach)

After winning 12 England youth caps, appearing in an FA Youth Cup final and making a scoring League debut against Chelsea, Scott netted 19 goals in 97 appearances for West Ham. With Villa he linked up on the left-flank with Phil Woosnam, a colleague of his at Upton Park, and in his two years in the 'other' claret and blue strip, Scott did well. He had pace, used both feet and delivered an excellent cross but perhaps played better on the south coast, adding a further 199 League appearances to his tally (12 goals).

SEALEY, LESLIE JESSE

Goalkeeper: 24 apps

Born: Bethnal Green, London, 29 September 1959 – *Died*: London, 19 August 2001

Career: Coventry City (apprentice, July 1975; professional, May 1977), Luton Town (£120,000, August 1983), Plymouth Argyle (loan, October 1984), Manchester United (loan, March 1990; free transfer, June 1990), VILLA (free, July 1991), Coventry City (loan, March 1992), Birmingham City (loan, October 1992), Manchester United (free, January 1993), Blackpool (free, July 1994), West Ham United (free, November 1994), Leyton Orient (non-contract, July 1996), West Ham United (non-contract, November 1996; later coach at Upton Park until his death)

Sealey's career spanned 21 years, during which time he served with 9 different clubs and amassed 568 senior appearances. He replaced the injured Nigel Spink for Villa during 1991–92 and five years later had his final outing as a West Ham substitute in a Premiership game against his former club Manchester United at Old Trafford in front of 55,249 fans. A real character, strong-willed, confident, aggressive, boisterous at times, even annoying and rather too vocal, Sealey was, without doubt, a very competent keeper. He was brought in for the 1990 FA Cup final replay against Crystal Palace after a poor first game showing by Jim Leighton and duly collected a winner's medal as Manchester United won 4–0. A year later he was on the losing side in the 1991 League Cup final but soon afterwards gained a winner's medal when United won the European Cup-winners' Cup final in Barcelona. Sealey suffered another League Cup disappointment when Villa beat United to lift the trophy in 1994. Earlier, as a Luton player, he had missed the 1988 League Cup final through injury, but was then a loser as Forest beat the Hatters in the final of the same competition 12 months later. No international honours for Sealey but plenty of memories. He died from a heart attack.

SELLARS, GEOFFREY

Outside-right: 2 apps
Born: Stockport, 20 May 1930
Career: Stockport and Cheshire Schools, Armed Forces during WW2, Altrincham (amateur, 1947), Leeds United (professional, April 1950), VILLA (July 1950), Stalybridge Celtic (£1,000, August 1951), Altrincham (August 1952; retired May 1954).

An orthodox winger, Sellars failed to make the first XI at Leeds and only appeared in two League games for Villa, against Arsenal and Derby during the first half of the 1950–51 season. Hardly a first-class competitor, he returned to non-League soccer in 1952.

SEWELL, JOHN

Inside-forward: 145 apps, 40 goals
Born: Kells Village, Whitehaven, 24 January 1927
Career: Kells Centre, Whitehaven Town; guest for Carlisle United and Workington during WW2; Notts County (signed, October 1944; professional, August 1945), Sheffield Wednesday (£34,500, March 1951), VILLA (£20,000, December 1955), Hull City (October 1959), Lusaka City/Rhodesia (player/coach, September 1961–May 1964); Zambia (coach, 1968–71); the Belgian Congo (coach, 1972–73); later worked as a car salesman for Bristol Street Motors in West Bridgford, Nottingham (1973–87)

Sewell won championship medals with Notts County, Division Three (S) in 1950, and Sheffield Wednesday, Division Two in 1952 and 1956. He was the subject of a record transfer from Meadow Lane to Hillsborough in 1951 and helped Villa win the FA Cup in 1957. He was also with a relegated League club on four occasions: Wednesday twice, Villa (in 1959) and Hull, and he played for England in those two defeats by Hungary, 6–3 at Wembley (in 1953) and 7–1 in Budapest (in 1954). He won 6 full caps, represented the Football League and toured Canada and North America with the FA in June 1950 (scoring 6 goals in 7 games including a hat-trick in a 9–0 win over Alberta). A very talented player, Sewell netted 92 goals in 175 games for Sheffield Wednesday, having earlier responded brilliantly to the promptings of Tommy Lawton at Notts County. He did great things in Villa's forward-line and in a fine career claimed almost 250 goals in 550 matches (228 in 510 League games) – all this despite suffering a baffling loss of form when least expected!

SHARP, ALBERT

Defender: 23 apps

Born: Hereford, 8 January 1876 – *Died*: Liverpool, 2 November 1949

Career: Clyde Henry School, Hereford Comrades (April 1893), Hereford Thistle (August 1894), Hereford Town (July 1895), Hereford Thistle (September 1896), VILLA (April 1897), Everton (August 1899), Southampton (May 1900), Everton (May 1901), Kirkdale (August 1904; reinstated as an amateur), Southport Central (January 1905; retired April 1907); Everton (joined board of directors, 1922)

Sharp was never in the same class as his brother John (q.v.). Honest and hard-working, he was versatile and a good athlete who performed consistently well for each club he served, making 22 appearances for Saints and 10 for Everton at top-class level. He was also a useful cricketer, and in 1900 averaged 40 with the bat for Herefordshire.

SHARP, JOHN SAMUEL

Outside-right: 24 apps, 15 goals

Born: Hereford, 15 February 1878 – *Died*: Wavertree, Liverpool, 27 January 1938

Career: Clyde Henry School (Hereford), Violet Boys' Club, Hereford Thistle (August 1895), VILLA (April, 1897), Everton (August 1899; retired May 1910); opened a sports shop in Liverpool, became a wealthy businessman and in 1922 joined the board of directors at Goodison Park (with his brother Bert, q.v.); later chairman of Everton

Sharp represented England at both cricket and football. Short, thickset, a 'Pocket Hercules', he did well with Villa before developing into an international player with Everton, gaining two full caps and representing the Football League. He was a regular in the Goodison Park side for 11 years, scoring 80 goals in 342 games and playing in 2 FA Cup finals (1906, 1907). The famous referee Jack Howcroft, in the game for 30 years, rated Sharp as the best outside-right he ever saw play, better than Billy Bassett, Billy Meredith and Stanley Matthews!

On the cricket field, Sharp played in three Test matches and hit a century against Australia at the Oval in 1909. He spent 26 years with Lancashire (1899–1925), scored over 22,700 runs (38 centuries), took 440 wickets and held 223 catches.

SHARPLES, JOHN

Defender: 13 apps

Born: Heath Town, Wolverhampton, 8 August 1934

Career: Heath Town FC, Walsall (amateur, August 1951), VILLA (amateur, May 1953; professional, October 1955), Walsall (August 1959), Darlaston (August 1964), Hednesford Town (August 1968)

The strongly built Sharples understudied Peter Aldis for three of his five years with Villa (spending the other two in the Army). He signed 'pro' forms just 24 hours before joining the forces, a deferment until he had completed his engineering apprenticeship. He went on to play in 130 games for Walsall, occupying both the full-back and centre-half positions and helping the Saddlers twice win promotion.

SHAW, GARY ROBERT
Forward: 204+8 apps, 80 goals
Born: Castle Bromwich, Birmingham, 21 January 1961
Career: Kingshurst Comprehensive School, North Warwickshire Boys, Erdington and Saltley Boys, Coleshill Town Colts, Coleshill Town, Warwickshire and District Schools, VILLA (apprentice, July 1977; professional, January 1979), Blackpool (loan, February 1988), BK Copenhagen/Denmark (May 1988), FC Klagenfurt/Austria (March–May 1989), Sheffield Wednesday (loan, August-September 1989), Walsall (February 1990), Kilmarnock (briefly), Shrewsbury Town (September 1990), Ernst Borel FC/Hong Kong (1991); retired on his return to England (1992); later became a football summariser on local radio

After doing so well, scoring goals aplenty, winning medals, Shaw's career was ruined over a period of four years (1983–87) when he had six knee operations! Although he tried to make a comeback by playing abroad, he was never able to commit himself to League action and quit in 1991 at the age of 30. Forming a brilliant partnership with Peter Withe, he netted 20 goals in 1980–81 when the League championship was won, struck 14 the following year and 24 in 1982–83. A European Cup and Super Cup-winner in 1982, he had made his debut at Bristol City in August 1978 and a year later grabbed his first hat-trick on the same ground in an FA Cup tie. Voted PFA 'Young Player of the Year' in 1981, Shaw received the European Cup 'Player of the Year' award in 1982, having earlier in his career gained nine youth and seven Under-21 caps for England, coming so close to winning a full cap in 1981 when he was the only Birmingham-born player in Villa's First Division championship-winning side.

SHELL, FRANCIS HARRY
Forward: 31 apps, 13 goals
Born: Hackney, London, 2 December 1912 – *Died*: Axminster, Devon, 20 July 1988
Career: Ilford and District Schools, Barking (April 1930), Beantree Athletic, Ford Sports/Dagenham (August 1936), VILLA (professional, May 1937); guest for Leicester City (1939–40), Northampton Town (1939–40), Revo Electric (1940), Walsall (1941–42), Notts County (1944–45), Hereford United (1945–46); Birmingham City (September 1946), Hereford United (June 1947), Mansfield Town (June 1947), Stafford Rangers (August 1948), Barry Town (March 1949), Chingford, Hinckley Athletic (August 1950), Birfield FC (player and groundsman; retired as player, March 1952);

groundsman at Newton Lawn Tennis Club, Moseley, Birmingham (from April 1952); VILLA (fourth-team trainer, August 1957–April 1960)

Shell, a big, strapping player, entered League soccer at the age of 24. He quickly adapted to the game and in 1937–38 formed a fine understanding with Frank Broome in Villa's side. His wife was the daughter of Jack Crisp, who played for Walsall, WBA, Leicester, Blackburn and Coventry either side of WW1.

SHELTON, GARY

Midfield: 26+1 apps, 8 goals

Born: Nottingham, 21 March 1958

Career: St Bernadette's School (Nottingham), Notts County Schools, Parkhead FC, Walsall (apprentice, June 1972; professional, March 1976), VILLA (£60,000, January 1978), Barry Town (guest, June 1977), Notts County (loan, March 1980), Sheffield Wednesday (£50,000, March 1982), Oxford United (£150,000, July 1987), Bristol City (August 1989), Rochdale (loan, February 1994), Chester City (July 1994, player/assistant manager/coach), West Bromwich Albion (coach, July 2000)

Capped once by England at Under-21 level, the creative and hard-working Shelton drew up an exceptionally fine record, appearing in over 550 matches and scoring 62 goals. He helped Sheffield Wednesday win promotion to the First Division in 1984.

SHUTT, HARTLEY GEORGE

Full-back: 42 apps

Born: Burnley, 18 July 1875 – *Died*: Brierfield, Lancashire, October, 1950

Career: Brierfield FC, Nelson (1894), Bolton Wanderers (briefly, 1895), Swindon Town (1896), Notts Rangers (1898), Millwall Athletic (briefly, 1899), VILLA (September 1900), Hucknall Town (May 1904), Beasley RCA (1906–07)

Effective and hard-tackling with a tremendous right foot, Shutt was a fine partner to Jimmy Crabtree in 1901–02, making 26 senior appearances after taking over from Howard Spencer. He lost his place when Spencer returned the following season and subsequently drifted down the scale. Before moving to Villa, he made 83 Southern League appearances for Swindon and 28 for Millwall.

SIDEBOTTOM, GEOFFREY

Goalkeeper: 88 apps

Born: Mapplewell, Yorkshire, 29 December 1936

Career: Mapplewell Village Youths, Wath Wanderers, Wolverhampton Wanderers (professional, January 1954), VILLA (February 1961), Scunthorpe United (January 1965), New York Royals/USA (1967), New York Generals/USA (1968); Columbia University/USA (coach), Brighton and Hove Albion (January 1969; retired, injured, May 1971)

Despite being told by his doctor not to play football because of a chest complaint, Sidebottom was a fine understudy to Bert Williams at Molineux before moving to Villa Park, where he became reserve to another ex-'Wolf', Nigel Sims. He gained a League Cup-winner's prize in 1961 and had a testimonial with Brighton in 1971, after failing to recover from a serious head injury suffered in a reserve game in October 1970.

SIMMONDS, HENRY RICHMOND

Defence: 10 apps

Born: Birmingham, June 1858 – *Died*: Handsworth, Birmingham, 3 August 1939

Career: Hockley St John's Athletic, Aston Waverley, Wesleyan Methodists, VILLA (July 1878; retired, injured, broken ankle, May 1890); played cricket for Aston Unity (1908–14)

Brother of Joseph (q.v.), Simmonds was an ever-present for Villa in 1880–81. A quality footballer, strong and resilient, always urging his team on, he played in ten FA Cup games for the club before injury ended his career. He represented the Birmingham Association against Sheffield, London and Scottish Counties (1880s).

SIMMONDS, JOSEPH OSCAR

Defender: 22 apps

Born: Birmingham, 20 April 1861 – *Died*: Birmingham, 8 April 1940

Career: Hockley Hill Council School, Key Hill Methodists, Hockley St John's Athletic, VILLA (August 1878; retired, injured, damaged shoulder, May 1887)

Slim-looking, nothing like his elder brother, Henry (q.v.), Simmonds was fast, aggressive when required, always driving forward. He wore a tight-fitting dazzling red polo-cap and consequently was dubbed 'Red Cap' by his team-mates. Only 5 ft 5 in. tall, he had great pluck and woe betide an opponent if his cap fell off! He was an FA Cup winner in 1887.

SIMMONS, DAVID JOHN

Striker: 13+6 apps, 7 goals

Born: Ryde, Isle of Wight, 24 October 1948

Career: Gosport Borough Schools, Gosport Boys, Arsenal (amateur, June 1963; professional, November 1965), Bournemouth (loan, November 1968), VILLA (£15,000, February 1969), Walsall (loan, October 1970), Colchester United (December 1970), Cambridge United (March 1973), Brentford (March 1974), Cambridge United (November 1975–May 1976)

As a youngster, Simmons escaped death after falling through a plate glass window, receiving multiple cuts and lacerations. He had a useful career in the lower divisions, scoring over 50 goals in almost 200 games (48 in 179 League matches). He didn't do much at Highbury, Bournemouth or indeed Villa, although he did score for the latter on his debut against Charlton in February 1969. He helped Colchester knock Leeds out of the FA Cup in 1971.

SIMPSON, WILLIAM SWAN

Wing-half: 29 apps, 1 goal
Born: Cowdenbeath, 1 May 1907 – *Died*: 1990
Career: Cowdenbeath and District Schools, Donibristle Colliery, Cowdenbeath YMCA, Musselburgh Bruntonians, Dunbar, Fulford White Rose, Clyde (April 1928), VILLA (£1,000, November 1931), Cowdenbeath (July 1935), Northampton Town (August 1936), Walsall (June 1937), Bromsgrove Rovers (August 1939); guest for Sutton Town (1940–41), Dunlop Sports (1941–42); later worked for Dunlop, then in business in Birmingham

A tall, slender player who loved to attack, Simpson won a junior international cap for Scotland against Ireland in March 1928 and at the time looked a useful prospect. However, he failed to do the business in the First Division with Villa, but later did well with Northampton (44 games) and Walsall (89 games, 6 goals). He played for Birmingham Works XI (1941). His brother-in-law, Jimmy Gemmell, played for Bury.

SIMS, NIGEL DAVID

Goalkeeper: 310 apps
Born: Coton-in-the-Elms, Burton-on-Trent, 9 August 1931
Career: Coton Swifts, Stapenhill, Wolverhampton Wanderers (amateur, August 1948; professional, September 1948), VILLA (March 1956), Arsenal (guest, May 1959), Peterborough United (September 1964), Toronto City/Canada (1965), Toronto Italia/Canada (April 1966; retired October 1966); later worked for a Wolverhampton-based insurance company

For his size and build, Sims was very agile. With Bert Williams as first-choice keeper at Molineux, he bided his time in the reserves, having fewer than 40 games, although he did win a 'Young' England cap against England in 1954 before transferring to Villa. He performed superbly well over the next eight years, gaining an FA Cup-winner's medal (1957), a Second Division championship medal (1960) and a League Cup-winner's tankard (1961). He also played for the Football League XI against the League of Ireland at Leeds in October 1957 and was voted Villa's 'Terrace Trophy' winner (1958). He now lives in Swansea.

SIMS, STEVEN FRANK

Defender: 47 apps
Born: Lincoln, 2 July 1957
Career: Lincoln County Schools, Lincoln United, Lincoln City (trial), Leicester City (apprentice, August 1973; professional, July 1974), Watford (£175,000, December 1978), Notts County (£50,000, September 1984), Watford (£50,000, October 1986), VILLA (£50,000, June 1987), Burton Albion

(June 1990), Lincoln City (non-contract, September–November 1990), Bournemouth (trial, February 1991), Boston FC (assistant manager, June 1991), Stafford Rangers (October 1991), Shepshed Albion (December 1991–May 1993)

A centre-half with a footballing father (Frank, a Lincoln City clubman in the 1950s), Sims made a rapid rise through the ranks at Leicester. He appeared in 87 first-class games for the Foxes, gained 10 England Under-21 caps and played in one 'B' international, having earlier represented his country as a youth-team player. He switched to Watford in 1978 for a then record outlay for a Third Division club and made over 150 League appearances for the Hornets in his first spell. He also did well at Meadow Lane (85 League games) before going back to Watford, from where he joined Villa in 1987 – signed by his old boss Graham Taylor. Partnering Martin Keown at the heart of the defence, Sims helped Villa win promotion from Division Two in his first season but struggled after that with injuries and was eventually released.

SINGLETON, HERBERT

Goalkeeper: 2 apps

Born: Manchester, 23 June 1900 – *Died*: 1958

Career: St Andrew's FC, California FC/USA, Buxton, Manchester Central, VILLA (trial, November 1923; professional, December 1923; retired after fracturing his skull in a reserve-team game in November 1926 – collided with his own full-back)

Very capable between the posts, Singleton (a junior international trialist for the Colours against the Whites in April 1925) was signed as cover for Tommy Jackson. A serious head injury ended his career.

SIX, DIDIER

Forward: 14+4 apps, 2 goals

Born: France, 21 August 1954

Career: Lens/France, Olympique Marseille/France, Valencia/Spain, RFC Bruges/Belgium, Strasbourg/France, Vfb Stuttgart/Germany, Mulhouse FC/France, VILLA (September 1984), Metz/France (June 1985–87); ran his own TV programme in Lille

Six had already scored 163 goals in 421 games in European League football (including 72 in 152 games for Spanish giants Valencia and 30 in one season for Stuttgart) before moving to Villa in 1984. Unfortunately he never settled in England, was always struggling to find his form and returned 'home' to France in 1985. Six, the first Frenchman to play in the Football League, won 52 caps for his country (13 goals). He also played in two World Cups.

SKEA, DAVID FREDERICK

Inside-forward: 1 app., 1 goal

Born: Arbroath, Angus, February 1871 – *Died*: Scotland, *circa* 1950

Career: Arbroath (August 1888), VILLA (July 1892), Dundee Thistle (April 1893), Darwen (July 1893), Bury (December 1893), Leicester Fosse (August 1894), Swindon Town (May 1896), New Brompton (£10, June 1897), Cowes/Isle of Wight (July 1899)

As he got older, Skea became more of a marksman than a creator, who netted Leicester's first-ever goal in the Football League, recorded the Foxes' first hat-trick at the same level and netted the club's first penalty! He went on to hit 37 goals in only 52 outings for Leicester – having earlier struggled with his previous clubs, notching just one goal in his only game for Villa against Notts County in December 1892. He later did well with Swindon and New Brompton (Gillingham) although his spell with Swindon was cut short following disciplinary measures taken by the club after he'd arrived late for training 'in an intoxicated condition'. Transfer-listed at £25, he spent six months out of the game before joining New Brompton.

SKILLER, LEON GEORGE FERDINAND

Goalkeeper: 1 app.

Born: Penzance, Cornwall, 11 December 1883 – *Died*: Penzance, Cornwall, July 1936

Career: Leytonstone (1903), South Weald FC, Leyton (1906), VILLA (September 1908), Swindon Town (July 1909; retired May 1922); later a coach driver in Penzance

After 54 games for Leyton, the long-legged Skiller, active on his line with a safe pair of hands, had just one game for Villa, deputising for Billy George against Nottingham Forest in January 1909. After leaving, he did well for Swindon, starring in more than 300 games for the Wiltshire club, 70 in the Football League.

SLADE, HOWARD CHARLES

Inside-forward: 3 apps

Born: Bath, 29 January 1891 – *Died*: Doncaster, 7 April 1971

Career: Bath City (August 1910), Stourbridge (July 1912), Nottingham Forest (trial, 1912), VILLA (June 1913), Huddersfield Town (March 1914); guest for Reading (1916); Middlesbrough (October 1922), Darlington (September 1925–May 1927), Folkestone (briefly); thereafter coached in Turkey, Venezuela, Mexico, Scandinavia; then at Rotherham United (1929), Aldershot (1930); Middlesex Schools Authority (instructor, October 1934–39); Crystal Palace (scout, then joint manager, 1950–51; chief scout, August 1951–June 1955); also played cricket for the Lockwood CC (Yorkshire) when at Huddersfield

A durable footballer, Slade's appearances for Villa were all in 1913–14. He was converted into a half-back at Huddersfield and played in 129 games for the Terriers, lining up in 2 FA Cup finals, gaining a loser's medal in 1920 (against Villa) and a winner's prize 2 years later (against Preston). He also helped the Yorkshire club gain promotion to the First Division in the initial post-war campaign. He broke his leg in November 1916 against Notts County and battled hard to regain full fitness. He held a full FA coaching badge.

SLOLEY, RICHARD

Inside-forward: 2 apps
Born: London, 17 January 1895 – *Died*: London, 1964
Career: Corinthians, Cambridge University, Brentford (1913–14), Corinthians (1917), Brentford (1918–19), VILLA (loan, October–November 1919), Corinthians (October 1919–May 1922)

Sloley, an England amateur international, was taken 'on loan' by Villa when senior players were absent through illness and injury. He was an Army lieutenant during WW1.

SLEEUWENHOEK, JOHN CORNELIUS

Centre-half: 260 apps, 1 goal
Born: Wednesfield, 26 February 1944 – *Died*: Birmingham, July 1989
Career: VILLA (junior, June 1959; professional, February 1961), Birmingham City (£45,000, November 1967), Torquay United (loan, March–May 1971), Oldham Athletic (July 1971–May 1972); played in the Cheshire League, for VILLA Old Stars and worked in the lottery office at Villa Park

Son of a Dutch parachute instructor, 'Tulip' Sleeuwenhoek was a fine defender, strong in the air, dominant on the ground. Brought up on cheese and stout, he won England honours at schoolboy, youth and Under-23 levels and also represented the Football League while collecting the Villa supporters' 'Terrace Trophy' award in 1964. Sidelined with a troublesome knee at St Andrew's, a weight problem caused him to quit League soccer. Sleeuwenhoek died from a heart attack, aged 45. His son, Kris, was a junior player with Wolves and Derby.

SMALL, BRYAN

Defender: 37+6 apps
Born: Birmingham, 15 November 1971
Career: VILLA (April 1988; professional, July 1990), Birmingham City (loan, September 1994), Bolton Wanderers (free, March 1996), Luton Town (loan, September 1997), Bradford City (loan, December 1997), Bury (free, January 1998), Stoke City (free, July 1998 to May 2000), Carlisle United (trial, August–September 2000), Brentford (trial, October 2000), Walsall (January 2001; retired, injured, July 2001)

Left wing-back Small, an England youth and Under-21 international (12 caps won at the latter level) was a useful performer who made over 100 senior appearances after leaving Villa.

SMART, HERBERT HORACE

Inside-left: 1 app.

Born: Smethwick, 24 April 1892 – *Died*: Birmingham, 1951

Career: Bilston United (1910), VILLA (January 1914); guest for Smethwick Carriage Works (1919), Leicester Fosse (1919); Wolverhampton Wanderers (December 1919), Hednesford Town (May 1920), Cannock Town (May 1922–June 1925); also assisted Dudley Town, Willenhall, Bloxwich Strollers

Smart was restricted in what he could do. Replacing Joe Bache at Newcastle in April 1914 for his only League game with Villa, he failed to make the grade at Wolves either!

SMART, THOMAS

Full-back: 452 apps, 8 goals

Born: Blackheath, 20 September 1896 – *Died*: 10 June 1968

Career: Rowley Regis Schools, Blackheath Town (1913), Army football (1915–18), Halesowen (July 1919), VILLA (January 1920), Brierley Hill Alliance (May 1934, then player/coach to May 1938), Blackheath Town (player/coach, August 1938–September 1939); later worked at Marsh and Baxter (sausage and pork-pie manufacturer) for 17 years

Three months after joining Villa from non-League football, Smart collected an FA Cup-winner's medal after Huddersfield had been beaten 1–0 in the 1920 final. He made great strides in top-class soccer and went on to become a real quality defender. Barrel-chested and nicknamed 'Tic', he was a fierce tackler, and his sheer size used to place a certain amount of apprehension in the eyes of the opposing forwards! One report stated that he was built like a 'buffalo and kicked like a mule'. In fact, he had a war cry 'Thik Hai' (Hindustani language) which he yelled out quite often when clearing his lines. He had picked this up during his Army service in India. Forming a formidable partnership in the Villa rearguard with Tommy Mort, Smart won five caps for England and in 1924 added a Cup runner's-up medal to his collection. He played in two international trials in 1929 – for The Rest versus England and Cradley Heath. Smart, who would often turn up for morning training on his bike wearing a flat cap, eventually handed over his position in the Villa side to Danny Blair. He served in the South Staffs Regiment during WW1, based in Greece, Belgium and India. His brother, Len, played for Luton, Wolves, Port Vale and Bournemouth.

SMITH, GEORGE

Utility: 5 apps

Born: Preston, 12 July 1879 – *Died*: Southampton, 3 July 1908

Career: St Christopher's/Preston, Leyland FC (1897), Preston North End (July 1899), VILLA (July 1901), Blackburn Rovers (October 1901), New

Brompton (December 1901), Plymouth Argyle (August 1906), Southampton (August 1907–April 1908)

Originally a half-back, Smith became a fine utility forward, able to occupy three different positions. A direct player, not at all flashy, he was a good, old-fashioned footballer who made over 125 appearances at competitive level, but managed only a handful with Villa. He died of pneumonia just before his 29th birthday.

SMITH, GORDON MELVILLE

Full-back: 92+4 apps

Born: Glasgow, 3 July 1954

Career: Glasgow schoolboy football, St Johnstone (amateur, June 1969; professional, July 1971), VILLA (August 1976), Tottenham Hotspur (£150,000, February 1979), Wolverhampton Wanderers (August 1982); South African football (June 1984); Pittsburgh Spirit/USA (January 1985), Barnet (season 1985–86; retired, injured, July 1986); now works for an advertising company in Glasgow

After representing his country at youth-team level, industrious defender Smith went on to gain four Scottish Under-23 caps. He did well north of the border before appearing in almost 100 senior games for Villa. The majority of his outings came in his first two seasons when he partnered John Gidman. He gained a League Cup-winner's medal as a substitute (1977) but then dropped out of favour, hence his transfer to Spurs, for whom he played in 67 first-class games, helping the Londoners re-establish themselves in the First Division. Stricken by injuries, he moved to Molineux in 1982 and was a member of the Wolves side that won promotion from Division Two. He then lost his place in the defence, and that led him to making the big decision to go overseas, where he did well for a number of years.

SMITH, HERBERT HENRY

Outside-right: 54 apps, 9 goals

Born: Small Heath, Birmingham, 17 December 1922 – *Died*: Birmingham, 11 January 1996

Career: Alston Road School (Bordesley Green), Birmingham Boys; served in Army under age, enlisted with the Royal Gloucesters, transferred to REME (Army), attached to the Derbyshire Regiment; Moor Green (August 1945), VILLA (professional, May 1947), Southend United (June 1954), Corby Town (November 1954), Moor Green (briefly), Hinckley Athletic (September 1956), Brush Sports (March 1958); later with Wolseley FC (works side, season 1960–61); then associated with the Mackadown Sports and Social Club, Lea Hall (Birmingham)

A small, pencil-slim winger with good pace and ability, known as 'Little Herbie' or 'Little Sport' by his team-mates, Smith (5 ft 3 in. tall and 9 st. in weight) could battle it out with the meanest and toughest defenders in the game. During his 7 years at Villa Park, despite an abundance of similar players, he performed well, having his best season in 1951–52 (26 outings). Making his debut for Villa in the FA Cup second replay against Bolton in January 1949, he scored the winner in extra time. He also starred in Villa's Central League side before transferring to Southend.

SMITH, LESLIE GEORGE FREDERICK

Outside-left: 197 apps, 37 goals
Born: Ealing, London, 23 March 1918 – *Died*: Lichfield, 20 May 1995
Career: St John's Grammar School (Brentford), Horn and Petersham FC, Brentford (junior, 1933), Wimbledon (August 1934), Hayes (July 1935), Brentford (professional, March 1936); guest for Chelsea, Leicester City (1941), Manchester City and West Bromwich Albion during WW2; VILLA (£7,500, October 1945), Brentford (June 1952), Kidderminster Harriers (player/manager, August 1953–June 1954), Wolverhampton Wanderers (scout, 1954–55); VILLA Old Stars (manager, 1960–65); ran an electrical business in Aston for many years

Les 'Schmidtz' Smith was Villa's 'Will-o'-the-Wisp' winger who thrilled the crowds with his precocious confidence, exquisite ball-control, wing wizardry, dash and a goalscoring and goal-making technique that earned him England recognition.

After appearing in Wimbledon's losing 1935 FA Amateur Cup final side, Smith starred in 13 wartime and Victory internationals as well as gaining one senior cap (1939). He also represented the FA in Romania, Italy and Yugoslavia, and played for the Combined Services and the RAF during WW2. Besides his senior appearances for Villa, he also had 22 outings (3 goals) in the transitional season of 1945–46. He made his Villa debut at Plymouth in November 1945 (League South) and his 'senior' bow followed in January 1946 when he scored in a 2–1 FA Cup defeat at Coventry. His Football League baptism in a Villa shirt arrived in August 1946 when Middlesbrough won 1–0 in the Midlands. Smith kept his place on the left-wing until 1951–52 when he was replaced by Billy Goffin. He played in over 80 games for Brentford.

SMITH, LESLIE JOSEPH

Outside-right: 130 apps, 25 goals
Born: Halesowen, 24 December 1927
Career: Wolverhampton Wanderers (amateur, June 1945; professional, April 1946), VILLA (£25,000, February 1956; retired, injured, January 1960)

Smith was a fast, clever and direct winger who made his League debut for Wolves in 1947–48. Owing to the form of Johnny Hancocks and Jimmy Mullen, he was mainly a reserve at Molineux and played in only four games when the championship was won in 1954. He finally broke through on a regular basis the following year, starring in 34 games when Wolves finished runners-up to Chelsea. After scoring over 20 goals in just under 100 outings for the

Wanderers, Smith moved to Villa, where he found less competition. With Jackie Sewell initially his partner on the right, he won an FA Cup-winner's medal in 1957 before an Achilles tendon injury forced him to retire. He now lives in Halesowen.

SMITH, STEPHEN

Outside-left: 194 apps, 42 goals

Born: Abbotts Langley, 14 January 1874 – *Died*: Benson, Oxfordshire, 19 May 1935

Career: Cannock and Rugeley Colliery, Cannock Town, Rugeley Ceal FC, Hednesford Town (September 1891), VILLA (August 1893), Portsmouth (May 1901), New Brompton (July 1906; then player/manager, December 1906–May 1908); lived in Portsmouth until 1932; then manager of Roke Stores, Benson (Oxfordshire)

Smith was an accomplished winger, very tricky, who could pass a ball with pinpoint accuracy and produce a stunning shot. A player who rose to the big occasion, he was signed by Fred Rinder after doing a ten-hour shift as a haulage machine operator at the coal-face. He shared the left-wing berth with Albert Woolley when Villa won the League title in 1893–94, and then figured prominently when the same prize was won four times in five seasons between 1896 and 1900. He also gained two FA Cup-winner's medals (1895, 1897) and was capped by England against Scotland in 1895. He helped Pompey win the Southern League title in 1902.

SOLANO, NOLBERTO ALBINO

Midfield: 10 apps

Born: Lima, Peru, 12 December 1974

Career: Cristal Alianza/Peru, Sporting Deportivo Municipal/Peru, Boca Juniors/Argentina, Newcastle United (£2,763,958, August 1998), VILLA (£1.5m, January 2004)

A Peruvian international right-sided midfielder with over 60 full caps to his name, Solano was a surprise signing by Villa boss David O'Leary, having previously scored almost 40 goals in well over 200 appearances for Newcastle. A fine ball-player with a strong shot, he made his debut in a 5–0 win at Leicester in January 2004.

SORENSEN, THOMAS

Goalkeeper: 45 apps

Born: Denmark, 12 June 1976

Career: OB Odense/Denmark, Sunderland (£500,000, August 1998), VILLA (£2m, August 2003)

After other clubs had shown an interest, Villa boss David O'Leary made Sorensen his second signing from the Stadium of Light. Capped over 30 times by his country at senior level, as well as playing in one 'B' and 6 Under-21 internationals, Sorensen – 6 ft 4 in. tall and 13 st. 10 lb in weight – helped

Sunderland win the First Division championship in 1999 and made 197 appearances for the Wearsiders. A fine shot-stopper with sound positional sense, who has been first choice for his country for the last three seasons, he made his debut for Villa against Portsmouth on the opening day of the 2003–04 Premiership season. Played in Euro 2004.

SOUTHGATE, GARETH

Defender: 243 apps, 9 goals
Born: Watford, 3 September 1970
Career: Crystal Palace (YTS, January 1987; professional, January 1989), VILLA
    (£2.5m, July 1995), Middlesbrough (£6.5m, July 2001)

A classy defender, calm, confident, a good header of the ball, clean tackler and a fine reader of situations, the unflappable Southgate made 191 appearances for Palace before joining Villa for a record fee – 12 months after helping the Eagles win the First Division title. He immediately slotted into Villa's defence, alongside Paul McGrath and later Ugo Ehiogu, Colin Calderwood, Gareth Barry, Ozalan Alpay and others. An England international (almost 60 caps), he unfortunately missed a crucial spot-kick in the penalty shoot-out with Germany in the Euro '96 semi-final at Wembley, but quickly put that disappointment behind him and went on to play in the World Cup finals of 1998 and Euro 2000. Southgate teamed up with former team-mates Ehiogu and George Boateng when he joined Middlesbrough and in 2003 he took his career appearance-tally (at club level) past the 500 mark before gaining a League Cup-winner's medal a year later.

SOUTHREN, THOMAS CANSFIELD

Outside-right: 72 apps, 7 goals
Born: Southwick, near Sunderland, 1 August 1927 – *Died*: Welwyn Garden
    City, Herts, 10 May 2004
Career: High Southwark and Handside Schools, Peartree Old Boys' Club
    (1941); served in Royal Navy during WW2; Kirkham RNAS; Peartree Old
    Boys, Arsenal (amateur, January 1946), West Ham United (professional,
    January 1949), VILLA (£12,000, December 1954), Bournemouth (October
    1958; released August 1960)

Southren gained a first-team place in West Ham's team in 1950 and was a member of the Hammers' side that won the Combination League and Cup double in 1954 and represented the London FA against the Berlin FA that same season. After scoring twice in 66 appearances for the Londoners, he joined Villa, signing on platform 6 of Euston Station. Decidedly quick, especially over 30–40 yards, he always tried to get to the bye-line before delivering his cross, high or low, and replaced Norman Lockhart on the wing, having a fine debut at Manchester United 3 days after his move, helping Villa to a 1–0 win. He made 64 Third Division (S) appearances for Bournemouth.

SPENCER, HOWARD

Full-back: 295 apps, 2 goals

Born: Edgbaston, Birmingham, 23 August 1875 – *Died*: Four Oaks, Sutton Coldfield, 14 January 1940

Career: Albert Road School, Handsworth (Birmingham), Stamford FC (1890), Birchfield All Saints (August 1891), Birchfield Trinity (January 1892), VILLA (amateur, April 1892; professional, June 1894; retired, November 1907); VILLA (director, July 1909–May 1936)

'Gentle Howard' Spencer was scrupulously fair – never known to commit a ruthless foul. His anticipation was his forte and he became one of the biggest names in football, referred to continuously as the 'Prince of Full-backs' during the pinnacle of his career (1895–1907). When he got into Villa's team he partnered Jim Welford and then became an excellent aide to Albert Evans – both pairings were quite brilliant at times.

Spencer captained club and country, winning six England caps after appearing in a junior international in 1894 – scant reward for his many superb and sterling displays at full-back. He won four League championship medals, played in two FA Cup-winning sides (leading Villa to victory in 1905), received two benefits (1900, 1906) and after retiring with a knee injury, continued to prosper as a partner in a firm of fuel merchants (Spencer and Abbon). An active member on the board of directors, he served Villa for 42 years.

SPIERS, CYRIL HENRY

Goalkeeper: 112 apps

Born: Witton, Birmingham 4 April 1902 – *Died*: 21 May 1967

Career: Deykin Avenue School, Aston Boys (three seasons), Midland Boys, Witton Star, Birchfield Boys' Brigade, The Swifts (Witton), Brookvale United, Soho Rovers, Handsworth Central, Halesowen (1919), VILLA (December 1920), Tottenham Hotspur (trial, November 1927; signed December 1927), Wolverhampton Wanderers (September 1933; retired May 1935; appointed coach/assistant manager, August 1935), Cardiff City (assistant manager, March 1939; manager, April 1939), Norwich City (manager, June 1946), Cardiff City (manager, December 1947–April 1954), Crystal Palace (manager, October 1954–June 1958), Leicester City (chief scout, September 1958–April 1962), Exeter City (manager, May 1962–February 1963), Leicester City (chief scout, February 1963–May 1965)

Spiers played in the intermediate and reserve sides before gaining a first-team place in 1922–23, displacing Tommy Jackson. But when Jackson regained his form, Spiers slipped back into the second XI before claiming the number-one spot again in 1924–25. Consistent and reliable, he was injured in 1926 and on regaining fitness was released. He made 186 appearances for Spurs, including 124 consecutively between November 1928 and October 1931. He also played for the Football League against the Scottish League in 1930 and was an international trialist in 1931, losing out to Harry Hibbs of Birmingham. He became assistant manager to Major Frank Buckley at Wolves and in 1939 received his first managerial appointment at Cardiff, later guiding the Welsh club into the First Division (1952).

SPINK, NIGEL PHILIP

Goalkeeper: 449+5 apps
Born: Chelmsford, 8 August 1958
Career: Chelmsford City Schools, West Ham United (schoolboy forms), Chelmsford City (1974), VILLA (£4,000, January 1977), West Bromwich Albion (free, January 1996), Millwall (£50,000, September 1997–May 2000); then goalkeeping coach with Birmingham City, Swindon Town and Northampton Town; Forest Green Rovers (August 2001, appointed joint-manager for season 2002–03)

Spink, an apprentice plasterer before becoming a goalkeeper, found himself third choice behind John Burridge and Jake Findlay when he joined Villa and was then knocked down to fourth when Jimmy Rimmer arrived. Unperturbed, 'Spinky' played in the intermediate and reserve sides before establishing himself in the first XI in 1982, having only made two senior appearances in the previous five years. His League debut came in December 1979 against Nottingham Forest and was followed by an unexpected substitute appearance in the 1982 European Cup final against Bayern Munich after Rimmer had left the field injured.

Powerfully built, 6 ft 2 in. tall and weighing 14 st. 10 lb, he could withstand the toughest of challenges, handled the ball well, was a fine shot-stopper, had great anticipation and was courageous as well as confident. He won one England cap, as a 'sub' against Australia in 1983, played in two 'B' internationals and helped Villa win promotion to the First Division in 1988 (the year he had his testimonial). He lost his place for a while to Les Sealey but regained it and went on to appear in over 450 games. In fact, he played in more League, League Cup and competitive games than any other Villa keeper. He played his last League game for Millwall at Wigan in January 2000 at the age of 41 years, 5 months, 7 days (his 540th appearance in major competitions). He is also a useful cricketer. He now lives in Sutton Coldfield.

STAINROD, SIMON ALLAN

Forward: 76+6 apps, 27 goals
Born: Sheffield, 1 February 1959
Career: Sheffield and South Yorkshire Boys, Sheffield United (apprentice, June 1974; professional, July 1976), Oldham Athletic (£60,000, March 1979), Queens Park Rangers (£275,000, November 1980), Sheffield Wednesday (£250,000, February 1985), VILLA (£250,000, September 1985), Stoke City (£90,000, December 1987–May 1988), Racing Club Strasbourg/France (1988–89), FC Rouen/France (1989–90), Falkirk (player, June 1990; later

player/caretaker manager), Dundee (player/caretaker manager, February 1992), Ayr United (manager, 1993–95)

Stainrod, who was already an established marksman when he joined Villa, having netted 97 goals in 336 matches, made a terrific start for his new club, bagging all 4 goals on his debut in a 4–1 League Cup win at Exeter in September 1985. Capped by England as a youth and bought essentially to replace Gary Shaw, he was an aggressive striker, who easily lost his temper but had a knack of being in the right place at the right time to snap up the half-chance. He netted a goal every three games for Villa and helped QPR win the Second Division title in 1983.

STARK, ROY HOWARD
Defender: 2 apps
Born: Stapleford, Nottingham, 28 November 1953
Career: Stapleford and Nottinghamshire Boys, VILLA (apprentice, June 1967; professional, June 1969; free transfer, May 1975); non-League football (August 1975–May 1980)

Able to play at full-back and centre-half, Stark made his League debut against Sheffield Wednesday in April 1974, two years after skippering the youngsters to victory in the FA Youth Cup final. He suffered with injuries during his eight years at Villa Park, undergoing two cartilage operations.

STARLING, RONALD WILLIAM
Inside-left: 99 apps, 12 goals
Born: Pelaw-on-Tyne, near Gateshead, 11 October 1909 – *Died*: Sheffield, 17 December 1991
Career: Durham County Schools, Newcastle United (trial, November 1923), Usworth Colliery (January 1924), Washington Colliery (September 1924), Hull City (amateur, June 1925; professional, August 1927), Newcastle United (£3,750, May 1930), Sheffield Wednesday (£3,250, June 1932), VILLA (£7,500, January 1937); guest for Northampton Town (1939–40), Hereford United (1940), Nottingham Forest (1939–40, 1941–42), Walsall (1939–42), Sheffield Wednesday (1940–41); Nottingham Forest (player-coach, July 1948–June 1950), Beighton FC (February–April 1951); later ran a newsagent's near Hillsborough

Starling was a great strategist whose tactics could completely turn the flow of a game. He possessed all the tricks in the trade and often produced them to the full on the field of play. At his peak he was rated better than the great Alex James. Nicknamed 'Flutterfoot', he had trials with Newcastle but was not accepted and went to work down the pit. After scoring 8 goals in one game and 45 in a season of junior football, Hull signed him in 1925. He secured 16 goals in 89 appearances for the Tigers before, ironically, moving to Newcastle! He struck 8 goals in 53 appearances for the Geordies and followed up with 31 in 193 outings for Sheffield Wednesday, whom he skippered to victory in the 1935

FA Cup final. In 1938 he helped Villa win the Second Division title and continued to play during WW2 (sometimes as a wing-half), eventually retiring with a record of 431 appearances (393 in the League) and 65 goals. He also played in 136 games for Villa during the hostilities; was capped twice by England against Scotland (1933, 1937) and also starred for an International XI against a District XI in September 1940. Starling played in four FA Cup semi-finals with different clubs in nine years: Hull (1930), Newcastle (1932), Sheffield Wednesday (1935) and Villa (1938). He could also preach a sermon as good as any vicar!

STAUNTON, STEPHEN

Utility: 335+15 apps, 19 goals
Born: Drogheda, Ireland, 19 January 1969
Career: Dundalk (1985), Liverpool (£20,000, September 1986), Bradford City (loan, November 1987), VILLA (£1.1m, August 1991), Liverpool (free, July 1998), Crystal Palace (loan, August–September 2000), VILLA (free, December 2000), Coventry City (free, August 2003)

Capped by the Republic of Ireland at youth, Under-21 (4 games) and more than 100 times at senior level (a national record), Staunton can play as an orthodox left-back, central defender or in midfield. A snip-of-a-signing by Liverpool, he made 90 appearances for the Merseysiders, was an FA Cup winner in 1989 and a League championship-winner 12 months later. Enticed to Villa by Ron Atkinson, he immediately made his mark with a string of splendid defensive displays. Using his sweet left foot to good effect, to the appreciation of the fans, Staunton added two League Cup-winner's medals to his collection before rejoining Liverpool. Surprisingly, he was brought back to Villa for a second spell halfway through the 2000–01 season and pushed his appearance-tally up to 350 before moving to Coventry.

STEPHENSON, CLEMENT

Inside-forward: 216 apps, 96 goals
Born: New Delaval, County Durham, 6 February 1890 – *Died*: Huddersfield, 24 October 1961
Career: Bedlington, New Delaval Villa, West Stanley (1908), Blyth Spartans (three months), Durham City (1909), VILLA (£175, March 1910), Stourbridge (loan, August 1910–February 1911); two years in Royal Naval Air Service (PT instructor at the Crystal Palace); guest for Leeds City (February 1919), South Shields and District (1919); Huddersfield Town (£3,000, March 1921; retired May 1929; then manager until May 1942); later a caterer in Huddersfield

Stephenson played in four FA Cup finals and was a manager in two other finals. He gained winner's medals with Villa in 1913 and 1920 and Huddersfield in 1922, was a loser in 1928 and managed the Terriers in the losing finals of 1930 and 1938.

Stephenson dreamed that Villa would win the 1913 final 1–0 and that Tommy Barber would head the goal. That's precisely what happened and Villa even missed a penalty after Stephenson had been brought down! Elder brother of George T. (q.v.) and James (q.v.), Stephenson gained experience with Stourbridge. He made rapid progress and scored on his League debut in a 4–0 win over Spurs. Going from strength to strength, he represented Birmingham against London in 1913 and gained his only England cap against Wales in 1924 (there should have been more). An expert schemer, he passed the ball with fine judgement, was no mean goalscorer, could shoot with both feet, had good pace and was never afraid to 'rough it' with the burly defenders. With Joe Bache his wing partner, then Harold Edgeley and Arthur Dorrell after that, Stephenson did superbly with Villa before embarking on a 21-year association with Huddersfield, first as a player, then as a manager. He rattled in 50 goals in 275 outings for the Yorkshire club and replaced Jack Chaplin as manager. He saw the FA Cup snatched away from his team in the dying seconds of extra time in the 1938 final when Preston's George Mutch scored a dubious penalty!

STEPHENSON, GEORGE HENRY
Outside-left: 4 apps, 1 goal
Born: Stillington, Durham, 29 September 1908 – *Died*: 1964
Career: Stillington and Stockton Schools, Carlton Iron Works FC, Stillington St John's, Durham City (junior, September 1927, then amateur; professional, February 1930), Leicester City (trial, March 1930), VILLA (trial, November 1930; signed April 1931), Bradford Park Avenue (briefly), Luton Town (July 1934), Leeds United (August 1939), guest for Luton Town (1940); did not feature after WW2

No relation to the other Stephensons, George was a left-winger, clever on the ball, who struggled to make an impact at Villa Park. He netted 58 goals in almost 200 League games for Luton.

STEPHENSON, GEORGE TERNENT
Inside-forward: 95 apps, 22 goals
Born: Horton, Northumberland, 3 September 1900 – *Died*: Derby, 18 August 1971
Career: Blyth Secondary School Juniors, County Durham Schools, Northumberland County football, Blyth Secondary School Seniors, New Delaval Juniors, New Delaval Villa, Leeds City (June 1919), VILLA (£250, November 1919 – signed at an auction held at the Metropole Hotel, Leeds, after the Yorkshire club had folded and its players were put up for sale), Stourbridge (loan, August 1920–March 1921), Derby County (£2,000, November 1927), Sheffield Wednesday (£2,500, February 1931), Preston North End (£1,500, July 1933), Charlton Athletic (£660, May 1934; retired, injured, May 1937; joined the coaching staff, also scout), Huddersfield Town (assistant manager, August 1947–March 1952); licensee of the Sportsman's

Inn, near Huddersfield (1954–56); Rolls Royce factory worker, Derby (1957–58); Derby County ('A' team coach, 1961–63)

A former grocer, smithy and pit-worker, Stephenson – like brother Clem (q.v.) – was an England international, who won three caps: in 1928 against France and Belgium (two goals) and in 1931 against France again – having starred in a junior match against Scotland in 1920. A brainy, cultured footballer, Stephenson scored 120 goals in 319 League games during his career, including four-timers in two First Division matches for Derby. Small in stature, with a big heart, he was a key member of the Preston side and helped Charlton win the Third Division (S) title. Stephenson scored virtually a goal every 4 games for Villa, his best season coming in 1926–27, when he scored 13 goals in 37 games. As a stern and respected manager, he found it hard going at times as Huddersfield continually battled against relegation and quit with the club heading towards Division Two. His son, Bob, played for Derby, Shrewsbury and Rochdale and was a wicket-keeper for Derbyshire and Hampshire.

STEPHENSON, JAMES

Forward: 32 apps, 1 goal

Born: New Delaval, 10 February 1895 – *Died*: Newcastle, February 1958

Career: New Delaval, VILLA (April 1914); served in Army during WW1; guest for Leeds City (April 1919); Sunderland (£3,000, May 1921), Watford (£500, May 1922), Queens Park Rangers (July 1927), Norwich City (briefly), Boston Town (August 1928), Ashington (October 1928), New Delaval Villa, Ashington (December 1930), New Delaval Villa (February 1931)

Only 5 ft 5 in. tall, Stephenson was a useful acquisition to the Villa ranks and deputised (most of the time) for Charlie Wallace on the right-wing. Six months after playing for the Birmingham County FA against the Scottish FA in March 1914, he made his League debut as an emergency centre-forward at Everton. His only goal for the club earned Villa a point at Bradford City in April 1915. Stephenson played 22 games for Sunderland, scored 18 times in 213 League games for Watford and was still playing when WW2 broke out.

STOBART, BARRY HENRY

Inside-forward: 53 apps, 20 goals

Born: Dodsworth, near Doncaster, 6 June 1938

Career: Dodsworth County School, Wath Wanderers, Wolverhampton Wanderers (amateur, June 1953; professional, December 1955), Manchester City (£20,000, August 1964), VILLA (£22,000, November 1964), Shrewsbury Town (£10,000, October 1967), Durban Spurs/South Africa (June 1967–May 1969), Willenhall Town (player, August 1970–May 1972; later manager, 1978–83), Dudley Town (manager, 1983–90); also ran his own greengrocer's shop in Ward Grove and had a window-cleaning business in Ettingshall

After only five senior appearances, Stobart was called into Wolves' 1960 FA

Cup final team against Blackburn, gaining a winner's medal after a 3–0 win. However, he found it hard to keep his place in the first XI, but stuck to his guns and remained at Molineux until 1964, scoring 22 goals in 54 games. After failing to settle at Maine Road, he joined Villa and attained a similar strike record to the one at Wolves. Struggling at times with an injury, he was sold to Shrewsbury after losing his place. As a manager, he guided Willenhall to the West Midlands League title and also to the 1981 FA Vase final (beaten by Whickham after extra time).

STOKES, ARTHUR WILBERFORCE

Defender: 13 apps, 1 goal

Born: West Bromwich, 12 April 1867 – *Died*: Smethwick, June 1939

Career: Bratt Street School (West Bromwich), White Hill FC, Wednesbury Old Athletic, VILLA (April 1892), Burton Swifts (March 1893), Walsall Town Swifts (August 1894; retired, injured, April 1895)

A strong-looking player, Stokes was an efficient tackler whose thoughtfulness was not always in evidence.

STONE, STEPHEN BRIAN

Midfield: 85+35 apps, 7 goals

Born: Gateshead, 20 August 1971

Career: Nottingham Forest (YTS, June 1987; professional, May 1989), VILLA (£5.5m, March 1999), Portsmouth (loan, October–November 2002; free, December 2002)

Stone appeared in 229 games (27 goals scored) for Forest, winning 9 England caps and a First Division championship medal (1998) before transferring to Villa after recovering from a knee problem. Unfortunately, his first full season was disappointing, Stone failing to establish himself in the team while suffering a back injury in the process. He came on as a late 'sub' in the 2000 FA Cup final. He did much better during the next campaign but a change of manager saw him leave. With Portsmouth (playing alongside ex-Villa man Paul Merson), he gained a First Division championship medal (2003).

STRANGE, EDMUND WALLACE

Left-half: 2 apps

Born: Bordesley Green, 12 March 1871 – *Died*: Birmingham, December 1925

Career: Small Heath Ravenshurst FC, Hoskins and Sewell FC, Small Heath, Langley Mill, Unity Gas, VILLA (August 1895), Langley St Michael's (September 1898; retired April 1899 due to a knee injury), VILLA (assistant secretary, August 1899–1925; also manager of the second XI)

A beautifully balanced footballer, Strange's career was dogged by injury. One of the game's gentlemen, he set up the goal that earned a point when making his debut against Stoke in April 1898. He guided Villa's second XI to the Birmingham and District League title eight seasons running (1903–10).

SUDDICK, JAMES
Inside-forward: 2 apps, 1 goal
Born: Middlesbrough, 17 August 1875 – *Died*: 1932
Career: VILLA (July 1897), Nottingham Forest (August 1898–April 1900), Thornaby, Middlesbrough (July 1902–May 1904), Thornaby (1904–05)
Reserve forward Suddick's only goal for Villa came in the 4–0 home win over Preston in February 1898. He scored four goals in fourteen starts for Forest and once in his only game for Middlesbrough in 1904.

SURTEES, ALBERT EDWARD
Inside- or centre-forward: 11 apps, 1 goal
Born: Willington Quay, 24 February 1902 – *Died*: 30 July 1963
Career: Percy Main School, North Eastern Marine, Rose Hill Villa, North Shields, Croxdale Villa, Spennymoor United, Durham City (February 1921), Preston Colliery (briefly), VILLA (February 1923), West Ham United (August 1924), St Andrew's FC/Victoria, Canada (1925), Southend United (November 1926), Clapton Orient (June 1927), Wellington Town (July 1928–May 1929)
Tall, strong and forceful, Surtees, an ex-miner, scored his only goal for Villa in a 3–0 home win over Burnley in December 1924 when he replaced Billy Walker. His younger brother, John, played in the 1930s for Middlesbrough, Portsmouth, Bournemouth, Northampton, Sheffield Wednesday and Nottingham Forest.

SWAIN, KENNETH
Right-back: 179 apps, 5 goals
Born: Birkenhead, 28 January 1952
Career: Liverpool, Birkenhead and Merseyside District Schools, Kirby Boys, Bolton Wanderers (schoolboy forms, 1967), Peckham Comprehensive and Streatham Schools, Shoreditch Teachers' Training College (Surrey), South East Counties Colleges, Wycombe Wanderers (amateur, April 1973), Chelsea (professional, August 1973), West Bromwich Albion (loan, November 1978), VILLA (£100,000, December 1978), Nottingham Forest (October 1982), Portsmouth (July 1985), West Bromwich Albion (loan, February–March 1988), Crewe Alexandra (August 1988–May 1989, then player/coach, assistant manager), Wigan Athletic (manager, 1993–94), Grimsby Town (reserve-team coach/assistant manager, 1995; caretaker manager, October 1996–May 1997); FA School of Excellence technical director; scouted for several clubs, including Nottingham Forest; senior FA coach (2000–01); qualified in handicrafts and PE at college
Swain played as a forward in the same Kirby Boys side as Dennis Mortimer before developing into a full-back. Sound in the tackle, with a steady nerve and excellent technique, he was a key member of Villa's League championship, European Cup and Super Cup-winning sides of 1981 and 1982. He replaced John Gidman in the side and when he left Mark Jones took over his role. Swain

helped Pompey win promotion from Division Two in 1987 and Crewe from Division Four two years later. During his playing days he amassed over 500 competitive appearances.

SWALES, NORMAN
Wing-half: 8 apps
Born: New Marske, Guisborough, 25 October 1908 – *Died*: 10 September 1961
Career: New Marske County School, Normandy Magnets, New Marske FC, Scarborough (briefly), Middlesbrough (amateur, then professional, December 1925), Scarborough (July 1927), VILLA (£1,000, November 1928), Durham City (June 1935), Colwyn Bay (August 1936; retired with knee injury, May 1937)
No mean ball-player, Swales made his League debut for Villa against Burnley in February 1929 when he deputised for Joe Tate. He died of cancer/Hodgkin's disease.

TAINTON, WALTER
Right-half: 1 app.
Born: Smethwick, 20 August 1882 – *Died*: Birmingham, 2 December 1937
Career: Smethwick Centaur, VILLA (April 1906), Birmingham Welfare (July 1908), Hockley Hill Methodists (1910–11); later worked for the Birmingham Health Department
Tainton was a reserve whose only League appearance was against Notts County in April 1907, when he replaced Sam Greenhalgh.

TALBOT, ALEXANDER DOUGLAS
Centre-half: 263 apps, 7 goals
Born: Cannock, 13 July 1902 – *Died*: Stourbridge, 13 August 1975
Career: West Hill School, West Cannock Colliery; played in Cannock Church and Chapel League during WW1; Hednesford Prims, Hednesford Town (1921), VILLA (£100, April 1923), Bradford Park Avenue (June 1936), Brierley Hill Alliance (February 1937), Stourbridge (February 1939; retired as a player, 1940; later manager to 1947); worked for the Austin Motor Company at Longbridge after WW2; ran his own dairy business in Stourbridge during the 1950s
A mixture of courage and culture, finesse and skilfully applied force made Talbot into a fine defender who was first choice in Villa's defence for a decade. Signed after completing a ten-hour shift down the pit, he became part of what has been described as the greatest Villa half-back line of all-time with Alex Gibson and Joe Tate playing either side of him. A reliable 'stopper' when he had to be, 'Tiny' Talbot represented the Football League against the Scottish League in 1933 but never won an England cap. He was rewarded with a benefit match by the club and was given his nickname because he was the shortest of that brilliant half-back line!

TATE, JOSEPH THOMAS

Wing-half: 193 apps, 4 goals

Born: Old Hill, 4 August 1904 – *Died*: Cradley Heath, 18 May 1973

Career: Stourbridge Council School, Birch Coppice Primitives, Grainger's Lane Primitives, Road Oak Steel Works/Brierley Hill, Cradley Heath (April 1923), VILLA (£400, April 1925), Brierley Hill Alliance (player/manager, May 1935; retired May 1937 after breaking his right leg playing against Moor Green); coach at Birmingham University (September 1937 – succeeded after WW2 by another ex-Villa player, Norman Young); later ran a tobacconist shop in Brierley Hill (started in 1936); also a fine cricketer, playing for the Warwickshire club and ground

Tate was an outstanding tactician who preferred to play the ball on the ground rather than giving it the big heave-ho! Described as being 'strong in attack and quick in recovery' he loved to participate in a triangular movement involving his inside-forward and winger or perhaps his full-back. A member of that great half-back trio (with Jimmy Gibson and Alec Talbot) – and the youngest of five brothers – he was an England trialist in 1925 (Whites against Colours) and went on to win three caps, against France, Belgium and Wales (1931 and 1932). He suffered with niggling injuries during the latter stages of his career, having only one first-team game during his last two seasons.

TAYLOR, IAN KENNETH

Midfield: 254+37 apps, 43 goals

Born: Birmingham, 4 June 1968

Career: Moor Green (August 1988), Port Vale (£15,000, professional, July 1992), Sheffield Wednesday (£1m, July 1994), VILLA (£1m, December 1994), Derby County (free, June 2003)

Taylor was the first player on Villa manager John Gregory's team sheet. A workaholic, whether playing as an anchorman or acting as the main driving force, he covered every blade of grass during a game. He had a terrific engine, and although he had to battle against ankle, knee and hamstring injuries, he always bounced back in style, giving nothing less than 100 per cent every time he took the field, being strong in the tackle with a phenomenal workrate. A Villa fan as a lad, he made 106 appearances for Port Vale (35 goals), helping them win the AWS in 1993; netted twice in 18 games for the Owls and with Villa gained a League Cup-winner's medal and an FA Cup runner's-up medal in 1996 and 2000 respectively.

TAYLOR, MARTIN SEYMOUR

Centre-forward: 1 app.

Born: Annfield Plain, Co. Durham, May 1899 – *Died*: 1962

Career: Annfield Plain, VILLA (June 1920), Scotswood (March 1922), Durham City (August 1922–May 1923)

A relatively unknown reserve with Villa, Taylor's only League game was against Preston in September 1921, when he deputised for Billy Dickson.

TEALE, SHAUN

Defender: 176+1 apps, 5 goals

Born: Southport, 10 March 1964

Career: Burscough (1984), Weymouth (August 1985), Bournemouth (£50,000, February 1989), VILLA (£300,000, July 1991), Tranmere Rovers (£450,000, August 1995), Preston North End (loan, February–March 1997), Motherwell (August 1998), Carlisle United (loan, February–May 2000), Southport (May 2000), Burscough (player/manager, May 2002), Northwich Victoria (manager, August 2003–April 2004)

Rugged, combative and able to occupy a variety of defensive positions including that of sweeper, Teale won a semi-professional cap for England before joining Bournemouth. A fearless competitor, scarred everywhere (he had stitches inserted all over his body due to various injuries), he appeared in 116 games for the Cherries and gained a League Cup-winner's medal with Villa in 1994. He lost his way at one stage before re-establishing himself in the side under Brian Little as the relegation battle hotted up towards the end of 1994–95. An ever-present at Prenton Park before losing his place in 1996–97, he was an FA Trophy winner with Burscough at Villa Park in 2003.

TEMPLETON, ROBERT BRYSON

Forward: 71 apps, 7 goals

Born: Coylton, 22 June 1879 – *Died*: Kilmarnock, Ayrshire, 2 November 1919

Career: Irvine Heatherall, Westmount Juveniles, Kilmarnock Roslyn (1896), Neilston Victoria, Kilmarnock Rugby XV (July 1897), VILLA (£250, May 1899), Newcastle United (£400, January 1903), Woolwich Arsenal (£250, December 1904), Celtic (£250, May 1906), Kilmarnock (October 1907), Fulham (August 1913–May 1914), Kilmarnock (April 1915); did not figure after WW1; later a publican in George Street, Kilmarnock, until his untimely death

A tremendously gifted player, Templeton was one of the characters of pre-WW1 football. Tall and thin, selfish but brilliant, he could play as an inside-forward and on both wings, preferring the left flank. He tended to be inconsistent at times, yet on his day was an exceptionally brilliant footballer who produced the goods on the big occasion. It was often claimed that Templeton was the cause of the Ibrox Park disaster in 1902 when several fans were killed. He was waltzing his way down the wing when the vast crowd swayed to see his dribbling skills – hence the collapse of a retaining wall and crush barriers. A real showman, Templeton was capped 11 times by Scotland, won both Scottish League championship and Scottish Cup-winner's medals with Celtic and appeared in that ill-fated international against England in 1902. He starred in well over 400 club games and scored 40 goals. He won a First Division championship medal in 1900, forming a fine partnership with Fred Wheldon and then Joe Bache before joining Newcastle.

In 1900 Templeton was suspended for insubordination, won the footballer's billiards championship while at Newcastle and in 1922 got into the cage at Bostock and Wombwell's menagerie and twisted the lion's tail for a bet. The proprietor awarded him a gold medal for his bravery! He died of a heart attack while putting on his boots for work.

TEWKESBURY, KENNETH CHARLES

Goalkeeper: 1 app.

Born: Hove, Sussex, 10 April 1909 – *Died*: Birmingham, 20 November 1970

Career: Birmingham University, Birmingham (October 1929), VILLA (December 1931), Notts County (September 1932), VILLA (January 1933), Bradford Park Avenue (July 1935), Walsall (February 1937; retired 1941); as manager, helped form Falmouth Town FC (1950); later worked for many years in Birmingham's jewellery quarter; gained his Bachelor of Science degree at Birmingham University (1927–28)

An England amateur international, Tewkesbury was reserve to Fred Biddlestone and Harry Morton during his time at Villa Park. His only first-team outing was against Newcastle in April 1933. He made 14 League appearances for Bradford and 75 for Walsall, and was capped 6 times at amateur level, winning his first in 1932 and his last 3 years later. He also played for England Amateurs against the Rest in 1935 and for an International XI against a District XI in 1940.

THOMAS, ROBERT SAMUEL

Full-back: 1 app.

Born: Newtown, Birmingham, April 1867 – *Died*: Edgbaston, Birmingham, March 1936

Career: Cocknage FC, VILLA (April 1888), Walsall Town (August 1889–May 1890)

Squarely built defender whose career was plagued by injury, Thomas' only first-team appearance for Villa came at Blackburn in a third-round FA Cup tie in March 1889.

THOMPSON, ALAN

Midfield: 46+14 apps, 5 goals

Born: Newcastle, 22 December 1973

Career: Newcastle United (YTS, June 1980; professional, March 1991), Bolton Wanderers (£250,000, July 1993), VILLA (£4.5m, June 1998), Celtic (£3.25m, September 2000)

Capped by England at both youth and Under-21 levels early in his career, Thompson was John Gregory's first signing as manager at Villa Park. Recruited to give the left side of midfield a more solid and combative look to it, he unfortunately struggled with ankle and hamstring injuries after a useful start. A dead-ball specialist, he packs a tremendous shot. After leaving Villa, he helped Celtic win the Scottish Premiership title in his first season at Parkhead, adding more medals to his collection during the subsequent years. He gained his first full England cap against Sweden in 2004.

THOMPSON, GARRY LINDSEY
Striker: 69+4 apps, 19 goals
Born: Kings Heath, Birmingham, 7 October 1959
Career: Brandwood and Maypole Schools, Coventry City (apprentice, July 1975; professional, June 1977), West Bromwich Albion (£225,000, February 1983), Sheffield Wednesday (£450,000, August 1985), VILLA (£400,000, July 1986), Watford (£150,000, October 1988), Crystal Palace (£200,000, March 1990), Queens Park Rangers (£125,000, August 1991), Cardiff City (free, July 1993), Northampton Town (free, February 1995; retired, May 1997, then reserve-team manager/coach), Brentford (briefly), Bristol Rovers (coach, July 1999; caretaker manager, January–May 2002), Brentford (assistant manager/coach, 2002–03, then manager to March 2004)

Rugged, determined, very efficient, strong in the air and on the ground, Thompson's career spanned twenty years and he played in all four divisions. He scored 49 goals in 158 appearances for Coventry while also gaining 6 England Under-21 caps. Nicknamed 'Thommo', he spent two and a half years with WBA, netting 45 times in 105 outings. Recruited by Graham Turner to replace Andy Gray, he formed a very useful striking partnership with Simon Stainrod and then Warren Aspinall, and when promotion was gained from Division Two in 1988 he had David Platt as his partner. Thompson retired with a record of 614 senior appearances and 164 goals. He was replaced as manager at Bristol Rovers by another ex-Villa player, Ray Graydon.

THOMPSON, JOHN GEORGE
Right-back: 28 apps
Born: Cramlington, Northumberland, July 1900 – *Died*: *circa* 1970
Career: Ashington (1918), VILLA (November 1919), Brighton and Hove Albion (August 1921), Chesterton (August 1924–May 1926); reinstated as an amateur with Tillings Works side (August 1927); later worked for a private car-hire firm

Thompson was a burly player, fearsome in the tackle, who did well for Villa. He struggled to gain a first-team place after the arrival of Tommy Smart, but went on to play 100 games for Brighton. He was awarded a benefit match in March 1926 (after suffering injury).

THOMPSON, THOMAS
Inside-forward: 165 apps, 76 goals
Born: Fencehouses, near Houghton-le-Spring, County Durham, 10 November 1929
Career: Lumley YMCA (1944), Newcastle United (£15, August 1946), VILLA (£12,000, September 1950), Preston North End (£28,500, June 1955), Stoke

City (£10,000, July 1961), Barrow (£5,000, March 1963; retired, May 1965); later became a carpenter in Preston

Thompson had a sound career, appearing in almost 450 League games and scoring 224 goals. One of the finest players in the game during the 1950s, his delicate touches, speed off the mark and expert finishing were his hallmarks. Small and stocky, he combined well with Colin Gibson, Johnny Dixon, Trevor Ford and Les Smith at Villa and was always looking for an opening, often trying his luck with long-range shots. Replaced by Jackie Sewell in the Villa forward-line, Thompson was capped twice by England, against Wales in 1952 and Scotland five years later; he also represented the Football League side and England 'B'. Nicknamed 'Toucher', he played superbly well alongside Tom Finney at Preston and then Stan Matthews at Stoke.

THOMSON, ROBERT GILLIES MCKENZIE
Inside-forward: 172 apps, 70 goals
Born: Dundee, 21 May 1937
Career: Dundee and Dunblane Schools, Albion Rovers (amateur, 1951), Airdrieonians (amateur, August 1952), Wolverhampton Wanderers (amateur, July 1953; professional, August 1954), VILLA (£8,000, June 1959), Birmingham City (September 1963), Stockport County (December 1967–May 1968), Bromsgrove Rovers (May 1968), Gornal (1970), Tamworth (1974), Halesowen (January 1977)

Thomson, unable to gain a first-team place at Molineux, was quickly into his stride with Villa, with whom he won a Second Division championship medal (1960) and the League Cup prize (1961) as well as collecting a runner's-up medal in the latter competition in 1963. As hard as nails, the chunky, wavy-haired Thomson hit another 25 goals in less than 130 games for the Blues. Keeping himself fit by playing squash and tennis, he now lives in Birmingham.

TIDMAN, OLIVER EUSTACE
Outside-left: 1 app.
Born: Margate, Kent, 16 May 1911
Career: Middlesex Wanderers, Tufnell Park (1928), Fulham (trial, 1931–32), VILLA (May 1932), Stockport County (May 1935–August 1936), Bristol Rovers (May 1936), Clapton Orient (July 1937), Chelmsford City (June 1938); guest for Southend United (1940–41), Watford (1940–41), Bournemouth (1941–42), Northampton Town (1943–44); retired May 1948

Tidman was a nimble player, brought in by Villa to cover for Eric Houghton and Frank Chester. His only appearance was in the 1–0 First Division win at Chelsea in February 1933. A year later Tidman played for the Birmingham County FA against the Scottish Juniors in a snowstorm at Dundee, his only representative honour. He scored 4 times in 25 games for Stockport and once in 16 for Bristol Rovers. Tidman retired to live in Bromley and is believed to be the oldest former Villa player alive today (2004).

TILER, BRIAN

Wing-half: 126+1 apps, 4 goals

Born: Whiston, near Rotherham, 15 March 1943 – *Died*: Italy, 30 June 1990

Career: Rotherham United (juniors, July 1958; professional, July 1962), VILLA (£50,000, December 1968), Atlanta Chiefs/NASL (1971), Portland Timbers/NASL (1972), Carlisle United (October 1972–May 1974), Wigan Athletic (coach/player/manager, July 1974–May 1976), Portland Timbers/NASL (manager/coach, 1976–77), Zambian national coach/manager (1977–79), Miami Americans/USA (coach/manager, 1979–81), San Diego Sockers/USA (coach/manager, 1982), Bournemouth (managing director/secretary, January 1984 until his death)

Tiler was the first player signed by Villa manager Tommy Docherty, who had been his boss at Millmoor. He made 212 League appearances for Rotherham United, where he developed into a solid and consistent wing-half. Tiler took over the captaincy at Villa and played in the 1971 League Cup final, having played sufficient games to qualify for a winner's medal a year later. He later helped Carlisle reach the First Division (1974), but with top-class football ready and waiting, the impatient streak in Tiler's nature saw him forego that dream as he moved into management with non-League Wigan Athletic, whom he guided to the Northern Premier League title in his first season at Springfield Park (1975). He then returned to the States to take charge of Portland Timbers, learning a bit about the marketing side of football while in America. He was then appointed coach/manager of the Zambian national team and successfully guided them through the qualification stages for the 1980 Olympic Games as well as organising a national coaching scheme in that African country. In 1982 he returned to Rotherham, where he formed his own company, Brian Tiler (Management), while also acting as an agent for the Zambia FA. He then did superbly well in his capacity as managing director of Bournemouth before he was tragically killed in a car crash in Italy. His Bournemouth colleague, Harry Redknapp, was in the vehicle as well, but only received minor injuries.

TILER, CARL

Defender: 13+2 apps, 1 goal

Born: Sheffield, 11 February 1970

Career: Barnsley (YTS, June 1986; professional, February 1988), Nottingham Forest (£1.4m, May 1991), Swindon Town (loan, November 1994), VILLA (£750,000, October 1995), Sheffield United (£650,000, March 1997), Everton (£500,000, November 1997), Charlton Athletic (£700,000, September 1998), Birmingham City (loan, February 2000), Portsmouth (£250,000, March 2001; released May 2003)

Strong, tall and dominant, Tiler had already gained 13 England Under-21 caps and made over 170 appearances, as well as spending 3 years in the shadows at Nottingham Forest before joining Villa. Unfortunately he suffered a hamstring injury on his debut against Everton and missed the remainder of the 1995–96 season. He scored his only Villa goal against his old club, Forest. Injury problems and the good form of Ugo Ehiogu and Gareth Southgate eventually led to Tiler moving to Sheffield United. He went on to appear in another 100-plus senior games, helping both Charlton and Pompey reach the Premiership.

TINDALL, MICHAEL CHADWICK

Midfield: 134+2 apps, 9 goals

Born: Acocks Green, Birmingham, 5 April 1941

Career: South Birmingham Boys, VILLA (amateur, April 1956; professional, April 1958), New York Americans/USA (loan, 1961), Walsall (June 1968–November 1968), Tamworth (December 1968–71); VILLA Old Stars (1975–88); later licensee of the Coach and Horses pub (Bromsgrove)

Capped eight times by England at youth international level, Tindall played in the final of the FIFA Youth Tournament in Luxembourg in 1958. Making his Villa debut in December 1959 against Hull, he had to fight for a place in the team with Alan Deakin, Jimmy McMorran and Ron Wylie and later Alan Baker and Phil Woosnam. He had the misfortune to suffer a broken leg against Spurs in 1964, but this did not curb his enthusiasm and although it was quite some time before he recovered, Tindall battled on to re-establish himself in the side in 1965–66.

TOWNSEND, ANDREW DAVID

Midfield: 175+1 apps, 11 goals

Born: Maidstone, Kent, 27 July 1963

Career: Welling United (August 1980), Weymouth (March 1984), Southampton (£35,000, January 1985), Norwich City (£300,000, August 1988), Chelsea (£1.2m, July 1990), VILLA (£2.1m, July 1993), Middlesbrough (£500,000, August 1997), West Bromwich Albion (£50,000, September 1999; retired, January 2000; then reserve coach to July 2000); now a TV pundit

Capped 70 times by the Republic of Ireland and once by the 'B' team, Townsend had an excellent career in top-class football. On his day he was an effective, hard-working performer, on a par with most of the leading professionals manning the same position. Before joining Villa, he had made over 100 appearances for Saints, 88 for the Canaries and 138 for Chelsea. He was already an established Eire international and quickly made his mark with Villa. His inspirational displays from centre-field sparked off many attacks, his experience and his presence on the field being appreciated to the full by the younger players in the side. Townsend, who gained two League Cup-winner's medals with Villa (1994, 1996) and skippered the side in the latter final, amassed over 175 first-team appearances before transferring to Middlesbrough. He helped 'Boro regain their Premiership status and played in 88 further matches before ending his career. He was replaced as reserve-team manager at Albion by ex-Villa player Gary Shelton. Townsend's father, Don, was a full-back with Charlton Athletic and Crystal Palace.

TRANTER, GEORGE HENRY
Right-half: 175 apps, 1 goal
Born: Quarry Bank, Brierley Hill, 8 April 1887 – *Died*: Dudley, September 1940
Career: Netherton Recreationalists, Brierley Hill Alliance (1902), Stourbridge (August 1904), VILLA (January 1905), Stourbridge (August 1919; retired, injured, June 1920)

Tranter was a tough defender who played for Birmingham against London in 1911. As hard as nails, he never shirked a tackle, was totally committed, had an infallibly cool temperament and was a good passer of the ball, very rarely hoofing it downfield – if he did, it was simply for safety purposes! He held his place in the Villa side for five years to 1912, scoring one goal against Notts County in a 1–1 League draw in November 1908. He hurt his knee in January 1914 and never played for the first team again, replaced by Tommy Barber.

TRAVERS, JAMES EDWARD (GEORGE)
Forward: 4 apps, 4 goals
Born: Newtown, Birmingham, 11 November 1888 – *Died*: Smethwick, 31 August 1946
Career: Bilston United (1904), Rowley United (1905), Wolverhampton Wanderers (July 1906), Birmingham (August 1907), VILLA (December 1908), Queens Park Rangers (May 1909), Leicester Fosse (August 1910), Barnsley (January 1911), Manchester United (February 1914); guest for Tottenham Hotspur (October 1915); Swindon Town (July 1919), Millwall Athletic (June 1920), Norwich City (October 1920), Gillingham (June 1921), Nuneaton Town (September 1921), Cradley St Luke's (November 1922), Pembroke Dock United (trial, October 1923), Bilston United (August 1929; retired May 1931); later lived and worked in Gillingham

Well-built, with good ability and a strong right-foot shot, Travers was a soccer nomad who never settled down in one place or, indeed, with any one club except Barnsley, for whom he made over 80 appearances, gaining an FA Cup-winner's medal in 1912. For Villa, he averaged a goal a game, bagging a hat-trick against Bury on Boxing Day 1908, when he deputised for Harry Hampton. He appeared in Millwall's first League game, against Bristol Rovers in August 1920, and scored in Norwich's first League win a few months later. He made over 250 career appearances and netted 75 goals. He served in the Army in Salonika during WW1, and played in various representative matches for his unit. In 1933, when living in Gillingham, he was charged with burglary.

TULLY, FREDERICK A. CHARLES
Forward: 7 apps
Born: St Pancras, London, July 1907 – *Died*: 1969
Career: Priory School, Tynemouth Schools, Rosehill Villa, Preston Colliery, Chaddleston Mental Hospital (North Staffs), VILLA (October 1926), Southampton (June 1933), Clapton Orient (June 1937–May 1939); guest for

Charlton Athletic (1939–40), Brighton and Hove Albion (1942–43); retired in 1945 to join his father as a carpenter in east London

Described in the press as a 'winger with thrust and enterprise', Tully – a short, stocky, busy footballer – could turn up anywhere in the forward-line! Mainly a reserve to Billy Armfield, Reg Chester, Arthur Dorrell, Eric Houghton, Jack Mandley and Dicky York at Villa, he later scored 9 goals in 109 games for Saints and netted 18 times in over 60 starts for Orient. An excellent club man, he did well in Villa's second XI.

TURNBULL, FREDERICK

Defender: 182+1 apps, 3 goals

Born: Wallsend, 28 August 1946

Career: Centre 64 FC/Blyth, VILLA (trial, August 1966; professional, September 1966), Halifax Town (loan, October–November 1969; retired, injured, May 1975); became self-employed in Blyth (Northumberland)

Despite being rather thin-looking, quiet and somewhat withdrawn in his ways, Turnbull was a fine, resolute, hard-tackling defender. He gained a League Cup runner's-up medal in 1971, collected a Third Division championship medal 12 months later and helped Villa consolidate themselves in the Second Division before injury forced him into early retirement, aged 28. He was awarded a testimonial match (Villa against WBA) in April 1976.

TURNER, GILBERT HORACE HUGO

Goalkeeper: 14 apps

Born: Bolton, Lancashire, 6 March 1877 – *Died*: Wolverhampton, July 1957

Career: Victoria Wesleyan Schoolboys, Victoria Wesleyan Juniors, Victoria Wesleyan Seniors, Bolton St Luke's (August 1904), Accrington Stanley, VILLA (January 1907), Pontypridd (1912–13), Everton (August 1913); Army football; Bury (season 1921–22); also a fine club cricketer for Halliwell

Tall and agile, Turner covered for Billy George and left the club unwillingly. He had his best run in the first team during September–October 1907, appearing in seven consecutive League games.

TYRRELL, JOSEPH JAMES

Inside-forward: 7 apps, 3 goals

Born: Stepney, London, 27 January 1932

Career: Littleton Council School (Evesham), Littleton Juniors, Littleton Rovers, Bretforton Old Boys, VILLA (amateur, June 1948; professional, May 1950), Millwall (March 1956), Bournemouth (June 1957), Folkestone (August 1959–May 1965)

Nurtured through Villa's nursery system, Tyrrell scored twice on his debut against WBA in April 1954. A purposeful player, he underwent a cartilage operation in 1955 and never impressed after that, although he did net 18 goals in 37 League games for Millwall.

VALE, ARCHIBALD FOSTER

Goalkeeper: 3 apps

Born: Kings Heath, Birmingham, July 1861– *Died*: Walsall, August 1937

Career: Edwardians FC/Birmingham, VILLA (August 1883), Erdington Lads' Club (September 1884), Walsall Royal Star (1888–90)

Big and sturdy, Vale was also safe and sure when the occasion demanded. He played in two 5–1 FA Cup wins for Villa, against Walsall Town Swifts and Stafford Road in November–December 1883, and in a 6–1 defeat by Glasgow Rangers in January 1884.

VARCO, PERCY SEYMOUR

Centre-forward: 10 apps, 2 goals

Born: Fowey, Cornwall, 17 April 1904 – *Died*: Fowey, 29 January 1982

Career: Fowey Council School, Fowey Town, Torquay United (October 1923), VILLA (£200, December 1923), Queens Park Rangers (June 1926), Norwich City (July 1927), Exeter City (February 1930), Brighton and Hove Albion (June 1932), St Austell (August 1933), St Balzey (August 1934; retired, injured, May 1936); later a fish merchant with two aquariums; had two terms in office as mayor of Fowey

Powerfully built and difficult to knock off the ball, a pen-picture in the 1920s described 'Saccho' Varco as a player who 'loses no time with the ball, fearless in attack and has a kick that sometimes makes one gasp. He goes for goal like a bull at a gatepost.'

He had a great first season with Norwich (29 goals in 41 League outings) and later netted 46 times in 90 games for Exeter.

VASSELL, DARIUS

Striker: 106+74 apps, 42 goals

Born: Birmingham, 13 June 1980

Career: Birmingham and District Schools, VILLA (YTS, June 1996; professional, April 1998)

Strong-running, hard-working, with pace and ability, Vassell graduated through the Villa ranks and after representing England youth, became a key member of his country's Under-21 squad, gaining ten caps before embarking on the senior international circuit. He has now played in 20 full internationals, including appearances in the 2002 World Cup and Euro 2004. Used regularly as a 'sub' during his first three seasons, he's now an established striker who has come off the bench more times than any other Villa player. He had the misfortune to miss from the spot in the vital penalty shoot-out against Portugal in Euro 2004.

VAUGHTON, OLIVER HOWARD

Inside-left: 26 apps, 15 goals

Born: Aston, Birmingham, 2 January 1861 *–Died*: Birmingham, January 1937

Career: Waterloo FC, Birmingham FC, Wednesbury Strollers, VILLA (August 1880; retired May 1888 due to a thigh injury); started his own silversmith's business in the jewellery quarter, Hockley, Birmingham, which still exists today; VILLA (vice president, 1923; president, June 1924; director, September 1924–December 1932; then life member of the club, from February 1933)

Vaughton, a key member of Villa's 1887 FA Cup-winning side, was regarded as one of the club's finest forwards during the 1880s, scoring a goal every two games before injury forced him to retire at the age of twenty-seven. With Arthur Brown, he was Villa's first international, capped by England against Ireland in February 1882 when he notched 5 goals in a 13–0 win. He added four more caps to his tally. Described as 'a roamer', Vaughton could also be erratic with his shooting but made up for that with his superb ball-skills. He 'dribbled like an angel', wrote one reporter! He formed a fine left-wing partnership with Eli Davis and, besides being an accomplished footballer (the people's favourite), Vaughton was also a competent ice-skater, winning the all-England title. He played cricket for Warwickshire and Staffordshire; was a County hockey player; a racing cyclist and a first-class swimmer. After the FA Cup was stolen from a shop window on Newtown Row in 1895, Vaughton's firm was asked to make a new one, at a cost of £25.

VINALL, ALBERT

Full-back: 11 apps

Born: Hockley, Birmingham, 6 March 1922

Career: Deykin Avenue School and Hockley Brook School, Ellisons Works, Norwich City (amateur, 1938), Southampton (amateur), VILLA (amateur, August 1939; professional, August 1946); served in the Royal Navy during WW2; Walsall (August 1954; retired, July 1957; continued as Colts' coach); VILLA (scout, August 1959–61)

Vinall – a solid performer – rendered yeoman service to Villa's Central League side but appeared in less than a dozen first-team games owing to WW2. His brother, Jack, played for Sunderland, Norwich, Luton, Coventry and Walsall, and also managed Worcester before scouting for Villa (mid-1950s). Albert's son, Micky, was a policeman in Handsworth, Birmingham (1966–76).

VOWDEN, GEOFFREY ALAN

Forward: 110+4 apps, 25 goals

Born: Barnsley, 27 April 1941

Career: Jersey football, Nottingham Forest (amateur, 1958; professional, January 1960), Birmingham City (£25,000, October 1964), VILLA (£12,500, March 1971), New York Cosmos/USA (June–August 1974), Kettering Town (player/assistant manager, July 1974); Saudi Arabia (coach, 1976–78); coached schoolboys and youths in Nottingham; Sheffield United (coach, 1980–81)

Vowden was a fine marksman who scored over 150 goals in under 500 matches spread over 14 years. He struck 40 times in 90 League games for Forest and 95 in 253 appearances for the Blues and was a Third Division championship-winner with Villa in 1972. A beautifully balanced player, he was strike partner to Andy Lochhead before moving to Kettering. Vowden was the first substitute to score a League hat-trick, doing so for the Blues against Huddersfield in 1968.

WAKEMAN, ALAN

Goalkeeper: 20 apps

Born: Leamore, Walsall, 20 November 1920 – *Died:* Stafford, 15 December 2002

Career: Elmore Green School, Leamore Boys, Walsall and District Schools, Bloxwich Strollers (amateur, 1935), VILLA (amateur, August 1937; professional, August 1938); guest for Hednesford Town (1939–40), Nottingham Forest (1940–42), Northampton Town and Notts County during WW2; Doncaster Rovers (July 1950), Shrewsbury Town (February 1953–May 1954), Bloxwich Strollers (manager, May 1954–April 1959), Shrewsbury Town (player, 1959), Walsall Wood (manager, August 1960–May 1967), Stratford Town (manager, 1968–69), Bilston Town (manager, August 1969–May 1970); then manager of the National Coal Board (Bridgetown Colliery); worked part-time in Villa Park offices; Armitage Town (manager, 1982–83)

Wakeman gained six England schoolboy caps as a centre-forward in 1934–35 (two as captain). Converted into a goalkeeper at Bloxwich Strollers, he joined Villa as deputy to Fred Biddlestone, with Joe Rutherford also challenging for a first-team place. Brave and competent, his career was severely interrupted by WW2, but he still made 183 appearances during the war, helping Villa win the Wartime League Cup (N) in 1944, having saved 3 penalties in the month of April 1943.

WALKER, RAYMOND

Midfield: 18+8 apps

Born: North Shields, 28 September 1963

Career: Mansfield and District Schools, Nottinghamshire Boys, VILLA (apprentice, July 1979; professional, September 1981), Port Vale (loan, September–November 1984; signed for £12,000, July 1986), Cambridge United (loan, September 1994; retired May 1996); Leek Town (July 1997; later player/coach, then caretaker manager), Newcastle Town (manager, 1998–99), Port Vale (coach, 1999–2000)

Walker, an England youth international, collected an FA Youth Cup-winner's medal in 1980, but with so many talented players at the club he found it hard to establish himself in the side and moved to Port Vale. He made 427 appearances and scored 43 goals for the Valiants, was chosen in the PFA Third Division sides for 1988 and 1989, and he was an AWS and Second Division championship-winner in the 1990s. Walker was fined £150 in 1988 after being sent off for stamping on the head of Grimsby's 20-year-old left-half Ian Toale.

WALKER, RICHARD MARTIN

Striker: 4+6 apps, 2 goals

Born: Birmingham, 8 November 1977

Career: VILLA (YTS, July 1994; professional, December 1995), Cambridge United (loan, December 1998–January 1999), Blackpool (loan, February–March 2001), Wycombe Wanderers (loan, September–October 2001), Blackpool (£50,000, December 2001), Northampton Town (July 2003)

Walker – a very pacy player on the ground and useful in the air – took full advantage of injuries to Dion Dublin and Darius Vassell to make his mark in Villa's first XI in 1999–2000.

WALKER, WILLIAM HENRY

Forward: 531 apps, 244 goals

Born: Wednesbury, 29 October 1897 – *Died*: Sheffield, 28 November 1964

Career: King's Hill School (Wednesbury), Walsall Boys, Fallings Heath, Hednesford Town, Darlaston, Wednesbury Old Park, VILLA (trial, 1913), Wednesbury Old Athletic, VILLA, (March 1915; professional, June 1920; retired November 1933); guest for Birmingham (1916–17), Wednesbury Old Park (1916–18); Sheffield Wednesday (manager, December 1933–November 1937), Chelmsford City (manager, January–October 1938), Nottingham Forest (manager, March 1939; retired July 1960, owing to illness; remained on the club's committee until his death); played cricket for Warwickshire club and ground; was a fine golfer, winning the Robin Hood Bowl and 36-hole Open Championship in June 1930

Walker scored 80 goals in the Walsall Boys' League in 1910–11 and after gaining experience in non-League soccer became an institution at Villa Park. He had tremendous on-the-ball ability and skippered Villa for 6 seasons (1926–32), scored 9 goals in 18 full England internationals and also led his country in a famous victory over Austria in 1932, a game regarded as one of the greatest internationals of all time. He also played in an international trial (England against the Rest at Tottenham in 1929) and captained the Staffs Jubilee FA side against the Football League in 1926. He netted twice on his Villa debut in the home third-round FA Cup tie against QPR in January 1920 and at the end of that season won an FA Cup-winner's medal. Unfortunately, he wasn't so lucky when Villa lost to Newcastle in the 1924 final. Walker possessed a cracking right- or left-foot shot, was also a fine header of the ball and, besides being a champion marksman, was also a superb tactician, who went on to net a record number of goals for Villa during his 18-plus years at the club. He secured eleven hat-tricks (nine League, two FA Cup); hit a four-timer against Arsenal in 1920 and is one of a dozen or so players, world-wide, to have scored a hat-trick of penalties, doing so for Villa against Bradford City (League), November 1921. His heroic feats were not always confined to his marksmanship, for he was an exceptionally talented goalkeeper, deputising between the posts on many occasions for club and country. With Arthur Dorrell as his left-wing partner at Villa, Walker was irresistible at times. He reached double figures in the scoring charts every season from 1919 to 1931, having his best campaign in 1920–21 (31 goals in 42 games). After retiring as a player, Walker took over as boss at Hillsborough and two years later (having kept the Owls in the First Division) he guided them to FA Cup glory over WBA. Twenty-four years later he repeated that feat with Nottingham Forest (2–1 winners over Luton), having earlier helped the Reds win promotion from the Third Division (S) in 1951 and the Second Division in 1957. He also played in six WW2 games for Forest as an emergency goalkeeper. Walker's father, George, was a full-back with Wolves.

WALLACE, CHARLES WILLIAM
Outside-right: 350 apps, 57 goals
Born: Southwick, near Sunderland, 20 January 1885 – *Died*: 7 January 1970
Career: Sunderland and District Schools, Southwick FC (1903), Crystal Palace (July 1905), VILLA (£500, May 1907), Oldham Athletic (£1,000, May 1921; retired April 1923); became a painter and decorator, also worked part-time for VILLA (in the boot-room, with the kit, as a scout, steward and mentor to the club's Junior Ordnance Corps team, late 1930s)

A speedy, direct winger, Wallace helped Villa win the League championship in 1910 and the FA Cup in 1913 and 1920. He had the misfortune to miss a penalty in the 1913 final against Sunderland but made amends by taking the corner from which Harold Edgley headed the winning goal. He won three England caps (against Ireland, Scotland and Wales), represented the Football League on five occasions and appeared in three international trials. After achieving a fine record with Villa, he spent two seasons with Oldham before retiring in 1923. A Villa man through and through, almost the whole of his career was attached to claret and blue – the colours of Southwick, Palace and Villa! As leader of Villa's Junior Ordnance Corps side, he guided them to the runner's-up spot in their respective League in 1939 and served the club for over 50 years.

WALSH, DAVID JOHN
Centre-forward: 114 apps, 40 goals
Born: Waterford, Ireland, 28 April 1923
Career: St Joseph's, Corinthians, Shelbourne (Waterford), Glen Rovers, Limerick, Shelbourne (Dublin), Linfield (1943), West Bromwich Albion (£3,500, May 1946), VILLA (£25,000, December 1950), Walsall (July

1955–May 1956), Worcester City (August 1956; retired May 1957); owned a sports shop/general store in Droitwich, later ran holiday homes at Thurlestone, Kingsbridge (from 1984)

A sharp-shooting Irish international, Walsh made a terrific start to his League career by scoring in each of his first six games for WBA at the start of the 1946–47 season. A player with an eye for goal, he continued to net regularly for the Baggies and was a key figure when promotion was gained in 1949. He went on to net a century of goals before moving to Villa for a record fee, signed to replace Trevor Ford. He scored practically a goal every three games before assisting Walsall and then Worcester. Nimble and decisive in front of goal, Walsh had the knack of being in the right spot at the right time. He netted 122 goals in Ireland, including 73 in 1945–46 for Linfield (61 in League and Cup), gaining both Irish League championship and Irish Cup medals, having earlier won the Irish Cup (1945). Capped 20 times for the Republic of Ireland and on 9 occasions for Northern Ireland, his record in League football was superb – 137 goals in 293 games. He still lives in Devon, and is a life member of the local Thurlestone golf club.

WALTERS, JOSEPH
Forward: 121 apps, 41 goals
Born: Stourbridge, 11 December 1886 – *Died*: New Moston, Manchester, 24 December 1923
Career: Wordsley Athletic (1900), Stourbridge (August 1902), VILLA (June 1905), Oldham Athletic (£900, June 1912); guest for Tottenham Hotspur reserves during WW1; Accrington Stanley (August 1920), Southend United (£200, September 1920), Millwall Athletic (May 1921), Rochdale (October 1922), Crewe Alexandra (November–December 1923)

Walters was a fine, consistent inside- or outside-left. An England junior international trialist (1911), he was clever, creative in style, possessed good pace, packed a fine shot in both feet and had a first-rate temperament. He helped Villa win the League title in 1910, netting a hat-trick in a 7–1 home win over Manchester United. He scored 36 goals in 110 senior outings for Oldham and during his career claimed over 100 goals in more than 425 games. Walters, who served in the Flying Corps in WW1, died of pneumonia before making his debut for Crewe.

WALTERS, MARK EVERTON
Winger: 207+18 apps, 48 goals
Born: Aston, Birmingham, 2 June 1964
Career: Hampton Junior and Holte Grammar Schools (Lozells, Birmingham), Aston and District Boys, Birmingham Schools, VILLA (apprentice, June 1980; professional, May 1982), Glasgow Rangers (£600,000, December 1987), Liverpool (£1.25m, August 1991), Stoke City (loan, March–April 1994), Wolverhampton Wanderers (loan, September–October 1994),

Southampton (free, January 1996), Swindon Town (free, July 1996), Bristol Rovers (November 1999), Ilkeston Town (July 2002), Dudley Town (September 2003)

Walters, who could occupy either flank, was a player with excellent pace, clever tricks and a telling shot, who centred with great precision, on the run or otherwise. He had one favourite trick whereby he used to drag his foot over the ball before gliding past a defender. After representing England at both schoolboy- and youth-team levels, he gained one full, one 'B' and nine Under-21 caps. An FA Youth Cup winner in 1980 and a European Super Cup winner in 1982, he collected three Scottish Premier League and two Skol League Cup-winner's medals with Rangers and then helped Liverpool win both the FA Cup and League Cup (1992, 1995). Walters' senior career realised over 750 appearances and almost 170 goals.

WARD, JOSEPH

Forward: 3 apps

Born: Glasgow, 25 November 1954

Career: Glasgow and District Schools, St Roch's (Glasgow), Clyde (amateur, August 1970; professional, November 1972), VILLA (£80,000, December 1978), Hibernian (£80,000, plus Des Bremner, September 1979), Dundee United (July 1980–May 1982)

Before joining Villa, Ward – a well-built striker – won both amateur and youth caps for Scotland as well as collecting a Second Division championship medal with Clyde (1978). Unfortunately he never settled down in England and returned home as part of the deal that brought Des Bremner to Villa Park.

WARING, THOMAS

Centre-forward: 226 apps, 167 goals

Born: Birkenhead, 12 October 1906 – *Died*: 20 December 1980

Career: Mersey Park Council School, Birkenhead and District Schools, Tranmere Colts (August 1922), Tranmere Celtic (July 1923), Tranmere Rovers (professional, February 1926), VILLA (£4,700, February 1928), Barnsley (November 1935), Wolverhampton Wanderers (July 1936), Tranmere Rovers (October 1936), Accrington Stanley (November 1939–July 1939), Bath City (August–September 1939); guest for New Brighton (1939–42), Wrexham (1940–43), Everton (1941–42), Crewe Alexandra (1942–43), VILLA (February 1944), also Grayson's FC/South Liverpool; Ellesmere Port Town (August 1946), Birkenhead Dockers FC (July 1948), Harrowby FC (August 1949–May 1950); also worked on Merseyside docks

Tall, long-striding, six feet of sinew, muscle and bone, 'Pongo' Waring was a wonderfully consistent goalscorer, supremely confident in his own ability. A colourful character, the stories about him, apocryphal or otherwise, are legion. A crowd of 23,440 saw him net a hat-trick on his debut for Villa in a 6–3 Central League win over Birmingham in February 1928 – soon after he'd scored 6 goals for Tranmere in an 11–0 win over Durham in a Third Division (N) game. A former chocolate-seller at Prenton Park, he succeeded Dixie Dean at Tranmere and two years later moved to Villa. Over the next decade he notched goals galore, including ten hat-tricks, nine in the First Division. An England international (5 caps: 1931–32), Waring hit a record 49 League goals (plus one in the FA Cup) in 1930–31, when he was dubbed the 'Gay Cavalier' as he streaked past defenders time and again to smash the ball into the net. Indeed, every kid around Villa Park wanted to be 'Pongo' Waring – for he was more popular than the Prime Minister at that time! He was sent off playing against Spurs in January 1934, and as he walked, head bowed, from the pitch he received a bigger cheer than the whole team would have got if they'd won the FA Cup! Waring, who didn't fit into Wolves' style of play (under Frank Buckley), was also called the 'Birkenhead Bombadier' and the 'Claret and Blue Torpedo'. During his career, he scored 245 goals in 362 League games. He gained just one medal at club level – helping Tranmere win the Third Division (N) title in 1938. In the 1990s, Kidderminster-based Villa fan John Peutherer bought his wife a racehorse and named it Pongo Waring.

WARNER, JAMES
Goalkeeper: 101 apps
Born: Lozells, Birmingham, 15 April 1865 – *Died*: Pittsburgh, USA, 7 November 1943
Career: Hampton Road School, Milton FC, VILLA (May 1886), Newton Heath (July 1892), Walsall Town Swifts (September 1893; retired, with a back injury, May 1894); Aston licensee (1891–93); later coach in Pittsburgh/USA (September 1907–May 1909)
Supple and shrewd, agile enough to reach (punch) the most difficult of shots (or headers) Warner played in two FA Cup finals for Villa, both against WBA, gaining a winner's medal in 1887 and a loser's in 1892. Rumours abounded that he 'sold' the latter game and as a result had his pub damaged by irate supporters. His last competitive game for Villa was, in fact, in that 1892 final. He infuriated Newton Heath's committee by failing to turn up for a game against Stoke that ended in a 7–1 defeat! He was suspended for 'carelessness' and played in only two more games. He died after falling down the stairs at his home in Pittsburgh.

WATKINS, ALFRED ERNEST
Inside-forward: 1 app.
Born: Llanwnnog, Montgomeryshire, 26 June 1878 – *Died*: Barking, Essex, 7 December 1957
Career: Caersws (1893), Chirk (1894), Oswestry (August 1895), Leicester Fosse (October 1897), VILLA (April 1899), Grimsby Town (February 1901), Millwall (May 1901), Southend United (August 1906–May 1907); later assistant station-master, and cemetery caretaker
The eldest of six brothers, Watkins relied on skill rather than graft and had an

almost languid approach to the game. Difficult to knock off the ball, he was a natural ball-player who could also occupy either the left-wing or left-half berths. He won five caps for Wales – his first with Leicester (1898) and his last with Millwall (1904) and two as a Villa player (1900). His only League game for Villa was a 2–1 win at Burnley in March 1900. He made over 130 appearances for Millwall in the Southern League. He died in a house fire. His brother, Walter 'Mart' Watkins (q.v.), also played for Villa.

WATKINS, ARTHUR DENNIS
Outside-right: 21 apps, 5 goals
Born: Loughborough, Leicestershire, 28 June 1912 – *Died*: 1983
Career: Stapleford (1927), Notts County (amateur, 1928–30), James and Barnes FC/Nottingham, Loughborough, VILLA (November 1932), Reading (July 1936–May 1940)
A cheeky but clever little winger, Watkins averaged a goal every four games for Villa. He often roughed it with the burly defenders who challenged him, but always had a smile on his face! He netted 22 goals in 86 League games for Reading.

WATKINS, WALTER MARTIN
Inside-forward: 6 apps
Born: Llanwnnog, Montgomeryshire, August 1880 – *Died*: Stoke-on-Trent, 14 May 1942
Career: Caersws (1894), Oswestry Town (1896), Stoke (August 1900), VILLA (£400, January 1904), Sunderland (October 1904), Crystal Palace (June 1905), Northampton Town (May 1906), Stoke (May 1907), Crewe Alexandra (July 1908), Stafford Rangers (1909–10), Tunstall (player/coach, 1910–11), Stoke (August 1911; retired May 1914)
Watkins was brought up on a farm with his elder brother, Alfred Watkins (q.v.). He made rapid progress and after joining Stoke, his career hardly faltered. He won 10 caps for Wales (3 with Villa) and appeared in more than 200 games at senior level, scoring over 70 goals. Described in 1901 as a 'smart player who marshalls his forces splendidly in midfield, keeps the game open and the wing men supplied with opportunities', he signed for Villa instead of Manchester City.

WATSON, STEPHEN CRAIG
Right-back: 51+3 apps, 1 goal
Born: North Shields, 1 April 1974
Career: North Shields schoolboy football, Newcastle United (apprentice, June 1990; professional, April 1991), VILLA (£4m, October 1998), Everton (£2.5m, July 2000)
Calm under pressure and a strong, forceful player who always gives 100 per cent every time he takes the field, before joining Villa Watson made 263 appearances

for Newcastle as well as gaining England honours at youth, Under-21 (12 caps won) and 'B' team level. He had a disappointing 1999–2000 season, hence his cut-price transfer to Goodison Park!

WATSON, WALTER
Outside-left: 3 apps
Born: Sheffield, November 1890 – *Died*: 1956
Career: Worksop Town (December 1911), VILLA (March 1912), Rotherham Town (July 1913), Worksop Town (1915–16); then served in WW1
Signed as cover for Horace Henshall, Watson made his League debut in a 6–0 home win over Manchester United in March 1912, assisting in three of the goals.

WATTS, WILLIAM HENRY
Utility: 2 apps
Born: Yardley, Birmingham, 12 April 1859 – *Died*: Birmingham, 28 September 1913
Career: Cocknage, VILLA (August 1880; retired, with knee injury, April 1882)
A versatile footballer, Watts played in two FA Cup games for Villa in 1880–81. A strapping footballer, his career ended prematurely. He died from pneumonia.

WELFORD, JAMES WILLIAM
Full-back: 83 apps, 1 goal
Born: Glasgow, 27 March 1869 – *Died*: Scotland, 1945
Career: Glasgow schoolboy football, Stockton (1886), Bishop Auckland (1890), Birmingham St George's (1892), VILLA (August 1893), Celtic (November 1896), Belfast Celtic (August 1900; retired, injured, May 1905); played cricket for the Warwickshire club and ground (1894–96)
Welford was the first Englishman to win both FA Cup and Scottish Cup-winner's medals – doing so with Villa (1895) and Celtic (1899). A sturdy defender, strong in the tackle, he partnered Howard Spencer before Albert Evans entered the fray in 1896. His only goal for Villa came in a 2–0 home League win over Bolton in December 1895.

WESTON, THOMAS
Full-back: 179 apps
Born: Halesowen, 23 August 1890 – *Died*: Stourbridge, 1952
Career: Red Hill School, Quarry Bank (1907), Old Hill Comrades (1908), Coombs Wood (1909), VILLA (professional, July 1911), Stoke (August 1921–November 1922), Stourbridge (December 1922; retired May 1924); later coached at schools in Stourbridge, Old Hill and Cradley Heath
Some fans considered Weston to be rather impetuous at times, wanting him to show more caution in his play, but he was undoubtedly a very fine footballer, strong-willed, competitive and solid. He introduced an element of dash into

Villa's defence where he formed an excellent partnership at full-back with first Tommy Lyons before WW1 and then with Tommy Smart, gaining an FA Cup-winner's medal in 1920. He was badly wounded in Ervilliers, France, during WW1 (1918).

WHATELEY, OLIVER

Inside-forward: 19 apps, 9 goals

Born: Coventry, 8 August 1861 – *Died*: Birmingham, October 1926

Career: Gladstone Unity, Coventry (1878), VILLA (July 1880; retired with face cancer, May 1888); underwent a successful operation in 1911 and during WW1 worked for the YMCA in Rouen (France)

Variable in performance, at his best 'Olly' Whateley was a formidable amateur who had an aggressive spirit in his general play. Possessing an excellent shot (reputed to be one of the hardest of his day), he often had a crack at goal from anywhere within reason! Nicknamed 'Daisy-cutter' because a lot of his efforts skimmed along the ground, Whateley helped to build the club up during the early 1880s. He won two England caps in 1883, against Ireland (scoring twice in a 7–0 win) and Scotland. An artist and designer by profession, the son of the Birmingham councillor James Whateley, he was in very poor health for many years prior to his death.

WHELDON, GEORGE FREDERICK

Inside-left: 140 apps, 74 goals

Born: Langley Green, Oldbury, 1 November 1869 – *Died*: St George's, Worcester, 13 January 1924

Career: Chance's Infants and Langley St Michael's Council Schools, Rood End White Star, Langley Green Victoria, West Bromwich Albion (trial, October–November 1888), Small Heath (February 1890), VILLA (£350, June, 1896), West Bromwich Albion (£100, August 1900), Queens Park Rangers (£400, December 1901), Portsmouth (£150, August 1902), Worcester City (July 1904–May 1906); played county cricket for Worcestershire and Carmarthenshire; later became a publican in Worcester

The youngest of ten children, Fred 'Diamond' Wheldon was a brilliant footballer, an exceptional talent, a tremendous goalscorer who went on to great things with club and country. Often seen wearing a pair of golfing stockings (instead of the footballing type), he scored 84 goals in 134 games for the Blues, helping them win the Second Division title and promotion in successive years (1893, 1894). In fact, Wheldon notched the Blues' first-ever League goal, against Burslem Port Vale in September 1892, and claimed the club's first penalty in the 2–2 draw with Villa in October 1894. But he wanted a bigger stage and in 1896 moved to Villa for a record fee. He impressed all and sundry with his performances, being instrumental in three League championship triumphs (1897, 1898, 1900) and the 1897 FA Cup final success as Villa achieved the double. Wheldon played four times for England (it should have been more) and in four inter-League games. He averaged a goal every two games for Villa and that gave him an overall record of 156 goals in 267 first-class outings for the two second-city clubs. He played in the first League game at The Hawthorns (for Albion against Derby on 3 September 1900) and became the first professional to appear at competitive level for three central West Midland clubs. He struggled with his form at Albion and eight months after they had been relegated to the Second Division he moved to QPR. Besides being a splendid footballer, Wheldon was also a fine cricketer. He scored almost 5,000 runs in 138 matches for Worcestershire (1899–1906) and averaged over 22.50 per innings. He also hit 3 centuries and took 95 catches, some as a wicketkeeper. His brother, Sam, played for WBA and his son, Norris, for Liverpool.

WHITEHOUSE, JAMES

Goalkeeper: 43 apps

Born: Birmingham, 9 April 1873 – *Died*: Birmingham, 7 February 1934

Career: Albion Swifts, Mitchell St George's (1890), Grimsby Town (June 1892), VILLA (£200, July 1896), Bedminster (May 1898), Grimsby Town (May 1899), Newton Heath (September 1900), Manchester City (February 1903), Third Lanark (September 1903), Hull City (July 1904), Southend United (July 1905–May 1907)

Tall and well-built, Whitehouse was a clean handler of the ball, a reliable last line of defence, who produced some excellent displays during his time with Villa. In an emergency, he also proved to be an above-average inside-forward. A double winner with Villa in 1897, he totalled 161 games in two separate spells with Grimsby.

WHITLEY, JOHN

Goalkeeper: 11 apps

Born: Seacombe, Cheshire, 20 April 1880 – *Died*: London, 1953

Career: Seacombe Swifts, Seacombe YMCA (May 1897), Darwen (January 1899), VILLA (May 1900), Everton (May 1902), Stoke (August 1905), Tottenham Hotspur (briefly, June 1905; registration cancelled, returned to Stoke), Leeds City (April 1906), Lincoln City (September 1906), Chelsea (July 1907; retired May 1914; then trainer until May 1939); served with the Royal Flying Corps during WW1

Whitley, sound and competent, deputised for Billy George during his time with Villa. He helped Chelsea win promotion to the First Division in 1912, making 138 appearances for the Londoners. As a trainer, he was a father figure to generations of young players at Stamford Bridge and his bald head and flapping coat-tails (as he raced on to the pitch) were very much part of the Chelsea scene during the inter-war years. He spent 32 years at the 'Bridge'.

WHITTAKER, SAMUEL SAMSON
Inside-forward: 58 apps, 6 goals
Born: Shelfield, Walsall, 12 August 1888 – *Died*: Wednesfield, 19 September 1952
Career: Shelfield Methodists, Aldridge Arms FC, Rushall Red Cross (1906), Bloxwich Strollers, VILLA (January 1908), Grimsby Town (February 1908; registration cancelled by FA as he had already signed for Villa), Walsall (May 1915), Walsall Wood (1915–17), Port Vale (1917–18), Walsall (August 1919), Walsall Wood (May 1921).

A hard-working player, with poise and penetration, Whittaker had his best season with Villa in 1911–12 when he starred in 27 matches. He had the knack of keeping his shorts clean after playing on the muddiest of pitches! He played in a Birmingham Association trial match in 1908.

WHITTINGHAM, GUY
Striker: 23+10 apps, 6 goals
Born: Evesham, 10 November 1964
Career: Yeovil Town, Army football, Portsmouth (June 1989), VILLA (£1.2m, August 1993), Wolverhampton Wanderers (loan, February 1994), Sheffield Wednesday (£700,000, December 1994), Wolverhampton Wanderers (loan, November 1998), Portsmouth (loan, January 1999), Watford (loan, March 1999), Portsmouth (free, July 1999), Peterborough United (August 2000), Oxford United (loan, September 2000), Portsmouth (player/coach/assistant manager, October 2000), Wycombe Wanderers (free, March 2001), Newport/Isle of Wight (August 2001)

Whittingham, strong and willing, never settled at Villa Park, yet during his senior career the former soldier (who was bought out of the Army by Portsmouth) netted over 150 goals in more than 400 competitive matches.

WHITTINGHAM, PETER
Midfield: 26+17 apps, 1 goal
Born: Nuneaton, 8 September 1984
Career: Coventry City (juniors), VILLA (YTS, April 2001; professional, November 2002)

An attacking midfielder or left wing-back, Whittingham made his debut for Villa against Newcastle United in front of 52,000 fans at St James' Park in April 2003. An England youth international (Under-19), and later named in his country's Under-21 squad, he helped Villa win the FA Youth Cup in 2002.

WILCOX, JOSEPH MITCHELL
Outside-right: 6 apps
Born: Stourbridge, 2 January 1886 – *Died*: Lichfield, August 1940
Career: Stourbridge Standard, Cradley Heath St Luke's, Dudley Town, VILLA (amateur, March 1906; professional, November 1907), Birmingham

(November 1908), Southampton (£250, May 1911); emigrated to Canada (summer 1912)

Quick and decisive, yet sometimes erratic with his crosses, Wilcox could 'manoeuvre astutely past his full-back'. After spending a year with Villa, he made almost 50 appearances for the Blues and 28 for Saints.

WILKES, ALBERT

Wing-half: 159 apps, 8 goals

Born: Birmingham, October 1874 – *Died*: Bromsgrove, 9 December 1936

Career: Walsall Street School (West Bromwich), West Bromwich Baptists, Oldbury Town, West Bromwich Albion (trial), Walsall (April 1895), VILLA (May 1898), Fulham (June 1907), Chesterfield (February 1909; retired May 1909); became a referee and later joined the board of directors at Villa Park (September 1934)

As a 'straight-as-a-die, no-nonsense' defender, Wilkes was renowned for his competitiveness and hard work. He possessed a formidable tackle, and was a fine helpmeet to his full-back, being scrupulously fair. Recipient of five England caps (1901–02) he gained two League championship medals (1899, 1900) and was all set to join WBA in 1906, the deal falling through at the eleventh hour. As well as being a fine footballer, Wilkes was also a marvellous singer and delighted thousands round the Midlands music halls in the 1920s. He also enjoyed swimming and received the Royal Humane Society's award for life-saving after diving into a West Bromwich park pool to save a young boy from drowning. His daughter received a similar prize when she saved a child from drowning in the sea at Aberdovey, Wales. After fire damaged his photographic studio in West Bromwich, he retired from football and had his studio modernised. Wilkes flourished in the trade, specialising in team groups as well as individual player profiles and action shots. After he died, the business remained in the family (run by his son, Albert junior) until the collection was sold to Colorsport (London) in the late 1970s.

WILKES, HARRY THEODORE

Goalkeeper: 57 apps

Born: Alcester, 19 June 1874 – *Died*: Stoke-on-Trent, 9 February 1921

Career: Congregational Unity (Redditch), Redditch Town (August 1891), VILLA (April 1893), Stoke (loan, March–April 1898), VILLA (April 1898), Stoke (August 1899; retired May 1903); later licensee of the Wharf Tavern, Stoke

Agile and brave, 'Badger' Wilkes, 6 ft 1 in. tall and 13 st. in weight, spent six years with Villa, collecting an FA Cup-winner's medal in 1895 and a League championship medal the following season. After being replaced by Jimmy Whitehouse, he went on to make 89 appearances for Stoke. In April 1913, a benefit match was arranged on his behalf after he'd fallen on hard times and was suffering with his health. His son, Tom, also kept goal for Stoke.

WILLIAMS, EVAN SAMUEL

Goalkeeper: 13 apps

Born: Dumbarton, Scotland, 15 July 1943

Career: St Michael's Boys' Club, Duntocher Juveniles, Vale of Leven (June 1962), Third Lanark (October 1964), Wolverhampton Wanderers (£5,000, March 1966), VILLA (loan, August–September 1969), Celtic (October 1969), Clyde (July 1974), Arbroath (reserves, August 1975), Falkirk (April 1976), Vale of Leven (manager, July 1976), Albion Rovers (assistant manager, February 1981)

Williams was a capable goalkeeper with good technique who acted as reserve to both Phil Parkes and Fred Davies at Molineux. He had 26 games for Third Lanark before joining Wolves and became the first loan signing made by Villa in 1969 (following an injury to John Dunn). He made 148 appearances for Celtic.

WILLIAMS, GARETH JAMES

Left-back/midfield: 6+8 apps

Born: Cowes, Isle of Wight, 12 March 1967

Career: Gosport Borough, VILLA (£30,000, January 1988), Barnsley (£200,000, August 1991), Hull City (loan, September 1992–January 1994), Bournemouth (non-contract, September 1994), Northampton Town (transfer, September 1994), Scarborough (August 1996), Hull City (free, November 1998), Scarborough (December 1998), Ilkeston Town (August 2001), Gainsborough Trinity (November 2001), Matlock Town (August 2002), Blyth Spartans (2003–04)

Williams, highly rated when he moved to Villa Park, unfortunately never settled or indeed established himself at the club, who made a profit of £170,000 when selling him to Barnsley! Over the next decade Williams amassed 325 appearances.

WILLIAMS, GARY

Left-back/midfield: 297+15 apps, 2 goals

Born: Wolverhampton, 17 June 1960

Career: St Alban's and Coppice High Schools, Wolverhampton and South Staffs District Boys, VILLA (apprentice, July 1976; professional, June 1978), Walsall (loan, March–April 1980), Leeds United (July 1987), Watford (January 1990), Bradford City (December 1991; retired May 1994)

A versatile player, Williams skippered Villa's youth team from the centre-half position in 1977–78 when they reached the FA Youth Cup final. After that he developed into a fine left-back who could also do a good job in midfield. He performed with consummate ease and authority and helped Villa win the League title in 1981, the European Cup and Super Cup in 1982 and was also in the Walsall team that gained promotion from Division Four in 1980. He lost his chance of an England Under-21 cap against the Republic of Ireland in 1981 through injury and never got another opportunity at international level. He quit top-class football with more than 500 appearances under his belt.

WILLIAMS, JOHN JAMES

Outside-right: 17 apps, 5 goals

Born: Aberdare, Glamorgan, 29 March 1911 – *Died*: Wrexham, 12 October 1987

Career: Aberaman, Llanelli (amateur, August 1931; professional, November 1932), Huddersfield Town (November 1932), VILLA (£2,000, November 1935), Ipswich Town (July 1936), Wrexham (November 1938–46); guest for Colwyn Bay (1945–46); Runcorn (August 1947–May 1948); later a storekeeper for Hunt's Capacitors (Wrexham)

Dark-haired and quick, Williams – 5 ft 5 in. tall, like so many other flank players – more than made up for his lack of height with guile and trickery. After scoring 14 goals in 50 League games for Huddersfield, he joined Villa, where he occupied the right-wing berth, allowing Eric Houghton to switch to the left. Doing well enough during his short stay at Villa Park, he later helped Ipswich win the Southern League title in 1937 and gain entry into the Football League, appearing in their first-ever Third Division (S) match against Southend in August 1938. He won his only Welsh cap as a Wrexham player against France in 1939.

WILLIAMS, WILLIAM HUGH

Left-back: 1 app.

Born: Wrexham, 6 September 1886 – *Died*: Chester, November 1957

Career: Chirk (May 1904), Wrexham (May 1909), VILLA (April 1912), Chirk (May 1915), Mold (August 1919), St Asaph (1920), Chester Lymphets (1921–22)

Ostensibly a reserve defender, strong and upright, Williams' only League game for Villa came in a 3–2 home win over Derby in April 1914, when he deputised for Tommy Weston.

WILLIS, JOHN JOHNSON

Outside-left: 1 app.

Born: East Boldon, Durham, 28 May 1934

Career: Boldon Colliery, Blackburn Rovers (amateur, July 1953; professional, August 1954); National Service (two years); Accrington Stanley (briefly), Mossley (December 1957), VILLA (£500, August 1958), Grimsby Town (trial, August 1959), Mossley (October 1959), Boldon FC (August 1960)

Reserve winger Willis played one League game for Blackburn and one for Villa, the latter against Wolves at Molineux in September 1958.

WILSON, ROBERT JOHN
Goalkeeper: 9 apps
Born: Small Heath, Birmingham, May 1943
Career: Bordesley Green Rovers, St Andrew's Boys' Club, VILLA (juniors, July 1958; professional, September 1961), Cardiff City (£2,000, August 1964), Bristol City (loan, October 1969), Exeter City (January 1970; retired May 1976)

Tall and lanky, Wilson spent most of his five years at Villa Park playing reserve-team soccer. However, he did go on to appear in over 350 senior matches for his three City clubs – Cardiff, Bristol and Exeter. He now lives in Devon.

WILSON, THOMAS CARTER
Utility forward: 2 apps
Born: Preston, 20 October 1877 – *Died*: Blackpool, 30 August 1940
Career: Fishwick Ramblers (Preston), Ashton-in-Makerfield, West Manchester, Ashton Town, Ashton North End, Oldham County (August 1896), Swindon Town (May 1897), Blackburn Rovers (May 1898), Swindon Town (May 1899), Millwall Athletic (May 1900), VILLA (April 1901), Queens Park Rangers (July 1902), Bolton Wanderers (May 1904), Leeds City (December 1906), Manchester United (February 1908); Chorley (manager, August 1912), Rochdale (chairman, October 1919; manager, July 1922–February 1923); married the daughter of an Oldham publican

Small, and compact, Wilson was very popular during his two spells with Swindon. He never got a chance at Villa Park, making only two appearances before moving to QPR. He played in 205 games during his career.

WINDMILL, JOSEPH WALTER
Half-back: 50 apps, 1 goal
Born: Halesowen, 8 June 1883 – *Died*: Kingswinford, 22 October 1927
Career: Saltley College (Birmingham), Halesowen, VILLA (April 1902; retired May 1910); then in teaching profession, becoming headmaster of Brook Street School, Wordsley (Stourbridge)

Windmill was part of a superb Villa middle-line between 1904 and 1906, lining up with Joe Pearson and Alec Leake. A fine player, he let the ball do the work and created many openings for his forwards with sweetly struck passes. An FA Cup winner in 1905, he was awarded the DCM and MC during WW1 when serving as a company sergeant major.

WINTON, DOUGLAS GEORGE
Full-back: 50 apps
Born: Perth, Scotland, October 1929
Career: Jeanfield Swifts (Perth), St Johnstone (trial), Perth Youth Club, Burnley (amateur, July 1945; professional, September 1947), VILLA (January 1959), Rochdale (June 1961; retired, injured, May 1965)

Capped by Scotland 'B' in 1957, Winton was first choice at Burnley for 12 years, making almost 200 appearances. His arrival at Villa Park, following the departure of Stan Lynn, allowed John Neal to switch flanks. Winton gave way to Charlie Aitken in 1961.

WITHE, PETER

Striker: 233 apps, 92 goals

Born: Liverpool, 30 August 1951

Career: All Hallow's School (Speke), Smith Coggins (1966), Skelmersdale (amateur, 1968–69), Smith Coggins (1969–70), Southport (amateur, July 1970; professional, August 1971), Preston North End (briefly, mid-1971), Barrow (trial, December 1971), Port Elizabeth/South Africa (1972), Arcadia Shepherds/South Africa (1973), Wolverhampton Wanderers (loan, October 1973; signed for £13,500, November 1973), Portland Timbers/USA (May 1975), Birmingham City (£50,000, August 1975), Nottingham Forest (£42,000, September 1976), Newcastle United (£200,000, August 1978), VILLA (£500,000, May 1980), Sheffield United (free, July 1985), Birmingham City (loan, September–November 1987), Huddersfield Town (player/coach, July 1988); VILLA (assistant manager/coach, January–October 1991), Wimbledon (manager, October 1991–January 1992), Port Vale (football in the community officer, August 1992–May 1995), VILLA (chief scout, 1997–99), Thailand (national team coach/soccer advisor, April 2000–October 2003)

Withe was a goalscoring nomad whose career spanned almost 20 years, during which time he netted over 200 goals in more than 600 appearances, serving with 15 different clubs.

He gained a First Division championship medal with Nottingham Forest in 1978 and added a second to his tally with Villa in 1981. He scored the winning goal in the 1982 European Cup final, netted twice in the Charity Shield game against Spurs at Wembley that same year, and won 11 England caps, the first against Brazil in 1981, the last against Sweden in 1986. A big favourite with the fans at Villa Park, Withe was the perfect foil to Gary Shaw and thrived on Tony Morley's crosses. Tremendous in the air, competent on the ground, he could hold the ball up with neat, close control: the perfect target man! He was assistant to manager Josef Venglos in 1991 and spent three hellish months at Plough Lane as boss of the Dons. Withe's brother, Chris, played for Bradford City and his son was on WBA's books.

WITHERS, COLIN CHARLES

Goalkeeper: 163 apps

Born: Erdington, Birmingham, 21 March 1940

Career: Erdington Albion, West Bromwich Albion (amateur, 1956–57), Birmingham City (professional, May 1957), VILLA (£18,000, November 1964), Lincoln City (June 1969), Go-Ahead Eagles, Deventer/Holland (July

1970), Atherstone Town (August 1973; retired May 1978); later became a hotelier in Blackpool, then a licensee in Bridgnorth

'Tiny' Withers – 6 ft 3 in. tall – conceded six goals on his League debut for Birmingham at Tottenham in 1960 and then let in four when making his debut for Villa on the same ground in 1964. Those games apart, he produced some excellent performances for both the Blues and Villa. An England schoolboy international, he played for Albion's third team, made 116 appearances for the Blues and took over from Geoff Sidebottom at Villa before losing his place to John Dunn.

WOLLASTON, ARTHUR WILBERT

Wing-half: 5 apps

Born: Shrewsbury, March 1865 – *Died*: Chirk, October 1933

Career: Layton Road Council School, Stafford Road FC (1886), VILLA (April 1888), Chirk (August 1890–May 1891)

A well-built player, Wollaston appeared in a handful of games for Villa in the club's first League season of 1888–89.

WOOD, ALFRED JOSIAH EDWARD

Utility: 111 apps, 7 goals

Born: Smallthorne, Burslem, Stoke-on-Trent, 30 June 1876 – *Died*: 5 April 1919

Career: Smallthorne Albion, Burslem Port Vale (December 1892), Southampton (July 1895), Stoke (October 1895), VILLA (March 1901), Derby County (May 1905), Bradford Park Avenue (May 1907; retired, injured, May 1908)

Wood could play on the left-wing, at inside-forward and in all three half-back positions. He made 65 appearances for Port Vale and more than 100 for Stoke before joining Villa as a replacement for Jas Cowan. He was placed in the left-half berth in his first full season (1901–02) and performed well alongside Tom Perry and Albert Wilkes. He later reverted to the pivotal role before transferring to Derby, having helped Villa take the runner's-up spot in the First Division in 1903. He made 58 League appearances for the Rams and 4 for Bradford before retiring in 1908. When Wood signed for Southampton, there was a dispute about his transfer from Vale. A commission cancelled the deal without Wood ever playing a single game for Saints.

WOOD, THOMAS

Wing-half: 71 apps, 12 goals

Born: Wednesbury, April 1908 – *Died*: 1970

Career: White Hill School (Wednesbury), Wednesbury United, Shrewsbury Town (August 1925), VILLA (February 1929), Newport County (November 1936; retired May 1945); guest for Walsall (1939–46), Hednesford Town (1941–42), West Bromwich Albion (1942–43), Wolverhampton Wanderers (1943–44), Crewe Alexandra (1945–46); Walsall (part-time trainer/coach, August 1946–49); thereafter was steward of the Wednesbury Bridge Street

Social Club for many years; also a champion crown green bowler, winning the Farcroft Floodlit tournament in Handsworth, Birmingham in 1933, beating 500 other contestants

'Smokey' or 'Splinter' Wood was a fine player with plenty of skill and resource, a very serviceable competitor and the dressing room comic who was initially 'first' reserve to Jimmy Gibson at Villa Park. He later turned out in various other positions, making over 70 appearances before adding over 100 more to his tally with Newport (25 goals).

WOODWARD, JOHN

Striker: 24+3 apps, 8 goals

Born: Tunstall, Stoke-on-Trent, 16 January 1947

Career: Tunstall Park, Stoke City (apprentice, June 1962; professional, October 1964), VILLA (£27,500, October 1966), Walsall (free, May 1969), Port Vale (£2,250, February 1973), Scunthorpe United (July 1975), Ostende FC/Belgium (May 1977), Kidderminster Harriers (August 1978–May 1979)

After just 11 outings for Stoke, swashbuckling striker 'Woodie' Woodward looked like being a terrific marksman in the First Division with Villa until he suffered a severe ankle injury during a game against WBA in October 1966. This knocked him back considerably and although he recovered full fitness he was never able to establish himself in the Villa side again. He notched 29 goals in 145 appearances for Walsall and netted 32 times in 95 outings for Port Vale. He did well in Belgium.

WOOLLEY, ALBERT

Outside-left: 24 apps, 13 goals

Born: Hockley, Birmingham, June 1870 – *Died*: Manchester, 3 February 1896

Career: Park Mills, VILLA (March 1892), Derby County (January 1895; retired through ill-heath, January 1896)

A wholehearted, enthusiastic winger, quick off the mark with a strong shot, Woolley scored twice on his League debut for Villa against Accrington in March 1892. He went on to hit three goals in six outings for the Rams before injury and illness ruined a promising career at the age of twenty-five. He died from pneumonia.

WOOSNAM, PHILIP ABRAHAM

Inside-left: 125 apps, 29 goals

Born: Caersws, Montgomeryshire, 22 December 1932

Career: Montgomeryshire Schools, Wrexham (amateur, 1947), UCNW, Bangor University (January 1951–53), Peritus FC (February-April 1951), Manchester City (amateur, July 1951; professional, June 1952), Army XI, Sutton United (1953–54), Middlesex Wanderers, Leyton Orient (amateur, March 1955; professional, December 1955), West Ham United (£30,000, November 1958), VILLA (£27,000, November 1962), Atlanta Chiefs/NASL (player/coach, 1966–68); then Commissioner of the North American Soccer League (1969–83)

Woosnam's footballing skills were recognised at an early age and after making rapid progress, he gained Welsh schoolboy and youth caps before entering Bangor University, captaining the varsity side to the Welsh Universities championship in 1952. Although he played in the Central League for Manchester City, it came as a surprise when he was released. He continued to play when possible and after graduating with a BSc degree from university, he joined the Royal Artillery as a second lieutenant to complete his National Service. On demob, Woosnam became a physics teacher in Leyton (London) and subsequently joined Orient, moving to West Ham as a professional. With the Hammers (where he linked up with Bobby Moore), his intelligent footballing skills came to the fore. An elegant and constructive player, sleek and slender-looking, with a crewcut hairstyle, Woosnam possessed craft rather than graft and used his brain rather than brawn. He played for London Select against Lausanne Sports in the semi-final of the Inter Cities Fairs Cup in 1957 and proceeded to score 27 goals in 147 appearances for Hammers, whom he helped establish in the First Division. Always one move ahead of his colleagues – and, indeed, his opponents – Woosnam went straight into Villa's first XI as partner to Harry Burrows, and did very well during his time at the club, teaming up in midfield with Alan Deakin, Mike Tindall and Ron Wylie. He took his total of full caps for Wales to 17 (gaining one with Orient, 14 with West Ham and 2 with Villa). In 1955 he was voted 'Amateur Footballer of the Year', represented the Football League and helped Orient win the Third Division (S) title in 1956. He was mainly responsible for introducing Franz Beckenbauer, Pele, George Best and others to USA football. When Woosnam joined West Ham, only three other players in British football had cost more money when switching clubs.

WORRELL, JOSEPH ERIC

Defender: 4 apps

Born: Amblecote, Stourbridge, July 1886 – *Died*: Worcester, 1970

Career: Wordsley Council School, Stourbridge Swifts (1906), Stourbridge (1912); Sutton Command (WW1); guest for Stourbridge (February 1919), VILLA (May 1919; signed permanently, August 1919), Stourbridge (August 1920), Darlaston (April 1921), Cradley Heath St Luke's (March 1922), Darlaston (August 1922), Netherton (December 1923), Kidderminster Harriers (August 1924), Brierley Hill (1927–28), Wellington Town (August 1928), Kidderminster Harriers (February 1929–May 1931)

Tough-looking, best suited to the hurly-burly of local Black Country soccer, Worrell stepped into League action with Villa following an injury to Frank Moss. He was almost 44 when he played his last game for Brierley Hill.

WRIGHT, ALAN GEOFFREY

Left-back: 325+5 apps, 5 goals

Born: Ashton-under-Lyme, 28 September 1971

Career: Blackpool (YTS, June 1987; professional, April 1989), Blackburn Rovers (£400,000, October 1991), VILLA (£1m, March 1995; free, May 2003), Glasgow Rangers (trial, June 2003), Middlesbrough (trial, July 2003; signed permanently, August 2003), Sheffield United (on loan, October–November 2003; signed permanently, January 2004)

At 5 ft 4 in. tall, Wright is one of the smallest defenders in the game – but what he loses in height, he makes up for in commitment. A very consistent performer, he made 131 appearances for Blackpool and 91 for Blackburn before joining Villa. A League Cup winner the following year, he hardly missed a match between 1995 and 2001 (absent only through injury) and, in fact, holds the Villa record for consecutive Premiership appearances – 79 between August 1997 and September 1999. He gained schoolboy and youth caps before playing in two Under-21 matches for England, against Spain and Denmark in 1993, all as a Blackburn player.

Wright was the youngest player ever to appear in a League game for Blackpool – aged 16 years, 217 days against Chesterfield in May 1988 (Trevor Sinclair surpassed it in August 1989).

WRIGHT, EDMUND

Goalkeeper: 2 apps

Born: Leytonstone, London, 7 March 1902 – *Died*: London, *circa* 1978

Career: Leyton and District Council Schools, Worcester City (briefly), High Wycombe (1918–19), VILLA (May 1919), Brentford (August 1921–May 1923)

Rather small at 5 ft 9 in., Wright was reserve to Sam Hardy, Jim Lee and Cyril Spiers during his time with Villa. He made his debut in front of 70,504 fans at Manchester United in December 1920 when Villa won 3–1.

WRIGHT, JOHN MICHAEL

Full-back: 314+3 apps, 1 goal

Born: Ellesmere Port, Cheshire, 25 September 1946

Career: Ellesmere Port Grammar School, Ellesmere Port, VILLA (apprentice, July 1962; professional, September 1963; retired, injured, May 1973); became an auction director/officer working briefly in engineering; granted a testimonial match in 1973–74

After amassing almost 150 senior appearances for Villa, England youth international Wright broke his leg at Middlesbrough in 1967. There was concern at the time regarding the seriousness of the injury, but he made a full recovery, regained his place in the side and went on to double his overall appearance-tally before retiring in 1973. His only League goal came in a 3–0 home win over Manchester City in September 1966. Wright played both rugby and soccer at school and was recommended to Villa by Bill Roberts, the man who had earlier 'coached' Joe Mercer. Capped by England at youth-team level, Wright took over from Cammie Fraser and held off Keith Bradley's challenge as he battled to retain his first-team spot. He did it splendidly and gained a Third Division championship medal in 1972 before handing over to John Gidman.

WYLIE, RONALD MAURICE

Inside-forward: 244 apps, 26 goals
Born: Glasgow, 6 August 1933
Career: Clydesdale Juniors (August 1947–March 1949), Notts County (amateur, April 1949; professional, September 1950), VILLA (£9,250, November 1958), Birmingham City (July 1965; retired May 1970, then a public relations officer at St Andrew's); VILLA (coach, June 1970–April 1972), Coventry City (coach, 1975, then assistant manager, 1978–81), Cyprus (coach), Bulova/Hong Kong (coach, 1982), West Bromwich Albion (manager, July 1982–February 1984), VILLA (reserve-team coach, February 1984–May 1987); scout for several clubs; VILLA (community officer, August 1990; later community liaison officer, August 1995)

The barrel-chested Wylie appeared in over 700 games during his 20-year playing career. He won two Scottish international caps at schoolboy level before joining ex-Villa star Eric Houghton at Notts County. He made over 200 appearances for the Magpies, playing alongside Tommy Lawton. Wylie was then Houghton's last signing before Villa sacked him in 1958. Two years later Wylie helped the team regain its First Division status with some superb performances and the following year was a League Cup winner. Voted 'Midland Footballer of the Year' in 1965, it was thought he was well past his best when he moved to St Andrew's, but Wylie surprised even himself by playing in almost 150 games for the Blues, skippering the team in the 1967 League Cup and 1968 FA Cup semi-finals. After succeeding Ronnie Allen as manager of WBA, he later rejoined Villa and in 2003 completed 25 years' service with the club.

YATES, HARRY RICHARD

Right-half: 29 apps
Born: Walsall, August 1861 – *Died*: Birmingham, *circa* 1932
Career: Walsall Swifts (April 1883), VILLA (July 1885), Walsall (August 1890; retired May 1898 after a long-term hip injury)

'Tubby' Yates, 14 st. in weight, was a solid defender with immense power. A strong, forceful tackler, he gained an FA Cup-winner's medal in 1897 and followed up with almost 50 outings for Walsall.

YATES, JOHN THOMSON
Left-half: 14 apps

Born: Burton-on-Irwell, near Manchester, 26 September 1903 – *Died:* 1980

Career: Manchester Central, Cottonopolis FC (local team), Boston Town (briefly), Coventry City (June 1921), Chesterfield (August 1923), Boston Town (June 1924), VILLA (May 1925), Queens Park Rangers (May 1929), Stourbridge (August 1931–May 1932)

Another hefty defender, Yates had boundless energy and was highly competitive, being described as 'an India rubber man'. Very mobile, full of vim and vigour, he played for Birmingham against Scotland in a junior international in April 1927 and deputised for Frank Moss in Villa's middle-line, but failed to make headway at Chesterfield.

YORK, RICHARD ERNEST
Outside-right: 390 apps, 86 goals

Born: Villa Cross, Handsworth, Birmingham, 25 April 1899 – *Died:* Handsworth, Birmingham, 9 December 1969

Career: Icknield Street Council School (Hockley), King Edward Grammar School (Aston), Friends Hall (Hockley), GEC Works, Birmingham Boys, Handsworth Royal, Birchfield Rangers, VILLA (amateur, March 1915; professional, May 1915); served in the Royal Flying Corps, WW1, receiving a commission; guest for Chelsea (as amateur) and Boscombe Town; George Robey's XI; VILLA (professional, August 1919), Port Vale (June 1931), Brierley Hill Alliance (August 1932–May 1934); VILLA (third team, 1948–49, also coach for a time); employed as a technical advisor (buildings) on the Birmingham War Damage Committee from 1942; later manager of a Coventry plumbing, building and decorating company; also director and captain of the Brecon Tennis Club

York was capped by England on two occasions as a schoolboy and later represented his country twice at senior level (1922, 1926). A player with tremendous speed, developed as a sprinter on the athletics track with Birchfield Harriers from the age of eight, he was an FA Cup winner with Villa in 1924, having made his debut at right-half against Sunderland in August 1919. He replaced Charlie Wallace on the right-wing during the second half of 1920–21 and was first choice until Jack Mandley arrived in 1931. An ever-present in 1926–27 and 1928–29, York played in 26 games for Port Vale.

YORKE, DWIGHT
Striker: 247+40 apps, 97 goals

Born: Canaan, Tobago, 3 November 1971

Career: Signal FC (Tobago), VILLA (£120,000, December 1989), Manchester United (£12.6m, August 1998), Blackburn Rovers (£2m, July 2002), Birmingham City (August 2004)

When Dwight Yorke joined Manchester United, he became the twelfth costliest footballer in the game's history and the second highest-priced player involved in a transfer between two British clubs. He shared the record (with Chris Sutton) of scoring what was then the fastest goal in the Premiership – after just 13 seconds for Manchester United against Coventry in September 1998. A buddy of West Indies Test cricketer Brian Lara, Yorke took time to establish himself in Villa's League side, eventually claiming his place in 1991–92, when he made 39 appearances and scored 16 goals. Positive with neat skills and a penetrative approach, he's a natural athlete with great balance and a useful right foot. A Trinidad and Tobago international (eight caps), Yorke won a League Cup-winner's medal with Villa (1996), helped United win three Premiership titles (1999, 2000, 2001) as well as the FA Cup and European Cup, also in 1999 when part of the treble-winning side.

YOUNG, ANDREW

Forward: 26 apps, 11 goals

Born: Darlington, 17 September 1896 – *Died*: 1964

Career: Darlington junior football, Blyth Spartans (May 1914), VILLA (November 1919), Arsenal (March 1922), Bournemouth (June 1927), Kidderminster Harriers (July 1928–May 1930)

Young proved to be a very useful forward, a player who loved a challenge and one who was totally committed. During his Villa days, he had to battle for a place up front with Billy Kirton, Harry Hampton and Billy Walker, and after leaving did well at Highbury, where he was converted into a half-back, holding that position for the rest of his career. He struck nine goals in seventy-one outings for the Gunners, helping their reserve side win two London Combination championships (1923, 1927) and also the London FA Challenge Cup (1924).

YOUNG, CHARLES FREDERICK

Defender: 11+1 apps

Born: Nicosia, Cyprus, 14 February 1958

Career: Chester Schoolboys, VILLA (apprentice, June 1974; professional, November 1975), Gillingham (£30,000, March 1978; retired, injured, May 1983)

The son of an English-born serviceman and a Welsh mother, both based in Cyprus, Young, 6 ft tall, was a strong and reliable player who deputised for Chris Nicholl and Leighton Phillips during his time with Villa. He played in 28 League games for Gillingham.

YOUNG, NORMAN JAMES

Full-back: 9 apps

Born: Kings Heath, Birmingham, March 1907 – *Died*: *circa* 1980

Career: Cobden Works FC (1922), Redditch Town (1923), VILLA (April 1926), Barnsley (July 1936), Brierley Hill Alliance (May 1937; retired during

WW2); later coach at Birmingham University (in succession to ex-Villa player Joe Tate)

Unyielding and efficient with a useful left foot but a swinging right one, Young appeared in 170 second-team games for Villa. In fact, he had to wait until mid-September 1935 (9 years after joining the club) before making his League debut, in a 5–1 home win over Preston. He played in 22 League matches for Barnsley.

YOUNG, WILLIAM JOHN

Forward: 3 apps

Born: Glasgow, 24 February 1956

Career: Clyde (trial, 1975), Arthurlie (1976–77), VILLA (professional, July 1978), Torquay United (October 1981–May 1983); non-League football in Scotland

Inside- or outside-left Willie Young played in three League games for Villa, the first in the number 10 shirt in front of 36,000 fans against Manchester United in October 1978. He went on to appear in 38 League matches for Torquay.

LATE NEWS

Prior to the start of the 2004–05 season, Aston Villa manager David O'Leary secured the following players to bolster his first-team squad.

BERSON, MATHIEU
A French midfielder, aged 24, signed from Nantes in August 2004 for £1.6m.

COLE, CARLTON MICHAEL
Striker, 6 ft 3 in. tall, born in Croydon on 12 November 1983, who was signed on a season-long loan from Chelsea in June 2004. Capped by England at youth and Under-21 levels, he joined Chelsea as a professional in October 2000 (after two years as a trainee) and was on loan to Wolverhampton Wanderers in November and December 2002, and Charlton Athletic last season (2003–04).

LAURSEN, MARTIN
Tall, stylish central defender, transferred from AC Milan for £3m in May 2004. A Danish international, he played in Euro 2004.

APPENDIX: ASTON VILLA'S MANAGERS AND CHAIRMEN

LIST OF VILLA'S MANAGERS:

Name	Term of Office
Jimmy McMullan*	June 1934–October 1936
Jimmy Hogan	November 1936–September 1939
Alex Massie*	September 1945–August 1950
George Martin	December 1950–August 1953
Eric Houghton*	September 1953–November 1958
Joe Mercer	December 1958–July 1964
Dick Taylor	July 1964–May 1967
Tommy Cummings	July 1967–November 1968
Arthur Cox+	November 1968–December 1968
Tommy Docherty	December 1968–January 1970
Vic Crowe*	January 1970–May 1974
Ron Saunders	June 1974–February 1982
Tony Barton	February 1982–May 1984
Graham Turner	July 1984–September 1986
Billy McNeill MBE	September 1986–May 1987
Graham Taylor OBE	July 1987–July 1990
Josef Venglos	July 1990–May 1991
Ron Atkinson*	July 1991–November 1994
Brian Little*	November 1994–February 1998
John Gregory*	February 1998–May 2003
David O'Leary	July 2003–

+ Cox was caretaker manager until Docherty arrived.

* Also registered as a player with the club.

NB: Prior to the appointment of Jimmy McMullan, the club's team affairs were run indirectly by the club secretary and a committee that included the captain. From 1884 to 1926, under the aegis of secretary George Ramsay, six First Division titles and five FA Cup finals were won by Villa.

LIST OF VILLA'S CHAIRMEN:

Joshua Margoschis	1885–94
William McGregor	1894–1902
Frederick W. Rinder	1902–25
John (Jack) Jones	1926–36
Frederick Normansell	1936–55
Christopher Buckley	1955–66
Norman Smith	1966–68
Douglas M. Ellis	1968–76
Sir William Dugdale	1976–79
Harold Kartz	1979–81
Ronald Bendall	1981–82
Douglas M. Ellis	1982–

BIBLIOGRAPHY

I have referred to several books to clarify certain relevant statistics including facts and figures, individual players' details and, indeed, stories and match reports from past seasons regarding Aston Villa FC. There are some conflicting facts, stats and other information in these sources, and I have made judgement as to what is likely to be correct.

Here is a list of publications I have consulted:

Betts, G. (1998), *The Villans: Day to Day Life at Villa Park* (Edinburgh: Mainstream)

FA Yearbook [1951–2000; published yearly] (London: The Football Association)

Gibbs, N. (1988), *England: The Football Facts* (Exeter: Facet Books)

Gibson, A. and W. Pickford (1905–06), *Association Football and the Men Who Made It*, 4 vols (London: Caxton Publishing Company)

Goldsworthy, M. (1969), *The Encyclopaedia of Association Football* (London: Robert Hale & Co.)

Hayes, D. (1997), *The Villa Park Encyclopaedia* (Edinburgh: Mainstream)

Hugman, B.J. (ed.) (1996), *PFA Footballers' Factfile, 1995–96* (London: Stanley Paul)

Hugman, B.J. (ed.) (1997–2000), *PFA Footballers' Factfiles, 1996–97 to 2000–01* (Hertfordshire: Queen Anne Press)

Hugman, B.J. (ed.) (2001), *PFA Footballers Who's Who, 2001–02* (Basildon: AFS)

Hugman, B.J. (ed.) (2002), *PFA Footballers Who's Who, 2002–03* (Hertfordshire: Queen Anne Press)

Hugman, B.J. (ed.) (2003), *PFA Footballers Who's Who, 2003–04* (Hertfordshire: Queen Anne Press)

Hugman, B.J. (ed.) (1998), *The PFA Premier and Football League Players' Records, 1946–1998* (Hertfordshire: Queen Anne Press)

Johnson, F. (1935), *Football Who's Who* (London: Associated Sporting Press)

Johnson, I. (1981), *The Aston Villa Story* (London: Arthur Baker Ltd)

Joyce, M. (2002), *Football League Players' Records, 1888–1939* (Nottingham: Tony Brown/SoccerData)

Lamming, D. and M. Farror (1972), *English Internationals Who's Who, 1872–1972* (London: Robert Hale & Co.)

Morris, P. (1960), *The History of a Great Football Club: Aston Villa* (London: Naldrett Press)

Pringler, A. and N. Fissler (1996), *Where Are They Now?* (London: Two Heads Publishing)

Rollin, J. (1995), *Soccer at War, 1939–45* (London: Willow Books Collins)

Spiller, R. (ed.) (1990), *AFS Football Who's Who: 1902–03, 1903–04, 1907–08, 1909–10* (Basildon: AFS)

Spinks, D. (1989), *The Aston Villa Quiz Book* (Edinburgh: Mainstream)

Williams, T. (ed.) (1992), *Football League Directory, 1993* (London: *Daily Mail*)

OTHER PUBLICATIONS:

AFS Bulletins (various)

Aston Villa home programmes (various) 1906–2004

Aston Villa reviews, magazines and supporters' handbooks (various)

Sports Argus annuals: 1950–68

I have also referred to several sporting newspapers; various club histories and *Who's Who's*, autobiographies and biographies of players and managers and general football reference books for confirmation of certain factual points.